HANDBOOK OF PROGRAMMING LANGUAGES, VOLUME II

Imperative Programming Languages

Peter H. Salus, Series Editor in Chief

M
T|P
MACMILLAN
TECHNICAL
PUBLISHING
U·S·A

Handbook of Programming Languages, Volume II: Imperative Programming Languages

Peter H. Salus, Series Editor in Chief

Published by:
Macmillan Technical Publishing
201 West 103rd Street
Indianapolis, IN 46290 USA

Copyright © 1998 by Macmillian Technical Publishing

FIRST EDITION

International Standard Book Number: 1-57870-009-4

Library of Congress Catalog Card Number: 97-81204

01   00   99   98   4   3   2   1

Interpretation of the printing code: The rightmost double-digit number is the year of the book's printing; the rightmost single-digit, the number of the book's printing. For example, the printing code 98-1 shows that the first printing of the book occurred in 1998.

Composed in Sabon and MCPdigital by Macmillan Technical Publishing

Printed in the United States of America

Trademark Acknowledgments 11/17/98

Warning and Disclaimer

Permissions

Chapter 2 copyright 1993, Association for Computing Machinery, Inc., and made available by the author as a courtesy. For further publication rights, contact ACM or the author. This article was presented at the Second History of Programming Language conference Cambridge, MA, April 1993.

Associate Publisher
Jim LeValley

Managing Editor
Caroline Roop

Executive Editors
Linda Engelman
Tom Stone

Acquisitions Editors
Jane K. Brownlow
Karen Wachs

Development Editor
Kitty Wilson Jarrett

Project Editor
Brad Herriman

Copy Editor
Kristine Simmons

Indexers
Chris Cleveland
Bront Davis

Team Coordinator
Amy Lewis

Manufacturing Coordinator
Brook Farling

Book Designer
Gary Adair

Cover Designer
Karen Ruggles

Production Team Supervisor
Daniela Raderstorf

Production
Mary Hunt
Laura A. Knox

Overview

Table of Contents

Foreword to the *Handbook of Programming Languages*

The aim of the *Handbook of Programming Languages* is to provide a single, comprehensive source of information concerning a variety of individual programming languages and methodologies for computing professionals. The *Handbook* is published in multiple volumes and covers a wide range of languages, organized by type and functionality.

The *Handbook* includes four volumes:

Volume I: Object-Oriented Programming Languages

This volume contains chapters on Smalltalk, C++, Eiffel, Ada95, Modula-3, and Java.

Volume II: Imperative Programming Languages

This volume contains chapters on Fortran, Pascal, Icon, and C, as well as a chapter on intermediate languages by Ron Cytron.

Volume III: Little Languages and Tools

This volume contains chapters on little languages and domain-specific languages, such as troff, awk, sed, Perl, Tcl and Tk, Python, and SQL. It also contains seminal work by Brian Kernighan and Lorinda Cherry as well as Jon Bentley and essays by Paul Hudak and Peter Langston.

Volume IV: Functional and Logic Programming Languages

This volume contains chapters on functional (Lisp, Scheme, Guile, and Emacs Lisp) and logic (Prolog) programming languages.

Natural, or human, languages appear to be about 10,000 years old. Symbolic, or formal, languages began in Sumer (a civilization of southern Iraq from about 3800 to 2300 BCE), where we find the oldest writing system, cuneiform. It was followed by Egyptian hieroglyphics (about 3000 BCE), the language of the Harappa in the Indus valley, the Chinese shell and bone inscriptions, and (in the Western hemisphere) the language of the Maya.

Writing systems abstract from speech and formalize that abstraction in their symbols. This may be done semantically (for example, hieroglyphs, English numerals, and symbols such as &) or phonologically (for example, alphabetic spelling).

In more recent times, further abstractions have become necessary: warning beacons, flags on sailing vessels, railway telegraph/semaphore, Morse code, and so forth.

Mechanical methods for calculating are very old, but they all involve symbolic abstraction. The abacus is probably the oldest of such constructions. The Chinese and Egyptians had this device nearly four millennia ago. The Mayans possessed it when the Spanish arrived. It was only a few years after Napier's discovery of logarithms (1614), and the use of his "bones" (marked ivory rods) for multiplication, that the slide rule was invented.

In 1642, at the age of 18, Blaise Pascal invented a calculator that could add and carry to aid his father, a tax collector. Almost 30 years later, in 1671, Leibniz took Pascal's machine a step further and built a prototype machine that could multiply using an ingenious device called the *stepped wheel*, which was still in use in mechanical calculators manufactured in the late 1940s. Leibniz demonstrated his calculator to the Royal Society in London in 1676.

The first commercially successful calculator was invented by Charles Xavier Thomas in 1820. By 1878, an astounding 1,500 had been sold—nearly 30 per year. They were still being manufactured by Darras in Paris after World War I. The Brunsviga adding machine, based on an 1875 patent by Frank Stephen Baldwin, which substituted a wheel with a variable number of protruding teeth for the Leibniz stepped wheel, sold an incredible 20,000 machines between 1892 and 1912—1,000 per year.

The first keyboard-driven calculator was patented in 1850 by D. D. Parmalee, and Dorr Eugene Felt's Comptometer—the first successful key-driven, multiple-order calculating machine—was patented in 1887.

In 1812, Charles Babbage came up with a notion for a different type of calculator, which he termed a *difference engine*. He was granted support by the British government in 1823. Work stopped in 1833, and the project was abandoned in 1842, the government having decided the cost was too great. From 1833 on, though, Babbage devoted himself to a different sort of machine, an analytical engine, that would automatically evaluate any mathematical formula. The various operations of the analytical engine were to be controlled by punched cards of the type used in the Jacquard loom. Though only a fraction of the construction appears to have been effected, Babbage's notes, drawings, and portions of the engine are in the Victoria and Albert Museum (as is the set of Napier's bones that belonged to Babbage).

The Jacquard loom, a successful attempt at increasing production through automation, was itself the result of several prior innovations: In 1725 Bouchon substituted an endless paper tape with perforations for the bunches of looped string. In 1728 Falcon substituted perforated cards, but attached them to strings, and in 1748, Jacques de Vaucanson combined the bands of perforated paper and the cards. The patterns on the cards were perforated by machines that cut on designs painted on by stencils. The programmed machine was born.

Over 100 years later, Herman Hollerith, a graduate of Columbia College in New York, recalled the existence of those perforated cards. Hollerith had just started work at the Census Bureau at a generous salary of $600 per year. There he was put to work on a survey of power and machinery used in manufacturing. But he also met John Shaw Billings, who was in charge of "vital statistics." One night at dinner, Billings complained about the recently invented but inadequate tabulating device of Charles Seaton, which had been used for the census of 1870. Billings felt that given the increased population, the 1880 census might not be completed in less than seven or eight years, and the 1890 census would still be incomplete in 1900. "There ought to be a machine for doing the purely mechanical work of tabulating population and similar statistics," Billings said. "We talked it over," Hollerith recalled 30 years later, "and I remember...he thought of using cards with the description of the individual shown by notches punched in the edge of the card." Hollerith thought about constructing a device to record and read such information and asked Billings to go into business with him. Billings was a cautious man and said no.

In 1882 Hollerith went to MIT as an instructor in mechanical engineering (he was then 22). Teaching at MIT gave him the time to work on his machine. He first considered putting the information on long strips of paper, but this proved impractical. In the summer of 1883, Hollerith took a train trip west. On the train he saw the "punch photograph," a way for conductors to punch passengers' descriptions onto tickets so they could check that the same individual was using the ticket throughout the trip; in this system things like gender and hair and eye color were encoded.

Hollerith patented his first machine in 1884 and an improved design in 1886, when he performed a trial by conducting the Baltimore census. On the basis of reports of the trial, New Jersey and New York placed orders for machines (to tally mortality rates). Hollerith and some business colleagues bid for the contract for the 1890 census and won it. The government of Austria ordered machines in 1890. Canada ordered five the next year. Italy and Norway followed, and then Russia. The machines were a clear success. Hollerith incorporated his Hollerith Electric Tabulating System as the Tabulating Machine Company in 1896; he reincorporated it in 1905.

Nearly 80 years passed before the computer industry moved beyond several of Hollerith's insights. First, so that operators would have no problem orienting the cards, he cut a corner from the upper right. Second, he *rented* the machines at a reasonable rate (the rental fees for the 1890 census were $750,000; the labor cost in 1880 had been $5 million), but *sold* the patented cards (more than 100 million between 1890 and 1895). Third, he adapted the census-counting to tally freight and passenger data for railroads. Hollerith effectively invented reusability.

Despite the fact that Thomas Watson said (in 1945), "I think there is a world market for about five computers," the first completed was one he had funded. Howard Aiken of Harvard, along with a small team, began in 1939 to put together a machine that exploited Babbage's principles. It consisted, when completed in 1944, of a 51-foot by 8-foot panel on which tape readers, relays, and rotary switches were mounted. Nearly all of the operations of the Harvard Mark I Calculator were controlled by mechanical switches, driven by a 4-horsepower motor.

The first all-electronic computer was the Electronic Numerical Integrator and Calculator. Completed by J. W. Mauchly and J. P. Eckert of the University of Pennsylvania in late 1945 and installed in 1946, it was commissioned by the Ballistics Research Laboratory (BRL) at the Aberdeen (Maryland) Proving Ground. It was—and will remain, I expect—the largest computing machine ever built: It was made up of 18,000 tubes and 1,500 relays. ENIAC was the electronic analogue of the Mark I, but ran several hundred times faster.

ENIAC had offspring in England, too. Maurice V. Wilkes and his group began planning their Electronic Delay Storage Automatic Calculator (EDSAC) in late 1946, on Wilkes's return from Pennsylvania, and began work at the University Mathematical Laboratory in Cambridge early in the new year. It was one fifth the size of ENIAC and based on ideas that John von Neumann had presented in a paper. When it performed its first fully automatic calculation in May 1949, EDSAC became the first electronic machine to be put into operation that had a high-speed memory (store) and I/O (input/output) devices. Within a few years, EDSAC's library contained more than 150 subroutines, according to Wilkes.

At virtually the same time, in Manchester, a team under M. H. A. Newman began work on a machine that was to embody the EDVAC concepts. F. C. Williams, who invented cathode ray tube storage, I. J. Good, who had worked on the Colossus code-breaking machine with Alan M. Turing, and Turing himself, joined the team. The Manchester Automatic Digital Machine prototype was built in 1948, and the definitive machine ran its first program in June 1949. MADM introduced to computing both the index register and pagination.

In the meantime, IBM had begun work on its Selective-Sequence
Electronic Calculator (SSEC). It is important to remember that while
EDSAC was the first electronic computer, the SSEC was the first
computer—it combined computation with a stored program. It was put
into operation at IBM headquarters in Manhattan early in 1948, cleverly
placed behind plate glass windows at street level so that pedestrians
could see it operate. It was a large machine with 13,000 tubes and
23,000 relays. Because all the arithmetic calculations were carried out by
the tubes, it was more than 100 times as fast as the Mark I. It also had
three different types of memory: a high-speed tube store, a larger capacity
in relays, and a vastly larger store on 80-column paper tape. Instructions
and input were punched on tape and there were 66 heads arranged so
that control was transferred automatically from one to the other. "It was
probably the first machine to have a conditional transfer of control
instruction in the sense that Babbage and Lady [Ada] Lovelace recommended," wrote B. W. Bowden in 1953. It did work for, among other
things, the Atomic Energy Commission, before being dismantled in
August 1952.

That very June, von Neumann and his colleagues completed Maniac at
the Institute for Advanced Studies in Princeton, New Jersey. It employed
the electrostatic memory invented by F. C. Williams and T. Kilburn,
which required a single cathode ray tube, instead of special storage tubes.

The next advance in hardware came at MIT's Whirlwind project, begun
by Jay Forrester in 1944. Whirlwind performed 20,000 single-address
operations per second on 16-digit words, employing a new type of electrostatic store in which 16 tubes each contained 256 binary digits. The
Algebraic Interpreter for the Whirlwind and A-2—developed by Grace
Murray Hopper for the UNIVAC—are likely the most important of the
machine-oriented languages.

The 704, originally the 701A, was released in 1954. It was the logical suc-
cessor to the IBM 701 (1952, 1953). The evolution of the 701 into the
704 was headed up by Gene Amdahl. The direct result of the 701/704 was
the beginning of work on Fortran (which stands for *formula translator*) by
John Backus at IBM in 1953. Work on the Fortran translator (we would
call it a compiler) began in 1955 and was completed in 1957. Fortran
was, without a doubt, the first programming language.

In December 1959, at the Eastern Joint Computer Conference at the
Statler Hotel in Boston, the three-year-old DEC unveiled the prototype of
its PDP-1 (Programmed Data Processor-1). It was priced at $120,000 and
deliveries began in November 1960.

The PDP-1 was an 18-bit machine with a memory capacity between 4,096 and 32,768 words. The PDP-1 had a memory cycle of 5 microseconds and a computing speed of 100,000 computations per second. It was the result of a project led by Benjamin Gurley and was composed of 3,500 transistors and 4,300 diodes. It had an editor, a macroassembler, and an ALGOL compiler, DECAL. It employed a paper tape reader for input and an IBM typewriter for output. The PDP-1 had the best cost/performance of any real-time computer of its generation. It was also the first commercial computer to come with a graphical display screen.

Just over 40 years ago there were no programming languages. In 1954 programming was still a function of hardware. Fortran was invented in 1957. It was soon being taught. By 1960, not only had COBOL and Lisp joined the roster, but so had others, many now thankfully forgotten. Over the past 40 years, nearly 4,000 computer languages have been produced. Only a tithe of these are in use today, but the growth and development of them has been progressive and organic.

There are a number of ways such languages can be taxonomized. One frequent classification is into machine languages (the natural language of a given device), assembly languages (in which common English words and abbreviations are used as input to the appropriate machine language), and high-level languages (which permit instructions that more closely resemble English instructions). Assembly languages are translators; high-level languages require conversion into machine language: These translators are called *compilers*. Among the high-level languages currently in use are C, C++, Eiffel, and Java.

Yet there is no guide for the overwhelmed programmer, who merely wants to get her job done. This *Handbook of Programming Languages* is intended to serve as an instant reference, a life-preserver, providing information to enable that programmer to make intelligent choices as to which languages to employ, enough information to enable him to program at a basic level, and references to further, more detailed information.

Peter H. Salus
Boston, February 1998

General Bibliography

Histories of Programming Languages
Bergin, T. J., and R. G. Gibson (Eds.). 1996. *History of programming languages*. Reading, MA: Addison-Wesley. Proceedings of ACM's Second History of Programming Languages Conference.

Sammet, J. A. 1969. *Programming languages: History and fundamentals.* Englewood Cliffs, NJ: Prentice Hall. An indispensable work.

Wexelblat, R. L. (Ed.). 1981. *History of programming languages.* New York: Academic Press. The proceedings of ACM's First History of Programming Languages Conference.

Reader on Programming Languages
Horowitz, E. 1987. *Programming languages: A grand tour* (3rd ed.). Rockville, MD: Computer Science Press.

Surveys and Guides to Programming Languages
Appleby, D. 1991. *Programming languages: Paradigm and practice.* New York: McGraw-Hill.

Bal, H. E., and D. Grune. 1994. *Programming language essentials.* Wokingham, England: Addison-Wesley.

Cezzar, R. 1995. *A guide to programming languages.* Norwood, MA: Artech House.

Sethi, R. 1996. *Programming languages: Concepts & constructs* (2nd ed.). Reading, MA: Addison-Wesley.

Stansifer, R. 1995. *The study of programming languages.* Englewood Cliffs, NJ: Prentice Hall.

Foreword to This Volume: Imperative Programming Languages

On the simplest level, imperative programming languages are those that manipulate data in a stepwise fashion. That is, they take sequential instructions (algorithms) and apply them to data of various kinds.

Imperative languages have a "do this, then do that" structure. These instructions or commands are usually called statements. Most of the data items in memory have names, which are used when manipulating those items. The properties of the data items are called types. Programmers specify the relationships among representations, types, data, and names in data declarations.

A data declaration imposes structure upon data and gives it a name. The imposed structure is a specified type; the name is an identifier. All data is stored as bits. The bit pattern and the structure determine the data item's value. The union of name, type and value is called a variable.

The work of Konrad Zuse is of tremendous value, but it lacked use and influence: For political reasons, Zuse's work wasn't published contemporaneously, and so the history of imperative languages begins with Fortran, proceeding to Snobol4, Icon, C, and Pascal. Fortran, it must be noted, was designed for a specific machine: the IBM 704. It quickly became extre-mely popular with scientists.

In C, a data declaration looks like:

```
int x, y;
```

This states that x and y are integers.

In Ada66 and Ada9x, this would be stated as:

```
I, J: Integer;
```

These languages can also initialize the data, assigning a real value:

```
int x = 3, y = 4;
```

Not all currently used imperative programming languages can be found in this volume. C++ is an imperative language; but it is also an object- oriented language, and I have made the (arbitrary) decision to place it in Volume I of this *Handbook*. Similarly, while CLOS is an object-oriented language, it also belongs in the Lisp family, and so I have placed it in Volume IV.

There are basically two kinds of imperative languages: those which focus on compilation, on speed of execution, and those which focus on the level and convenience of the programmer—focus on compilation or on interpretation. Icon is most likely the best instance of an interpretation-oriented language.

This volume will concentrate on languages in use in 1996/97. This includes the first true programming language (Fortran), as well as C, Pascal, and Icon; Modula-3 and Ada95 have been placed in Volume I.

Although it is but 40 years between Fortran and Limbo, more than 4,000 programming languages have been proposed and/or developed in that time. That averages at two per week! I can only compare this luxuriance to that of the Permian explosion, millions of years ago.

Prehistory

The first true computer (ENIAC, 1946) wasn't electronic: it was electro-mechanical, with many thousands of glass tubes and many mechanical relays. It used a "stored program," as did the early Manchester (UK) computers. It was followed rapidly by Aiken's (and IBM's) "Automatic Sequence Controlled Calculator" at Harvard (also 1946). The SSC had more than "2,200 counter wheels for storage and summation and 3,300 relay components for control circuitry...[it] was 51 feet long and 8 feet high. It weighed about 5 tons"[1]. A decade later, we were still working with punched cards and plugwires.

While ENIAC and its relatives were computers, they were not addressable by means of languages, any more than the punched cards of a Jacquard loom were addressing the mechanical loom. With one exception, the "programmers" of the 1940s were individuals who wrote out instructions on large sheets of paper which were "translated" to the machinery by means of registers and cables (plugwires)

The sole exception was a German engineer, Konrad Zuse, who was in exile in Switzerland. Zuse designed "Plankakuel," a programming language. It featured structured values, variables, and procedures with parameters. Unfortunately, the Second World War and other events prevented Plankalkuel from becoming known for nearly 25 years. Bal and Grune note that had Zuse's work become known, "present-day programming languages might have looked different." But it must be admitted that Plankalkuel wasn't efficient.

However, in the 1950s, IBM (and other companies) were interested in leveraging the power of their machines. In order to gain the greatest machine advantage from their computers in executing mathematical calcu-lations (the principal use of computation), programmers spent most of their time converting numerical material into assembler instructions. These first higher-level languages were called Autocodes. They were extremely limited in their range and could handle a few relatively simple formulae.

---

[1]Bashe, C.J., L. R. Johnson, J. H. Palmer, & Emerson W. Pugh. 1986. IBM's early computers. Cambridge, MA: MIT Press.

And so the stage was set for IBM to set up a group, headed by John Backus, in 1953; in 1955, the group began its "six month" job of writing a compiler. They finished in 1957. The report was published late that year, and by spring 1958, IBM's formula translator (Fortran) was being taught.

> *Peter H. Salus*
> Boston, February 1998

Dedication

This *Handbook* is dedicated to John Backus, James Gosling, Adele Goldberg, Ralph Griswold, Brian Kernighan, John McCarthy, Bertrand Meyer, Dennis Ritchie, Bjarne Stroustrup, and the memory of Joe Ossanna, without whose efforts most of these languages wouldn't exist.

Acknowledgments

Many individuals deserve mention where this enormous *Handbook* is concerned. First of all, Tom Stone, who abetted my thinking and then effected a contract prior to deserting me for another publisher; next, Jim LeValley and Don Fowley at Macmillan, for being willing to take a chance on this project. I'd also like to thank Linda Engelman, Tracy Hughes, Amy Lewis, Jane Brownlow, Karen Wachs, and Kitty Jarrett at Macmillan.

In addition to the many authors, I'd like to thank Lou Katz, Stuart McRobert, Len Tower, and Brent Welch for their advice, patience, and friendship.

My gratitude to the ACM, to Addison-Wesley Longman, to MIT Press, to O'Reilly & Associates, and to the Waite Group for permissions to reprint various materials is enormous.

The errors and omissions are mine.

About the Series Editor

Peter H. Salus

Peter H. Salus is the author of *A Quarter Century of UNIX* (1994) and *Casting the Net: From ARPANET to Internet and Beyond* (1995). He is an internationally recognized expert and has been the keynote speaker at Uniforum Canada, the UKUUG, the NLUUG, and the OTA (Belgium) in the past few years. He has been executive director of the USENIX Association and of the Sun User Group and vice president of the Free Software Foundation. He was the managing editor of *Computing Systems* (MIT Press) from 1987 to 1996. He writes on a variety of computing topics in a number of magazines. His Ph.D. in linguistics (New York University, 1963) has led him from natural languages to computer languages.

About the Authors

Walt Brainerd

Walt Brainerd received the third Ph.D. in computing sciences awarded in the United States. He has taught at Columbia University and the University of New Mexico and worked for Burroughs and the Los Alamos National Laboratory.

Walt has been a member of the Fortran national and international standards committees for more than 20 years. He served as director of technical work for X3J3 during the development of Fortran 90 and was the document editor.

He is currently President of Unicomp, Inc., which specializes in consulting and training in high performance computing. He maintains the definitive Web site for information about Fortran (http://www.fortran.com/fortran) and can be reached at walt@fortran.com.

Ron Cytron

Ron Cytron received a B.S. in electrical engineering from Rice University in 1980. His graduate studies at the University of Illinois at Urbana-Champaign resulted in an M.S. in 1982 and a Ph.D. in 1984, both in computer science. Ron joined the Parallel Translation (PTRAN) project at the IBM Research Division, Thomas J. Watson Research Center in 1984, where he investigated various aspects of program analysis and optimization, with an emphasis on parallel architectures. His research there also included algorithms for constructing and using Static Single Assignment (SSA) form, an intermediate representation now in widespread use. Ron joined the staff of Washington University in 1991 and is now an associate professor in the Computer Science Department.

His research interests include program analysis, optimization, and transformation; optimization of object-oriented languages; intermediate representations; network software; and electronic voting systems.

Ralph E. Griswold

Ralph E. Griswold received his Ph.D. in electrical engineering from Stanford University in 1962. From then until 1970, he was a member of the technical staff at Bell Laboratories, where he became head of the Programming Research and Development Department and led the group that designed and implemented the SNOBOL programming languages.

In 1971 he moved to the University of Arizona, where he founded the Department of Computer Science. His work on programming languages continued, leading to the SL5 and Icon programming languages. He presently is Regents' Professor Emeritus.

Glenn Grotzinger

Glenn Grotzinger is a graduate of Central Missouri State University in computer information science. He is currently programming COBOL on a temporary basis.

Dennis M. Ritchie

Dennis M. Ritchie is head of the System Software Research Department in the Computing Science Research Center of Bell Labs, the research and development arm of Lucent Technologies.

Ritchie received his bachelor's and advanced degrees in physics and applied mathematics from Harvard University. The subject of his 1968 doctoral thesis was subrecursive hierarchies of functions.

Ritchie joined Bell Laboratories in 1967, where he contributed to the Multics project. Subsequently, he aided Ken Thompson in creating the UNIX operating system. After UNIX had become well established in the Bell System and in a number of educational, government, and commercial installations, Ritchie and Steven C. Johnson transported the operating system to another hardware architecture, thus demonstrating its portability and laying the groundwork for the widespread growth of the UNIX system. The Seventh Edition system from the Bell Laboratories research group contributed to the development of what has now become UNIX System V and was the basis for the Berkeley system distributions.

Early in the development of UNIX, Ritchie added data types and new syntax to Thompson's B language, thus producing the new language C. This language is the foundation for the portability of UNIX, and it has become widely used in other contexts as well.

Steve Summit

Steve Summit is a software engineer specializing in C and UNIX, which he has enjoyed using for approximately 15 years. He is the author of the comprehensive Internet FAQ list on C. He currently lives, writes, teaches, and works in Seattle, Washington.

PART I
Fortran

CHAPTER 1

Fortran

by Walt Brainerd

1.1. Introduction

For a programming language, Fortran has been around a long time. It was one of the first widely used high-level languages, as well as the first programming language to be standardized. It is still the premier language for scientific and engineering computing applications.

The first section of this chapter presents a brief history of the development and standardization of Fortran and the related languages HPF and F. Much of the material in this section has been adapted from *The Fortran 95 Handbook* (Adams, Brainerd, Martin, Smith, & Wagener, 1997) with permission from the authors. The remaining sections illustrate major features of the language, primarily by giving examples with accompanying explanations; much of this material has been adapted from the *Programmer's Guide to F* (Brainerd, Goldberg, & Adams, 1996) with the permission of the authors.

1.1.1. History

1.1.1.1. Initial Development of Fortran

In 1954, a project was begun under the leadership of John Backus at IBM to develop an "automatic programming" system that would convert programs written in a mathematical notation to machine instructions for the IBM 704 computer. Many were skeptical about the success of the project because, at the time, computer memories were so small and expensive and execution time so valuable that it was believed necessary for the compiled program to be almost as efficient as that produced by a good assembly language programmer.

This project produced the first Fortran compiler, which was delivered to a customer in 1957. It was a great success by any reasonable criterion. The efficiency of the code generated by the compiler surprised even some of its authors. A more important achievement, but one that took longer to realize, was that programmers could express their computations in a more natural way. This increased productivity and permitted the programmer to write a program that could be maintained and enhanced more easily than an assembly language program.

About one year after the introduction of the first Fortran compiler, IBM introduced Fortran II. One of the most important changes in Fortran II was the addition of subroutines that could be compiled independently. Thus, Fortran changed substantially even during its first year; it has been changing continually ever since.

1.1.1.2. Standardization

By the early 1960s, many computer vendors had implemented a Fortran compiler. They all included special features not found in the original IBM compiler. These features usually were included to meet the needs and requests of the users and thus provide an inducement for the customer to buy computer systems from the vendor providing the best compiler. Because the language was young, a special added feature could be tested to see if it was a good long-term addition to the language. Unfortunately, the profusion of dialects of Fortran prevented programs written for one computer from being transported to a different computer system.

At about this time, the American Standards Association (ASA), later to become the American National Standards Institute (ANSI), began a project of standardizing many aspects of data processing. Someone had the daring idea of standardizing programming languages. A committee, which became X3J3 and is now J3, was formed to develop a standard for Fortran. This standard was adopted in 1966; after the adoption of Fortran 77, it became known as Fortran 66 to distinguish the two versions.

The language continued to develop after 1966, along with general knowledge in the areas of programming, language design, and computer design. Work on a revision of Fortran 66 was completed in 1977 (hence the name Fortran 77) and officially published in 1978 (ANSI, 1978; Brainerd, 1978). The most significant features introduced in this version were the character data type, the if-then-else construct, and many new input/output facilities, such as direct access files and the open statement.

Except for the character data type, most of these features had been implemented in many compilers or preprocessors. During this revision, Hollerith data was removed because the character data type is a far superior facility. Although this idea of removing features did not seem controversial when Fortran 77 was introduced, it proved to be controversial later—so much so that no Fortran 77 features were removed in Fortran 90.

Fortran 77, developed by X3J3, was an ANSI standard—an American National Standard. At about this time, the International Standards Organization (ISO) began to mature in the computing language area and adopted Fortran 77 as an international standard; the ISO standard was identical to the ANSI standard and in fact consisted of one page that referenced the ANSI standard.

As soon as the technical development of Fortran 77 was completed, X3J3 and its ISO counterpart WG5 (SC22/WG5) teamed up for the next revision, which was called Fortran 90. Fortran 90 was an ISO standard first, which the U.S. adopted, word for word, as an ANSI standard. Although X3J3 did the technical work on Fortran 90 and produced the standard document, the torch had been passed regarding the "owner" of the Fortran standard; that owner, for Fortran 90 and forevermore, is ISO.

Fortran 90 (ISO, 1991) was a major advance over Fortran 77. It included a greatly liberalized source form, a complete set of iteration and selection control structures, enhanced numeric facilities (e.g., the environmental intrinsic functions), a comprehensive data-parallel array language, data structures (including dynamic structures), user-defined types and operators, procedure extensions (e.g., recursion, internal procedures, explicit procedure interfaces, and user-defined generic procedures), module encapsulation (with powerful data-hiding features), data-type kind parameters (e.g., to regularize the different "kinds" of reals, provide the corresponding kinds of complex, accommodate different kinds of character, and resolve overloads in a simple way), dynamic objects (e.g., allocatable arrays), and some I/O extensions (e.g., namelist and nonadvancing I/O). The concept of "obsolescent" features was introduced, and a handful of Fortran 77 features were so identified. But removal of significant numbers of archaic features was controversial, so no features were actually removed. A standard-conforming Fortran 77 program is a standard-conforming Fortran 90 program with the same interpretation.

Fortran 95 (ISO, 1997), specified by WG5 and produced by X3J3, represents a minor revision to Fortran 90. Most of the changes correct and clarify what was in Fortran 90. However, a few significant features, such as pure functions and the forall construct and statement, were added because they are considered important contributions from high performance Fortran. A few (but not all) of the features designated as obsolescent in Fortran 90 have been removed from Fortran 95.

1.1.2. Fortran 95—the Language of Modern Choice

Fortran 95 should be the language of choice for modern applications development. This section sketches why and shows how Fortran 95 can serve this role while accommodating the 40-year Fortran tradition (and application base).

Fortran 95 is a minor extension of Fortran 90; the changes from Fortran 90 are limited primarily to correcting a few errors and inconsistencies in Fortran 90 and timely strengthening of data-parallel array operations. Fortran 95 therefore supports (most of) Fortran 77 and the vast libraries of such "legacy Fortran code."

Fortran is famous for its efficiency and prowess for numerical computation. These strengths form two of the basic principles guiding Fortran 95. In addition, inherited from Fortran 90 are the principles of high performance data-parallel array operations and efficient data abstraction. These four fundamental principles, the way they are implemented, and their supporting cast of modern features make Fortran 95 a clean, pleasant language to use for applications requiring either high performance or modern programming techniques, or both.

The Fortran 95 data-parallel array operations constitute a valuable programming paradigm for scalable parallel architectures, especially for array-oriented applications such as many scientific and engineering models.

Dynamically allocatable arrays alleviate many of the deficiencies of those older versions of Fortran with static memory allocation. Pointers provide efficient subobject aliases as well as facilitate the use of dynamic structures such as linked lists and trees. Optimization is preserved in the face of pointers by requiring a target to be designated as such.

Much modern programming involves the definition of arbitrary data types (classes), arbitrary operations on these types, and appropriate data hiding. These capabilities are provided cleanly and efficiently in Fortran 95 by derived data types, flexible procedure overloading and operator definition, and powerful packaging facilities (modules). These provide most object-oriented programming capabilities, except for automatic operator inheritance, in a user-friendly manner.

These are described in detail in subsequent sections.

With support of high-performance computing, modern programming techniques, and legacy code, Fortran 95 represents an unbeatable combination for application development at the close of the 20th century with its rapidly changing computer technology.

1.1.3. Fortran 90 Compatibility

Because of the large investment in existing software written in Fortran, X3J3 and WG5 decided to include almost all of Fortran 90 in Fortran 95. (Recall that all of Fortran 77 was included in Fortran 90.) The Fortran 90 features deleted in Fortran 95 are

- Real and double precision do variables

- Branching to an end if statement from outside its if block

- pause statement

- assign, assigned go to, and assigned format

- h edit descriptor

In all other ways, Fortran 95 is compatible with Fortran 90.

1.1.4. Extensibility

User-defined data types, operators, and assignment provide ways for the programmer to extend Fortran. These facilities allow the programmer to create abstract data types by defining new types and the operations to be performed on them. Fortran modules provide a convenient way to package these new data types and their operations. Modules can be used by the same user in different applications or may be distributed to a number of users on the same or different projects. This provides effective practical support for object-oriented programming, as well as enhancing both economy and efficiency.

1.1.5. The Fortran 95 Language Standard

The Fortran 95 standard (ISO, 1997) describes the syntax and semantics of the Fortran programming language but only certain, not all, aspects of the Fortran processing system. When specifications are not covered by the standard, the interpretation is processor dependent—that is, the processor defines the interpretation, but the interpretations for any two processors need not be the same. Programs that rely on processor-dependent interpretations typically are not portable.

The specifications included in the standard are

- The syntax of Fortran statements and forms for Fortran programs
- The semantics of Fortran statements and the semantics of Fortran programs
- Specifications for correct input data
- Appearance of standard output data

The specifications not defined in the standard are

- The way in which Fortran compilers are written
- Operating-system facilities defining the computing system
- Methods used to transfer data to and from peripheral storage devices and the nature of the peripheral devices
- Behavior of extensions implemented by vendors
- The size and complexity of a Fortran program and its data
- The hardware or firmware used to run the program
- The way values are represented and the way numeric values are computed
- The physical representation of data
- The characteristics of tapes, disks, and various storage media

1.1.5.1. Program Conformance to the Standard

A program conforms to the standard if the statements are all syntactically correct, execution of the program causes no violations of the standard (for example, numerical overflow), and the input data is all in the correct form. A program that uses a vendor extension is not standard conforming and may not be portable.

1.1.5.2. Processor Conformance to the Standard

In the Fortran 95 standard, the term *processor* means the combination of a Fortran compiler and the computing system that executes the code. A processor conforms to the standard if it correctly processes any standard-conforming program, provided the Fortran program is not too large or complex for the computer system in question. Except for certain restrictions in format specifications, the processor must be able to flag any non-standard syntax used in the program. This includes the capability to flag any extensions available in the vendor software (including deleted features) and used in the program. The standard also requires that the processor flag, with appropriate explanation, the following:

- Obsolescent features

- Kind values not supported

- Characters not permitted by the processor

- Illegal source form

- Violations of the scope rules for names, labels, operators, and assignment symbols

Rules for the form of the output are less stringent than for other features of the language in the sense that the processor may have some options about the format of the output and the programmer may not have complete control over which of these options is used.

A processor may include extensions not in the standard; if it processes standard-conforming programs according to the standard, it is considered to be a standard-conforming processor.

1.1.5.3. Portability

One of the main purposes of a standard is to describe how to write portable programs. However, there are some things that are standard conforming but not portable. An example is a program that computes a very large number such as 10^{10000}. Certain computing systems will not accommodate a number this large. Thus, such a number could be a part of a standard-conforming program but may not run on all systems and thus may not be portable. Another example is a program that uses a deeper nesting of control constructs than is allowed by a particular compiler.

1.1.5.4. A Permissive Standard

The primary purpose of the Fortran standard is to describe a language with the property that, if a programmer uses the language, it minimizes the difficulties of porting programs from one computer system to another. To handle the somewhat contradictory goal of permitting experimentation and development of the language, the standard is permissive: That is, a processor can conform to the standard even if it allows features that are not described in the standard. This has its good and bad aspects.

On the positive side, it allows implementers to experiment with features not in the standard; if they are successful and prove useful, they can become candidates for standardization during the next revision. Thus, a vendor of a compiler may choose to add some features not found in the standard and still conform to the standard by correctly processing all the features that are described in the standard.

On the negative side, the burden is on the programmer to know and avoid these extra features when the program is to be ported to a different computer system. The programmer is given some help with this problem in that a Fortran processor is required to recognize and warn the programmer about syntactic constructs in a program that do not conform to the standard. A good Fortran programmer's manual also points out non-standard features with some technique, such as shading on the page. But there is no real substitute for knowledge of the standard language itself.

1.1.6. Fortran 2000

The next Fortran standard, due to be completed in the year 2002, is now under development. As of this writing, details of the features are not known, but the major topics being considered include

- Floating-point exception handling

- More allocatable objects

- Interoperability with C

- Interval arithmetic

- Parameterized derived types

- Object-oriented features

- Pointers to procedures

- Asynchronous I/O

- Derived-type I/O

1.1.7. HPF

HPF (Koelbel, Loveman, Schreiber, Steele, & Zosel, 1993) is a set of extensions to Fortran to assist in enhancing the performance of Fortran programs, particularly on computers with multiple processors and distributed memory. The most important feature of the language is a set of directives that indicate how data (particularly arrays) are to be distributed among the multiple memories associated with the processors of the system. HPF was developed by a consortium of interested parties, both vendors and users, and it is not a standard adopted by one of the official standards bodies, such as ISO or IEEE. HPF compilers are available for a number of systems.

To give just one simple example, the HPF directives in the following code fragments indicate that if there are eight processors, then jupiter(1:125) is mapped to the first processor, jupiter(126:250) is mapped to the second processor, and so on:

```
real, dimension (1000) :: jupiter
!HPF$ distribute (block) :: jupiter
```

In the next example, saturn(1:150) is mapped to processor 1, saturn(151:300) is mapped to processor 2, and so on:

```
real, dimension (1000) :: saturn
!HPF$ distribute (block (150)) :: saturn
```

There must be at least

$$\left\lceil \frac{1000}{150} \right\rceil$$

processors (or seven processors, in this case); if there are eight processors, the seventh has only 100 elements, saturn(901:1000), and the eighth none.

For more information on HPF, go to

http://www.crpc.rice.edu/HPFF/home.html.

1.1.8. F

F (Adams, Brainerd, Martin, & Smith, 1996; Brainerd, Goldberg, & Adams, 1996) is a clean, elegant, but powerful subset of Fortran that contains all the modern features of the language but does not contain older features that have more modern replacements. Also, many redundancies are eliminated, such as one of the two source forms and all but one of the many ways to declare variables. Thus, F is perfect for developing new Fortran code and for teaching programming. Most of the examples in this book conform to F. F books and compilers for most major computing systems are inexpensive and can be purchased from Imagine1, Inc. (http://www.imagine1.com/imagine1).

1.2. An Overview of the Fortran Language

The remaining sections illustrate the major features of Fortran 95, primarily with the use of examples. In this exposition, there is not sufficient space to discuss the detailed rules about how to use the features. Most of the features discussed are part of the F subset (Brainerd, Goldberg, & Adams, 1996); these are the features that should be learned in programming courses and the features that should be used by professional programmers when writing new code or modifying old code.

The first example is a program that prints the result of an addition:

```
program calculation_1
   print *, 84 + 13
end program calculation_1
```

The program `calculation_1` tells the computer to add the numbers 84 and 13 and then to print the sum, 97.

1.2.1. The Form of a Fortran Program

A Fortran program consists of a sequence of statements; these statements are written on lines that may contain from 0 to 132 characters.

1.2.1.1. Continued Statements

Often a Fortran statement fits on one line, but a statement can be continued onto multiple lines if the last character of the line to be continued is an ampersand (`&`):

```
print *,  &
      "I hope this is the right answer."
```

A statement cannot have more than 40 lines.

A statement cannot be broken in the middle of a keyword, a name, or a constant. If it is necessary to break a long character string, use the concatenation operator (`//`), as shown in the following example:

```
print *,  &
      "This is a line that contains a really, "  //  &
      "really, really, long character string."
```

The important fact is that, in the absence of a continuation symbol, the end of a line marks the end of a statement.

Each Fortran statement (except the assignment statements) begins with a keyword, such as `print`, that identifies the kind of statement it is.

1.2.1.2. Significant Blank Characters

Blank characters are significant in a Fortran program. In general, they must not occur within items that normally are not typed with blanks in English text, such as names and numbers. On the other hand, they usually must be used between two items that look like words. For example, in the first line of a program, the keyword `program` and the name of the program must be separated by one or more blanks, as in

```
program add_2
```

Keywords and names such as `print` and `number` must contain no blank characters, but keywords consisting of more than one English word may contain blanks between the words, as in the statement

```
end do
```

Two or more consecutive blanks are always equivalent to one blank unless they are in a character string.

1.2.1.3. Comments
Any occurrence of the exclamation symbol (!) other than within a character string or a comment marks the beginning of a comment. The comment is terminated by the end of the line. All comments are ignored.

Because comments are ignored, it is permissible to place a comment after the ampersand continuation symbol without impairing the continuation:

```
real :: x, &    ! measured value
       xbar     ! smoothed value
```

1.2.1.4. The Fortran Character Set
A Fortran statement is a sequence of characters. The characters of the Fortran character set consist of the uppercase letters A to Z, the lowercase letters a to z, the digits 0 to 9, the underscore (_), and the special characters in Table 1.1.

Table 1.1. The Fortran special characters.

Character	Name of Character
	Blank
:	Colon
=	Equals
!	Exclamation point
+	Plus
"	Quotation mark or quote
–	Minus
%	Percent
*	Asterisk

continues

Table 1.1. Continued.

Character	Name of Character
&	Ampersand
/	Slash
;	Semicolon
(	Left parenthesis
<	Less than
)	Right parenthesis
>	Greater than
,	Comma
?	Question mark
.	Decimal point or period
$	Currency symbol
'	Apostrophe or single quote

The character set contains all required characters but may contain additional characters, such as the nonprintable characters tab or bell or additional printable characters, such as {.

These additional characters may appear in a Fortran program only within a comment or character constant.

Two of the characters, $ and ?, have no special use, and the currency symbol need not display or print as $ in all implementations.

1.2.2. The program Statement

Each Fortran program must begin with a program statement. It consists of the keyword program followed by a program name of the programmer's choosing. A name must start with a letter and consist of at most 31 letters, digits, and underscores. Other Fortran names also follow these rules.

1.2.3. The end program Statement

The end program statement begins with the keywords end program, followed by the name of the program. Every Fortran program must have an end program statement as its last statement.

1.2.4. Intrinsic Data Types

The five intrinsic (in other words, built-in) data types in Fortran are integer, real, complex, logical, and character. Each data type has a set of values that may be represented in that type and operations that can be performed on those values.

1.2.4.1. The Integer Type

The integer type is used to represent values that are whole numbers. An integer constant is a string containing only the digits 0 to 9, possibly followed by an underscore (_) and a named integer constant, which designates the kind parameter, as described in section 1.2.5. The following are examples of integer constants:

```
23   0   1234567   42_short   42_long
```

1.2.4.2. The Real Type

There are two forms of a real constant. The first is called *positional form* because the place value of each digit is determined by its position relative to the decimal point. The positional form of a real constant consists of an integer followed by a decimal point followed by a string of digits representing the fractional part of the value, possibly followed by an underscore and a kind parameter. Assuming that double and quad are names of integer constants that are permissible real kinds on the Fortran system being used, all the following are real constants written in positional form:

```
13.5           0.1234567      123.45678
00.30_double   3.0            0.1234567_quad
```

The exponential form of a real number consists of a real number written in positional form followed by the letter e and an optionally signed integer (without a kind parameter) and optionally followed by an underscore and kind parameter. The letter e is read as "times 10 to the power" and the integer following the e is a power of 10 to be multiplied by the number preceding the e. For example, 23.4e5 represents 23.4×10^5. Another example is 1.0e9_double, which is one billion with kind parameter double.

1.2.4.3. The Complex Type

The Fortran complex type is used to represent the mathematical complex numbers. A complex constant is written as two (possibly signed) real numbers, separated by a comma and enclosed in parentheses. Examples of complex constants are

```
(1.0, -1.0)
(-1.0, 3.1e-27)
(3.14_double, -7.0_double)
```

1.2.4.4. Arithmetic Operators

The operators that may be used to combine two numeric values (integer, real, or complex) include +, -, *, /, and **. Except for **, these symbols have their usual mathematical meaning indicating addition, subtraction, multiplication, and division. The two asterisks indicate exponentiation.

Integer division always produces an integer result obtained by chopping off any fractional part of the mathematical result. For example, the value of 23 / 2 is 11.

1.2.4.5. Relational Operators

Numeric (and character) values may be compared with the relational operators <, <=, ==, /=, >=, and >. The result of a relational operator is type logical.

1.2.4.6. Mixed-Mode Expressions

The two operands of a numeric operator do not have to be the same data type; when they are different, one is converted to the type of the other prior to executing the operation. If one is type integer and the other is type real, the integer is converted to a real value; if one is type integer and the other is type complex, the integer is converted to a complex value; if one is type real and the other is type complex, the real is converted to a complex value. As an example, the value of the expression 23.0 / 2 is 11.5. If the two operands have different kind parameters, the number whose kind parameter specifies lesser precision is converted to the kind with greater precision before the operation is performed.

1.2.4.7. The Logical Type

The logical type is used to represent the two truth values true and false.

A logical constant is either .true. or .false., possibly followed by an underscore and a kind parameter.

The operators that may be used to combine logical values are .not., .and., .or., .eqv., and .neqv..

To give one simple example, the value of .false. .eqv. .false. is true.

1.2.4.8. The Character Type

The character type is used to represent strings of characters. The form of a character constant is a sequence of any characters representable in the computer delimited by quotation marks. If a quotation mark is to occur in the character string, it is represented by two quotation marks with no intervening characters:

```
"He said, ""Don't tread on me."""
```

There is only one character operator that produces a character result: concatenation. For example, the value of "John Q. " // "Public" is the string "John Q.Public", with no blank after the period.

1.2.5. Kind Parameters

Kind parameters provide a way to parameterize the selection of different possible machine representations for each of the intrinsic data types. If the programmer is careful, this provides a mechanism for making the selection of numeric precision and range portable.

Each intrinsic data type (integer, real, complex, characters, and logical) has a parameter, called its kind parameter, associated with it. A kind parameter is intended to designate a machine representation for a particular data type. As an example, an implementation might have three real kinds, informally known as single, double, and quadruple precision.

The kind parameter is an integer. These numbers are processor dependent so that kind parameters 1, 2, and 3 might be single, double, and quadruple precision; on a different system, kind parameters 4, 8, and 16 could be used for the same things.

There are at least two real and complex kinds and at least one kind for the other data types.

Note that the value of the kind parameter has nothing to do with the number of decimal digits of precision or range.

The intrinsic functions `selected_int_kind` and `selected_real_kind` can be used to select an appropriate kind for a variable or a named constant. These functions provide the means for making a program portable in cases where values need to be computed with a certain specified precision that may use single precision on one machine but require double precision on another machine.

When a kind parameter is a part of another constant, it follows the underscore at the end of the constant (except character, in which case it precedes the underscore and constant):

```
12345_short
1.345_very_precise
.true._enough
ascii_"first_name"
```

1.2.6. Parameters/Named Constants

A parameter is a named constant. Each parameter must be declared in a type statement. Type statements appear between the program statement and the beginning of the executable part of the program. Type statements also are used to give names to variables and indicate their data type.

Each parameter declaration consists of a keyword specifying an intrinsic type, followed by a comma and the keyword parameter, followed by two colons. To the right of the double colon is a list of names, each followed by an assignment and the expression giving the parameter value. The initialization assignments are separated by commas:

```
real, parameter :: pi = 3.14159, e = 2.71828
integer, parameter :: number_of_states = 50, &
                      number_of_senators = 2 * number_of_states
```

The value of a parameter is fixed by its declaration and cannot change during execution of a program.

1.2.7. Rules for Names

number_of_states and number_of_senators are names. The following are the rules for names of parameters as well as all other names in a program:

- The first character of the name must be a letter.

- The remaining characters may be any mixture of letters, digits, or underscore characters (_).

- There may be at most 31 characters in a name.

1.2.8. Variables

The value of a parameter is fixed by its declaration and cannot change during execution of a program. On the other hand, if the keyword parameter is omitted, the objects being declared become variables and their values can be changed at any time.

Thus, the following declares count to be an integer variable:

```
integer :: count
```

Variables may have a particular hardware representation by putting kind= followed by a named constant in parentheses after the keyword representing the data type:

```
integer, parameter :: more_precision = 2
real (kind = more_precision) :: dpq, x, long
```

A character variable also has a length. The keyword character may be followed by len= and an integer value indicating the number of characters in the character string in parentheses:

```
character (len = 20) :: name
```

Instead of an integer, the length of a dummy argument of type character may be * (meaning "assumed from the actual argument").

1.2.9. Attributes

In addition to the data type, a variable may be given several other attributes in a type declaration statement. Examples are pointer and save. Table 1.2 indicates these attributes and which of them make sense together.

TABLE 1.2. *Attribute compatibility.*

If two attributes can appear in the same type declaration statement, a check mark (✓) appears at their intersection in the chart. An × indicates incompatibility.

Attribute compatibility	Initialization	ALLOCATABLE	DIMENSION	EXTERNAL	INTENT	INTRINSIC	OPTIONAL	PARAMETER	POINTER	PRIVATE	PUBLIC	SAVE	TARGET
Initialization		X	✓	X	X	X	X	✓	✓	✓	✓	✓	✓
ALLOCATABLE	X		✓	X	X	X	X	X	X	✓	✓	✓	✓
DIMENSION	✓	✓		X	✓	X	✓	✓	✓	✓	✓	✓	✓
EXTERNAL	X	X	X		X	X	✓	X	X	✓	✓	X	X
INTENT	X	X	✓	X		X	✓	X	X	X	X	X	✓
INTRINSIC	X	X	X	X	X		X	X	X	✓	✓	X	X
OPTIONAL	X	X	✓	✓	✓	X		X	✓	X	X	X	✓
PARAMETER	✓	X	✓	X	X	X	X		X	✓	✓	X	X
POINTER	✓	X	✓	X	X	X	✓	X		✓	✓	✓	X
PRIVATE	✓	✓	✓	✓	X	✓	X	✓	✓		X	✓	✓
PUBLIC	✓	✓	✓	✓	X	✓	X	✓	✓	X		✓	✓
SAVE	✓	✓	✓	X	X	X	X	X	✓	✓	✓		✓
TARGET	✓	✓	✓	X	✓	X	✓	X	X	✓	✓	✓	

1.2.10. Intrinsic Functions

There are many built-in or intrinsic functions and a few built-in subroutines. To use the functions, simply type the name of the function followed by the arguments to the function, enclosed in parentheses. For example, abs(x) produces the absolute value of x, and max(a,b,c) yields the maximum of the values of a, b, and c.

Two of the more commonly used subroutines are date_and_time and random_number.

1.2.11. Expressions

An expression can be used to indicate many sorts of computations and manipulations of data values.

1.2.11.1. Primaries

The basic component of an expression is a primary. Primaries are combined with operations and grouped with parentheses to indicate how values are to be computed. A primary is a constant, variable, function reference, array element, array section, structure component, substring, array constructor, structure constructor, or an expression enclosed in parentheses.

1.2.11.2. The Interpretation of Expressions

When more than one operation occurs in an expression, parentheses and the precedence of the operations determine the operands to which the operations are applied. Operations with the highest precedence are applied first to the operand or operands immediately adjacent to the operator. For example, because * has higher precedence than +, in the expression a + b * c, the multiplication is first applied to its operands b and c; then the result of this computation is used as an operand by adding it to the value of a.

When two operators have the same precedence, they are applied left to right, except for exponentiation, which is applied right to left. Thus, the value of 9 - 4 - 3 is 5 - 3 = 2, but the value of 2 ** 3 ** 2 is 2^9 = 512.

Table 1.3 shows the operations with the highest precedence at the top of the list and the ones with the lowest precedence at the bottom.

Table 1.3. Operator precedence.

Operator	Precedence
User-defined unary operation	Highest
**	.
* or /	.
unary + or -	.
binary + or -	.
//	.
==, /=, <, <=, >, >=	.
.not.	.
.and.	.
.or.	.
.eqv. or .neqv.	.
User-defined binary operation	Lowest

1.2.11.3. The Evaluation of Expressions

After it has been determined by the use of parentheses and precedence of operations which operations are to be performed on which operands, the computer may evaluate the expression by doing the computations in any order that is mathematically equivalent to the one indicated by the correct interpretation—except that it must evaluate each subexpression within parentheses before combining it with any other value. For example, the interpretation of the expression a + b + c indicates that a and b are to be added and the result added to c. Once this interpretation is made, it can be determined that a mathematically equivalent result will be obtained by first adding b and c and then adding this sum to a. Thus, the computer may do the computation either way. However, if the programmer writes the expression (a + b) + c, the computer must first do the computation as required by the parentheses.

1.2.12. Assignment

The assignment statement is the most common way of giving a variable a value. An assignment statement consists of a variable, an equals sign (=), and an expression. The expression is evaluated and assigned to the variable.

An example of an assignment statement is

```
x = a + 2 * sin (b)
```

The variable on the left-hand side may be an array, an array element, an array section, a substring, or a structure component.

Complete agreement of the variable and expression type and kind is not always required. In some cases, the data type or kind parameter of the expression may be converted to assign it to the variable. If the variable on the left-hand side is any numeric type, the expression may be any numeric type and any kind. If the variable is type character, the expression must be type character, and they must be the same kind. If the variable is type logical, the expression must be type logical but may be any kind. If the variable is a derived type, the expression must be the same derived type. All of these rules apply to assignment as provided by the system (intrinsic assignment); it is possible to extend the meaning of assignment to other cases.

1.2.13. Control Constructs

Almost any useful program has the properties that some collections of statements are executed many times, and different sequences of statements are executed depending on the values of the input data.

The Fortran statements that control which statements are executed, together with the statements executed, are called control constructs.

There are three kinds of control constructs—the `if` construct, the `case` construct, and the `do` construct.

1.2.13.1. Statement Blocks
A collection of statements whose execution is controlled by one of the control constructs is called a block. For example, the statements between an `if` statement and the next matching `else if` statement form a block. Transferring control into a block from outside is not allowed, but it is possible to leave a `do` construct with a transfer of control, such as an `exit` or `cycle` statement. Any block may contain a complete `if`, `case`, or `do` construct so that these constructs can be nested to any level.

1.2.13.2. The `if` Construct
The `if` construct is a simple and elegant decision construct that permits the selection of one of a number of blocks during execution of a program. Some simple examples follow:

```
if (dice <= 3 .or. dice == 12) then
    print *, "You lose!"
else if (dice == 7 .or. dice == 11) then
    print *, "You win!"
else
    print *, "You have to keep rolling until you get"
    print *, "either a 7 or a", dice
end if

!  30 days has September, April, June, and November
if (month == 9 .or. month == 4 .or. &
    month == 6 .or. month == 11) then
    number_of_days = 30
!  All the rest have 31, except February
else if (month == 1 .or. month == 3 .or. &
    month == 5 .or. month == 7 .or. &
    month == 8 .or. month == 10 .or. &
    month == 12) then
    number_of_days = 31
else if (month == 2) then
    if (leap_year) then
        number_of_days = 29
    else
        number_of_days = 28
    end if
else
    print *, month, "is not the number of a month."
end if
```

The logical expressions in the `if` statement and the `else if` statements are tested until one is found to be true. Then the block following the statement containing that test is executed, which completes execution of the `if` construct. If all logical conditions are false, the block following the `else` statement is executed (if there is one).

1.2.13.3. The `case` Construct

The `case` construct is somewhat similar to the `if` construct in that it permits selection of one of a number of different alternative blocks of instructions, providing a streamlined syntax for an important special case of a multiway selection.

The `case` construct is executed by evaluating the expression in the `select case` statement. Then the expressions in the `case` statements are examined until one is found with a value or range that includes the value of the expression. The block of statements following this `case` statement is executed, completing execution of the entire `case` construct. Unlike `if` constructs, no more than one `case` statement can match the value of the expression. If no `case` statement matches the value of the expression and there is a `case default` statement, the block following the `case default` statement is executed.

Any of the items in the list of values in the `case` statement can be a range of values, indicated by the lower bound and upper bound separated by a colon (`:`). The `case` expression matches this item if the value of the expression is greater than or equal to the lower bound and less than or equal to the upper bound.

Some simple examples follow:

```
select case (dice)
   case (2:3, 12)
      print *, "You lose!"
   case (7, 11)
      print *, "You win!"
   case default
      print *, "You have to keep rolling until you get"
      print *, "either a 7 or a ", dice
end select

select case (traffic_light)
   case ("red")
      print *, "Stop"
   case ("yellow")
      print *, "Caution"
   case ("green")
      print *, "Go"
   case default
      print *, "Illegal value:", traffic_light
end select

select case (month)
   ! 30 days has September, April, June, and November
   case (9, 4, 6, 11)
      number_of_days = 30
```

```
    !  All the rest have 31, except February
    case (1, 3, 5, 7, 8, 10, 12)
        number_of_days = 31
    case (2)
        if (leap_year) then
            number_of_days = 29
        else
            number_of_days = 28
        end if
    case default
        print *, month, " is not the number of a month."
end select

select case (symbol)
    case ("a":"z")
        category = "lowercase letter"
    case ("A":"Z")
        category = "uppercase letter"
    case ("0":"9")
        category = "digit"
    case default
        category = "other"
end select
```

1.2.13.4. The do Construct

The looping construct in Fortran is the do construct. The general form of the do construct is

```
do loop control
    block of statements
end do
```

The block of statements, called the loop body or do construct body, is executed repeatedly as indicated by the loop control.

There are three types of loop control. In one instance, the loop control is missing, in which case the loop is executed until some explicit instruction in the do body such as an exit statement terminates the loop. In the second type of loop control, a variable takes on a progression of values until some limit is reached. The third type is executed while a logical expression is true.

Construct Names

A do construct may have a construct name on its first statement. It consists of an ordinary Fortran name followed by a colon. The end do statement that ends the construct must be followed by the same construct name. This permits more complete checking that do constructs are nested properly and provides a means of exiting or cycling more than one level of nested loop.

The `exit` Statement

The `exit` statement causes termination of execution of a loop. If the keyword `exit` is followed by the name of a `do` construct, that named loop (and all loops nested within it) is exited.

The `cycle` Statement

The `cycle` statement causes termination of the execution of one iteration of a loop. If the keyword `cycle` is followed by the name of a construct, all loops nested within that named loop are exited and control is transferred back to the beginning of the block of statements that comprise the named `do` construct.

Loops with No Loop Control

For a `do` construct with no loop control, the block of statements between the `do` statement and the matching `end do` statement is executed repeatedly until an `exit` statement causes it to terminate.

Suppose you want to print out all powers of 2 that are less than 1000. This is done with a simple `do` construct with no loop control and an `exit` statement:

```
program some_powers_of_2

    integer :: power_of_2

    power_of_2 = 1   ! The zero power of 2
    print_power: do
        print *, power_of_2
        power_of_2 = 2 * power_of_2
        if (power_of_2 >= 1000) then
            exit print_power
        end if
    end do print_power
end program some_powers_of_2
```

Loop Control with a `do` Variable

This type of loop control provides a simple means of assigning successive values to a variable each time an iteration of a loop is executed. A simple example that prints the squares and cubes of the integers 1 to 20 follows:

```
do number = 1, 20
    print *, number, number ** 2, number ** 3
end do
```

The `do while` Construct

The `do while` form of the `do` construct allows a loop to be executed as long as a logical condition is true. This is illustrated by a simple example of a loop that is executed until some iterative process converges:

```
converged = .false.
do while (.not. converged)
   call iter_8 (data, converged)
end do
```

1.2.14. Modules and Procedures

Modules provide a place to put data declarations so that they can be used and shared by programs. Modules also provide the place to put a procedure, which is either a function or a subroutine, and to put definitions of user-defined types; these are basic building blocks of a program and are usually used by more than one part of a program.

Modules are especially useful when building a package or library of data and procedures that may be accessible to many different programs.

1.2.14.1. Modules

A module is a program unit that is not executed directly but contains data specifications and procedures that may be utilized by other program units via the use statement.

Writing and Using Modules

To begin with a simple example, one use of a module is to include the definition of constants that might be useful in programs. The module math_module contains the values of pi, e, and g; of course, it could contain many more useful constants:

```
module math_module

   real, public, parameter :: pi = &
      3.1415926535897932384626433832795028841972
   real, public, parameter :: e = &
      2.7182818284590452353602874713526624977572
   real, public, parameter :: g = &
      0.5772156649015328606065120900824024310422

end module math_module
```

Any program that needs these constants can simply use the module:

```
program circle

   use math_module
   real :: radius, area

   radius = 2.2
   area = pi * radius ** 2
   print *, area

end program circle
```

It is also possible to declare variables in a module. The module `declarations_module` declares logical variables `flag_1` and `flag_2`, which could then be used in any program that uses the module:

```
module declarations_module

    logical, public :: flag_1, flag_2
end module declarations_module
```

Any program or procedures that use a module share the values of variables declared in the module. Thus, changing the value of such a variable in one procedure causes it to change in all procedures that use the module:

```
program using_modules

    use declarations_module
    logical, parameter :: f = .false.
    flag_1 = f
    flag_2 = .not. f
    . . .
end program using_modules
```

The form of a typical module is

```
module module name
    use statements
    private
    access statements
    type definitions
    type declarations
contains
    subroutines and functions
end module module name
```

The access statement consists of either `private` or `public` followed by a colon and a list of the names of procedures in the module. The access determines whether the procedure is available outside the module. Other entities, such as types, variables, and parameters, may have `public` or `private` as an attribute.

The use Statement

The simple form of the `use` statement is just the keyword `use` followed by a module to be used. However, with the `use` statement, there are two ways to affect the way that names in a module are accessed by another program unit. The first is that the names used in the module may be changed in the program unit using the module. For example, in a subroutine using module `math_module`, the programmer may rename the variable `e` to the longer name `logarithm_base` with the `use` statement:

```
use math_module, logarithm_base => e
```

Any number of rename clauses may appear in the use statement, but any name in the module can be renamed only once.

The second way to affect the objects accessed in a module is to have an only clause in the use statement. In the program circle, only the constant pi is needed. It is possible to prevent other names in the module from conflicting with names in the program; this can be accomplished with the use statement:

```
use math_module, only : pi
```

If, in addition, it is desirable to use and rename the parameter e to loga-rithm_base, this can be done with the statement

```
use math_module, only : pi, logarithm_base => e
```

1.2.14.2. Procedures

There are two kinds of procedures: functions and subroutines. A function looks much like a Fortran program, except that it begins with the keyword function instead of the keyword program. Once written, a function is used just like the built-in functions to compute a value that may be used in any expression. A subroutine also looks like a program or a function, except that the first line begins with the keyword subroutine. A subroutine may be used to perform any computation and is invoked by executing a call statement.

Functions and subroutines whose first statements begin with the keyword recursive are permitted to call themselves directly or indirectly; recursion is used to write clear and simple programs for what might otherwise be difficult programming tasks.

Argument Intent

In Fortran, you may indicate the intent of use of each dummy argument of a subroutine or function unless it is a pointer or dummy procedure. The intent may be in, which means that the dummy argument cannot be changed within the procedure; it may be out, which means that the actual argument must not be used until given a value in the procedure and is usually used to pass a value back to the calling program; or it may be in out, which means that the dummy argument is expected both to receive an initial value from and return a value to the corresponding actual argu-ment. Thus, for dummy arguments with intent out or in out, the corre-sponding actual argument must be a variable.

Keyword Arguments

With the use of keyword arguments, it is not necessary to put the arguments in the correct order, but it is necessary to know the names of the
dummy arguments. Suppose series_sum (m, n) is a function that sums the
integers from m to n, inclusive. Then, the statement

```
print *, series_sum (400, 700)
```

prints the value of 400 + 401 + ... + 700. The same computation may be
made using the statement

```
print *, series_sum (n = 700, m = 400)
```

Optional Arguments

In the sample computation of an arithmetic series, a common occurrence
would be that the value of m is 1. It is possible to indicate that certain
arguments to a procedure are optional arguments in the sense that they
do not have to be present when the procedure is called.

An optional argument must be declared to be such within the procedure;
usually, there would be some statements within the procedure to test the
presence of the optional argument on a particular call and perhaps do
something different if it is not there. In the example, if the function
series_sum is called without the argument m, the value 1 is used. To do
this, the intrinsic function present is used:

```
function series_sum (m, n) result (series_sum_result)

    integer, optional, intent (in) :: m
    integer, intent (in) :: n
    integer :: series_sum

      series_sum_result = n * (n + 1) / 2 end if
    if (present (m)) then
      series_sum_result = series_sum_result - (m - 1) * m / 2 if (present(m)) then
    else
    end if

end function series_sum
```

The result clause names the variable series_sum_result as the one to hold
the function result returned to the calling program. It is required in a
recursive function but is optional, otherwise.

This new version of the function can now be called with any of the following statements, all of which compute the same sum:

```
print *, series_sum (1, 700)
print *, series_sum (n = 700)
print *, series_sum (n = 700, m = 1)
print *, series_sum (m = 1, n = 700)
```

1.2.14.3. Pure Procedures

With the advent of parallel processing, problems associated with side effects become decidedly more pronounced than in a single processor environment. This is the case in calling a function in a `forall` construct, for example, in which the execution order is indeterminate. For the computational result to be determinate, the function must not have side effects such as changing values in common or writing intermediate results to a file. Pure procedures are intended to disallow the side effects that impact determinancy. Pure procedures have a number of other advantages as well, such as making possible the use of user-defined functions in specification expressions.

All the intrinsic functions and the `mvbits` intrinsic subroutine are pure procedures. The prefix specification `pure` in a user-defined function or subroutine statement specifies that procedure to be pure. There are four contexts in which a procedure must be pure:

- A function referenced in a `forall` construct

- A function referenced in a specification statement

- A procedure that is passed as an actual argument to a pure procedure

- A procedure referenced in the body of a pure procedure (including those referenced by a defined operator or defined assignment)

1.2.14.4. Elemental Procedures

The purpose of elemental procedures is to allow the programmer to define a procedure with scalar arguments and the `elemental` keyword that can be called with array arguments of any rank.

An elemental procedure has all scalar dummy arguments; in addition, an elemental function delivers a scalar result. The expressive power of elemental procedures comes from the provision that the actual arguments may be arrays of any rank, as long as all the actual arguments in a given call to an elemental procedure are in general conformable. The result of an elemental call having array actual arguments is the same as would have been obtained if the procedure had been applied separately, in any order (including simultaneously), to the corresponding elements of each argument.

The prefix specification `elemental` in a user-defined function or subroutine statement specifies that procedure to be elemental. Here is an example:

```
elemental function vip_calc(x, y)

    real :: vip_calc
    real, intent(in) :: x, y
        . . .
end function vip_calc

    x = vip_calc(1.1, 2.2)  ! A call to vip_calc with scalar arguments
    ax = vip_calc(a(1:n), b(1:n))
! The result of this call is an array
!   conformable with a(1:n) and b(1:n).
```

1.2.15. Arrays

The name of an array obeys the same rules as an ordinary variable name. Each array must be declared in the declaration section of program, module, or procedure. A name is declared to be an array by putting the dimension attribute in a type statement followed by a range of subscripts, enclosed in parentheses:

```
real, dimension (1 : 9) :: x, y
logical, dimension (-99 : 99) :: yes_no
```

In a function or subroutine, the range of a dummy argument may consist of just the colon, possibly preceded by a lower bound, and the subscript range is determined by the corresponding actual argument passed to the procedure. This sort of dummy argument is called an assumed-shape array. If no lower bound is given, the subscript range is from 1 to the size of the array, in each dimension:

```
subroutine s (d)
    integer, dimension (:, :, 0:), intent (in) :: d
```

An array of character strings may be declared in a form such as the following:

```
character (len = 8), dimension (0 : 17) :: char_list
```

In this example, the variable char_list is an array of 18 character strings, each of length 8.

The shape of an array is a list of the number of elements in each dimension. A 9×7 array has shape (9,7); the array char_list declared above has shape (18); and the array declared by

```
integer, dimension (9, 0:99, -99:99) :: iii
```

has shape (9,100,199). When only one number is given in a dimension declaration in place of a subscript range, it is used as the upper subscript bound and the lower bound is 1.

The shape of a scalar is a list with no elements in it. The shape of a scalar or array can be computed using the shape intrinsic function.

1.2.15.1. Array Constructors

An array constructor is a convenient way to give an array a set of values. An array constructor is a list of values, separated by commas and delimited by the pair of two-character symbols (/ and /).

There are three possible forms for the array constructor values:

- A scalar expression, as in

```
x (1:4) = (/ 1.2, 3.5, 1.1, 1.5 /)
```

- An array expression, as in

```
x (1:4) = (/ a (i, 1:2), a (i+1, 2:3) /)
```

- An implied do loop, as in

```
x (1:4) = (/ (sqrt (real (i)), i = 1, 4) /)
```

If there are no values specified in an array constructor, the resulting array is zero sized. The values of the components must have the same type and type parameters (kind and length). The rank of an array constructor is always one; however, the reshape intrinsic function can be used to define rank-two to rank-seven arrays from the array constructor values where

```
reshape ( (/ 1, 2, 3, 4, 5, 6 /), (/ 2, 3 /) )
```

is the 2 × 3 array

$$\begin{bmatrix} 1\ 3\ 5 \\ 2\ 4\ 6 \end{bmatrix}$$

1.2.15.2. Dynamic Arrays

By giving an array the allocatable or pointer attribute, memory may be allocated for the array during execution of the program:

```
real, dimension (:,:), allocatable :: data_array
   . . .
read *, n
allocate (data_array (n,n+1))
```

The deallocate statement may be used to free the allocated storage.

1.2.15.3. Array Sections

Sometimes, only a portion of the elements of an array is needed for a computation. It is possible to refer to a selected portion of an array, called an array section.

For example, if v is a one-dimensional array of ten numbers, then

    v (0:4)

represents elements v(0), v(1), v(2), v(3), and v(4) and

    v (3:7:2)

represents elements v(3), v(5), and v(7).

Another way of selecting a section of an array is to use a vector subscript. A vector subscript is an integer array expression of rank one. For example, if iv is an array of three integers, 3, 7, and 2, and x is an array of 9 real numbers 1.1, 2.2, ... 9.9, the value of x(iv) is the list of three numbers 3.3, 7.7, and 2.2—the third, seventh, and second elements of x.

1.2.15.4. Array Assignment

Array assignment is permitted under two circumstances: when the array expression on the right has exactly the same shape as the array on the left, and when the expression on the right is a scalar. The term for this is that the expression on the right of the equals is conformable to the variable on the left. Note that, for example, if a is a 9×9 array, the section a(2:4,5:8) is the same shape as a(3:5,1:4), so the assignment

    a (2:4, 5:8) = a (3:5, 1:4)

is valid, but the assignment

    a (1:4, 1:3) = a (1:3, 1:4)

is not valid because even though there are 12 elements in the array on each side of the assignment, the left side has shape (4,3) and the right side has shape (3,4).

When a scalar is assigned to an array, the value of the scalar is assigned to every element of the array. Thus, for example, the statement

    m (k+1:n, k) = 0

sets the elements m(k+1,k), m(k+2,k), ... m(n,k) to 0.

1.2.15.5. Intrinsic Operators

All of the intrinsic operators and many of the intrinsic functions may be applied to arrays, operating independently on each element of the array. For example, the expression `abs(a(k:n,k))` results in a one-dimensional array of `n-k+1` non-negative real values. A binary operation, such as `*`, may be applied only to two arrays of the same shape or an array and a scalar. It multiplies corresponding elements of the two arrays or multiplies the elements of the array by the scalar. The assignment statement

```
a (k, k:n+1) = a (k, k:n+1) / pivot
```

divides each element of `a(k,k:n+1)` by the real scalar value `pivot`. In essence, a scalar value may be considered an array of the appropriate size and shape with all its entries equal to the value of the scalar.

1.2.15.6. Masked Array Assignment—The `where` Construct

The `where` construct may be used to assign values to only those elements of an array where a logical condition is true. For example, the following statement sets the elements of `b` to `0` in those positions where the corresponding element of `a` is negative:

```
where (a < 0)
   b = 0
end where
```

The other elements of `b` are unchanged. `a` and `b` must be arrays of the same shape. The logical condition in parentheses is an array of logical values conformable to each array in the assignment statement. In the preceding example, comparison of an array of values with a scalar produces the array of logical values.

The `where` construct permits any number of array assignments to be done under control of the same logical array, and the `elsewhere` statement within a `where` construct permits array assignments to be done where the logical expression is false. The following statements assign to the integer array `size_category` an indication of the size of the elements of `b`:

```
real, dimension (m,n) :: b
integer, dimension (m,n) :: a
    . . .
where (abs(b) > huge (b)/100.0)
   a = 3
elsewhere (abs(b) > 10.0*epsilon (b))
   a = 2
elsewhere
   a = 1
end where
```

Within a `where` construct, only array assignments and nested `where` constructs are permitted. The shape of all arrays in the assignment statements must conform to the shape of the logical expression following the keyword `where`. The assignments are executed in the order they are written—first those in the `where` block, then those in the `elsewhere` block.

1.2.15.7. Indexed Parallel Array Assignment—The `forall` Construct

The `forall` construct provides a mechanism to specify an indexed parallel assignment of values to an array for the following sorts of formulas often found in mathematical treatises:

$$a_{ij} = i + j, \text{ for } i = 1 \text{ to } n, j = 1 \text{ to } m$$

or

$$a_{ii} = b_i, \text{ for } i = 1 \text{ to } n$$

The first formula can be translated into nested `do` loops:

```
do j = 1, m
   do i = 1, n
      a(i,j) = i + j
   end do
end do
```

This formulation does not allow for the optimization that can be achieved on some computers when array notation is used.

The `forall` statement makes use of array element and section references to express such calculations more naturally and at the same time indicate computations that may be executed in parallel:

```
forall (i=1:n, j=1:m)
   a(i,j) = i+j
end forall
```

The second formula cannot be expressed with array section notation, but a `forall` statement can be used to assign the elements of the array `b` of rank one to the diagonal of array `a`:

```
forall (i=1:n)
   a(i,i) = b(i)
end forall
```

The following are permitted in a `forall` body:

- Assignment statements

- Pointer assignment statements

- `where` constructs

- `forall` constructs

The `forall` statement resembles a loop construct, but its evaluation rules treat the statements within the construct as indexed parallel operations, in which a particular statement is executed for all selected index values before the next statement in the `forall` body is executed. As such, it is not a control construct, but a special kind of parallel assignment statement. On the other hand, a `do` construct executes each statement in its range in order for a particular index value and then returns to the first statement in the range to repeat the computations for the next index value.

Sometimes it is desirable to exclude some elements from taking part in a calculation. Thus, an optional mask expression may appear in a `forall` header:

```
forall (i=1:n, j=1:m, a(i)<9.0 .and. b(j)<9.0)
   c(i,j) = a(i) + b(j)
end forall
```

1.2.15.8. Calculating Probabilities

Consider the problem of calculating the probability that a throw of two dice will yield a 7 or an 11. The resulting program uses the built-in subroutine `random_number` to generate random numbers between 0 and 1.

When the argument to the built-in subroutine `random_number` is a real array, the array is filled with a collection of real numbers each greater than or equal to 0 and less than 1. The subroutine `random_int`, which calls `random_number`, returns an array of integers from low to high:

```
module random_module

    public :: random_int

    contains

    subroutine random_int (value, low, high)

        integer, dimension (:), intent (out) :: value
        integer, intent (in) :: low, high
        real, dimension (:), allocatable :: uniform_random_value

        allocate (uniform_random_value (size (value)))
        call random_number (uniform_random_value)
        value = int ((high - low + 1) * uniform_random_value + low)
        deallocate (uniform_random_value)

    end subroutine random_int

end module random_module

program seven_11

    use random_module
```

```
integer, parameter :: number_of_rolls = 1000
integer, dimension (number_of_rolls) :: dice, die_1, die_2
integer :: wins

call random_int (die_1, 1, 6)
call random_int (die_2, 1, 6)
dice = die_1 + die_2
wins = count ((dice == 7) .or. (dice == 11))

print "(a, f6.2)", &
    "The percentage of rolls that are 7 or 11 is", &
    100.0 * real (wins) / real (number_of_rolls)

end program seven_11
```

The built-in function `count` returns the number of true values in any logical array; in this case, the value in the array is true if the corresponding value in the array dice is 7 or 11.

1.2.16. Character Data

Each object of type character has a fixed length, which is the number of characters that the string has. For example, the declaration

```
character (len = 7) :: string_7
```

declares the variable `string_7` to be a character string of length 7. It is possible to have an array of character strings, all of the same length. The following declares `string_array` to be a $5 \times 9 \times 7$ array of character strings of length 20:

```
character (len = 20), dimension (5,9,7) :: string_array
```

It is possible for a character string to have length 0.

Character dummy arguments may have their length designated as an asterisk, indicating that their length will be determined by the corresponding actual argument.

1.2.16.1. Character Parameters

A character constant may be given a name using the parameter attribute. As a simple example, the program `hello` prints a character parameter or named character constant, instead of a literal character constant:

```
program hello
    character (len = *), parameter :: &
        message = "Hello, I am a computer."
    print *, message
end program hello
```

Note that the name of the character parameter must be declared, just like a character variable, but the length may be declared as an asterisk indicating that the length is to be determined from the value of the string.

1.2.16.2. Character Constants

A character constant is enclosed in quotation marks (double quotes). It may have a kind parameter, which precedes the opening quote:

```
greek_"μικονσσ"
```

1.2.16.3. Substrings

A substring of a character string is any consecutive sequence of characters in the string. There is a convenient way to refer to any contiguous subsequence of characters of a character string. This is done by writing after any character variable or array element two integer expressions that give the positions of the first and last characters in the substring. These two expressions are separated by a colon and enclosed in parentheses. An example is string(k:m), where the values of k and m are positive integers less than or equal to the length of string and k≤m. If k>m, the result is the null string. For example if c = "crunch",

```
c (2 : 4) is run
c (1 : 6) is crunch
c (3 : 2) is the null string
c (2 : 7) is illegal
c (5 : 5) is c
```

The last example illustrates how to refer to a single character of a string.

1.2.16.4. Concatenation

The only built-in operation that can be performed on strings that produces a string result is concatenation. The symbol for concatenation is two slashes (//).

1.2.17. Structures and Derived Types

A structure is a collection of values, not necessarily of the same type. The objects that make up a structure are called its components. The components of a structure are identified by Fortran names.

An example of the use of a structure might be provided by a simple text editor, such as the one supplied with many BASIC programming language systems. Each line in a BASIC program consists of a line number and one or more statements. One way to do this is to have an object called line consisting of two components, an integer line_number, and a character string statement. The entire program would then be an array of these structures, one for each line.

The components of a structure may be arrays or other structures. The elements of an array may be a structure. The elements of an array may not be arrays, but this functionality can be achieved with an array whose elements are structures whose only component is an array or by a higher dimensional (rank) array.

1.2.17.1. Derived Types

As was mentioned previously, there are five intrinsic Fortran data types: integer, real, complex, logical, and character. A programmer may define a new data type, called a derived type. A derived type can be used only to define a structure. Conversely, a structure can occur in a program only as a value of some derived type.

A type definition begins with the keyword type, possibly followed by the private or public accessibility attribute, followed by two colons (::) and the name of the type being defined. The components of the type are given in the form of ordinary type declarations. The type definition ends with the keywords end type, followed by the name of the type being defined.

A definition of a type that would be useful for the BASIC editor is

```
type, public :: line
    integer :: line_number
    character (len = line_length) :: text
end type line
```

where line_length is an integer parameter (named constant).

1.2.17.2. Declaring and Using Structures

Given the type definition for line, a variable new_line that could be used to represent one line of the program can then be declared by

```
type (line) :: new_line
```

As shown in this example, a variable is declared to be a derived type with a declaration that is similar to the declaration of a variable of intrinsic type, except that the name of the intrinsic type is replaced by the keyword type and the name of the type in parentheses.

An entire BASIC program to be edited could be represented by a single variable declared to be an array of values of type line:

```
type (line), dimension (max_lines) :: basic_program
```

1.2.17.3. Referencing Structure Components

A component of a structure is referenced by writing the name of the structure followed by a percent sign (%) and then the name of the component. Suppose new_line is a variable declared to be type line as shown previously. Then the line number of the line is referenced by the expression

```
new_line % line_number
```

1.2.17.4. Structure Constructors

Each derived-type declaration creates a structure constructor, whose name is the same as that of the derived type. For example, if you define a type named boa, you have a boa constructor. This constructor may be used much like a function to create a structure of the named type. The arguments are values to be placed in the individual components of the structure. For example, using the type line, a value for new_line may be assigned with the statement

```
new_line = line (previous_line_number + 1, "LET A = B")
```

1.2.18. Extending Fortran

In Fortran, the programmer can create generic procedures, define new operators, and extend the definition of intrinsic functions, existing operators, and assignment. These features will be illustrated by constructing a new data type for computing with large integers.

The Fortran intrinsic integer type has a limit on the size of numbers it can represent; the largest integer can be determined on any Fortran system as the value of the intrinsic function huge(0). A typical limit is $2^{31}-1$, which is 2,147,483,647. This problem can be solved by creating a new data type, called big_integer, deciding which operations are needed, and writing procedures that perform the operations on values of this type. All of this will be placed in a module called big_integers.

1.2.18.1. The Type Definition for Big Integers

The first task is to decide how these large integers will be represented. Although a linked list of digits is a possibility, it seems more straightforward to use an array of ordinary Fortran integers. The only remaining thing to decide is how much of a big integer to put into each element of the array. One possibility is to put as large a number into each element as possible. To make it easier to conceptualize with simple examples, I store one decimal digit in each element. However, because the abstract data type paradigm is followed, changing the representation so that larger integers are stored in each array element can be implemented easily without changing the programs that use the big_integer module.

The following type definition example does the job. This type definition uses a parameter nr_of_digits that has arbitrarily been set to 100, which allows decimal numbers with up to 100 digits to be represented using this scheme. The parameter nr_of_digits has the private attribute, which means it cannot be accessed outside the module:

```
integer, parameter, private :: nr_of_digits = 100

type, public :: big_integer
   private
   integer, dimension (0 : nr_of_digits) :: digit
end type big_integer
```

The array `digit` has 101 elements: `digit(0)` holds the ones digit, `digit(1)` holds the tens digit, `digit(2)` holds the hundreds digit, and so on. The extra element in the array is used to check for overflow. If any value other than 0 gets put into the largest element, that is considered to exceed the largest `big_integer` value, and after we have extended the intrinsic function `huge`, the value is set to the largest possible big integer. The `private` statement indicates that we don't want anybody that uses the module to be able to access the component digit of a variable of type `big_integer`, even though the type itself is public; we provide all the operations necessary to compute with such values.

The next thing to do is to define some operations for big integers. The first necessary operations assign values to a big integer and print the value of a big integer. Let's take care of the printing first. The following subroutine prints the value of a big integer. It takes advantage of the fact that each element of the array digit is one decimal digit. This subroutine `print_big` is inside the module `big_integers`, so it has access to all the data and procedures in the module:

```
subroutine print_big (b)

   type (big_integer), intent (in) :: b
   integer :: n, first_significant_digit
   character (len = 10) :: format

   ! Find first significant digit
   first_significant_digit = 0   ! In case b = 0
   do n = nr_of_digits, 1, -1
      if (b % digit (n) /= 0) then
         first_significant_digit = n
         exit
      end if
   end do

   ! Set format = "(<first_significant_digit+1>i1)"
   write (unit = format, fmt = "(a, i6, a)")  &
         "(", first_significant_digit + 1, "i1)"
   print format,  &
         b % digit (first_significant_digit : 0 : -1)

end subroutine print_big
```

The basic strategy is to print the digits in `i1` format, where each digit occupies one character position in the output, but first the leftmost nonzero digit must be located, both to compute the multiplier in the format specification and to avoid printing long strings of leading zeros. This way, there is also no problem if the parameter nr_of_digits is changed.

Another interesting feature is that we use a formatted write to a character variable to convert an integer subscript to character form for inclusion in an edit descriptor. In effect, we calculate the appropriate print format on-the-fly.

To test this subroutine, we need a way to assign values to a big integer. One possibility is to write a procedure that assigns an ordinary Fortran integer to a big integer, but this limits the size of the integer that can be assigned. A second possibility is to write the integer as a character string consisting of only digits 0–9. (We are not allowing negative numbers.) This is done by the subroutine big_gets_char(b,c) that assigns the integer represented by the character string c to the big integer b. If c contains a character other than one of the digits or c contains more digits than can be stored in b, the value huge(b) is assigned:

```
subroutine big_gets_char (b, c)

    type (big_integer), intent (out) :: b
    character (len = *), intent (in) :: c
    integer :: n, i

    if (len (c) > nr_of_digits) then
        b = huge (b)
        return
    end if

    b % digit = 0
    n = 0
    do i = len (c), 1, -1
        b % digit (n) = index ("0123456789", c (i:i)) - 1
        if (b % digit (n) == -1) then
            b = huge (b)
            return
        end if
        n = n + 1
    end do

end subroutine big_gets_char
```

The name for the subroutine big_gets_char was picked because it converts a character string to a big integer. This is like intrinsic assignment that converts an integer to a real value when necessary. Indeed, it is possible to use the assignment statement to do the conversion from character to big integer. It is done by extending assignment. The following interface block is placed in the module big_integers to indicate that the module procedure big_gets_char is to be used to extend assignment to the case

where the variable on the left side of the assignment is a big integer and
the expression on the right side is a character expression:

```
public :: assignment (=)
private :: big_gets_char

interface assignment (=)
    module procedure big_gets_char
end interface
```

Here is what the module big_integers looks like so far:

```
module big_integers_module

integer, parameter, private :: nr_of_decimal_digits = 100

type, public :: big_integer
    private
    integer, dimension (0 : nr_of_digits) :: digit
end type big_integer

interface assignment (=)
    module procedure big_gets_char
end interface

public :: assignment (=)
private :: big_gets_char

"contains"

subroutine big_gets_char (b, c)
    . . .
end subroutine big_gets_char

subroutine print_big (b)
    . . .
end subroutine print_big

end module big_integers_module
```

Any user of the module can use the assignment statement instead of calling a subroutine, which makes the program a lot easier to understand:

```
program test_big_1

    use big_integers_module
    type (big_integer) :: b1

    b1 = "71234567890987654321"
    call print_big (b1)
    b1 = "123456789+987654321"    ! Will be huge(b) = 99999...
    call print_big (b1)

end program test_big_1
```

With conversion from character strings to big integers using the assignment statement, there is no need to have the subroutine `big_gets_char` available. It is declared `private`.

1.2.18.2. Extending Intrinsic Functions to Big Integers

Many of the Fortran intrinsic functions manipulate numeric values, and it is reasonable to extend some of them, such as `modulo` and `sqrt`, to have big integer arguments. This is done by writing an interface block and the function to do the computation. This is illustrated by extending the intrinsic function `huge` so that when given a big integer as argument, it returns the largest possible big integer. This function is tested by the program `test_big_2`:

```
module big_integers_module

    intrinsic huge
    public :: huge
        . . .
    interface huge
        module procedure huge_big
    end interface
        . . .

contains
    . . .

function huge_big (b)   result (huge_big_result)

    type (big_integer), intent (in) :: b
    type (big_integer) :: huge_big_result

    huge_big_result % digit (0 : nr_of_digits - 1) = 9
    huge_big_result % digit (nr_of_digits) = 0

end function huge_big
    . . .
end module big_integers_module

program test_big_2

    use big_integers_module
    type (big_integer) :: b1
    call print_big (huge (b1))

end program test_big_2
```

1.2.18.3. Adding Big Integers

Now that we can assign to a big integer variable and print its value, it would be nice to be able to perform some computations with big integers. Addition can be done with a function that adds just like we do with pencil and paper, adding two digits at a time and keeping track of any carry-over, starting with the rightmost digits. The function `big_plus_big` does this:

```
function big_plus_big (x, y) result (big_plus_big_result)

    type (big_integer), intent (in) :: x, y
    type (big_integer) :: big_plus_big_result
    integer :: carry, temp_sum, n

    carry = 0
    do n = 0, nr_of_digits
        temp_sum = x % digit (n) + y % digit (n) + carry
        big_plus_big_result % digit (n) = modulo (temp_sum, 10)
        carry = temp_sum / 10
    end do

    if (big_plus_big_result % digit(nr_of_digits) /= 0 &
        .or. carry /= 0) then
        big_plus_big_result = huge (big_plus_big_result)
    end if

end function big_plus_big
```

We now extend the meaning of addition to our own newly defined type, big_integer. This is done with another interface block, this time with the keyword operator, followed by the operator being extended. The + operator is public, but the subroutine big_plus_big is private:

```
interface operator (+)
    module procedure big_plus_big
end interface
```

The use of the + operator to add two big integers is tested by the program test_big_3:

```
program test_big_3

    use big_integers_module
    type (big_integer) :: b1, b2

    b1 = "1234567890987654321"
    b2 = "9876543210123456789"
    call print_big (b1 + b2)
end program test_big_3
```

The value printed by this program is

```
11111111101111111110
```

1.2.19. Pointer Variables

In Fortran, a pointer variable or simply a pointer is best thought of as a free-floating name that can be associated dynamically with or aliased to some data object. The data object already may have one or more other names, or it may be an unnamed object.

Syntactically, a pointer is just any sort of variable that has been given the pointer attribute in a declaration. A variable with the pointer attribute may be used just like any ordinary variable, but it may be used in some additional ways as well.

To understand how Fortran pointers work, it is almost always better to think of them simply as aliases. Another possibility is to think of the pointers as descriptors, sufficient to describe a row of a matrix, for example.

1.2.19.1. The Use of Pointers
Each pointer in a program is in one of three states:

- It may be undefined, which is the condition of all pointers at the beginning of a program.

- It may be null, which means that it is not the alias of any data object.

- It may be associated, which means that it is the alias of some target data object.

The terms *disassociated* and *not associated* are used when a pointer is in state 1 or state 2. The associated intrinsic inquiry function distinguishes between states 2 and 3 only; its arguments must not be undefined.

1.2.19.2. The Pointer Assignment Statement
A variable with the pointer attribute may be an object more complicated than a simple variable. It may be an array or structure, for example. The following declares v to be a pointer to a one-dimensional array of reals:

```
real, dimension (:), pointer :: v
```

With v so declared, it may be used to alias any one-dimensional array of reals, including a row or column of some two-dimensional array of reals where

```
v => real_array (4, :)
```

makes v an alias of the fourth row of the array real_array. real_array must have the target attribute for this to be legal:

```
real, dimension (100, 100), target :: real_array
```

Once a variable with the pointer attribute is an alias for some data object—that is, it is pointing to something—it may be used in the same way that any other variable may be used. For the preceding example, using v,

```
print *, v
```

has the same effect as

```
print *, real_array (4, :)
```

and the assignment statement

```
v = 0
```

has the effect setting all the elements of the fourth row of the array real_array to 0.

1.2.19.3. The allocate and deallocate Statements

With the allocate statement, it is possible to create space for a value and cause a pointer variable to refer to that space. The space has no name other than the pointer mentioned in the allocate statement. For example, if p1 is declared by

```
real, pointer :: p1
```

the statement

```
allocate (p1)
```

creates space for one real number and makes p1 an alias for that space. No real value is stored in the space by the allocate statement, so it is necessary to assign a value to p1 before it can be used, just as with any other real variable.

The deallocate statement throws away the space pointed to by its argument and makes its argument null (state 2) where

```
deallocate (p1)
```

disassociates p1 from any target and nullifies it.

1.2.19.4. The null Function

At the beginning of a program, a pointer variable (just as all other variables) is not defined unless it is initialized with the null intrinsic function. A pointer variable must not be referenced to produce a value when it is not defined, but it is sometimes desirable to have a pointer variable be in the state of not pointing to anything, which might signify the last item in a linked list, for example. This occurs when it is nullified, which creates a condition that may be tested and assigned to other pointers by pointer assignment (=>). The following statement nullifies p1:

```
p1 => null ()
```

If p1 is null, then executing the pointer assignment

```
p2 => p1
```

causes p2 to be null also.

1.2.19.5. The associated **Intrinsic Function**

The associated intrinsic function can be used to determine if a pointer variable is pointing to, or is an alias for, another object. To use this function, the pointer variable must be defined; that is, it must either be the alias of some data object or be null. The associated function indicates which of these two cases is true; thus it provides the means of testing if a pointer is null.

The associated function may have a second argument. If the second argument is a target, the value of the function indicates whether the first argument is an alias of the second argument. If the second argument is a pointer, it must be defined; in this case, the value of the function is true if both pointers are null or if they are both aliases of the same target. For example, the expression

```
associated (p1, r)
```

indicates whether p1 is an alias of r, and the expression

```
associated (p1, p2)
```

indicates whether p1 and p2 are both aliases of the same thing or they are both null.

1.2.19.6. Trees

An efficient sorting program can be constructed using a data structure that is a binary tree. The resulting program, tree_sort, has an expected running time proportional to $n \log_2 n$.

It is quite difficult to write nonrecursive programs to process trees, so we will think of trees as recursive structures. Using this approach, a binary tree of integers is either empty or an integer, followed by two binary trees of integers, called the left subtree and right subtree.

Sorting with Trees

To sort numbers with a tree, we will construct a special kind of ordered binary tree with the property that the number at the top or root node of the tree is greater than all the numbers in its left subtree and less than or equal to all the numbers in its right subtree. This property will hold not only for the most accessible node at the top of the tree, but for all nodes of the tree.

The sorting process consists of inserting the values to be sorted, one at a time, into the tree (after starting with and empty tree) and then printing the values in the tree in the correct (infix) order.

Type Declarations for Trees

The declaration for the node of a tree must contain two pointers, one to the left subtree and

```
type, public :: node
    integer :: value
    type (node), pointer :: left, right
end type node
```

The subroutine that inserts a new number into the tree is a straightforward implementation of the following informal recipe: If the tree is empty, make the new entry the only node of the tree; if the tree is not empty and the number to be inserted is less than the number at the root, insert the number in the left subtree; otherwise, insert the number in the right subtree.

The recipe for printing the nodes of the tree follows from the way the tree has been built: It is simply to print in order the values in the left subtree of the root, print the value at the root node, and then print in order the values in the right subtree. This subroutine is shown in the following complete module and program that sort a file of integers by reading them all in, constructing an ordered binary tree, and then printing out the values in the tree in order:

```
module tree_module

public :: insert, print_tree

    type, public :: node
        integer :: value
        type (node), pointer :: left, right
    end type node

contains

    recursive subroutine insert (t, number)

        type (node), pointer :: t   ! A tree
        integer, intent (in) :: number

        ! If (sub)tree is empty, put number at root
        if (.not. associated (t)) then
            allocate (t)
            t % value = number
            t % left => null ()
            t % right => null ()
        ! Otherwise, insert into correct subtree
        else if (number < t % value) then
            call insert (t % left, number)
        else
            call insert (t % right, number)
        end if

    end subroutine insert
```

```
recursive subroutine print_tree (t)
! Print tree in infix order

    type (node), pointer :: t  ! A tree

    if (associated (t)) then
        call print_tree (t % left)
        print *, t % value
        call print_tree (t % right)
    end if

end subroutine print_tree

end module tree_module

program tree_sort
! Sorts a file of integers by building a
! tree, sorted in infix order.
! This sort has expected behavior n log n,
! but worst case (input is sorted) n ** 2.

    use tree_module

    type (node), pointer :: t  ! A tree
    integer :: number, ios

    t => null ()   ! Start with empty tree
    do
        read (unit = *, fmt = *, iostat = ios) number
        if (ios < 0) then
            exit
        end if
        call insert (t, number) ! Put next number in tree
    end do
    ! Print nodes of tree in infix order
    call print_tree (t)

end program tree_sort
```

1.2.20. Input and Output

The input/output statements are

```
read

print

write

open

close

inquire

backspace

endfile

rewind
```

The read, write, and print statements are the ones that do the data transfer; the open and close statements deal with the connection between an input/output unit and a file; the inquire statement provides the means to find out things about a file or unit; and the backspace, endfile, and rewind statements affect the position of the file.

Input and output operations deal with collections of data called files. The data in files are organized into records, which may correspond to lines on a computer terminal, lines on a printout, or parts of a disk file. The descriptions of records and file are to be considered abstractions and do not necessarily represent the way data is stored physically on any particular device.

1.2.20.1. Records

There are two kinds of records—data records and endfile records. A data record is a sequence of values. The values in a data record may be represented in one of two ways: formatted or unformatted. If the values are characters readable by a person, each character is one value and the data is formatted. For example, the statement

```
write (unit=*, fmt="(i1, a, i2)") 6, ",", 11
```

produces a record containing the following four character values: 6,11.

Unformatted data consists of values usually represented just as they are stored in computer memory.

Formatted Records

A formatted record is one that contains only formatted data. A formatted record may be created by a person typing at a terminal or by a Fortran program that converts values stored internally into character strings that form readable representations of those values. When formatted data is read into the computer, the characters must be converted to the computer's internal representation of values, which is often a binary representation. Even character values may be converted from one character representation in the record to another internal representation. The length of a formatted record is the number of characters in it; the length may be zero.

Unformatted Records

An unformatted record is one that contains only unformatted data. Unformatted records usually are created by running a Fortran program, although, with the knowledge of how to form the bit patterns correctly, they could be created by other means. Unformatted data often requires less space on an external device. Also, it is usually faster to read and write unformatted data because no conversion is required. However, it is not as suitable for reading by humans, and usually it is not suitable for transferring data from one computer to another because the internal representation of values is machine dependent. The length of an unformatted data record depends on the number of values in it but is measured in some processor-dependent units such as machine words; the length may be zero. The length of an unformatted record that will be produced by a particular output list may be determined by the `inquire` statement.

Endfile Records

The other kind of record is the endfile record, which, at least conceptually, has no values and no length. There can be at most one endfile record in a file and it must be the last record. It is used to mark the end of a file.

1.2.20.2. Files

A file is a collection of records. The records of a file must be either all formatted or all unformatted, except that the file may contain an endfile record as the last record. A file may have a name, but the length of the names and the characters that may be used in the names depends on the system being used. The set of names that are allowed often is determined by the operating system as well as the Fortran compiler.

A distinction is made between files that are located on an external device, such as a disk, and files in memory accessible to the program. The two kinds of files are external files and internal files.

An external file usually is stored on a peripheral device, such as a tape, a disk, or a computer terminal. For each external file, there is a set of allowed access methods, a set of allowed forms (formatted or unformatted), a set of allowed actions, and a set of allowed record lengths. How these characteristics are established depends on the computer system you are using, but usually they are determined by a combination of requests by the user of the file and actions by the operating system.

Internal files are stored in memory as values of character variables. The character values may be created using all the usual means of assigning character values, or they may be created with an output statement using the variable as an internal file. If the variable is a scalar, the file has just one record; if the variable is an array, the file has one record for each element of the array. The length of the record is the number of characters declared or assumed for the character variable. Only formatted sequential access is permitted on internal files.

For example, if `char_array` is an array of two character strings declared by

```
character (len = 7), dimension (2) :: char_array
```

the statement

```
write (unit = char_array, fmt = "(f7.5, /, f7.5)") 10/3.0, 10/6.0
```

produces the same effect as the assignment statements

```
char_array (1) = "3.33333"
char_array (2) = "1.66667"
```

An internal file was used to construct the format to print big integers in section 1.2.18.1.

1.2.20.3. File Access Methods

There are two access methods for external files: sequential access and direct access. Sequential access to the records in the file begins with the first record of the file and proceeds sequentially to the second record, and then to the next record, record by record. The records are accessed in the order that they appear in the file. It is not possible to begin at some particular record within the file without reading from the current record down to that record in sequential order.

When a file is accessed sequentially, the records are read and written sequentially. For example, if the records are written in any arbitrary order using direct access and then read using sequential access, the records are read beginning with the first record of the file, regardless of when it was written.

When a file is accessed directly, the records are selected by record number. Using this identification, the records may be read or written in any order. For example, it is possible to write record number 47 first and then write record number 13.

Each file has a set of permissible access methods, which usually means that it may be accessed either sequentially or directly.

1.2.20.4. Advancing and Nonadvancing I/O

Advancing input/output is record oriented. Completion of an input/output operation always positions the file at the end of a record. Nonadvancing input/output is character oriented. After reading and writing, the file position may be between characters within a record. Nonadvancing input/output is used by the program char_count, which counts the number of characters in a file:

```
program char_count
    integer, parameter :: end_of_record = -2
    integer, parameter :: end_of_file = -1
    character (len = 1) :: c
    integer :: character_count, ios

    character_count = 0
    do
        read (unit = *, fmt = "(a)", advance = "no", iostat = ios) c
        if (ios == end_of_record) then
            cycle
        else if (ios == end_of_file) then
            exit
        else
            character_count = character_count + 1
        end if
    end do

    print *, "The number of characters in the file is", character_count
end program char_count
```

This program also illustrates the use of the iostat specifier to test for end of record and end of file. The values -1 and -2 are common, but not universal.

1.2.20.5. Data Transfer Statements

The data transfer statements are the read, write, and print statements. You have already seen examples of various kinds of data transfer statements. The general forms for the data transfer statements are as follows. Optional parts of a statement appear in square brackets.

```
read ( io-control-spec-list ) [ input-item-list ]
read format [ , input-item-list ]
write ( io-control-spec-list ) [ output-item-list ]
print format [ , output-item-list ]
```

Some examples of data transfer statements are

```
read (unit = 9, iostat = is) x
write (unit = 6, rec = 14) y
read "(f10.2)", z
print *, zt
```

The Format Specifier

The format specifier (format in the form for the print statement and the short form of the read statement) may be a character expression indicating explicit formatting or an asterisk (*) indicating list-directed or default formatting.

The Control Information List

The input/output control specification list must contain a unit specifier of the form

```
unit = io-unit
```

and may contain at most one each of the following optional items:

```
fmt = format
rec = scalar-integer-expr
iostat = scalar-default-integer-variable
advance = scalar-character-expr
size = scalar-default-integer-variable
```

The Input/Output List

The input/output list consists basically of variables in a read statement and expressions in a write or print statement.

1.2.20.6. The open Statement

The open statement establishes a connection between a unit and an external file and determines the connection properties. After this is done, the file can be used for data transfers (reading and writing) using the unit number. It is not necessary to execute an open statement for files that are preconnected to a unit. Examples are

```
open (unit = 9, iostat = ios, status = "scratch", &
      action = "readwrite")
open (unit = 8, access = "direct", file = "plot_data", &
      status = "old", action = "read")
```

1.2.20.7. The close Statement

Execution of a close statement terminates the connection of a file to a unit. Any connections not closed explicitly by a close statement are closed by the operating system when the program terminates. Examples are

```
close (unit = 9)
close (unit = 8, iostat = ir, status = "keep")
```

1.2.20.8. The inquire Statement

The inquire statement provides the capability of determining information about a file's existence, connection, access method, or other properties during execution of a program. For each property inquired about, a scalar variable of default kind is supplied; that variable is given a value that answers the inquiry. The variable may be tested and optional execution paths selected in a program based on the answer returned. A file inquiry may be made by unit number, by the file name, or by an output list that might be used in an unformatted direct-access output statement. Examples of the `inquire` statement are

```
inquire (unit = 9, exist = ex)
inquire (file = "t123", opened = op, access = ac)
inquire (iolength = iolen)  x, y, cat
```

1.2.20.9. File-Positioning Statements

Execution of a data transfer usually changes the position of a file. In addition, there are three statements whose main purpose is to change the position of a file. The `backspace` statement reverts the position backward by one record. The `rewind` statement moves the position to the beginning of the file. The `endfile` statement writes an endfile record and positions the file after the endfile record. Examples of file-positioning statements are

```
backspace (unit = 8, iostat = status)
rewind (unit = 10)
endfile (unit = 10, iostat = ierr)
```

1.2.20.10. Formatting

Data usually is stored in memory as the values of variables in some binary form. For example, the integer 6 may be stored as 0000000000000110, where the 1s and 0s represent bits. On the other hand, formatted data records in a file consist of characters. Thus, when data is read from a formatted record, it must be converted from characters to the internal representation, and when data is written to a formatted record, it must be converted from the internal representation into a string of characters. A format specification provides the information needed to determine how these conversions are to be performed. The format specification is basically a list of edit descriptors, one for each data value in the input/output list of the data transfer statement. The following examples use formatting:

```
read (unit = *, fmt = "(5e10.1, i10)") max_values, k
print "(a, 2i5)", "The two values are: ", n(1), n(2)
```

1.2.20.11. List-Directed Formatting

List-directed formatting, also called *default formatting*, is selected by using an asterisk (*) in place of an explicit format specification in a `read`, `write`, or `print` statement. List-directed editing occurs based on the type of each list item. Examples are

```
read (unit = 5, fmt = *) a, b, c
print *, x(1:n)
```

1.3. More Information About Fortran

Fortran's web site contains a great deal of information, including the Fortran FAQ (frequently asked questions), information about current standardization projects, pointers to software (much of it free), and information about compilers from most Fortran vendors:

```
http://www.fortran.com/fortran
```

1.4. References

Adams, J. C., W. S. Brainerd, J. T. Martin, B. T. Smith, and J. L. Wagener. 1997. *The Fortran 95 handbook*. Cambridge, MA: MIT Press.

Adams, J. C., W. S. Brainerd, J. T. Martin, B. T. Smith, and J. L. Wagener. 1992. *The Fortran 90 handbook*. New York: McGraw-Hill.

Adams, J. C., W. S. Brainerd, J. T. Martin, and B. T. Smith. 1996. *The key features of F.* Albuquerque, NM: Unicomp.

Adams, J. C., W. S. Brainerd, J. T. Martin, and B. T. Smith. 1995. *Fortran top 90—Ninety key features of Fortran 90*. Albuquerque, NM: Unicomp.

American National Standards Institute. 1978. *American national standard programming language FORTRAN*, ANSI X3.9-1978, New York.

Brainerd, W. S. (Ed.). 1978. Fortran 77. *Communications of the ACM*. 21(10):806–820.

Brainerd, W. S., C. H. Goldberg, and J. C. Adams. 1996. *Programmer's guide to F.* Albuquerque, NM: Unicomp.

Brainerd, W. S., C. H. Goldberg, and J. C. Adams. 1995. *Programmer's guide to Fortran 90* (3rd ed.) New York: Springer-Verlag.

Fortran 90 (Special Issue). *Computer standards & interfaces*. 18(4).

Greenfield, M. H. 1982. *History of Fortran standardization*. Proceedings of the 1982 National Computer Conference, AFIPS Press, Arlington, VA.

International Standards Organization. 1997. *ISO/IEC 1539: 1997, Information technology—Programming languages—Fortran*. Geneva, Switzerland: Author.

International Standards Organization. 1994. *ISO/IEC 1539-2: 1994, Varying length character strings in Fortran.* Geneva, Switzerland.

Koelbel, C. H., D. B. Loveman, R. S. Schreiber, G. L. Steele, Jr., and M. E. Zosel. 1993. *High performance Fortran handbook.* Cambridge, MA: MIT Press.

A programming language for information processing on automatic data-processing systems. 1964. *Communications of the ACM* 7(10):591–625.

PART II
C

CHAPTER 2

The Development of the C Language[1]

by Dennis M. Ritchie

2.1. Introduction

This chapter details the development of the C programming language, the influences on it, and the conditions under which it was created. For the sake of brevity, I omit full descriptions of C itself, its parent B (Johnson & Kernighan, 1973), and its grandparent BCPL (Richards & Whitbey-Strevens, 1979) and instead concentrate on characteristic elements of each language and how they evolved.

C came into being in the years 1969–1973, in parallel with the early development of the UNIX operating system; the most creative period occurred during 1972. Another spate of changes peaked between 1977 and 1979, when portability of the UNIX system was being demonstrated. In the middle of this second period, the first widely available description of the language appeared: *The C Programming Language*, often called the white book or K&R (Kernighan & Ritchie, 1978). Finally, in the mid-1980s, the language was officially standardized by the ANSI X3J11 committee, which made further changes. Until the early 1980s, although compilers existed for a variety of machine architectures and operating systems, the language was almost exclusively associated with UNIX. More recently, its use has spread more widely, and today, it is among the languages most commonly used throughout the computer industry.

2.2. History

2.2.1. The Setting

The late 1960s were a turbulent era for computer systems research at Bell Laboratories (Kernighan & Ritchie, 1978; Ritchie, 1984). The company was pulling out of the Multics project (Organick, 1975), which had started as a joint venture of MIT, General Electric, and Bell Labs. By 1969, Bell Labs management, and even the researchers, came to believe that the promises of Multics could be fulfilled only too late and too expensively. Even before the GE-645 Multics machine was removed from the premises, an informal group, led primarily by Ken Thompson, had begun investigating alternatives.

Thompson wanted to create a comfortable computing environment constructed according to his own design, using whatever means were available. His plans, it is evident in retrospect, incorporated many of the innovative aspects of Multics, including an explicit notion of a process as a locus of control, a tree-structured file system, a command interpreter as user-level program, simple representation of text files, and generalized access to devices. They excluded other aspects of Multics, such as unified access to memory and to files. At the start, he and the rest of us deferred another pioneering (although not original) element of Multics, namely writing almost exclusively in a higher-level language. PL/I, the implementation language of Multics, was not much to our tastes, but we were also using other languages, including BCPL, and we regretted losing the advantages of writing programs in a language above the level of assembler, such as ease of writing and clarity of understanding. At the time, we did not put much weight on portability; interest in this arose later.

Thompson was faced with a hardware environment cramped and spartan even for the time: The DEC PDP-7 on which he started in 1968 was a machine with 8KB 18-bit words of memory and no software useful to him. Although he wanted to use a higher–level language, he wrote the original UNIX system in PDP-7 assembler. Initially, he did not even program on the PDP-7 itself but instead used a set of macros for the GEMAP assembler on a GE-635 machine. A postprocessor generated a paper tape readable by the PDP-7.

These tapes were carried from the GE machine to the PDP-7 for testing until a primitive UNIX kernel, an editor, an assembler, a simple shell (command interpreter), and a few utilities (such as the UNIX rm, cat, and cp commands) were completed. After this point, the operating system was self-supporting: Programs could be written and tested without resort to paper tape, and development continued on the PDP-7 itself.

Thompson's PDP-7 assembler simplified even DEC's in that it evaluated expressions and emitted the corresponding bits. There were no libraries and no loader or link editor: The entire source of a program was presented to the assembler, and the output file with a fixed name that emerged was directly executable. (This name, a.out, explains a bit of UNIX etymology; it is the output of the assembler. Even after the system gained a linker and a means of specifying another name explicitly, it was retained as the default executable result of a compilation.)

Not long after UNIX first ran on the PDP-7, in 1969, Doug McIlroy created the new system's first higher–level language: an implementation of McClure's TMG (McClure, 1965). TMG is a language for writing compilers (more generally, *transmogrifiers*) in a top-down, recursive-descent style that combines context–free syntax notation with procedural elements. McIlroy and Bob Morris had used TMG to write the early PL/I compiler for Multics.

Challenged by McIlroy's feat in reproducing TMG, Thompson decided that UNIX—possibly it had not even been named yet—needed a system programming language. After a rapidly scuttled attempt at Fortran, he created a language of his own, which he called B. B can be thought of as C without types; more accurately, it is BCPL squeezed into 8KB of memory and filtered through Thompson's brain. Its name most probably represents a contraction of BCPL, although an alternate theory holds that it derives from Bon (Thompson, ca. 1969), an unrelated language created by Thompson during the Multics days. Bon in turn was named either after his wife Bonnie or (according to an encyclopedia quotation in its manual) after a religion whose rituals involve the murmuring of magic formulas.

2.2.2. Origins: The Languages

BCPL was designed by Martin Richards in the mid–1960s while he was visiting MIT. It was used during the early 1970s for several interesting projects, among them the OS6 operating system at Oxford (Stoy & Strachey, 1972) and parts of the seminal Alto work at Xerox PARC (Thacker, McCreight, Lampson, Sproull, & Boggs, 1979). We became familiar with it because the MIT CTSS system (Corbato, Merwin-Dagget, & Daley, 1962) on which Richards worked was used for Multics development. The original BCPL compiler was transported both to Multics and to the GE–635 GECOS system by Rudd Canaday and others at Bell Labs (Canaday & Ritchie, 1969); during the final throes of Multics's life at Bell Labs and immediately after, it was the language of choice among the group of people who would later become involved with UNIX.

BCPL, B, and C all fit firmly in the traditional procedural family typified by Fortran and Algol 60. They are particularly oriented toward system programming, are small and compactly described, and are amenable to translation by simple compilers. They are close to the machine in that the abstractions they introduce are readily grounded in the concrete data types and operations supplied by conventional computers, and they rely on library routines for input/output and other interactions with an operating system. With less success, they also use library procedures to specify interesting control constructs such as co-routines and procedure closures. At the same time, their abstractions lie at a sufficiently high level that, with care, portability between machines can be achieved.

BCPL, B, and C differ syntactically in many details, but broadly, they are similar. Programs consist of a sequence of global declarations and function (procedure) declarations. Procedures can be nested in BCPL but may not refer to nonstatic objects defined in containing procedures. B and C avoid this restriction by imposing a more severe one: no nested procedures at all. Each of the languages (except for earliest versions of B) recognizes separate compilation and provides a means for including text from named files.

Several syntactic and lexical mechanisms of BCPL are more elegant and regular than those of B and C. For example, BCPL's procedure and data declarations have a more uniform structure, and it supplies a more complete set of looping constructs. Although BCPL programs are notionally supplied from an undelimited stream of characters, clever rules allow most semicolons to be elided after statements that end on a line boundary. B and C omit this convenience and end most statements with semicolons. In spite of the differences, most of the statements and operators of BCPL map directly into corresponding B and C.

Some of the structural differences between BCPL and B stemmed from limitations on intermediate memory. For example, BCPL declarations may take the form

```
let P1 be command
and P2 be command
and P3 be command
    ...
```

where the program text represented by *command* contains whole procedures. The subdeclarations are connected and occur simultaneously, so the name P3 is known inside procedure P1. Similarly, BCPL can package a group of declarations and statements into an expression that yields a value, for example

```
E1 := valof $( declarations ; commands ; resultis E2 $) + 1
```

The BCPL compiler readily handled such constructs by storing and analyzing a parsed representation of the entire program in memory before producing output. Storage limitations on the B compiler demanded a one–pass technique in which output was generated as soon as possible, and the syntactic redesign that made this possible was carried forward into C.

Certain less pleasant aspects of BCPL owed to its own technological problems and were consciously avoided in the design of B. For example, BCPL uses a global vector mechanism for communicating between separately compiled programs. In this scheme, the programmer explicitly associates the name of each externally visible procedure and data object with a numeric offset in the global vector; the linkage is accomplished in the compiled code by using these numeric offsets. B evaded this inconvenience initially by insisting that the entire program be presented all at once to the compiler. Later implementations of B, and all those of C, use a conventional linker to resolve external names occurring in files compiled separately, instead of placing the burden of assigning offsets on the programmer.

Other fiddles in the transition from BCPL to B were introduced as a matter of taste, and some remain controversial (for example, the decision to use the single character = for assignment instead of :=). Similarly, B uses /* */ to enclose comments, whereas BCPL uses // to ignore text up to the end of the line. The legacy of PL/I is evident here. (C++ has resurrected the BCPL comment convention.) Fortran influenced the syntax of declarations: B declarations begin with a specifier such as auto or static, followed by a list of names, and C not only followed this style but also ornamented it by placing its type keywords at the start of declarations.

Not every difference between the BCPL language documented in Richards and Whitbey-Strevens's book (1979) and B was deliberate; we started from an earlier version of BCPL (Richards, 1967). For example, the endcase that escapes from a BCPL switchon statement was not present in the language when we learned it in the 1960s, so the overloading of the break keyword to escape from the B and C switch statement owes to divergent evolution rather than conscious change.

In contrast to the pervasive syntax variation that occurred during the creation of B, the core semantic content of BCPL, its type structure, and expression evaluation rules remained intact. Both languages are typeless, or rather have a single data type, the word, or cell, a fixed–length bit pattern. Memory in these languages consists of a linear array of such cells, and the meaning of the contents of a cell depends on the operation applied. The + operator, for example, simply adds its operands using the machine's integer

add instruction, and the other arithmetic operations are equally uncon-
scious of the actual meaning of their operands. Because memory is a linear
array, it is possible to interpret the value in a cell as an index in this array,
and BCPL supplies an operator for this purpose. In the original language,
it was spelled rv, and later !, whereas B uses the unary *. Thus, if p is a
cell containing the index of (or address of, or pointer to) another cell, *p
refers to the contents of the pointed-to cell, either as a value in an expression or as the target of an assignment.

Because pointers in BCPL and B are merely integer indices in the memory
array, arithmetic on them is meaningful: If p is the address of a cell, then
p+1 is the address of the next cell. This convention is the basis for the
semantics of arrays in both languages. When in BCPL, one writes

```
let V = vec 10
```

or in B,

```
auto V[10];
```

the effect is the same: A cell named v is allocated, then another group of
10 contiguous cells is set aside, and the memory index of the first of these
is placed into v. By a general rule, in B, the expression

```
*(V+i)
```

adds v and i and refers to the ith location after v. Both BCPL and B each
add special notation to sweeten such array accesses; in B, an equivalent
expression is

```
V[i]
```

and in BCPL

```
V!i
```

This approach to arrays was unusual even at the time; C would later
assimilate it in an even less conventional way.

None of BCPL, B, or C supports character data strongly in the language;
each treats strings much like vectors of integers and supplements general
rules by a few conventions. In both BCPL and B, a string literal denotes
the address of a static area initialized with the characters of the string,
packed into cells. In BCPL, the first packed byte contains the number of
characters in the string; in B, there is no count and strings are terminated
by a special character, which B spelled *e. This change was made partially
to avoid the limitation on the length of a string caused by holding the
count in an 8- or 9-bit slot and partly because maintaining the count
seemed, in our experience, less convenient than using a terminator.

Individual characters in a BCPL string were usually manipulated by spreading the string out into another array, one character per cell, and then repacking it later; B provided corresponding routines, but people more often used other library functions that accessed or replaced individual characters in a string.

2.2.3. More History

After the TMG version of B was working, Thompson rewrote B in itself (a bootstrapping step). During development, he continually struggled against memory limitations: Each language addition inflated the compiler so it could barely fit, but each rewrite taking advantage of the feature reduced its size. For example, B introduced generalized assignment operators, using x=+y to add y to x. The notation came from Algol 68 (van Wijngaarden, et al., 1975) via McIlroy, who had incorporated it into his version of TMG. (In B and early C, the operator was spelled =+ instead of +=; this mistake, repaired in 1976, was induced by a seductively easy way of handling the first form in B's lexical analyzer.)

Thompson went a step further by inventing the ++ and -- operators, which increment or decrement; their prefix or postfix position determines whether the alteration occurs before or after noting the value of the operand. They were not in the earliest versions of B but appeared along the way. People often guess that they were created to use the autoincrement and autodecrement address modes provided by the DEC PDP-11 on which C and UNIX first became popular. This is historically impossible because there was no PDP-11 when B was developed. The PDP-7, however, did have a few autoincrement memory cells with the property that an indirect memory reference through them incremented the cell. This feature probably suggested such operators to Thompson; the generalization to make them both prefix and postfix was his own. Indeed, the autoincrement cells were not used directly in implementation of the operators, and a stronger motivation for the innovation was probably his observation that the translation of ++x was smaller than that of x=x+1.

The B compiler on the PDP-7 did not generate machine instructions, but instead threaded code (Bell, 1972), an interpretive scheme in which the compiler's output consists of a sequence of addresses of code fragments that perform the elementary operations. The operations typically, but in particular for B, act on a simple stack machine.

On the PDP-7 UNIX system, only a few things were written in B except B itself because the machine was too small and too slow to do more than experiment; rewriting the operating system and the utilities wholly into B was too expensive a step to seem feasible. At some point, Thompson relieved the address–space crunch by offering a virtual B compiler that allowed the interpreted program to occupy more than 8 KB by paging the code and data within the interpreter, but it was too slow to be practical for the common utilities. Still, some utilities written in B appeared, including an early version of the variable–precision calculator dc familiar to UNIX users (McIlroy & Kernighan, 1979). The most ambitious enterprise I undertook was a genuine cross-compiler that translated B to GE-635 machine instructions, not threaded code. It was a small tour de force: a full B compiler, written in its own language and generating code for a 36-bit mainframe, that ran on an 18-bit machine with 4 KB words of user address space. This project was possible only because of the simplicity of the B language and its runtime system.

Although we entertained occasional thoughts about implementing one of the major languages of the time such as Fortran, PL/I, or Algol 68, such a project seemed hopelessly large for our resources: Much simpler and smaller tools were called for. All these languages influenced our work, but it was more fun to do things on our own.

By 1970, the UNIX project had shown enough promise that we were able to acquire the new DEC PDP-11. The processor was among the first of its line delivered by DEC, and three months passed before its disk arrived. Making B programs run on it using the threaded technique required only writing the code fragments for the operators and a simple assembler that I coded in B; soon, dc became the first interesting program to be tested, before any operating system, on our PDP-11. Almost as rapidly, still waiting for the disk, Thompson recoded the UNIX kernel and some basic commands in PDP-11 assembly language. Of the 24 KB of memory on the machine, the earliest PDP-11 UNIX system used 12 KB for the operating system, a tiny space for user programs, and the remainder as a RAM disk. This version was only for testing, not for real work; the machine marked time by enumerating closed knight's tours on chess boards of various sizes. Once its disk appeared, we quickly migrated to it after transliterating assembly–language commands to the PDP-11 dialect and porting those already in B.

By 1971, our miniature computer center was beginning to have users. We all wanted to create interesting software more easily. Using assembler was dreary enough that B, despite its performance problems, had been supplemented by a small library of useful service routines and was being used for more and more new programs. Among the more notable results of this period was Steve Johnson's first version of the Yacc parser–generator (Johnson, 1979a).

2.3. The Development of C

2.3.1. The Problems of B

The machines on which we first used BCPL and then B were word-addressed, and these languages' single data type, the cell, comfortably equated with the hardware machine word. The advent of the PDP–11 exposed several inadequacies of B's semantic model. First, its character-handling mechanisms, inherited with few changes from BCPL, were clumsy: Using library procedures to spread packed strings into individual cells and then repack, or to access and replace individual characters, began to feel awkward, even silly, on a byte-oriented machine.

Second, although the original PDP-11 did not provide for floating–point arithmetic, the manufacturer promised that it would soon be available. Floating-point operations had been added to BCPL in our Multics and GCOS compilers by defining special operators, but the mechanism was possible only because on the relevant machines, a single word was large enough to contain a floating–point number; this was not true on the 16-bit PDP-11.

Finally, the B and BCPL model implied overhead in dealing with pointers: The language rules, by defining a pointer as an index in an array of words, forced pointers to be represented as word indices. Each pointer reference generated a runtime scale conversion from the pointer to the byte address expected by the hardware.

For all these reasons, it seemed that a typing scheme was necessary to cope with characters and byte addressing and to prepare for the coming floating-point hardware. Other issues, particularly type safety and interface checking, did not seem as important then as they became later.

Aside from the problems with the language itself, the B compiler's threaded-code technique yielded programs so much slower than their assembly-language counterparts that we discounted the possibility of recoding the operating system or its central utilities in B.

In 1971, I began to extend the B language by adding a character type and also rewrote its compiler to generate PDP-11 machine instructions instead of threaded code. Thus, the transition from B to C was contemporaneous with the creation of a compiler capable of producing programs fast and small enough to compete with assembly language. I called the slightly extended language NB for new B.

2.3.2. Embryonic C

NB existed so briefly that no full description of it was written. It supplied the types int and char, arrays of them, and pointers to them, declared in a style typified by

```
int i, j;
char c, d;
int iarray[10];
int ipointer[];
char carray[10];
char cpointer[];
```

The semantics of arrays remained exactly as in B and BCPL: The declarations of iarray and carray create cells dynamically initialized with a value pointing to the first of a sequence of 10 integers and characters. The declarations for ipointer and cpointer omit the size to assert that no storage should be allocated automatically. Within procedures, the language's interpretation of the pointers was identical to that of the array variables: A pointer declaration created a cell differing from an array declaration only in that the programmer was expected to assign a referent, instead of letting the compiler allocate the space and initialize the cell.

Values stored in the cells bound to array and pointer names were the machine addresses, measured in bytes, of the corresponding storage area. Therefore, indirection through a pointer implied no runtime overhead to scale the pointer from word to byte offset. On the other hand, the machine code for array subscripting and pointer arithmetic now depended on the type of the array or the pointer: To compute iarray[i] or ipointer+i implied scaling the addend i by the size of the object referred to.

These semantics represented an easy transition from B, and I experimented with them for some months. Problems became evident when I tried to extend the type notation, especially to add structured (record) types. Structures, it seemed, should map in an intuitive way onto memory in the machine, but in a structure containing an array, there was no good place to stash the pointer containing the base of the array, nor any convenient way to arrange that it be initialized. For example, the directory entries of early UNIX systems might be described in C as

```
struct {
        int     inumber;
        char    name[14];
};
```

I wanted the structure not merely to characterize an abstract object but also to describe a collection of bits that might be read from a directory.

Where could the compiler hide the pointer to name that the semantics demanded? Even if structures were thought of more abstractly, and the space for pointers could be hidden somehow, how could I handle the technical problem of properly initializing these pointers when allocating a complicated object, perhaps one that specified structures containing arrays containing structures to arbitrary depth?

The solution constituted the crucial jump in the evolutionary chain between typeless BCPL and typed C. It eliminated the materialization of the pointer in storage and instead caused the creation of the pointer when the array name is mentioned in an expression. The rule, which survives in today's C, is that values of array type are converted, when they appear in expressions, into pointers to the first of the objects making up the array.

This invention enabled most existing B code to continue to work, despite the underlying shift in the language's semantics. The few programs that assigned new values to an array name to adjust its origin—possible in B and BCPL, meaningless in C—were easily repaired. More important, the new language retained a coherent and workable (if unusual) explanation of the semantics of arrays while opening the way to a more comprehensive type structure.

The second innovation that most clearly distinguishes C from its predecessors is this fuller type structure and especially its expression in the syntax of declarations. NB offered the basic types int and char, together with arrays of them, and pointers to them, but no further ways of composition. Generalization was required: Given an object of any type, it should be possible to describe a new object that gathers several into an array, yields it from a function, or is a pointer to it.

For each object of such a composed type, there was already a way to mention the underlying object: Index the array, call the function, and use the indirection operator on the pointer. Analogical reasoning led to a declaration syntax for names mirroring that of the expression syntax in which the names typically appear. Thus,

```
int i, *pi, **ppi;
```

declares an integer, a pointer to an integer, and a pointer to a pointer to an integer. The syntax of these declarations reflects the observation that i, *pi, and **ppi all yield an int type when used in an expression. Similarly,

```
int f(), *f(), (*f)();
```

declares a function returning an integer, a function returning a pointer to
an integer, and a pointer to a function returning an integer;

```
int *api[10], (*pai)[10];
```

declares an array of pointers to integers and a pointer to an array of integers. In all these cases, the declaration of a variable resembles its usage in
an expression whose type is the one named at the head of the declaration.

The scheme of type composition adopted by C owes considerable debt to
Algol 68, although it did not, perhaps, emerge in a form that Algol's
adherents would approve of. The central notion I captured from Algol
was a type structure based on atomic types (including structures), composed into arrays, pointers (references), and functions (procedures). Algol
68's concept of unions and casts also had an influence that appeared later.

After creating the type system, the associated syntax, and the compiler
for the new language, I felt that it deserved a new name; NB seemed
insufficiently distinctive. I decided to follow the single–letter style and
called it C, leaving open the question whether the name represented a
progression through the alphabet or through the letters in BCPL.

2.3.3. Neonatal C

Rapid changes continued after the language had been named—for
example, the introduction of the && and ¦¦ operators. In BCPL and B, the
evaluation of expressions depends on context: Within if and other conditional statements that compare an expression's value with zero, these
languages place a special interpretation on the and (&) and or (¦) operators. In ordinary contexts, they operate bitwise, but in the B statement

```
if (e1 & e2) ...
```

the compiler must evaluate e1 and whether it is nonzero; evaluate e2, and
whether it too is nonzero; elaborate the statement dependent on the if.
The requirement descends recursively on & and ¦ operators within e1 and
e2. The short–circuit semantics of the Boolean operators in such
truth–value context seemed desirable, but the overloading of the operators was difficult to explain and use. At the suggestion of Alan Snyder, I
introduced the && and ¦¦ operators to make the mechanism more explicit.

Their tardy introduction explains an infelicity of C's precedence rules. In
B, one writes

```
if (a==b & c) ...
```

to check whether a equals b and c is nonzero; in such a conditional expression, it is better that & have lower precedence than ==. In converting from B to C, one wants to replace & with && in such a statement; to make the conversion less painful, we decided to keep the precedence of the & operator the same relative to == and merely split the precedence of && slightly from &. Today, it seems that it would have been preferable to move the relative precedences of & and == and thereby simplify a common C idiom: To test a masked value against another value, one must write

```
if ((a&mask) == b) ...
```

where the inner parentheses are required but easily forgotten.

Many other changes occurred around 1972–1973, but the most important was the introduction of the preprocessor, partly at the urging of Alan Snyder (1974) but also in recognition of the utility of the file-inclusion mechanisms available in BCPL and PL/I. Its original version was exceedingly simple and provided only included files and simple string replacements: #include and #define of parameterless macros. Soon thereafter, it was extended, mostly by Mike Lesk and then by John Reiser, to incorporate macros with arguments and conditional compilation. The preprocessor was originally considered an optional adjunct to the language itself. Indeed, for some years, it was not even invoked unless the source program contained a special signal at its beginning. This attitude persisted and explains both the incomplete integration of the syntax of the preprocessor with the rest of the language and the imprecision of its description in early reference manuals.

2.3.4. Portability

By early 1973, the essentials of modern C were complete. The language and compiler were strong enough to permit us to rewrite the UNIX kernel for the PDP-11 in C during the summer of that year. (Thompson had made a brief attempt to produce a system coded in an early version of C before structures in 1972 but gave up the effort.) Also during this period, the compiler was retargeted to other nearby machines, particularly the Honeywell 635 and IBM 360/370; because the language could not live in isolation, the prototypes for the modern libraries were developed. In particular, Lesk (1973) wrote "A Portable I/O Package," which was later reworked to become "The C Standard I/O Routines." In 1978, Brian Kernighan and I published *The C Programming Language* (Kernighan & Ritchie, 1978). Although it did not describe some additions that soon became common, this book served as the language reference until a formal standard was adopted more than 10 years later. Although we worked closely together on this book, there was a clear division of labor: Kernighan wrote almost all the expository material, and I was responsible for the appendix containing the reference manual and the chapter on interfacing with the UNIX system.

During 1973–1980, the language grew a bit: The type structure gained unsigned, long, union, and enumeration types, and structures became nearly first-class objects (lacking only a notation for literals). Equally important developments appeared in its environment and the accompanying technology. Writing the UNIX kernel in C had given us enough confidence in the language's usefulness and efficiency that we began to recode the system's utilities and tools as well and then to move the most interesting among them to the other platforms. As described in "Portability of C Programs and the UNIX System" (Johnson & Ritchie, 1978), we discovered that the hardest problems in propagating UNIX tools lay not in the interaction of the C language with new hardware, but in adapting to the existing software of other operating systems. Thus Steve Johnson began to work on pcc, a C compiler intended to be easy to retarget to new machines (Johnson, 1978) while he, Thompson, and I began to move the UNIX system itself to the Interdata 8/32 computer.

The language changes during this period, especially around 1977, were largely focused on considerations of portability and type safety in an effort to cope with the problems we foresaw and observed in moving a considerable body of code to the new Interdata platform. C at that time still manifested strong signs of its typeless origins. Pointers, for example, were barely distinguished from integral memory indices in early language manuals or extant code; the similarity of the arithmetic properties of character pointers and unsigned integers made it hard to resist the temptation to identify them. The unsigned types were added to make unsigned arithmetic available without confusing it with pointer manipulation. Similarly, the early language condoned assignments between integers and pointers, but this practice began to be discouraged; a notation for type conversions (called casts from the example of Algol 68) was invented to specify type conversions more explicitly. Beguiled by the example of PL/I, early C did not tie structure pointers firmly to the structures they pointed to and permitted programmers to write `pointer->member` almost without regard to the type of pointer; such an expression was taken uncritically as a reference to a region of memory designated by the pointer, whereas the member name specified only an offset and a type.

Although the first edition of K&R described most of the rules that brought C's type structure to its present form, many programs written in the older, more relaxed style persisted and so did compilers that tolerated it. To encourage people to pay more attention to the official language rules, to detect legal but suspicious constructions, and to help find interface mismatches undetectable with simple mechanisms for separate compilation, Steve Johnson adapted his pcc compiler to produce lint (Johnson, 1979), which scanned a set of files and remarked on dubious constructions.

2.3.5. Growth in Usage

The success of our portability experiment on the Interdata 8/32 soon led to another by Tom London and John Reiser on the DEC VAX 11/780. This machine became much more popular than the Interdata, and UNIX and the C language began to spread rapidly, both within AT&T and outside. Although by the middle 1970s UNIX was in use by a variety of projects within the Bell System as well as a small group of research–oriented industrial, academic, and government organizations outside our company, its real growth began only after portability had been achieved. Of particular note were the System III and System V versions of the system from the emerging Computer Systems division of AT&T, based on work by the company's development and research groups and the BSD series of releases by the University of California at Berkeley that derived from research organizations in Bell Laboratories.

During the 1980s, the use of the C language spread widely, and compilers became available on nearly every machine architecture and operating system; in particular, it became popular as a programming tool for personal computers, both for manufacturers of commercial software for these machines and for end users interested in programming. At the start of the decade, nearly every compiler was based on Johnson's pcc; by 1985, there were many independently produced compiler products.

2.3.6. Standardization

By 1982, it was clear that C needed formal standardization. The best approximation to a standard, the first edition of K&R, no longer described the language in actual use; in particular, it mentioned neither the void nor enum types. Although it foreshadowed the newer approach to structures, only after it was published did the language support assigning them, passing them to and from functions, and associating the names of members firmly with the structure or union containing them. Although compilers distributed by AT&T incorporated these changes, and most of the purveyors of compilers not based on pcc quickly picked them up, there remained no complete, authoritative description of the language.

The first edition of K&R was also insufficiently precise on many details of the language, and it became increasingly impractical to regard pcc as a reference compiler; it did not perfectly embody even the language described by K&R, let alone subsequent extensions. Finally, the incipient use of C in projects subject to commercial and government contract meant that the imprimatur of an official standard was important. Thus (at the urging of M. D. McIlroy), ANSI established the X3J11 committee under the direction of CBEMA in the summer of 1983 with the goal of producing a C standard. X3J11 produced its report (ANSI, 1989) at the end of 1989, and subsequently, this standard was accepted by ISO as ISO/IEC 9899–1990.

From the beginning, the X3J11 committee took a cautious, conservative view of language extensions. Much to my satisfaction, they took their goal seriously: to develop a clear, consistent, and unambiguous standard for the C programming language that codifies the common, existing definition of C and that promotes the portability of user programs across C language environments (ANSI, 1989). The committee realized that mere promulgation of a standard does not make the world change.

X3J11 introduced only one genuinely important change to the language itself: It incorporated the types of formal arguments in the type signature of a function, using syntax borrowed from C++ (Stroustrup, 1986). In the old style, external functions were declared like this:

```
double sin();
```

which says only that sin is a function returning a double (that is, double–precision floating–point) value. In the new style, this better rendered

```
double sin(double);
```

to make the argument type explicit and thus encourage better type checking and appropriate conversion. Even this addition, although it produced a noticeably better language, caused difficulties. The committee justifiably felt that simply outlawing old-style function definitions and declarations was not feasible, yet also agreed that the new forms were better. The inevitable compromise was as good as it could have been, although the language definition is complicated by permitting both forms, and writers of portable software must contend with compilers not yet brought up to standard.

X3J11 also introduced a host of smaller additions and adjustments—for example, the type qualifiers const and volatile and slightly different type promotion rules. Nevertheless, the standardization process did not change the character of the language. In particular, the C standard did not attempt to specify formally the language semantics, so there can be dispute over fine points; nevertheless, it successfully accounted for changes in usage since the original description and is sufficiently precise to base implementations on it.

Thus the core C language escaped nearly unscathed from the standardization process, and the standard emerged more as a better, careful codification than a new invention. More important changes took place in the language's surroundings: the preprocessor and the library. The preprocessor performs macro substitution using conventions distinct from the rest of the language. Its interaction with the compiler had never been well described, and X3J11 attempted to remedy the situation. The result is noticeably better than the explanation in the first edition of K&R; besides being more comprehensive, it provides operations, such as token concatenation, previously available only by accidents of implementation.

X3J11 correctly believed that a full and careful description of a standard C library was as important as its work on the language itself. The C language itself does not provide for input/output or any other interaction with the outside world and thus depends on a set of standard procedures. At the time of publication of K&R, C was thought of mainly as the system programming language of UNIX; although we provided examples of library routines intended to be readily transportable to other operating systems, underlying support from UNIX was implicitly understood. Thus, the X3J11 committee spent much of its time designing and documenting a set of library routines required to be available in all conforming implementations.

By the rules of the standards process, the current activity of the X3J11 committee is confined to issuing interpretations on the existing standard. However, an informal group originally convened by Rex Jaeschke as NCEG (Numerical C Extensions Group) has been officially accepted as subgroup X3J11.1, and they continue to consider extensions to C. As the name implies, many of these possible extensions are intended to make the language more suitable for numerical use: for example, adding multidimensional arrays whose bounds are dynamically determined, incorporating facilities for dealing with IEEE arithmetic, and making the language more effective on machines with vector or other advanced architectural features. Not all the possible extensions are specifically numerical; they include a notation for structure literals.

2.3.7. Successors

C and even B have several direct descendants, although they do not rival Pascal in generating progeny. One side branch developed early. When Steve Johnson visited the University of Waterloo on sabbatical in 1972, he brought B with him. It became popular on the Honeywell machines there and later spawned Eh and Zed (the Canadian answers to "What follows B?"). When Johnson returned to Bell Labs in 1973, he was disconcerted to find that the language whose seeds he brought to Canada had evolved back home; even his own yacc program had been rewritten in C by Alan Snyder.

More recent descendants of C proper include Concurrent C (Gehani & Roome, 1989), Objective C (Cox & Novobilski, 1986), C* (Thinking Machines Corporation, 1990), and especially C++ (Stroustrup, 1986). The language is also widely used as an intermediate representation (essentially, as a portable assembly language) for a wide variety of compilers, both for direct descendants such as C++ and independent languages such as Modula-3 (Nelson, 1991) and Eiffel (Meyer, 1988).

2.3.8. Critique

Two ideas are most characteristic of C among languages of its class: the relationship between arrays and pointers and the way in which declaration syntax mimics expression syntax. They are also among its most frequently criticized features and often serve as stumbling blocks to the beginner. In both cases, historical accidents or mistakes have exacerbated their difficulty. The most important of these has been the tolerance of C compilers to errors in type. As should be clear from the history, C evolved from typeless languages. It did not suddenly appear to its earliest users and developers as an entirely new language with its own rules; instead, we continually had to adapt existing programs as the language developed and make allowance for an existing body of code. (Later, the ANSI X3J11 committee standardizing C would face the same problem.)

Compilers in 1977, and even well after, did not complain about usages such as assigning between integers and pointers or using objects of the wrong type to refer to structure members. Although the language definition presented in the first edition of K&R was reasonably (although not completely) coherent in its treatment of type rules, that book admitted that existing compilers didn't enforce them. Moreover, some rules designed to ease early transitions contributed to later confusion. For example, the empty square brackets in the function declaration

```
int f(a) int a[]; { ... }
```

are a living fossil, a remnant of NB's way of declaring a pointer; a is, in this special case only, interpreted in C as a pointer. The notation survived in part for the sake of compatibility, in part under the rationalization that it would allow programmers to communicate to their readers an intent to pass f a pointer generated from an array, rather than a reference to a single integer. Unfortunately, it serves as much to confuse the learner as to alert the reader.

In K&R C, supplying arguments of the proper type to a function call was the responsibility of the programmer, and the extant compilers did not check for type agreement. The failure of the original language to include argument types in the type signature of a function was a significant weakness, indeed the one that required the X3J11 committee's boldest and most painful innovation to repair. The early design is explained (if not justified) by my avoidance of technological problems, especially cross-checking between separately compiled source files, and my incomplete assimilation of the implications of moving between an untyped to a typed language. The lint program, mentioned earlier, tried to alleviate the problem: Among its other functions, lint checks the consistency and coherency of a whole program by scanning a set of source files, comparing the types of function arguments used in calls with those in their definitions.

An accident of syntax contributed to the perceived complexity of the language. The indirection operator, spelled * in C, is syntactically a unary prefix operator, just as in BCPL and B. This works well in simple expressions, but in more complex cases, parentheses are required to direct the parsing. For example, to distinguish indirection through the value returned by a function from calling a function designated by a pointer, one writes *fp() and (*pf)(). The style used in expressions carries through to declarations, so the names might be declared

```
int *fp();
int (*pf)();
```

In more ornate but still realistic cases, things become worse:

```
int *(*pfp)();
```

is a pointer to a function returning a pointer to an integer. There are two effects occurring. Most important, C has a relatively rich set of ways of describing types (compared, say, with Pascal). Declarations in languages as expressive as C Algol 68, for example, describe objects equally hard to understand, simply because the objects themselves are complex. A second effect owes to details of the syntax. Declarations in C must be read in an inside-out style that many find difficult to grasp (Anderson, 1980). Sethi (1981) observed that many of the nested declarations and expressions would become simpler if the indirection operator had been taken as a postfix operator instead of prefix, but by then, it was too late to change.

In spite of its difficulties, I believe that C's approach to declarations remains plausible and I am comfortable with it; it is a useful unifying principle.

The other characteristic feature of C—its treatment of arrays—is more suspect on practical grounds, although it also has real virtues. Although the relationship between pointers and arrays is unusual, it can be learned. Moreover, the language shows considerable power to describe important concepts, for example, vectors whose length varies at runtime with only a few basic rules and conventions. In particular, character strings are handled by the same mechanisms as any other array, plus the convention that a null character terminates a string. It is interesting to compare C's approach with that of two nearly contemporaneous languages, Algol 68 and Pascal (Jensen & Wirth, 1974). Arrays in Algol 68 either have fixed bounds, or are flexible: Considerable mechanism is required both in the language definition and in compilers to accommodate flexible arrays (and not all compilers fully implement them). Original Pascal had only fixed–sized arrays and strings, and this proved confining (Kernighan, 1981). Later, this was partially fixed, although the resulting language is not yet universally available.

C treats strings as arrays of characters conventionally terminated by a marker. Aside from one special rule about initialization by string literals, the semantics of strings are fully subsumed by more general rules governing all arrays, and as a result, the language is simpler to describe and to translate than one incorporating the string as a unique data type. Some costs accrue from its approach: Certain string operations are more expensive than in other designs because application code or a library routine must occasionally search for the end of a string, because few built-in operations are available, and because the burden of storage management for strings falls more heavily on the user. Nevertheless, C's approach to strings works well.

On the other hand, C's treatment of arrays in general (not just strings) has unfortunate implications both for optimization and for future extensions. The prevalence of pointers in C programs, whether those declared explicitly or arising from arrays, means that optimizers must be cautious and must use careful dataflow techniques to achieve good results. Sophisticated compilers can understand what most pointers can possibly change, but some important usages remain difficult to analyze. For example, functions with pointer arguments derived from arrays are hard to compile into efficient code on vector machines because it is seldom possible to determine that one argument pointer does not overlap data also referred to by another argument or accessible externally. More fundamentally, the definition of C so specifically describes the semantics of arrays that changes or extensions treating arrays as more primitive objects, and permitting operations on them as wholes, become hard to fit into the existing language. Even extensions to permit the declaration and use of multidimensional arrays whose size is determined dynamically are not entirely straightforward (MacDonald, 1989; Ritchie, 1990), although they would make it much easier to write numerical libraries in C. Thus, C covers the most important uses of strings and arrays arising in practice by a uniform and simple mechanism but leaves problems for highly efficient implementations and for extensions.

Many smaller infelicities exist in the language and its description besides those discussed previously, of course. There are also general criticisms to be lodged that transcend detailed points. Chief among these is that the language and its generally expected environment provide little help for writing very large systems. The naming structure provides only two main levels, external (visible everywhere) and internal (within a single procedure). An intermediate level of visibility (within a single file of data and procedures) is weakly tied to the language definition. Thus, there is little direct support for modularization, and project designers are forced to create their own conventions.

Similarly, C itself provides two durations of storage: automatic objects that exist while control resides in or below a procedure and static, existing throughout execution of a program. Off-stack, dynamically allocated storage is provided only by a library routine and the burden of managing it is placed on the programmer: C is hostile to automatic garbage collection.

2.4. Whence Success?

C has become successful to an extent far surpassing any early expectations. What qualities contributed to its widespread use?

Doubtless, the success of UNIX itself was the most important factor; it made the language available to hundreds of thousands of people. Conversely, of course, UNIX's use of C and its consequent portability to a wide variety of machines was important in the system's success. But the language's invasion of other environments suggests more fundamental merits.

Despite some aspects mysterious to the beginner and occasionally even to the adept, C remains a simple and small language, translatable with simple and small compilers. Its types and operations are well-grounded in those provided by real machines, and for people used to how computers work, learning the idioms for generating time- and space-efficient programs is not difficult. At the same time, the language is sufficiently abstracted from machine details that program portability can be achieved.

Equally important, C and its central library support always remained in touch with a real environment. It was not designed in isolation to prove a point, or to serve as an example, but as a tool to write programs that did useful things; it was always meant to interact with a larger operating system and was regarded as a tool to build larger tools. A parsimonious, pragmatic approach influenced the things that went into C: It covers the essential needs of many programmers but does not try to supply too much.

Finally, despite the changes that it has undergone since its first published description, which was admittedly informal and incomplete, the actual C language as seen by millions of users using many different compilers has remained remarkably stable and unified compared to those of similarly widespread currency, for example, Pascal and Fortran. There are differing dialects of C—most noticeably those described by the older K&R and the newer Standard C—but on the whole, C has remained freer of proprietary extensions than other languages. Perhaps the most significant extensions are the `far` and `near` pointer qualifications intended to deal with peculiarities of some Intel processors. Although C was not originally designed with portability as a prime goal, it succeeded in expressing programs, even including operating systems, on machines ranging from the smallest personal computers through the mightiest supercomputers.

C is quirky, flawed, and an enormous success. Although accidents of history surely helped, it evidently satisfied a need for a system implementation language efficient enough to displace assembly language, yet sufficiently abstract and fluent to describe algorithms and interactions in a wide variety of environments.

2.5. Acknowledgments

It is worth summarizing compactly the roles of the direct contributors to today's C language. Ken Thompson created the B language in 1969–1970; it was derived directly from Martin Richards's BCPL. Dennis Ritchie turned B into C during 1971–1973, keeping most of B's syntax while adding types and many other changes and writing the first compiler. Ritchie, Alan Snyder, Steven C. Johnson, Michael Lesk, and Thompson contributed language ideas during 1972–1977, and Johnson's portable compiler remains widely used. During this period, the collection of library routines grew considerably, thanks to these people and many others at Bell Laboratories. In 1978, Kernighan and Ritchie wrote the book that became the language definition for several years. Beginning in 1983, the ANSI X3J11 committee standardized the language. Especially notable in keeping its efforts on track were its officers Jim Brodie, Tom Plum, and P. J. Plauger and the successive draft redactors, Larry Rosler and Dave Prosser.

I thank Brian Kernighan, Doug McIlroy, Dave Prosser, Peter Nelson, Rob Pike, Ken Thompson, and HOPL's referees for advice in the preparation of this paper.

2.6. References

American National Standards Institute. 1989. American national standard for information systems programming language C. New York: Author.

Anderson, B. 1980. Type syntax in the language C: An object lesson in syntactic innovation. *SIGPLAN Notices* 15(3):21–27.

Bell, J. R. 1972. Threaded code. *ACM* 16(6):370–372.

Canaday, R. H., and D. M. Ritchie. May 1969. *Bell Laboratories BCPL.* AT&T Bell Laboratories internal memorandum.

Corbato, F. J., M. Merwin–Dagget, and R. C. Daley. 1962. *An experimental time–sharing system.* AFIPS Conference Proceedings, pp. 335–344.

Cox, B. J., and A. J. Novobilski. 1986. *Object–oriented programming: An evolutionary approach.* Reading, MA: Addison–Wesley.

Gehani, N. H., and W. D. Roome. 1989. *Concurrent C.* Summit, NJ: Silicon Press.

Jensen, K., and N. Wirth. 1974. *Pascal user manual and report* (2nd ed.). New York: Springer–Verlag.

Johnson, S. C. January 1978. *A portable compiler: Theory and practice.* Proceedings of the 5th ACM POPL Symposium.

Johnson, S. C. 1979. Yet another compiler–compiler. In M. D. McIlroy and B. W. Kernighan (Eds.), *UNIX programmer's manual, seventh edition* (Vol. 2A). Murray Hill, NJ: AT&T Bell Laboratories.

Johnson, S. C. 1979. Lint, a program checker. In M. D. McIlroy and B. W. Kernighan (Eds.), *UNIX programmer's manual, seventh edition* (Vol. 2B). Murray Hill, NJ: AT&T Bell Laboratories.

Johnson, S. C., and B. W. Kernighan. 1973. *The programming language B*. Computer Science Technical Report #8, AT&T Bell Laboratories, Murray Hill, NJ.

Johnson, S. C., and D. M. Ritchie. 1978. Portability of C programs and the UNIX system. *Bell Systems Technical Journal* 57(6).

Kernighan, B. W. 1981. *Why Pascal is not my favorite programming language*. Computer Science Technical Report #100, AT&T Bell Laboratories, Murray Hill, NJ.

Kernighan, B. W., and D. M. Ritchie. 1978. *The C programming language*. Englewood Cliffs, NJ: Prentice Hall.

Lesk, M. E. 1973. *A portable I/O package*. AT&T Bell Laboratories internal memorandum, Murray Hill, NJ.

MacDonald, T. 1989. Arrays of variable length. *Journal of C. Lang. Trans.* 1(3):215–233.

McClure, R. M. 1965. TMG—A syntax-directed compiler. *Proceedings of the 20th ACM National Conference*, pp. 262–274.

McIlroy, M. D. 1960. Macro instruction extensions of compiler languages. *ACM* 3(4):214–220.

McIlroy, M. D., and B. W. Kernighan (Eds.). 1979. *UNIX programmer's manual, seventh edition* (Vol. 1). Murray Hill, NJ: AT&T Bell Laboratories.

Meyer, B. 1988. *Object–oriented software construction*. Englewood Cliffs, NJ: Prentice Hall.

Nelson, G. 1991. *Systems programming with Modula–3*. Englewood Cliffs, NJ: Prentice–Hall.

Organick, E. I. 1975. *The Multics system: An examination of its structure*. Cambridge, MA: MIT Press.

Richards, M. 1967. *The BCPL reference manual.* MIT Project MAC Memorandum M–352, Cambridge, MA.

Richards, M., and C. Whitbey–Strevens. 1979. *BCPL: The language and its compiler.* Cambridge, England: Cambridge University Press.

Ritchie, D. M. 1978. UNIX: A retrospective. *Bell Systems Technical Journal* 57(6).

Ritchie, D. M. 1984. The evolution of the UNIX time–sharing system. *AT&T Bell Laboratories Technical Journal* 63(8).

Ritchie, D. M. 1990. Variable–size arrays in C. *Journal of C Lang. Trans.* 2(2):81–86.

Sethi, R. 1981. Uniform syntax for type expressions and declarators. *Software Practice and Experience* 11(6)623–628.

Snyder, A. 1974. *A portable compiler for the language C.* Cambridge, MA: MIT Press.

Stoy, J. E., and C. Strachey. 1972. OS6—An experimental operating system for a small computer. Part I: General principles and structure. *Comp. Journal* 15:117–124.

Stroustrup, B. 1986. *The C++ programming language.* Reading, MA: Addison–Wesley.

Thacker, C. P., E. M. McCreight, B. W. Lampson, R. F. Sproull, and D. R. Boggs. 1982. Alto: A personal computer. In D. Sieworek, C. G. Bell, A. Newell (Eds.), *Computer structures: Principles and examples.* New York: McGraw–Hill.

Thinking Machines Corporation. 1990. *C* programming guide.* Cambridge, MA: Author.

Thompson, K. ca. 1969. *Bon—An interactive language.* AT&T Bell Laboratories internal memorandum, Murray Hill, NJ.

van Wijngaarden, A., B. J. Mailloux, J. E. Peck, C. H. Koster, M. Sintzoff, C. Lindsey, L. G. Meertens, and R. G. Fisker. 1975. Revised report on the algorithmic language Algol 68. *Acta Informatica* 5:1–236.

CHAPTER 3

C Programming

by Steve Summit

3.1. Introduction

C is an extremely popular, relatively low-level, procedural programming language. As the language has evolved, its definition has passed through several stages, representing distinct dialects of the language. As of 1998, the vast majority of C programming is performed in accordance with the ANSI/ISO C Standard, first ratified as ANSI X3.159 in 1989 and then as ISO/IEC 9989 in 1990. The description in this chapter is primarily of the C language as defined in that standard, with notes concerning a few aspects of pre-ANSI C (also known as "K&R" C, after Kernighan & Ritchie, 1988), and of some changes that can be anticipated in the next revision of the C Standard (known informally as "C9X" and expected to be finalized in the next few years). The C Standard was amended significantly in 1994 by Normative Addendum 1 ("NA1"), and those changes are reflected in this chapter.

The history and philosophy of C are covered in Chapter 2 of this volume, so we will not dwell further on those topics here. Without further ado, then, we will proceed immediately with two sample programs, to set the stage for a reasonably complete treatment of the language in later sections.

3.1.1. Sample Programs

The traditional first C program is one that prints a certain well-worn phrase to the standard output device:

```
#include <stdio.h>

int main()
{
        printf("Hello, world!\n");
        return 0;
}
```

This tiny example displays many of the features of any C program. The syntax int main() { ... } defines a function named main with return type int. If the function accepted any parameters, they would be listed in the first pair of parentheses. The braces ({}) surround the body of the function, which in this case consists of just two statements. The first is an expression statement; the expression consists of a call to the standard library function printf, which generates formatted strings to the standard output device (typically the user's screen). This call to printf prints a single, constant string, the only unusual feature of which is the two-character sequence \n, which is an escape sequence indicating end-of-line. The second statement is a return statement, by which the function gives up control and optionally returns a value (in this case, the constant 0). A function with the name main is distinguished by being the first function called when a C program begins execution. When main returns, the program terminates, and main's return value becomes the exit status of the program. (By convention, an exit status of 0 indicates success.) The first line of the program, #include <stdio.h>, calls for the inclusion of some declarations and definitions relating to the I/O functions in the Standard C library; this line is required since the function calls printf.

As a slightly more realistic example, here is a program that prints the first 10 Fibonacci numbers:

```c
#include <stdio.h>

int fib(int);

main()
{
        int i;

        for(i = 1; i <= 10; i = i + 1)
                {
                int f = fib(i);
                printf("%d\n", f);
                }

        return 0;
}

/* compute nth Fibonacci number */

int fib(int n)
{
        int i;
        int fibonacci = 0, prev = 1;

        for(i = 1; i <= n; i = i + 1)
                {
                int tmp = fibonacci;
```

```
        fibonacci = fibonacci + prev;
        prev = tmp;
        }

    return fibonacci;
}
```

This program defines two functions: one named `main`, as before, and one named `fib`. The line `int fib(int)` is a forward declaration for the user-defined function `fib`, indicating that it accepts one argument of type `int`, and returns a value of type `int`. The line `int i;` is a declaration of a local variable, of type `int`, named `i`. The line

```
for(i = 1; i <= 10; i = i + 1)
```

sets up a loop that steps the variable `i` through the values 1 to 10 (inclusive). The body of the loop, enclosed in another pair of braces, consists of a declaration of a block-local variable `f`, a call to the function `fib`, and a call to `printf`. In this call to `printf`, the string to be printed includes the two-character sequence `%d`, which indicates that the value of another `int` argument passed to `printf`, in this case the variable `f`, should be inserted as a decimal integer (replacing the two characters `%d` in the output).

The line `/* compute nth Fibonacci number */` is a comment; any text between the characters `/*` and `*/` is ignored by the compiler. Below that is the definition of the function `fib`, consisting of several more local variable declarations, another `for` loop, and a `return` statement that returns the Fibonacci number computed. One limitation of the function as written is that C's `int` type has a guaranteed range of just ±32,767. If this function were to be used to compute Fibonacci numbers past the 23rd, its return type and the types of its local variables would have to be adjusted, probably to the type `long int`, which has a considerably larger range. (Also, the `fib` function as written is not terribly efficient; an improved version can be found in section 3.5.3.)

3.1.2. Lexical Issues

The top-level syntax of a C program consists of a series of global definitions and declarations, of functions, global variables, and data types. For the most part, the syntax is free-form; whitespace and line breaks are ignored except as they serve to separate adjacent tokens. Comments serve as whitespace.

The most significant exception to the free-form rule concerns preprocessor directives. These all begin with the character `#`, and must stand alone on a line. Both sample programs above contain one example of a preprocessor directive: the line `#include <stdio.h>`.

(On those rare occasions when it is necessary to continue a logical source line across multiple physical lines, the backslash (\) can be used as a continuation character at the ends of physical lines. Such continuation is generally only needed in preprocessor `#define` lines; see section 3.8.2.)

We now proceed with detailed explanations of the four fundamental syntactic elements of C programs: declarations (including types and constants), expressions, statements, and functions. Section 3.6 discusses the special topic of pointers, and section 3.7 describes user-defined data structures. Section 3.8 covers the C preprocessor. Section 3.9 introduces the C runtime environment. Finally, section 3.10 lists the functions in C's standard library.

3.2. Basic Types, Constants, and Declarations

C is a strongly typed language. With a few exceptions (which modern practice discourages making use of), all variables and functions must be declared before use. The reasons for predeclarations of variables and functions are the usual ones: to make life easier on the compiler, to help catch programmer errors (e.g., misspelled names), and to encourage a thoughtful selection of the appropriate type for each variable.

3.2.1. Basic Types

It is useful to think of a type in a somewhat mathematical sense: as a (finite) set of values upon which certain operations may be performed. C has a handful of basic types and several open-ended mechanisms for creating derived types. We cover the basic types first.

The most common types in typical C programs are certainly the integers. C's basic `int` type holds integers in at least the range ±32,767; type `int` is typically implemented as a machine word of a natural size, so it is usually the most efficient type in terms of calculation speed and memory bus cycles.

The basic `int` type can be extended in two orthogonal ways. Firstly, the size modifiers `short` and `long` request integers that are potentially smaller and larger than plain `int`. The `short int` type has a range of at least ±32,767, which is the same as plain `int`; the distinction is that `short int` is likely to be smaller (and so to occupy less memory in arrays or other large data structures) on machines where plain `int` is larger than its guaranteed minimum range. The type that is guaranteed to be larger is `long int`, which has a guaranteed minimum range of ±2,147,483,647 (or $2^{31}-1$).

From these guaranteed minimum ranges, we can see that types `int` and `short int` are both at least 16 bits in size, whereas `long int` is at least 32 bits. The exact sizes of these types vary from machine to machine and from compiler to compiler, and it is generally difficult to declare a variable with an exact size. It is wise, therefore, not to be too concerned about the exact size of a particular data type, as this is an implementation detail that can be thought of as best left to the compiler. Similarly, it is implementation-defined how the individual bytes of integer values are arranged in memory, and how negative numbers are represented (e.g., in two's complement or some other representation).

The second mode of extension is that unsigned versions of all of the integer types exist, indicated by the keyword `unsigned`. The `unsigned` types obviously hold only positive integers but are of the same size as their signed counterparts. The minimum range of types `unsigned int` and `unsigned short int` is 0–65,535, and of `unsigned long int` is 0–4,294,967,295 (which is $2^{32}-1$). It is also guaranteed that if arithmetic on an unsigned value overflows, or if an attempt is made to store a negative or overlarge value into an unsigned variable, the result is computed modulo the range of the corresponding type, without incurring any traps or exceptions. (Overflow on signed types, on the other hand, yields undefined behavior.) Thus, on a machine for which the range of `unsigned int` is 0–65,535, all arithmetic yielding an unsigned `int` result is computed modulo 65,536.

For symmetry, the keyword `signed` can be used to explicitly indicate a signed integer, although because this is the default for integers, the keyword is infrequently needed. (It can be useful with characters, as mentioned below, and with bit-fields, as discussed in section 3.7.4.)

When one of the modifiers `short`, `long`, `signed`, or `unsigned` is used, the keyword `int` is optional. Thus, the types can also be referred to as short, long, unsigned, unsigned short, unsigned long, and so on. (These "shorthand" forms are considerably more popular, and there is no stigma attached to their use.)

Under some compilers, a doubled modifier `long long` indicates an extra-long type, essentially of at least 64 bits, and this extension is likely to be incorporated into the next revision of the C Standard.

Running a close second in popularity to the integer types is the character type because C is often used for text processing. Characters are stored as small integers, using the mapping defined by the machine's native character set. Characters can, therefore, be thought of as tiny integer values, and they are not uncommonly used for this purpose. The basic character type is char. As for the integers, the modifier keywords signed and unsigned can be used to explicitly request signed or unsigned characters, but unlike the integers, a plain char can be signed or unsigned, depending on the implementation's choice. The keyword signed can, therefore, be significant in the declaration of a character object. Characters have a guaranteed minimum range of ±127 if they are signed, and 0–255 if they are unsigned. In any case, the characters in C's basic source and basic execution sets (roughly speaking, the 52 upper- and lowercase English letters, the 10 digits, and the 29 punctuation characters used in C) are all guaranteed to have positive values (as they do in ASCII). However, any extended characters (such as those in the ISO8859-1 Latin-1 character set, or the extended character sets of MS-DOS or Macintosh systems) are likely to have values that appear negative if characters are signed.

To summarize, then, the four integral types, and their guaranteed minimum ranges in both their signed and unsigned variants, are as follow:

	signed	unsigned
char	±127	0–255
short	±32,767	0–65,535
int	±32,767	0–65,535
long	±2,147,483,647	0–4,294,967,295

The integral types have the widest range of supported operations, including arithmetic, comparison, and "bitwise" operators, all of which are covered in later sections.

C also has three floating-point types: the single-precision float, the double-precision double, and the extended-precision long double. The absolute minimum range of these types is $\pm 10^{37}$, with the equivalent of at least 6 decimal digits' worth of precision for type float, and 10 digits for double and long double. Most machines provide more range and/or precision (but note that type long double is not in fact guaranteed to have any more precision or range than plain double).

The allowable operations on floating-point values are somewhat fewer than for integral variables; only arithmetic operations and comparisons are supported.

Finally, C has one "placeholder" type, void, which is used in a few situations in which a type is required but no values are expected. In the mathematical sense, type void has no values in its range and supports no operations. Type void is used in the parameter list of functions that accept no parameters, as the return value of functions that return no values (i.e., "procedures"), as an explicit indication that the result of an expression is being discarded, and in its pointer form as a "generic" pointer type (i.e., when the actual type pointed to is not precisely known). All of these uses are discussed later.

In addition to these basic types, there are any number of auxiliary and derived types, some defined by the language and some defined by the programmer. One that deserves mention here is wchar_t, which is a type that can hold wide characters, characters from extended or multinational character sets that would not fit in a char.

3.2.2. Constants

Source-code constants take several forms, roughly paralleling the several basic types listed in the preceding section.

Integer constants are indicated in the obvious way by simple digit sequences: 0, 1, 23, 456. Integer constants are in decimal (base 10) by default, but may be entered in octal (base 8) by prepending a leading 0 (digit zero), or in hexadecimal (base 16) by prepending a leading 0x or 0X. (The hexadecimal digits are 0–9 and the letters a–f or A–F). Thus, 010 and 0377 are octal constants, and 0x10, 0x1abc, and 0XFEED are hexadecimal constants. The constants 100, 0144, and 0x64 all have the same value, one hundred decimal.

Integer constants are of type int by default, unless they are too large to be represented in a plain int on the particular machine, in which case they are automatically assumed to be long and/or unsigned, as necessary. (Octal and hexadecimal constants have a preference for unsigned.) It is occasionally necessary to force a constant to be of a certain type; this can be done with the suffixes l (lowercase letter *l*) or L for long, and u or U for unsigned. So 1L is explicitly long, 2u is explicitly unsigned, and 3ul is explicitly unsigned long.

A decimal-point character (.) indicates a floating-point constant, as in 3.14. The letter e or E may also be used to indicate exponential notation: 1.23e4 is 1.23×10^4, or 12,300. A constant is floating point if it includes a decimal point (.) or e (or E) or both; digits may precede or follow the decimal point, or both. A sign (+ or -) may follow the letter e; `1.23e-4` is 1.23×10^{-4}, or 0.000123.

Floating-point constants are of type `double` by default. A suffix f or F may be appended to force type `float`, or 1 (again, letter *l*) or L may be suffixed to indicate `long double`.

A character constant consists of a character surrounded by single quotes (also known as apostrophes): `'A'`, `'2'`, `' '` (space). Several character escape sequences are available; all begin with the backslash (\), and all represent one character even though they occupy two (or more) characters in the constant. The character escape sequences are as follow:

`\a`	"alert" or bell
`\b`	backspace
`\f`	form feed
`\n`	newline
`\r`	carriage return
`\t`	horizontal tab
`\v`	vertical tab
`\'`	single quote (apostrophe)
`\"`	double quote
`\\`	backslash
`\0`	the "null character"; the character with the value `0` (used as a string terminator; see below)
`\nnn`	the character with the octal value *nnn* (1–3 octal digits)
`\xnn`	the character with the hexadecimal value *nn* (1 or more hexadecimal digits)

For example, the constants `'\n'`, `'\177'`, `'\xff'`, and `'\''` are all character constants, consisting of a newline character, the character with value `0177` (127 decimal), the character with value `0xff` (255 decimal), and a single quote, respectively.

A character constant has type `int`. (This represents one significant difference between C and C++.)

It is theoretically permissible to place multiple characters within one character constant, as in `'ab'`, although the result is implementation-defined and of questionable utility.

C has no formal string type, but there is considerable support in the language for a particular representation of strings: the characters in the string are simply stored consecutively in an array of `char`. The actual length of the string (which is often less than the size of the array) is recorded by terminating the string with a special character. The character with the value 0 is reserved for this purpose; it is represented as `\0` (which is, of course, a special case of the `\nnn` notation). This terminating character is also called the "null character."

The language supports constants for these strings, termed *string literals* (or, informally, simply *string constants*). The value of a string literal is an unnamed, unmodifiable array containing the requested characters and the terminating `\0`, which the compiler automatically appends. Examples of valid string constants are `"Hello, world!"`, `"abc"`, `"A"`, and `""` (the latter being the empty string, sometimes called the null string, and consisting solely of the terminating null character). Adjacent string literals are concatenated at compile time; for example, `"ab"` `"cd"` results in `"abcd"`. (This concatenation is useful when extremely long strings must be split across source lines.)

When you are working with wide characters, an `L` may be prepended to a character constant to give it type `wchar_t`, or to a string literal to give it type "array of `wchar_t`." Examples are `L'A'` and `L"abc"` (or, depending on the sophistication of the development environment, `L'æ'` or `L"ïöü"`).

Notice that character constants and string constants are distinct, even when a particular string constant happens to contain a single character. That is, `'A'` and `"A"` are very different (the latter is an array containing two characters, A and `\0`). Also, notice that although characters are represented internally as small integers that are the characters' values in the machine's character set, a digit character typically does not have its own value; the constants 2 and `'2'` are very different (the latter has the value 50 in ASCII). Finally, a string containing digits is different from the number it might seem to represent; the string `"123"` is not the number 123 (although C's `atoi` function would convert the string `"123"` to the integer 123; see section 3.10.4.2.1).

3.2.3. Declarations

As mentioned previously, C is strongly typed and requires that all variables be declared before use. The syntax of a simple declaration is

```
type identifier ;
```

where `type` is one of the basic types from section 3.2.1 or one of the user-defined types described in sections 3.2.9 and 3.7, and `identifier` is the name of the variable to be declared. For example,

```
int i;
```

declares an `int` variable named `i`, and

```
double degreescentigrade;
```

declares a `double` variable named `degreescentigrade`.

It is also possible to declare several variables, of the same base type, within the same declaration; multiple identifiers are separated by commas:

```
int j, k;
```

Furthermore, it is also possible to specify an initial value (an *initializer*):

```
float f1 = 1.2;
double d1 = 3.4, d2 = 5.6;
```

The initializer can be one of the constants from section 3.2.2, or a more general expression. (Depending on the particular variable being declared, the expression may have to be a constant expression as described in section 3.3.12. See also section 3.2.8.)

Rather than a simple identifier, a declaration can include a more complex declarator which indicates that an array or some other derived type is being declared rather than a simple variable. Later sections describe the additional type qualifiers and storage-class specifiers that can be used to adjust the meaning of a declaration. A more complete skeletal syntax for a declaration, incorporating all of these possibilities, is

```
[sc] [qualifier] type declarator [=init] [, declarator [=init]...] ;
```

where *sc* is the storage-class and brackets ([ ]) surround optional elements. (Actually, there is considerably more freedom in the arrangement of the *sc*, `qualifier`, and `type` than is indicated in the above skeleton, but placing the *sc* in other than the first position is discouraged.)

3.2.4. Identifiers

A C programmer has fairly wide latitude in choosing names (identifiers) for variables, functions, and other entities. Furthermore, it is possible to use the same name in several contexts at once because each name is known in a particular scope and namespace. (Briefly, *scope* refers to the part of a program in which an identifier is known, and the existence of multiple namespaces allows names for different entities—for example,

variables and user-defined data structures—to be distinguished.)
Although most of the examples in the previous section were simple names
like i or f1, the actual rules are as follow:

- An identifier must consist of alphabetic characters, digits, and/or underscore characters.

- An identifier must begin with an alphabetic character or under-score.

- Identifiers may be arbitrarily long, but the compiler is not required to consider more than the first 31 characters as significant.

- Case is usually significant.

- For external (i.e., "global") identifiers, some compilers (or, more precisely, some linkers) may not consider more than the first six characters as significant, and may disregard case.

- An identifier must not match a language keyword.

- Certain patterns of identifiers (including most beginning with underscores) are reserved in certain scopes and namespaces.

- The names of standard library functions, or names reserved for possible future extensions to the standard library, may not be used for user-defined global variables or functions. (Roughly speaking, the "future extensions" names are those beginning with mem, str, is, to, or wcs, followed by a lowercase letter.)

- When the standard headers associated with library functions are included, the macro and type names defined by those headers are, of course reserved. (These names, too, include some future extension patterns, such as most macros beginning with SIG if <signal.h> is included, or most macros beginning with E if <errno.h> is included.)

- Some compilers may allow additional characters (such as $) in identifiers, but these are nonstandard extensions.

3.2.5. Array Declarations

Besides single, simple variables, it is also possible to declare arrays, which are the first example of C's derived types. An array is indicated in a declaration by a pair of square brackets containing a constant expression that gives the desired number of elements in the array. For example,

```
int a[10];
```

declares an array a of 10 ints. All arrays in C are 0-based, so the 10 elements of the array a are numbered from 0 to 9.

In the preceding declaration, the syntax a[10] is the declarator. It contains the identifier to be declared, a, and also additional information about the variable's type, namely that it is an array of 10 elements. This example shows that the complete type of a variable is determined by a combination of the type name appearing at the beginning of the declaration, and any additional information found in the declarator. Functions and pointers are the other two derived types in C; the declarators for those types are described in sections 3.5.2, 3.6.1, and 3.6.7.

Array dimensions must be compile-time constants; C does not directly support variable-size arrays. (The programmer can, however, easily simulate them using pointers and dynamic memory allocation; see section 3.6.6.) C does not directly support multidimensional arrays, but these too can be readily simulated by declaring arrays of arrays.

Array types are somewhat constrained in their use; in particular, it is not possible to perform operations such as assignment on entire arrays at once. (The special handling of arrays is discussed in section 3.6.5.)

3.2.6. Scope, Duration, Linkage, and Storage Classes

An extra keyword, called the *storage-class*, can be added to a declaration (usually at the beginning) in order to control certain aspects of a variable's scope, duration, and linkage. To illustrate the use of storage classes, we must first look at how scope, duration, and linkage work in the absence of storage classes.

The *scope* or *visibility* of a variable's identifier is controlled by the placement of the variable's declaration. Variables declared within a function (or more locally, within a block; see section 4) have local scope, and are visible only within that function (or block). Variables declared outside of any function, on the other hand, have some degree of global scope, and are potentially visible to many functions.

The *duration* or *lifetime* of a variable determines when storage for it is allocated and deallocated. By default, local variables have *automatic* duration. This means that they spring into existence when the function containing them is called and disappear when the function returns. Variables declared outside functions, however, have static duration: They are created when the program is first invoked, and persist until the program terminates.

The automatic allocation of local variables means that if a function is called recursively, each invocation is allocated its own copies of all local variables, which therefore do not conflict with each other. Because automatic variables disappear when the containing function returns, they do not retain their values from call to call.

Global variables (and functions) can be used in programs that are built from multiple source files. A global variable or function may be referenced, via an *external declaration*, from many places in potentially many source files, but it must have exactly one *defining instance*, in exactly one source file. The term *linkage* refers to the process of matching up the references to global variables and functions, wherever they may appear, with their unique definitions.

All of the preceding attributes of a declaration may be modified by means of the storage-class specifier. The first storage-class to discuss is static, which has two different uses. When used in a declaration of a variable outside any function (an otherwise global variable), it limits the scope of that variable to the source file in which it is declared, and prevents it from being accessed from other source files. By default, outside a function, a declaration like

```
int globalvar;
```

declares a truly global variable that can potentially be accessed from any source file. With the addition of the keyword static, however,

```
static int privatevar;
```

the declaration is of a variable that, though global to its source file and accessible to any function in that source file, is *not* accessible to any function in any other source file. Functions can also be declared with the storage-class static, with the same result: A static function becomes private to its containing source file.

The second use of the storage-class specifier static is in controlling the duration of local variables. Inside a function, as mentioned, a declaration is by default of a variable with local scope and automatic duration. With the addition of the keyword static, however, the variable achieves static duration, meaning that it does not come and go as the function is called and returns, and that it does not lose its value between invocations of the function. Instead, it is created just once, when the program begins execution, and lasts as long as the program does. (This also means that one copy of the variable is shared among any recursive invocations of the function. See section 3.5.3 for a realistic example.)

The storage-class specifier `extern` is used in distinguishing between defining instances and external declarations of global variables and functions. Roughly speaking, a declaration not containing the storage-class `extern` is a defining instance, and a declaration with the storage-class `extern` is an external declaration. Section 3.5.4 discusses these two forms of declarations in more detail.

So far, we have mentioned two storage-class specifiers, `static` and `extern`. There are five storage-class specifiers in all, summarized here:

- `static`—For a variable declared outside any function, or for a function, indicates that the variable or function is to be private to the containing source file. For a local variable, indicates that the variable is to have static duration.

- `extern`—Indicates (with one exception) that a declaration is an external declaration of a variable or function defined elsewhere. (The exception is that a declaration containing an explicit initializer is a defining instance even if it contains the storage-class `extern`, although there is little use to be made of this exception.)

- `register`— For a local variable or function parameter, indicates that the variable should be assigned to a machine register, if possible, for greater efficiency. A variable declared `register` may not have its address taken with the `&` operator (see section 3.6.2); for a related reason, arrays may not be assigned to registers. The use of the `register` keyword has greatly diminished in importance as compilers have gotten better at detecting heavily used variables and automatically assigning them to machine registers.

- `auto`— For a local variable, indicates that the variable should have automatic duration. Because automatic duration is the default for local variables, this storage-class specifier is almost never used. (It is a holdover from C's predecessor language B.)

- `typedef`— Indicates that the identifier declared by the declaration is *not* of an actual variable or function, but rather is to be a synonym for the type that the variable or function would have had. See section 3.2.9.

If a declaration includes an explicit storage-class specifier, the type may be omitted, and defaults to `int`. Thus,

```
register r;
```

is a declaration of an `int` variable r, which should be placed in a machine register, and

```
extern a[];
```

is an external declaration of an array of `int`s. (The size is omitted because it is set, elsewhere, by the defining declaration of the array.)

3.2.7. Type Qualifiers

The final piece of the declaration scheme is the *type qualifier*, which can be used to specify two attributes of a variable's storage, in a way independent of and orthogonal to any storage-class. The two type qualifiers are

- `const`—Indicates that a location will not be written to during the running of the program, such that it may be placed in read-only storage. A `const` object may be assigned a value only by initialization. The compiler attempts to warn about attempts to modify `const` objects.

  (A `const` object is, however, *not* a compile-time constant; it is a run-time object that will not be modified. A `const` object cannot be used where a constant expression is required, such as in an array dimension. This is another significant difference from C++.)

- `volatile`—Indicates that a location may change its value other than as written to by the program, or that it otherwise has peculiar access semantics. The canonical example of a `volatile` location is a memory-mapped I/O register, which may have a different value each time it is read from, or may cause output operations to be performed when it is written to. The effect of the `volatile` qualifier is typically to suppress optimizations that would rearrange or eliminate loads or stores of the affected variable.

Simple examples of these type qualifiers in use are

```
const float pi = 3.14;
```

and

```
volatile int diskcsr;
```

Type qualifiers are distinct from storage classes because, in complex pointer declarations, it is possible for either the pointer itself or the pointed-to location to be qualified. (See section 3.6.1.)

If a declaration includes a type qualifier, the type may be omitted, and defaults to `int`. Thus,

```
const x = 10;
```

declares a nonwritable `int` variable named x with the value 10.

3.2.8. Initialization

As mentioned in section 3.2.3, the declaration of a variable may contain an initial value, termed an *initializer*. The allowable forms of initializers (and the default initialization, in the absence of an explicit initializer) depend on the type and duration of the variable.

The initializer for a variable with static duration must be a *constant expression*, either a single constant or an expression composed ultimately of constants (see section 3.3.12). In general, the initializer is computed at compile time, and arrangements are made to copy the value into the variable at program startup. In the absence of an explicit initializer, a variable with static duration is initialized to 0, just as if the programmer had written "= 0". (The initialization is to the value 0; the default initialization of a floating-point or pointer value is therefore not necessarily all-bits-0.)

The initializer for a variable with automatic duration may be any expression. The initializer is recomputed and reassigned each time the containing function is called (or control flow enters the top of the containing block). Any expression that could have been assigned to the variable using a conventional assignment may also appear as its initializer. In the absence of an explicit initializer, a variable with automatic duration is not initialized at all, and typically contains garbage. It is an error to attempt to use the value of an uninitialized local variable, but it is sometimes a subtle error, because in some cases the program may "happen" to work. (For example, most machines allocate local variables on a stack, and many operating systems provide programs with stack space that is initially all zero.)

It is also possible to initialize arrays; the initialization takes the form of a brace-enclosed, comma-separated list of values:

```
int a[10] = {1, 2, 3, 4, 5, 6, 7, 8, 9, 10};
```

The individual initializers must all be constant expressions; they cannot contain function calls and the like. There must not be more initializers than there are elements in the array. If there are fewer, the remaining elements are initialized to 0 (as was the case for uninitialized static variables, and in this case, whether the array is static or automatic). When the declaration for an array includes an initialization list, the size of the array may be omitted, and the compiler computes it automatically it by counting the initializers. For example,

```
int b[] = {1, 2, 3};
```

declares an array of three elements, just as if the programmer had written `int b[3]`.

The initializer for a character array may be a string literal:

```
char str[] = "Hello, world!";
```

The interpretation is the obvious one: The array is initialized with characters from the string literal. As before, the array size is inferred from the size of the initializer (which includes the implicit trailing \0) if the declared size is missing, and the array is filled with trailing 0's (i.e., \0 characters) if the explicit array size is larger than the initializer. (It is also possible, though rarely useful, for the explicitly given size to match the apparent length of the string literal initializer exactly, in which case the terminating \0 is omitted.)

3.2.9. Type Definitions

When the storage-class `typedef` appears in a declaration, as in

```
typedef int integer;
```

it indicates that the identifier, in this case, `integer`, is not to be declared as an object or function, but is rather to become a synonym for the type described by the rest of the declaration. In this example, the identifier `integer` becomes a synonym for the type `int`, and can thereafter (as long as the name `integer` remains in scope) be used in other declarations and elsewhere, just as a built-in type could:

```
integer i;
integer a[10];
```

Type definitions are most useful in building complicated derived types (see section 3.6.7). They may also be useful for documentation and software engineering purposes.

Type definitions create synonyms or aliases; they do not create new types, and the compiler is not obligated to diagnose mismatches. This means that when they are used for documentation and software engineering purposes, they are essentially advisory, not enforced. For example, if the

programmer wishes to define two distinct classes of integers named pyrus
and citrus

```
typedef int pyrus;
typedef int citrus;
```

and then to declare variables that are to hold values of these classes

```
pyrus apple;
citrus orange;
```

an assignment such as

```
apple = orange;
```

though presumably meaningless and undesirable in the programmer's
type scheme, would not necessarily be diagnosed by the compiler.

The language predefines a few auxiliary types that are typically implemented using typedef and that provide good examples of its use. size_t,
for instance, is an unsigned integer type used for holding the size, in
bytes, of objects and other memory regions. It might be implemented as

```
typedef unsigned int size_t;
```

on some machines, and as

```
typedef unsigned long int size_t;
```

on others, depending on architectural considerations. However, code that
declares variables, function parameters, and so on as being of type size_t
should work without change even when compiled on different machines.
Other examples of predefined types are FILE, time_t, ptrdiff_t, and wchar_t
(see sections 3.10.1, 3.10.6, 3.10.11, and 3.10.17).

3.3. Expressions

As far as the compiler is concerned, the primary purpose of an expression
in C is to compute a new value. The programmer is more concerned with
side effects; in the process of computing a value, most expressions assign
new values to variables or other objects, or call functions that perform
I/O or have other lasting, visible effects.

C's expression syntax is relatively rich, with a large number of operators.
It is also quite general: With a few exceptions, anywhere that an expression may appear, it may be an arbitrarily complicated expression. C programmers routinely make use of this flexibility, preferring to construct

large expressions that compute values and work with them immediately rather than, say, assigning them to temporary variables to be used in succeeding expressions.

So as to appreciate the potential complexity of C expressions, neither getting lost in them nor falsely imagining any unnecessary restrictions, it is useful to think of them recursively: An expression is either a simple, primitive expression, or it is an expression built up from subexpressions (which are, of course, themselves expressions) and operators. The size and complexity of an expression is therefore, in principle, infinite: Any expression, no matter how complicated, can always be treated as a subexpression and combined with more operators and other subexpressions to form an even larger expression.

The first expressions to look at are the *primary expressions,* which can be thought of as beginning the recursive process of building expressions. (Roughly speaking, a primary expression is one of the "simple, primitive expressions" informally referred to previously.) Next, we cover most of the operators that can be used to build expressions out of primary expressions or subexpressions. (The remaining few operators are discussed in later sections on pointers and data structures.)

3.3.1. Primary Expressions

The most basic, primitive expression, perhaps the most fundamental input for any computation, is a constant, of any of the forms described in section 3.2.2. That is, the forms

```
1     023     0x45     678L     '9'     "ten"
```

which you might first think of as constants, are also simple expressions, and can be used as such.

Almost as basic as a primary expression is the name (or identifier) of a variable. When the name of a variable appears in an expression in a context in which its value is needed, the interpretation is the obvious one: The value of the variable is fetched.

Also in the class of primary expressions are array references. The syntax a[0] refers to element number 0 of the array a; a[1] refers to element number 1; a[i] refers to element number i, and so on. Like constants and simple variable references, these array references can appear anywhere in expressions, and when they appear in contexts in which a value is required, the indicated element of the array is fetched. The subscript within the brackets can itself be an arbitrarily complicated expression; we may refer to not only a[0] or a[i] but also more complicated references such as a[b + f(c*d + 1, e)] or even a[b[c]].

A function call is also a primary expression, and contributes to the surrounding expression the value returned by the function. The arguments passed to the function, if any, may also be arbitrarily complicated subexpressions.

3.3.2. Arithmetic Operators

The basic arithmetic operators in C, as in many other languages, are +, -, *, and /, which are respectively addition, subtraction, multiplication, and division. These are all binary operators, combining two subexpressions to form a larger expression. They can all be used with integer or floating-point operands. (The + and - operators can also be used with pointers, as discussed in section 3.6.3.) The minus sign (-) can also be used as a unary negation operator, meaning that it is applied to just one operand; the expression -a simply negates the value of a, and is equivalent to 0 - a. For symmetry, the + operator can also be used in a unary form, although there is rarely any reason to do so.

The division operator, /, has the not-uncommon property that it operates in one of two different ways, depending on whether its operands are integers or floating-point values. If both its operands are integers, an integer division is performed, and the remainder is discarded. This means that 7 / 2 is 3 (not 3.5, not 3 1/2, not "three remainder one"). If either or both of the operands are floating-point values, however, floating-point division is performed, yielding a floating-point result. Therefore, the divisions 7.0/2, 7/2.0, and 7.0/2.0 all yield 3.5. When floating-point division is required in a particular situation, therefore, it is necessary to ensure that one of the operands is a floating-point constant or a variable of floating-point type, or to use an explicit type conversion (see section 3.3.11).

(As a matter of curiosity, C uses * and / for multiplication and division for the same reason that most conventional computer languages do: the symbols × and ÷ do not appear on most computer keyboards or in the ASCII character set.)

Included in the category of arithmetic operators is a fifth operator, the "remainder" or *modulus* operator %. The % operator may be applied only to integers, and yields the remainder that is left when the two operands are divided. Therefore, 7 % 2 is 1, 123 % 100 is 23, and 4 % 2 is 0. Among other things, the % operator is useful for determining whether one number is an even multiple of another, in which case the remainder when dividing the first by the second is 0.

One caveat: Integer division and the modulus operator are not precisely defined when one or both of the operands are negative. On different machines, -7 / 2 might give -3 or -4, and -7 % 2 might give 1 or -1. (However, it is guaranteed that for any integers a and b, (a/b)*b + (a%b) is equal to a, as long as b is not 0, of course.)

When evaluating expressions, C applies rules of *precedence* and *associativity*, just as most computer languages do, and as are present in the rules of algebra. (However, "associativity" has a significantly different meaning in programming than it does in mathematics.) Multiplication, division, and the modulus operator all have higher precedence than addition and subtraction, which means that the expression

```
a + b * c
```

is interpreted as

```
a + (b * c)
```

In other words, the operators *, /, and % "bind more tightly" than + and -. (One might also say that the multiplication in a + b * c happens "before" the addition, but as mentioned in section 3.3.9, using words like "before" when discussing precedence can be misleading.) Unary operators, including unary -, have the highest precedence of all, which means that

```
-a + b
```

is interpreted as

```
(-a) + b
```

not -(a + b).

The five binary operators in this section all "group" from left to right, which means that

```
a + b + c
```

is interpreted as

```
(a + b) + c
```

and that

```
a - b - c
```

is interpreted as

```
(a - b) - c
```

not as a - (b - c). Choosing a particular interpretation for subtraction and division is obviously significant, but it can also make a difference for addition and multiplication. For example, in the expression a + b + c, if it is the case that b + c would overflow, but (a + b) + c would not (perhaps a is -1, b is 1, and c is 32767), the programmer can be assured that overflow will not occur even in the absence of explicit parentheses.

To override the default precedence or associativity and force a particular interpretation, explicit parentheses can be used; for example, the expression

```
(a + b) * c
```

requests that a be added to b and the result multiplied by c.

3.3.3. Assignment Operators

Assignments in C are not distinguished statements. They are ordinary expressions; the assignment operator = is an ordinary binary operator. (This is in keeping with C's emphasis on expressions.) Placed between two subexpressions, the assignment operator = assigns the value of the right-hand subexpression to the location named by the left. For example,

```
a = b + 1
```

evaluates the subexpression b + 1 and assigns it to the variable a.

Note that although a is the name of a variable, here its value is not fetched. Because it appears on the left-hand side of an assignment operator, it serves as the destination for a value, not a source.

Like any other expression, an assignment expression has a value. If an assignment expression appears as a subexpression within some larger expression, the value passed on to the surrounding expression is simply the value that was assigned to the left-hand side. For example, the expression

```
f(a = b + 1)
```

assigns the value b + 1 to a and then passes that same value as an argument to the function f.

An assignment expression is an example of an expression with a side effect. Besides computing a value, an assignment expression also causes a change to the state of the program, by virtue of the fact that it modifies a variable by assigning a new value to it.

The assignment operator has very low precedence, so an expression like

```
a = b + 1
```

is interpreted as

```
a = (b + 1)
```

which is certainly what was meant. The assignment operator associates (groups) from right to left, so an expression like

```
a = b = 0
```

is interpreted as

```
a = (b = 0)
```

and therefore sets a to the same value it sets b. (An expression like a = b = 0 is a common, compact idiom for assigning the same value to several variables at once.)

Obviously, the left-hand side of an assignment expression must represent a value that can be assigned to. It may be an ordinary variable, or an element of an array, or certain other location-designating expressions. But it may not be the name of a variable that was declared const, or an entire array, or an expression that only computes a value. (As a counterexample, the expression a + 1 = b is meaningless.)

As in most computer languages, the assignment operator indicates an active assignment of a value to a location; it does not represent a test for or assertion of equality. (Some languages use notations like := for assignment, in order to make this distinction more evident.) The expression

```
i = i + 1
```

is a meaningful and extremely common idiom (though not as commonly written in this form in C). The interpretation is as before: The expression i + 1 is evaluated, and the result assigned to i, giving it a value one greater than it had before.

3.3.4. Relational and Logical Operators
C provides the usual set of operators for performing relational comparisons and logical or "boolean" operations. These operations are once again performed by ordinary operators in the context of ordinary expressions. The relational operators are as follow:

Operator	Description
<	less than
<=	less than or equal to
>	greater than
>=	greater than or equal to
==	equal to
!=	not equal to

These are all binary operators, comparing their two operands and returning a true or false result. They can be used not only with numerical quantities, but also with pointers, as discussed in section 3.6.3. (Also, we may again note that the notations <=, >=, and != are used at least in part because few keyboards or common character sets contain the symbols ≤, ≥, and ≠.)

A trivial example is

```
a == b
```

which has the value true if a and b are equal, and false otherwise.

It is important to notice that the equality-testing operator is ==, not one = by itself! Accidentally writing something like

```
if(a = b)
```

is a common error, which most certainly does not test whether a and b are equal, but rather sets them to be equal. (The condition tested would then be whether the value assigned was true or false.)

True and false values can be combined, using the logical or boolean operators, which are as follow:

Operator	Description
&&	logical AND
||	logical OR
!	logical NOT (unary)

For example, the expression

```
a == 2 || a == 3
```

represents (or, stated another way, tests the truth or falsehood of) the condition "a is equal to 2 or a is equal to 3". The expression

```
x > 0 && x < 10
```

tests whether x is between 0 and 10 (representing the condition that a mathematician would express as 0 < x < 10, although this form of expression is not meaningful in C).

The unary ! operator negates the truth of its (single) operand. The expression

```
!(a > b && c > d)
```

is true if it is not the case that a is greater than b and c is greater than d. (Logicians know that by applying De Morgan's theorem, the preceding expression can be transformed to the equivalent a <= b || c <= d.)

The && and || operators have an additional property, known as "short circuiting." If the left-hand side of the && operator is false, the result can never be true, so the right-hand side is not evaluated at all in that case. Similarly, if the left-hand side of the || operator is true, the result can never be false, so the right-hand side is not evaluated. Therefore, an expression like

```
n != 0 && sum/n > 0
```

is safe; if n is 0, no divide-by-0 will occur.

The precedence of the binary logical operators is lower than that of the relational operators; expressions like

```
a == 2 || a == 3
```

and

```
x > 0 && x < 10
```

are interpreted as

```
(a == 2) || (a == 3)
```

and

```
(x > 0) && (x < 10)
```

as you would expect. As is traditional in boolean algebra, the precedence of && is higher than ||, so

```
a > b || c > d && e > f
```

is interpreted as

```
a > b || (c > d && e > f)
```

As always, explicit parentheses can be used to force a particular interpretation. For example, a common idiom in C is

```
(c = getchar()) != EOF
```

which calls the function getchar, assigns its return value to the variable c, and also compares it to the constant EOF. Because the precedence of = is lower than !=, the parentheses are required to achieve the desired interpretation. (See section 3.3.9 for a complete precedence table.)

How does C represent true and false values? By definition, any value that is not equal to zero is true, whereas a value that compares equal to 0 is false. So the operation of the && operator can be paraphrased as "if the left-hand operand is not zero and the right-hand operand is not zero, return a nonzero result."

Although any nonzero value is considered to be true, the operators of this section always generate the value 1 for truth. For example, the operation of &&, ||, and ! can be summarized in this truth table:

a	b	a && b	a || b	!a	!b
0	0	0	0	1	1
0	nonzero	0	1	1	0
nonzero	0	0	1	0	1
nonzero	nonzero	1	1	0	0

(Returning to a previous example, the incorrect expression

```
0 < x < 10
```

always yields true, regardless of the value of x, because it is interpreted as

```
(0 < x) < 10
```

The first < yields either 0 or 1, which is certainly less than 10.)

Because true and false are represented as zero and nonzero, it is possible to effectively store truth values in ordinary variables. Variables of several types may be chosen, although char and int are most popular. (C has no predefined bool type.) For example, having declared and initialized

```
int xbetween = (x > 0 && x < 10);
```

the variable xbetween now contains a nonzero value (specifically, 1) if x is between 0 and 10, and zero otherwise. (In the initialization, the parentheses are unnecessary, but are inserted for clarity.) Later, the variable xbetween could be used in a context in which a true/false value was expected:

```
if(xbetween)
    ...
```

Furthermore, because the interpretation of true is simply "not equal to 0," any value (whether it is thought of as being a true/false value) may be tested for zero/nonzero by placing it in a conditional context. If the variable nitems contains a number of items, the test

```
if(nitems) ...
```

does something if nitems is not 0. An earlier example, which tested whether an average existed and was greater than zero (without ever dividing by zero), could have been written

```
n && sum/n > 0
```

Opinions differ on whether testing ordinary variables in this way is good style, but the idiom is often seen and must be recognized.

In summary: When a value is being tested for truth or falsehood, any nonzero value is considered true, but when an operator of this section generates a true value, it generates the value 1. However, many functions that conceptually return true/false values return true values other than 1, so it is never a good idea to test a conceptually boolean value for equality with the constant 1. That is, don't write if(isalpha(c) == 1); write if (isalpha(c)) instead. (See section 3.10.3 for information on isalpha and related functions.)

3.3.5. Bitwise Operators

The *bitwise operators* operate conceptually on the individual bits of binary numbers. They are perhaps the lowest level of C's operators, closest to the machine instructions that might otherwise be accessed only through assembly language. However, these operators find plenty of uses in higher-level algorithms and are used in a number of common idioms as well.

The &, |, and ^ operators perform boolean operations across the individual bits of two operands. The & operator performs bitwise AND, the | operator performs bitwise OR, and the ^ operator performs bitwise exclusive-OR (XOR). The truth tables for these operators can be summarized as follows:

```
    0x0011          0x0011          0x0011
  & 0x0101        | 0x0101        ^ 0x0101
  --------        --------        --------
    0x0001          0x0111          0x0110
```

A bit in the result of a bitwise AND operator is 1 if the corresponding bits in the first and second operands are both 1 (otherwise, the resulting bit is 0). A bit in the result of a bitwise OR operator is 1 if the corresponding bits in either the first or second operands (or both) are 1. A bit in the result of a bitwise XOR operator is 1 if one of the corresponding bits in either the first or second operands (but not both) is 1. (The preceding three examples use carefully chosen hexadecimal constants that suggest base-2 numbers, though they are not. As a fourth example, `0x7d & 0x5e` yields `0x5a`.)

The unary ~ operator takes the one's complement of its operand, changing all 0 bits to 1 and 1 bits to 0. On a machine with 16-bit ints, `~0x0101` is `0xfefe`.

The left- and right-shift operators << and >> shift their left operands left or right by a number of bits given by their right operands. The expression `0x0101 >> 4` yields `0x0010`, and the expression `0x1234 << 1` yields `0x2468`. Bits that are shifted away are discarded. The left-shift operator << always fills with 0 bits at the right. The right-shift operator >> fills with 0 bits at the left if the left operand has an unsigned type. If the left operand is signed, it is implementation defined whether the right-shift operator shifts in 0 bits or copies of the sign bit. The results are undefined if the right operand is negative or is greater than or equal to the size of the left operand in bits.

The bitwise operators are commonly used to encode a set of 1-bit flags within an integer. The expression `flags = flags | 0x10` sets the fifth bit from the right in `flags` to 1 (whether it was 1 or not). The expression `flags = flags & ~0x10` clears the fifth bit to 0. (The expression `~0x10` is preferable in this application to `0xffef` or `0xfffffef` because it is independent of the size of an `int`.) The expression `flags & 0x10` tests the fifth bit, yielding a zero value if the fifth bit is 0 and a nonzero value if it is 1, and can therefore be used directly in conditionals, as in `if(flags & 0x10) ....` It is also possible to construct bit masks "on the fly" by using the shift operators: the mask `0x10` could be computed from its (0-based) bit number using `0x01 << 4`.

The bitwise operators can also be used to extract subfields from integer values. For example, the expression `val & 0x0ff0` extracts the middle 8 bits from a (presumably) 16-bit value. By using the properties of binary numbers, these masks, too, can be computed on-the-fly. The expression `(1 << 6) - 1` yields the mask `0x3f`, which could be used to extract the low-order 6 bits of an integer. The expression `((1 << 8) - 1) << 4` yields the mask `0x0ff0`.

The exclusive-OR operator ^ has an "information preserving" property (roughly speaking, it changes as many 0's to 1's as it changes 1's to 0's), which makes it useful in several situations. Returning to the bit flags example, the expression `flags = flags ^ 0x10` toggles the fifth bit from 0 to 1 or from 1 to 0. If `val` is a data value and `key` is an encryption key, the expression `xval = val ^ key` yields a scrambled value `xval` with the property that the original value can be recovered simply by computing `xval ^ key`. (This rudimentary example has almost no security, but it forms the basis of many useful encryption algorithms, especially those that are self inverse.) If `val1`, `val2`, and `val3` are three values that are to be transmitted via an unreliable communications channel, the expression `val4x = val1 ^ val2 ^ val3` computes a fourth value, which, if it is transmitted along with the first three, can be used to recover any of them. For example, if it is discovered that `val2` was damaged in transit, the expression `val1 ^ val3 ^ val4x` recovers `val2`.

The precedence of the bitwise operators is not always obvious; in particular, the precedence of &, ^, and | is quite low (below +, ==, <<, and so on). A condition of the form `if(val & 0xf == 5)` does not behave as intended, if the intent was the condition that is correctly written as `if((val & 0xf) == 5)`. See the table in section 3.3.9 for complete information on the precedence of these operators.

3.3.6. Compound Assignment Operators
Patterns of the form

```
i = i + 1
```

turn up frequently in programming. C provides 10 shorthand assignment operators to simplify these patterns. Any expression of the form `v = v op e`, where `op` is one of the binary operators +, -, *, /, %, &, |, ^, <<, or >>, can be replaced with `v op= e`. Thus, `i += 1` is equivalent to `i = i + 1` and increments `i` by 1, `j -= 2` decrements `j` by 2, `x *= 10` multiplies `x` by 10 (in place), and `y %= 10` replaces `y` by its remainder when divided by 10. These assignment operators are particularly useful when the expression designating the object being modified is more complicated; for example,

```
tab[a + b + 2*c + d[e]] += 1
```

is clearly easier to write, read, and verify as correct than the longhand form

```
tab[a + b + 2*c + d[e]] = tab[a + b + 2*c + d[e]] + 1
```

Moreover, in the form using the assignment operator, the expression designating the object being modified is evaluated only once (which is natural because it appears only once). For example, in the slightly modified example

```
tab[a + b + 2*c + f(e)] += 1
```

the function `f()` is called only once. The assignment forms of the bitwise operators are also commonly seen; for example, the operations of setting, clearing, and toggling a bit can be succinctly expressed as `flags |= 0x10`, `flags &= ~0x10`, and `flags ^= 0x10`.

As was the case for the simple assignment operator =, expressions involving the compound assignment operators all yield values, namely the new values assigned to the left-hand side.

3.3.7. Autoincrement and Autodecrement Operators

C has two more shorthand increment and decrement operators. The assignment operators of the preceding section allow the general expression a = b *op* c to be simplified when a and b are identical, but these two operators allow a further simplification when *op* is + or - and c is 1. The expression ++v is equivalent to v = v + 1 (and, hence, to v += 1), and the expression --v is equivalent to v = v - 1.

Like all expressions in C, expressions involving ++ and -- yield values and can be used as subexpressions within larger expressions. The value of the expression ++i is the incremented value of i (as would be expected based on examination of the equivalent forms i += 1 and i = i + 1). However, the ++ and -- operators can also be used in two alternative forms, with significantly different results. Used as postfixed unary operators, as in i++ and j--, the value yielded to the surrounding expression (if any) is the old value, before the increment or decrement. Thus, the statement

```
a[i++] = 0;
```

is equivalent to the two statements

```
a[i] = 0;
i = i + 1;
```

and the statement

```
b[++i] = 0;
```

is equivalent to the two statements

```
i = i + 1;
b[i] = 0;
```

The only difference between the prefix and postfix forms is the value given up to the surrounding expression. Therefore, when there is no surrounding expression (when an expression involving ++ or -- stands alone, as in i++;), it makes no difference which form is used.

Because they modify the stored values of their operands, we say that the increment and decrement operators, too, produce side effects. Not only does the expression ++i generate the value i+1 for use in a surrounding expression, it also assigns this new value back to i. Thus, it is unnecessary (and, in fact, utterly incorrect) to write

```
i = ++i;          /* WRONG */
```

The expression ++i all by itself is sufficient to assign the incremented value back to i. To increment i using an assignment operator, use i = i + 1 or i += 1. See section 3.3.9 for additional caveats concerning ++ and other operators with side effects.

3.3.8. Conditional and Comma Operators

Two more operators that don't fit into any of the preceding categories are the conditional and comma operators. The conditional operator (which is a *ternary* operator, because unlike unary and binary operators, it takes three operands) is essentially an if/else statement buried in an expression. The expression c ? a : b has the value a if the condition c evaluates to nonzero (i.e., true), and the value b if c evaluates to 0. For example, the expression

```
m = (r > 0) ? a + 1 : b - 1
```

is equivalent to the code

```
if(r > 0)
        m = a + 1;
else    m = b - 1;
```

The expression

```
a > b ? a : b
```

computes the maximum of a and b.

The conditional operator always evaluates its first operand (the conditional subexpression) first, and evaluates only one of its second and third operands as appropriate. Like the && and || operators, it can therefore be safely used when the order of evaluation is important and must be constrained. For example, the expression

```
avg = (n > 0) ? sum / n : 0
```

does not divide by 0 even if n is 0.

The comma operator evaluates two subexpressions, discarding the value of the first one and returning the value of the second. For example, the expression

```
a = 1, b = 2
```

assigns 1 to a and then assigns 2 to b. The final value of the expression is 2.

The comma operator is used where two expressions must be evaluated in sequence in a context in which (syntactically) one expression is expected. Its only common use is in the first or third controlling expression of a for loop (see section 3.4.5).

Note that the commas which separate the arguments in a function call are not comma operators. (Among other things, the commas in a function call do not impose a defined order of evaluation.)

3.3.9. Precedence and Order of Evaluation

We've mentioned at several points that C's operators have the usual precedence and associativity relations defining how they bind to their operands—for example, that the expression a + b * c is parsed by the compiler as if it had been written as a + (b * c). This table summarizes the precedence (highest to lowest) and grouping of all of C's operators (including those having to do with pointers and structures that are formally introduced in sections 3.6 and 3.7).

Class	Operators	Associativity
primary	array [] . -> function-call ()	left-to-right
postfix unary	++ --	left-to-right
prefix unary	++ -- & * + - ~ ! sizeof cast	right-to-left
multiplicative	* / %	left-to-right
additive	+ -	left-to-right
shift	<< >>	left-to-right
relational	< > <= >=	left-to-right
equality	== !=	left-to-right
bitwise AND	&	left-to-right
exclusive OR	^	left-to-right

Class	Operators	Associativity
bitwise OR	`|`	left-to-right
logical AND	`&&`	left-to-right
logical OR	`||`	left-to-right
conditional	`?:`	right-to-left
assignment	`=  *=  /=  %=  +=  -=` `<<=  >>=  &=  ^=  |=`	right-to-left
comma	`,`	left-to-right

Although it can be convenient to say things like "due to precedence, multiplication takes place before addition," it is important to realize that not all aspects of evaluation order are predetermined in C. Precedence and associativity may determine the order of evaluation of operators, but when the operands of a given operator are themselves nontrivial subexpressions, there is nothing in general to tell us the order in which those subexpressions themselves will be evaluated. In the expression

```
a * b + c * d
```

the addition happens last, but we do not know the relative order of the two multiplications. In the expression

```
a[i++] + b[j++] * c[k++]
```

the addition happens after the multiplication, but the three increments could occur in any order, either before or after the other operations. (If the compiler chose to perform the increments first, it would save the old values of i, j, and k somewhere and use them as the subscripts.) In the expression

```
f() + g() * h()
```

the three functions could be called in any order.

The fact that evaluation order is underdetermined means that certain expressions must be avoided. One example is

```
a[i] = i++
```

which may look reasonable until we ask whether the i in a[i] is the old or the incremented value. The question is unanswerable: The C Standard says that it is undefined to modify a variable or location, and try to use its value at another point, unless it is definitively known which of these actions will occur first. A similar prohibition applies to modifying the same object twice within an expression, as in i++ * i++.

Use and modification of the same variable is, of course, permitted when the old value is being used to compute the new; otherwise, familiar and reasonable idioms such as i = i + 1 would be illegal. There is also a special exception for the &&, ||, ?:, and comma operators; these four each imply a sequence point after evaluation of their first operand, meaning that the first operand is guaranteed to be completely evaluated before any part of the second is evaluated (if the second operand—or, in the case of the ?: operator, the third operand—is evaluated at all).

Except when using one of those operators, therefore, it is best not to try to predict the exact order of evaluation within an expression. In particular, it is not possible in the general case to determine the exact sequence of one expression's side effects.

It is tempting to argue that these undefined expressions must be evaluated in some order by any given compiler, and to perform experiments to determine what that order might be. It is perilous, however, to make use of any information so gained in an actual program because there is obviously no guarantee that different compilers (or even the same compiler, under different circumstances) will produce the same results.

A good rule of thumb to follow is that, as mentioned, and with the exception of the four operators that do provide specific guarantees, the only constraints on the actual order of evaluation within an expression are those required in order for the final, topmost value of the expression to be correct. Subexpressions within the expression may in general be evaluated in any order, and any side effects may occur in any order. When, for whatever reason, more control over expression evaluation is needed, the safest approach is often to use separate statements because statements do (by definition) provide absolute control over their order of execution. For example, rather than writing a[i] = i++, write either

```
a[i] = i - 1;
i++;
```

or

```
a[i] = i;
i++;
```

or

```
a[i] = i + 1;
i++;
```

depending on whether a[i] should receive the previous, current, or next value of i.

3.3.10. Default Conversions

C has a simple but general set of rules for performing automatic conversions when values of different types participate in an expression, or when a value of one type is assigned to a variable of a different type. In an assignment, automatic conversions are performed if the types are both numeric, or if they are certain assignment-compatible types of pointers. In a mixed-mode arithmetic operation expression, the general rule is that most operators always operate on two values of the same type, such that when values of dissimilar types meet across a binary operator, one or both are promoted to a common type before the operation takes place. The promotion is to the largest of the floating-point types involved if either operand is floating-point, or to long if either operand is long, and/or to unsigned if either operand is unsigned.

There is a certain bias in the language towards types int and double. (Some of this bias is historical and is gradually being removed.) Many compilers perform all floating-point arithmetic in type double, and the math-related library functions (see section 3.10.5) all use type double. All arithmetic always takes place using at least type int; types char and short int are always promoted to int before being operated on.

The promotion of unsigned values can be tricky: When a seemingly smaller unsigned type is promoted to a larger type, the exact promotion depends on the actual sizes of the types involved, which is machine dependent. The goal is to preserve the value being promoted. For example, if an unsigned short value is being promoted to int, and if type int is in fact bigger than type short int, then the promotion is to int, but if the two types are the same size, the promotion is to unsigned int. This rule, though it sounds reasonable enough as stated here, can lead to surprises, so care must be taken when writing expressions that involve mixtures of small and large, signed and unsigned operands.

As a simple example of the default promotion rules, given the declarations

```
int i;
long int li;
float f;
double d;
```

the expression i + li causes i to be promoted to long int, the expression i + f causes i to be promoted to float, and the expression li + d causes li to be promoted to double. The assignment d = i causes an implicit conversion of i's value to double, and the assignment i = d causes an implicit conversion of d's value to int.

Conversions from smaller integral types to larger are, of course, always exact. If the types are signed, sign extension occurs so that the value is preserved. (Sign extension occasionally causes surprising results if the value being manipulated is not being thought of as an integer value, but rather as a bit pattern.) Conversions from integral types to floating point are usually exact, except perhaps if a very large `long int` value cannot be represented with full precision in the floating-point type.

Conversions from floating point to integer always involve simple truncation of the fractional part, as long as the whole number part can be represented by the destination integer. (The result is otherwise undefined; note too that truncation of a value such as 3.99999 yields a result very different than rounding would.) A conversion of a larger integer to a smaller one is undefined if the smaller integer is signed and cannot represent the value. If the smaller integer is unsigned, however, the conversion is performed modulo the range of the unsigned destination. (That is, on a machine with 16-bit `short int`s, the assignment in

```
unsigned short int us;
long int li = 123456;
us = li;
```

is equivalent to

```
us = li % 65536;
```

and yields 57,920.)

These rules produce reasonable, expected results in most circumstances. Care must be taken in a few situations, however. First of all, the destination or context of an expression is never considered when deciding how the expression should be evaluated; the evaluation is always determined strictly by the two operands of each operator. In the code

```
int i = 1000, j = 2000;
long int li;
li = i * j;                     /*WRONG*/
```

the multiplication is carried out using `int`s, and may overflow, even though the destination is a `long int`. In the code

```
int i = 15, j = 4;
float f;
f = i / j;                      /* WRONG, if 3.75 is wanted */
```

an integer division is performed, resulting in the value 3, even though the destination is a `float`. Explicitly typed constants or explicit conversion operators (as described in the next section) can be used to achieve the desired result in these situations.

3.3.11. Explicit Conversions

Explicit type conversions are performed by means of *casts*. A cast is a parenthesized type name that is used as a unary operator. For example, the simple expression

```
(float)i
```

converts i's value to type float. The cast might be used to force floating-point division:

```
f = i / (float)j;
```

(Because floating-point division is performed if either operand is floating point, only one cast is required.)

The type name that appears in a cast is actually a stripped-down declaration, minus the identifier name. An identifierless declarator may appear in the type name in a cast in order to perform pointer conversions, as described in section 3.6.3.

Although the type void has, by definition, no values, it is permissible to "cast an expression to void," although the only purpose of doing so is the documentary one of indicating explicitly that a value is being ignored. For example, in the statement

```
(void)printf("Hello, world!\n");
```

the return value of printf is explicitly discarded; the (void) cast may additionally disable a zealous compiler's warning about the discarded return value. (Of course, a call without the cast would not be incorrect, either.)

In modern C programming, the use of explicit casts is generally discouraged. The existence of function prototypes and void pointers (see sections 3.5.3 and 3.6.6) has removed most of the needs for explicit conversions that arose in traditional C programming. When a cast is used just to "shut the compiler up" (that is, in an attempt to silence some warning that the programmer believes is extraneous or unimportant), it is usually the case that the resulting code is less portable than it could be, and that another alternative, without an explicit cast, exists and is to be preferred. About the only good remaining uses for explicit casts are in forcing floating-point division (as in the example just above), forcing long arithmetic (as in li = i * (long)j;), performing the occasional explicit conversion to unsigned to prevent sign extension, and performing the occasional explicit pointer conversion when "generic" pointers are being used (see section 3.10.4.4.1 for an example).

3.3.12. Constant Expressions

In several circumstances, C requires a constant expression, one that can be evaluated at compile time. Constant expressions are required for array dimensions, case labels (see section 3.4.3), and the initializers for static-duration variables, arrays, and other aggregate variables (i.e., structures and unions). Constant expressions must obviously involve only compile-time constants; they cannot contain any function calls or variable references (even to variables declared const). It follows that the assignment operators and ++ and -- may also not appear. (Section 3.6.3 mentions a few constraints on constant expressions involving pointers.)

3.4. Statements

Statements are the discrete steps of a C program. By default, simple statements are executed one after the other, but the usual collection of conditional and looping constructs is available and can be used to arrange for more interesting and useful control flow patterns.

Anywhere that a simple statement may appear, it is also possible to put a block of several statements. A block consists of a pair of braces ({}) enclosing zero or more statements. Declarations may appear at the beginning of the block; these declare identifiers are local to that block (and thus have even narrower scope than the local variables in the surrounding function or block).

3.4.1. Expression Statements

The simplest and most common statements in C are expression statements. As the name implies, an expression statement consists of an expression; in fact, the only syntactic difference between an expression and an expression statement is that an expression statement is terminated by a semicolon. (The semicolon is a statement terminator in C; it is not a separator as it is in Pascal, for example.)

By the definition of an expression statement, any expression can be made into a statement by putting a semicolon after it. For example, an assignment expression becomes a useful statement:

```
a = b + c;
```

A single function call becomes a useful statement, even if nothing is done with its return value, as long as the function does something interesting:

```
printf("Hello, world!\n");
```

More generally, an expression statement is useful if it performs (either directly, or indirectly through a function call) at least one side effect. An expression statement that computes a value but does nothing with it, as in

```
a + b;
```

is syntactically valid but useless because the computed value is conceptually discarded. (In this case, some compilers would emit code to evaluate the expression and some would not, and some would issue a warning.)

Closely related to the expression statement is the empty or null statement. (In fact, it can be said that an empty statement is an expression statement, if the expression is considered optional.) An empty statement is a single semicolon, used where a statement is syntactically required but there is no work to be done, as in a loop with no body or a label at the end of a block. For example, this loop finds the end of a string:

```
for(i = 0; string[i] != '\0'; i++)
    ;
```

3.4.2. if Statements

An if statement arranges that a subsidiary statement (or block of statements) is executed or not executed, depending on some condition. The syntax is simple:

```
if(n > 0)
    average = sum / n;
```

If the condition in the parentheses is true (nonzero), the statement is executed. If the condition is false, the statement is skipped; execution continues with the following statement (if any).

Optionally, an if statement may include an else clause, containing a statement to be executed if the condition is not true:

```
if(n > 0)
    average = sum / n;
else
    average = 0;
```

If n is greater than 0, the average is set to the quotient sum / n; otherwise, the average is set to 0. In either case, execution continues with the statement(s) further down.

When several statements are to be executed or not executed together, they can be enclosed in braces to form a block statement:

```
if(a > b)
    {
    t = a;
    a = b;
    b = t;
    }
```

Now, if the condition is true, all three statements are executed; if it is false, all three are skipped. (The result of this example is that a and b are swapped, if necessary, to ensure that b is greater than or equal to a.) Of course, a block statement may appear in the else clause as well:

```
if(n > 0)
        average = sum / n;
else    {
        printf("n is 0!\n");
        average = 0;
        }
```

Syntactically, both the if clause and the else clause are statements; a block is permissible because, syntactically, a block is a statement.

Blocks are, of course, typically indented from the left margin to make their structure more visually apparent, although it is important to remember that the compiler ignores this indentation (because C is a free-form language). Many styles of indentation and brace placement have been devised, and although it is impossible to prescribe one as "best," there is some value in consistency. (The indentation style used in this chapter is representative but is neither the most nor the least popular of the common styles.)

if statements can (just like all of C's statements) be nested arbitrarily. For example, this fragment prints a rough indication of a direction of travel, assuming that y represents the northward component and x the eastward component:

```
if(x > 0)
        if(y > 0)
                printf("northeast");
        else    printf("southeast");
else    if(y > 0)
                printf("northwest");
        else    printf("southwest");
```

(Obviously, an improved version would handle the cases of x == 0 and y == 0.) However, "bushy" if/else trees like this one can become unreadable because it becomes increasingly difficult to match up the else's correctly. Comments can help, but it is worthwhile to seek cleaner alternatives (such as table lookup) when a large, complicated if/then structure becomes unwieldy.

Another arrangement (and one much easier to read than a "bushy" tree) is a cascading chain of ifs and elses:

```
if(T < 32)
         printf("ice");
else if(T < 212)
         printf("water");
else     printf("steam");
```

The sequence reads (and executes) naturally: The conditions are tested in order, and the code associated with the first matching condition is executed. (After a matching condition is found, we know that all following branches are skipped.)

Caution is necessary, however, when if statements are nested in yet another way. Consider the following code:

```
if(n >= 0)
         if(n > 0)
                  average = sum / n;
else
         printf("n is negative!\n");
```

Which of the two if clauses should the lone else clause be paired with? The indentation (and the wording in the printf call) suggests that the last message is to be printed if n is not greater than or equal to 0. This code, however, is an example of the "dangling else" problem. In C, as in most languages, the rule is that an else clause is always associated with the nearest if. (Once again, the indentation is immaterial.) In other words, the compiler interprets the code as if it had been written

```
if(n >= 0)
         {
         if(n > 0)
                  average = sum / n;
         else
                  printf("n is negative!\n");
         }
```

and the code thus interpreted does not have the desired effect. Explicit braces can, however, always be used to make the programmer's intentions explicit:

```
if(n >= 0)
         {
         if(n > 0)
                  average = sum / n;
         }
else
         printf("n is negative!\n");
```

As a general rule, it is best to use explicit braces when the body of an `if` statement (or other control-flow construct) is any more complicated than a single, simple statement. (Some programmers prefer to use explicit blocks in all control-flow constructs.)

3.4.3. switch Statements

When a cascaded `if`/`else` chain repeatedly compares the same variable against a fixed set of targets, as in

```
if(x == 2)
        statement1;
else if(x == 3)
        statement2;
else if(x == 5 || x == 7)
        statement3;
else    statement4;
```

an alternate construction, the `switch` statement, is available. It looks like this:

```
switch(x)
        {
case 2:
        statement1;
        break;
case 3:
        statement2;
        break;
case 5:
case 7:
        statement3;
        break;
default:
        statement4;
        break;
}
```

Conceptually, the expression in the parentheses (here, the variable x) is evaluated once and compared to each of the `case` labels. The code corresponding to a match is executed. If there is no match, the `default` case is executed if it is present; otherwise, the entire `switch` statement is skipped, with none of the cases executed.

The keyword `break` marks the end of each case. These `break` statements are important: Without them, the interpretation is that execution should flow through from case to case. (This "fall-through" behavior can be a nuisance, but it is a traditional and now fixed part of the language.) The `case` labels may appear in any order. The `default` case need not be present, nor need it be last; regardless of its position, it always catches those values not matched by any of the explicit cases. None of the case labels may be duplicated. The case labels must all be compile-time constants. It is possible to attach multiple case labels to one block of code, as in the preceding example.

As the preceding discussion illustrates, the switch statement is somewhat limited. It can switch only on integral expressions, and the targets must all be explicitly listed. There is no way to trigger a match on a range of targets, except by listing them all explicitly. Nevertheless, for applications that do fall within the switch statement's restrictions, it is a useful convenience. (As you might guess based on those restrictions, most compilers attempt to generate code corresponding to a jump table or the equivalent rather than perform a long chain of comparisons.)

Strictly speaking, the syntax of the switch statement is the keyword switch followed by a parenthesized expression followed by a single statement. In practice, the statement is invariably a brace-enclosed block. Like any block, it may contain local variables, but these are necessarily declared before the first case label and statement. Consequently, any initializers on those variables are never applied.

3.4.4. while Loops

C has three kinds of loop constructions available, the simplest of which is the while loop. It is a test-at-the-top loop (analogous to Pascal's while/do loop). The syntax is similar to an if statement:

```
while( condition )
        statement
```

In fact, the action of a while loop is similar to an if statement as well, except that after each execution of the statement, the condition is tested again, and if it is still true, the condition is performed again. (If the condition is initially false, the body of the loop is not executed at all.) A classic example of a while loop is this one, which reads characters as long as the end-of-file marker EOF is not seen:

```
while((c = getchar()) != EOF)
        process character...
```

(The expression is one that first appeared in section 3.3.4; it simultaneously assigns the character read by getchar to the variable c and compares it to the constant EOF.)

One way of writing an infinite loop (which either does not terminate at all, or does so only abnormally; see section 3.4.7) is to use a constant, true condition:

```
while(1)
    ...
```

3.4.5. for Loops

The for loop is usually used to step some variable through a sequence of values. (It is analogous to the for/to/do loop in Pascal, to the do loop in Fortran, and to the for/to/step loop in BASIC.) The syntax is the most general of C's loops:

```
for( expr1 ; expr2 ; expr3 )
        statement
```

$expr_1$ is the *initialization* expression; it is executed exactly once, before execution of the loop begins. $expr_2$ is the *test* expression. Like the controlling expression in a while loop, its value is tested before each trip through the body of the loop, and a trip is made only if the expression evaluates to nonzero. (If the expression is initially false, no trips at all are made.) $expr_3$ is the *increment* expression. It is executed after each trip through the loop, before testing for another trip. Like the expressions in expression statements, $expr_1$ and $expr_3$ must have side effects in order to be useful.

For example, the elementary for loop

```
for(i = 0; i < 10; i++)
        printf("%d\n", i);
```

initializes i to 0, loops as long as i is less than 10, and increments i by one after each trip through the loop. Ten values of i are therefore printed, from 0 to 9, inclusive.

Because the three expressions that control a for loop are arbitrary, it is possible to arrange for any arithmetic or geometric sequence (or even, as we see in section 3.7.6, for nonnumeric sequences). Here are several more examples:

Loop	*Range*
`for(i = 1; i <= 10; i++)`	1, 2, 3, ... 10
`for(i = 2; i <= 10; i += 2)`	2, 4, 6, ... 10
`for(i = 10; i > 0; i--)`	10, 9, 8, ... 1
`for(i = 1; i < 1000; i *= 2)`	1, 2, 4, 8, ... 512
`for(i = 2; i < 100; i = i * i)`	2, 4, 16

The form exemplified by

```
for(i = 0; i < 10; i++)
```

with an initial value of 0 and a less-than condition, is most common in C, in part because arrays are 0-based.

The three expressions that control a for loop are collected at the top for convenience, not because they or the variables they manipulate are privileged in any way. After exit from the loop, the control variable retains its final value (generally, the first value that caused the test expression to fail). In addition, the control variable may be modified within the loop (although any such modification should be made judiciously, as it can easily lead to impenetrable code).

It is possible to arrange for two (or more) variables to be manipulated by one for loop. Doing so is one use of the comma operator. Here is a simple example:

```
for(i = 1, j = 10; i < j; i++, j--) ...
```

In this case, *expr₁* is

```
i = 1, j = 10
```

which initializes i to 1 and then initializes j to 10. Similarly, *expr₃* is

```
i++, j--
```

All three of the controlling expressions in a for loop are optional. If the initialization expression (*expr₁*) is omitted, there is no explicit initialization; any variables used in the loop (or the other controlling expressions) have presumably been initialized beforehand. If the increment expression (*expr₃*) is omitted, there is no explicit increment step; any updating of the loop variable(s) is presumably taken care of by code within the body of the loop. Finally, if the test expression (*expr₂*) is omitted, it is simply assumed to be true, and the loop becomes an infinite one (again, unless terminated by abnormal means). If any expressions are omitted, the semicolons remain. Thus, another form of infinite loop in C is

```
for(;;)
      ...
```

The while and for loops share certain similarities, and it is possible to implement one in terms of the other. The two fragments

```
                                      expr1;
for( expr1 ; expr2 ; expr3 )          while ( expr2 )
      {                                     {
      statements                            statements
      }                                     expr3 ;
                                            }
```

behave almost identically (differing only in the presence of a `continue` statement; see section 3.4.7). As a general rule, it is appropriate to use a `for` loop when one or two variables, following an initialize/test/increment pattern, play a prominent role in controlling a loop, and to use a `while` loop otherwise. (In particular, it is poor style to jam three unrelated expressions into the controlling expressions of a `for` loop.)

3.4.6. `do`/`while` Loops

Finally, C has a test-at-the-bottom loop (analogous to the `repeat`/`until` loop of Pascal, but with the sense of the test reversed). The syntax is

```
do statement
while( expression );
```

Note the trailing semicolon. In practice, the statement is almost always a brace-enclosed block. Here is an example that generates (in reverse order) the digits in the base-10 representation of the number `n`:

```
do      {
        putdigit(n % 10);
        n = n / 10;
        } while(n > 0);
```

In this example, the at-least-once behavior of the `do`/`while` loop is desirable (and distinctly preferable to the behavior of the `while` loop); it ensures that one digit is generated even if `n` is initially `0`. (The example assumes that the hypothetical function `putdigit` actually does something with the generated digits and also assumes that `n` is nonnegative.)

3.4.7. `break` and `continue`

Frequently, it is necessary to modify the behavior of a loop slightly. Under certain conditions, it may be necessary to break out of a loop early, before its normal termination condition is met. Under certain conditions, it may be necessary to jump immediately to the next iteration through a loop, without completing the current one. The `break` and `continue` statements provide these capabilities. (In effect, both `break` and `continue` are constrained forms of `goto`, but they are favored in structured programming precisely because they are constrained.)

We have seen the `break` statement already, in the context of the `switch` statement. The `break` statement causes an immediate exit from the nearest enclosing loop or `switch` statement. For example, to read up to 10 lines of text from the file pointer `fp` using the `fgets` function, we might write this loop:

```
char lines[10][80];
int i;
for(i = 0; i < 10; i++)
        { if(fgets(lines[i], 80, fp) == NULL)
                break;
        }
```

If `fgets` returns a null pointer, signifying end-of-file, we use the `break` statement to exit the loop early, because it will be impossible to read all 10 lines. (See section 3.10.1 for more information on file pointers and `fgets`.)

The `continue` statement causes an immediate jump back to the head of a loop. The loop's test expression is immediately executed, and if still true, another trip through the loop is taken. In a `for` loop, the increment expression is also executed, just as if execution had reached the end of the loop body normally.

Continuing the previous example, if the 10 lines of text are to be processed in some way, except for those that begin with a # character (which are to be treated, as is common in many data file formats, as comments), we might rewrite the loop like this:

```
for(i = 0; i < 10; i++)
        {
        if(fgets(lines[i], 80, fp) == NULL)
                break;
        if(lines[i][0] == '#')
                continue;
        ...other processing...
        }
```

If a line begins with #, the *other processing* is not performed. (Exactly 10 lines are read in any case, however, because `continue` does imply execution of the `for` loop's increment expression. To read 10 noncomment lines, possibly reading more than 10 lines total, would require a different loop.)

We can summarize the operation of the `break` and `continue` statements with these three skeletal loops (after Kernighan and Ritchie):

```
while(expr)          for(e1; e2; e3)         do
    {                    {                       {
    body ;               body ;                  body ;
cont:    ;           cont:    ;              cont:    ;
    }                    }                       }
                                             while(expr);
brk:                 brk:                    brk:
```

In each case, a `continue` statement implies a jump to the label `cont`, and a `break` statement implies a jump to the label `brk`. (This example brings out the one discrepancy in the comparison, made in section 3.4.5, between a for loop and the apparently equivalent while loop. In the pair of examples in section 3.4.5, a continue statement would cause $expr_3$ to be skipped in the while loop, but it is always executed in the for loop.)

The break and continue statements work only on the innermost containing loop or (in the case of break) switch statement. When one loop is nested inside another, there is no way to specify that a break or continue within the inner loop should break or continue the outer one. When a switch statement is nested inside a loop, a break statement inside the switch terminates one case of the switch, but a continue statement continues the loop. (Neither the break nor continue statements have any effect on an enclosing or intervening if statement, however.)

Stylistically, break and continue statements are preferred when their use simplifies the normal processing case(s) within a loop. A continue statement could, in principle, always be replaced by inverting the test and placing the remainder of the loop body (which would have been skipped by a continue) into an if statement, at the cost of an extra level of indentation. A break statement could, in principle, always be replaced by adding extra tests and boolean control variables, at the cost of those extra tests and variables.

It is also possible to terminate a loop abnormally by using a goto statement (see the next section) or by returning from the containing function. For example, the body of a function that searches an array for a particular value, returning the index of the value or ·1 if it cannot be found, might be written like this:

```
for(i = 0; i < arraysize; i++)
        { if(array[i] == value)
                return i;        /* found */
        }
return -1;                       /* loop completed, so not found */
```

3.4.8. goto Statements

For fully general, unconstrained branching, C does provide the goto statement, although it is somewhat discouraged and rarely seen.

A label, which will presumably be the target of a goto, can be attached to any statement:

```
        statement1;
        statement2;
        if(condition)
                {
                statement3;
                }
        statement4;
end:    statement5;
```

The syntax for a label is simply an identifier followed by a colon. The rules for label names are the same as for any identifiers. Labels have their own namespace, and they have a scope extending throughout the enclosing function. (For obvious reasons, labels never enjoy a restricted scope in inner blocks.)

The syntax of the `goto` statement is simply

```
goto label ;
```

Fleshing out the preceding example, we might have the following:

```
     statement1;
     statement2;
     if(condition)
          {
          statement3;
          goto end;
          }
     statement4;
end: statement5;
```

In this hypothetical example, if the condition is true, *statement3* is executed, and then control immediately transfers to the end, executing only *statement5*, bypassing *statement4*. (In this case, of course, it would apparently also have been possible to have placed *statement4* in an `else` clause of the `if` statement.)

`goto` statements are typically used, if at all, to effect breaks or continues out of nested loops, or to jump to the end of some segment of code (often to ensure that common cleanup actions—for example, *statement5* in the example—are performed even when normal processing is skipped over due to some exceptional condition).

When a label is attached to a statement in an inner block (e.g., in an `if` or `loop` statement body), it is possible to jump into the loop. However, any initializers on variables declared within that block are not applied, so the practice of jumping into blocks is discouraged.

`goto` statements work only within a single function. A limited form of jumping between functions is provided by the library functions `setjmp` and `longjmp` (see section 3.10.8).

3.4.9. return Statements
The `return` statement terminates an invocation of a function, returning control to the function's caller and optionally returning a value. The `return` statement is discussed further in the next section.

3.5. Functions

The function is the principal unit of modularity in a C program. Ideally, a function constitutes a "black box," performing some operation that is useful to the rest of the program, but in such a way that the details of its operation need not be known to its callers. The only pieces of information a caller should need to know about a function are (1) its name, (2) the arguments it requires (if any), and (3) the type of its return value (if any).

Because C supports separate compilation, it is also possible to achieve another degree of modularity by grouping related functions and global variables into one source file, and arranging that those which are private to the module are visible (and accessible) only within that source file. (As described in section 3.2.6, the private variables and functions would be declared static.)

3.5.1. Defining Functions

The basic syntax for a function in C is

```
return-type function-name ( parameter-list )
{
            local-variable-declarations
            statements
}
```

The *return-type* declares the type of value to be returned by the function. The *parameter-list* declares the number and types of the arguments to be accepted by the function, as well as giving a name by which each is known within the function. The body of the function consists of declarations for any local variables, followed by the statements that actually do the work of the function. (The function body, including its enclosing braces, therefore matches the syntax for a block statement as described in section 3.4.)

As it happens, the italicized parts in the preceding skeleton, with the obvious exception of the function name, are all optional. If the return type is omitted, it defaults to int. If the parameter list is empty, it indicates a function that accepts no arguments at all. It is also possible for the body of the function to be empty, although this situation typically arises only during a program's early development, when some functions are temporarily "stubbed out."

When a function returns no value, it must be declared with the explicit return type void. When a function accepts no arguments, that fact can be explicitly indicated by placing the single keyword void in the parameter list (without any parameter names, of course). Modern practice is to use an explicit int for functions that return int and an explicit void in the parameter list for functions that accept no arguments.

Here is a complete example of a function definition:

```
int gcd(int a, int b)
{
        int t;
        while(b != 0)
                {
                t = a % b;
                a = b;
                b = t;
                }
        return a;
}
```

The function returns an int and accepts two int parameters, which it refers to by the identifiers a and b. The function declares one local variable, t. (Incidentally, what the function does is to compute the greatest common divisor of a and b, using Euclid's classic algorithm.)

The line

```
return a;
```

is a simple return statement; it causes the current function to relinquish control back to its caller, and it also supplies the return value. The value in a return statement can be any expression; it is converted to the return type of the function if necessary. Many programmers parenthesize the expression, although this is not required.

In a void-valued function, of course, there is no return value, so the expression would be omitted from the return statement. A void-valued function may also return by "falling off the end"—that is, by having its control flow reach the final } of the function.

(The expression in a return statement is disallowed in void-valued functions. However, because type void did not always exist, the expression is optional, not mandatory, in other functions. Needless to say, it is usually an error for a function that should return a value to execute a return statement without one, although not all compilers complain about this error.)

It is possible for a function to accept a varying number of arguments. (An obvious example is `printf`.) Variable arguments are indicated by three dots (an *ellipsis*) at the end of the function's parameter list:

```
return-type function-name ( fixed-arguments, ...)
{
              body-of-function
}
```

The mechanism by which a function accesses its variable arguments is described in section 3.10.10. A variable-arguments function must accept at least one known argument, which means that the ellipsis cannot appear alone as the parameter list. There is no way to specify the type or types of the variable arguments; the caller must supply them correctly, and the function must somehow know their type(s) in order to fetch them correctly. (For example, `printf` intuits the expected number and type of its variable arguments by parsing its format string.)

An older, nonprototyped, "pre-ANSI" form of function definition is also permitted and is occasionally seen. The syntax looks like this:

```
return-type function-name ( parameter-name-list )
parameter-declarations
{
              local-variable-declarations
              statements
}
```

Only the names of the parameters appear between the parentheses; their types are given by conventional-looking declarations between the close parenthesis and the opening brace of the function body. Named but undeclared parameters default to type `int`. In this older style, the beginning of the `gcd` function might look like this:

```
int gcd(a, b)
int a, b;
{
...
```

Also, in this old function-definition style, the compiler assumes that any parameters of types `char`, `short int`, or `float` are actually passed as `int` or `double`, according to the default argument promotions described in section 3.5.3.

3.5.2. Declaring Functions

It is usually appropriate to declare functions before calling them, to ensure that the compiler generates the correct calling sequences, and so that the compiler can check that the programmer has supplied the correct number (and type) of arguments. A complete declaration for a function takes the form of an external function prototype declaration:

```
extern return-type function-name ( parameter-type-list );
```

For example, a declaration of the gcd function of the preceding section might look like this:

```
extern int gcd(int, int);
```

The function declaration differs from the definition in three respects:

- It is preceded by the storage-class specifier extern.

- The parameter names are omitted.

- It is terminated by a semicolon where the brace-enclosed body in the definition would be.

In fact, only the third point is vital; the presence of the semicolon is sufficient for the compiler to distinguish function declarations from definitions. Accordingly, the keyword extern is optional in function declarations, and names for the parameters may be supplied, if desired. (Named parameters in function prototype declarations can be useful for documentary purposes.)

As for function definitions, an ellipsis (. . .) at the end of the parameter list in a function declaration indicates that the function accepts a varying number of additional arguments.

Corresponding to the pre-ANSI form of function definition, there is an old, nonprototyped form of function declaration, as well:

```
extern return-type function-name ( );
```

Only the return type of the function is specified; no information about the function's expected parameter list is supplied. Unlike function definitions, the empty parentheses in an old-style external function declaration indicate an unspecified (quite possibly nonzero) number of arguments. To explicitly declare a function as accepting no arguments, the prototype form, with the keyword void in the place of the parameter list, must be used.

Due to the default argument promotions (mentioned in section 3.5.1 and described in section 3.5.3), the correct external function prototype declaration for a function defined in the old style but with "narrow" parameters must be written carefully. The correct prototype specifies the widened versions of the parameters. For example, the function

```
int oldfunc(x, y, z)
char x;
short y;
float z;
{ ... }
```

has the corresponding external function prototype declaration

```
extern int oldfunc(int, int, double);
```

Function prototype declarations are optional in some circumstances and required in others (as discussed in section 3.5.3), but modern practice is to use them at all times. Function prototype declarations are usually arranged to appear at the beginning of each source file (supplying declarations for all functions called anywhere in that source file). Rather than typing multiple function declarations into many source files separately, it is usually convenient to type them into a separate header file once and insert them into each source file by means of header file inclusion, discussed in section 3.8.1. This practice is strongly recommended.

3.5.3. Calling Functions

A function may be called anywhere in any expression (with the exception of constant expressions). A function call consists of the name of the function followed by a pair of parentheses containing the comma-separated list of actual arguments to be passed to the function. (The parentheses are required even if there are no arguments.) At some point during the evaluation of the expression (unless evaluation has been short-circuited by the &&, II, or ?: operators), the expressions denoting the arguments are themselves evaluated, the resulting values passed to the function, and the function's return value propagated to the rest of the expression, in the natural and obvious ways. Simple examples of function calls are

```
c = sqrt(a * a + b * b);
```

and

```
x = gcd(5535, 8241);
```

C uses *pass by value* function-call semantics. With one (apparent) exception, the function receives copies of the values of its arguments, and these copies act essentially as local variables within the function, referred to by the names given in the parameter list of the function's definition. This means that a function cannot alter the values of ordinary variables passed to it as arguments. For example, if we were to write

```
int x = 20, y = 55;
int z = gcd(x, y);
```

the variables x and y would not be affected by the call to gcd, even though the implementation of gcd in section 3.5.1 assigned new values to its parameters a and b. (It is perfectly legal for a function to modify its parameters, as that sample gcd function does, if it is useful to the function to do so, and as long as the modified value is not expected to be propagated back to the caller.)

The one exception to the preceding rule concerns arrays. When a function is called with an array as an argument, a copy of the entire array is not made. Instead, the called function receives a *reference* to the caller's array, and any modifications made to the array by the called function do affect the caller's array. (As described in section 3.6.5, the "reference" takes the form of a pointer.)

The details of C's function calling mechanism differ depending on the form (if any) of declaration that has been seen for a particular function. Broken down to finest detail, there are four cases:

- *No declaration for the function is in scope.* The function is assumed to return int and to have parameters implied by the arguments it is actually called with. Several default argument promotions are applied to the actual arguments: Arguments of type char and short int (or their unsigned variants) are promoted to int or unsigned int, and arguments of type float are promoted to double. (Because they can undergo these promotions, the three types char, short int, and float are often referred to as "narrow" types.) If the arguments actually passed do not turn out to be compatible with the number or type of the parameters expected by the function, or if the actual return type is not int, the results are undefined.

- *A nonprototyped declaration for the function is in scope.* The declaration gives the return type of the function but not the expected types of its arguments. As for the first case, the function is assumed to have parameters implied by the actual arguments. The same default argument promotions are performed.

- *A prototype declaration for the function is in scope, specifying a fixed number of arguments.* Each argument is converted, as if by assignment, to the type of the corresponding parameter. If a conversion is impossible, the compiler reports an error. If there are more or fewer arguments than are specified in the parameter list, the compiler reports an error. The default argument promotions are not performed; arguments may be passed as char, short int, or float if their corresponding parameters have those types. The prototype also gives the return type of the function.

- *A prototype declaration for the function is in scope, specifying a variable number of arguments.* For the "fixed" arguments, declared explicitly in the prototype, the arguments are converted to the expected types and passed exactly as for the third case. If any are incompatible, or if there are fewer arguments than expected, the compiler reports an error. The additional arguments (if present) are promoted and passed according to the default argument promotions of the first and second cases.

These four cases and their defined handling lead to several rules and guidelines:

- It is safest to use the modern, ANSI-style function definition syntax, and to ensure that external function prototype declarations are in scope for all function calls. Most compilers can now be set to warn about functions called without prototypes in scope.

- Functions that accept "narrow" parameters must be called with prototypes in scope (and must be defined using the ANSI syntax).

- It is possible to mix old-style function definitions with ANSI prototype declarations, but doing so results in several additional caveats. "Narrow" parameters must either be avoided or carefully adjusted in prototypes, and variable-length argument lists may not be used or must be written entirely in the ANSI syntax. Many programmers recommend avoiding narrow parameters in any case, or recommend against mixing definition and declaration styles.

- Functions accepting a variable number of arguments must be defined using the ANSI syntax and must always be called with external function prototypes in scope.

- The arguments in variable-length argument lists are always promoted according to the default argument promotions; they are never passed as `char`, `short int`, or `float`.

Functions may be defined and manipulated with fair (though not ultimate) flexibility. It is possible to define and manipulate pointers to functions, and to call functions via pointers, as discussed in section 3.6.7. It is perfectly acceptable for a function to call itself, either directly or indirectly; C explicitly supports recursion. All functions have their non-`static` local variables allocated using a stack discipline, so multiple invocations of a function can coexist. Functions cannot be nested, however, and there is no mechanism (e.g., along the lines of Lisp's lambda) for generating functions at runtime.

We will close this section with three more examples, all of which happen to be recursive. Here is the digit-printing example of section 3.4.6, written recursively:

```
void printdigs(int n)
{
        if(n == 0)
                return;
        printdigs(n / 10);
        putdigit(n % 10);
}
```

(Because this function calls itself recursively before outputting a digit, it generates the digits in the correct, left-to-right order. This function, however, does not have the desirable property of section 3.4.6's do/while loop; it prints nothing for the number zero.)

Here is a recursive implementation of the gcd function of section 3.5.1:

```
int gcd(int a, int b)
{
        if(b == 0)
                return a;
        else    return gcd(b, a % b);
}
```

Finally, here is the fib function from section 3.1.1 written recursively. To avoid the notorious recursive explosion that a naïve recursive Fibonacci function exhibits, this implementation maintains an array of the Fibonacci numbers it has already computed so that it can return them immediately, without recursive calls. This technique also provides a good example of the use of local, static variables:

```
int fib(int n)
{
        static int fibs[24] = {0, 1};
        if(n < 0 || n >= 24)
                return -1;
        if(fibs[n] == 0 && n > 0)
                fibs[n] = fib(n-1) + fib(n-2);
        return fibs[n];
}
```

The array is prefilled with 0 and 1; all other elements are initialized by default to 0 and computed by the function when needed. An array of size 24 (0–23) suffices, because the 24th Fibonacci number, 46,368, cannot portably be represented in a plain int.

3.5.4. Global Variables and External Declarations

We have seen (in section 3.2.6) that the placement of the declaration of a variable, either within or without a function, determines whether the variable is local or global. We have also discussed a distinction between a defining instance (of a variable or function) and an external declaration. Finally, we have mentioned that C is arranged to support separate compilation: The various functions and global variables making up a program may be placed in separate source files, compiled individually, and then linked together. The linker (which may or may not be a part of the C compiler proper) takes care of resolving functions and variables defined in one module and referenced in another, as long as the programmer has arranged the declarations and definitions correctly. When a function or variable is global (and, in C, all functions are global), it may be necessary to refer to that function or variable from within a source file other than the one in which the function or variable is defined. Because C compilers typically take the notion of separate compilation quite literally (that is, each source file is compiled in isolation, with no knowledge of the others), it is necessary, within each source file, to give the compiler sufficient information about functions and variables that are referred to but defined elsewhere. This information is provided in the form of external declarations.

Syntactically, a C program consists at the top level of nothing but declarations, of functions and global variables. We can speak of two subsets of declarations:

- A defining instance is a declaration that actually "creates" the declared function or variable. The defining instance of a global variable allocates space for the variable and may supply an initial value. The defining instance of a function supplies the function's body.

- An external declaration refers to a variable or function that has been defined (that is, has its defining instance) elsewhere.

Before accessing a global variable, one of these declarations (a defining instance or an external declaration) must have been seen by the compiler. Before calling a function, a declaration may have been seen by the compiler; declarations are required under some circumstances and recommended in others, as discussed in section 3.5.3.

The exact scope of a declaration extends from its appearance in the source file onward, either to the end of the function or block (for local variables) or to the end of the source file (for globals). The placement of declarations is therefore significant: In order to refer to a global variable or call a function with its prototype in effect, the relevant declaration must already have been seen by the compiler—that is, must appear earlier in the source file than the reference—and must still be in scope.

An external declaration does not necessarily refer to a function or variable that is defined in another source file; it merely refers to a function or variable that is defined somewhere else, perhaps elsewhere in the same source file. When multiple interrelated functions are placed in the same source file, two broad arrangement strategies are possible:

- "Top-down": A source file begins with external declarations for all functions called within the source file. Then come the functions themselves, arranged in the same order as the function-call hierarchy: top-level functions first, followed by the functions they call. The external declarations at the top of the file are necessary so that declarations are in scope by the time the calls within the top-level function appear; at least some of those calls will presumably be to lower-level functions for which definitions have not been seen yet. The external declarations at the top of the file do not necessarily refer to functions defined in other source file(s); some or all are of functions that are defined later in the same source file.

- "Bottom-up": The functions in a source file are arranged in the reverse order of the function-call hierarchy: lowest-level functions first, followed by the higher-level functions that call them. Fewer external function declarations are required, because by the time a higher-level function appears, actual definitions may already have been seen for some or all of the lower-level functions that are to be called.

In either case, external declarations may still be required for called functions that are defined in other source files. External declarations may also be required when the function-call hierarchy is not strict (e.g., if it contains cycles). Finally, although we have spoken of the external declarations as appearing within the source file, they are often placed in header files, in which case all that appears in the main source file is the `#include` directive, which references the header file. (See section 3.8.1.)

3.6. Pointers and Arrays

Pointers are C's reference types. Besides providing extra levels of indirection, they are also indispensable in dynamic memory allocation and, when portability is not a concern, in accessing memory or other hardware at a very low level.

Conceptually, at a high level, we say that a pointer "points to" some other object or function. Pointers are themselves objects, and like all objects, they have types: The type of a pointer defines the types of objects (or functions) to which it can point and that result when the pointer is indirected upon (that is, when the value pointed to by the pointer is accessed). At a lower level, it is possible to think of pointers as machine addresses (with which, in fact, they are almost invariably implemented).

Additionally, there is one "generic" object pointer type that may be used as a container for object pointers of unspecified type, and there is a special null pointer value (or, more precisely, potentially one null pointer value for each pointer type) that points reliably nowhere, and that will never compare equal to a pointer to any actual object or function.

3.6.1. Pointer Declarations

Pointers are declared by using asterisks in the declarator. For example, a simple pointer declaration is

```
int *ip;
```

This declares the variable `ip` as a pointer, of type "pointer to int." One way of interpreting this declaration is that, as we'll see, when the indirection or "contents of" operator is applied to the pointer variable `ip`, the expression `*ip` will refer to an `int`.

Because the asterisk indicating a pointer is part of the declarator, not of the base type, it must be repeated if several pointer variables are being declared at once. That is, the correct way to declare two pointer variables in the same declaration is with a line like

```
int *ip1, *ip2;
```

This declaration can be contrasted with the line

```
int *p, q;
```

which declares `p` as type pointer-to-`int` and `q` as type `int`.

When type qualifiers are used in pointer declarations, their placement is significant. The declaration

```
const int *ptrtoconst;
```

declares `ptrtoconst` as type "pointer to const int." The declaration

```
int * const constptr;
```

on the other hand, declares `constptr` as type "const pointer to int." (These declarations have to be read "inside out" to make sense.) It is permissible to modify the `int` to which `constptr` points (that is, `*constptr`), and it is permissible to modify `ptrtoconst` to make it point to other const ints, but it is not permissible to modify `constptr` (the pointer itself) or `*ptrtoconst` (the pointed-to value). Pointers to constant values (e.g., `const char *`) are often used as function arguments, documenting (and in most cases ensuring) that the function does not use a particular pointer to modify any data in the caller. (See section 3.10 for many examples.)

The process by which pointer types are derived from other types is general, and it is quite possible to construct pointers to pointers (or pointers to pointers to pointers, and so on). For example, a pointer-to-pointer-to-int might be declared with

```
int **ipp;
```

It is important to recognize that a pointer variable (like any variable) cannot be used until it is initialized—that is, until some pointer value is assigned to it. The integer pointer variable ip, for example, although it has the capacity to point at integer values elsewhere in memory, does not, upon first being declared by the preceding declaration, point to any actual int-sized memory location yet. To use a pointer variable before it is initialized is as incorrect as to use any other variable before it is initialized.

3.6.2. Basic Pointer Operations

Pointer values are generated with the unary & operator, which we will refer to as the "pointer to" operator, although many programmers call it the "address of" operator. Applied to any object or function, the & operator generates a pointer to that object, which we might then assign to a pointer variable. For example, given the int variable

```
int i = 5;
```

we can apply the & operator to it and assign the resulting pointer to the pointer variable ip using the simple assignment

```
ip = &i;
```

We say that ip now points to i; it is useful to visualize the situation with a picture like this:

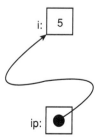

Notice that there is a very important difference between the contents of a pointer variable and what the pointer points to. In the example just given, the contents of the pointer variable ip consist of a pointer (represented in the figure by an arrow), while what that pointer points to is an int object containing the value 5, which happens also to be the variable i. (Notice also that the & operator has two different meanings, depending on whether it is used as a unary or binary operator. It is in this respect similar to the - operator, and as we'll shortly see, to the * operator.)

After a pointer has been set to point somewhere, we access the value pointed to with the unary indirection or "contents of" operator, *. Continuing with the ip example, if we write

```
printf("%d\n", *ip);
```

the second argument to printf, the expression *ip, means "fetch the value pointed to by ip." Because ip is of type pointer-to-int, the compiler assumes that the value pointed to is an int. (And an int is expected by the printf format specifier %d, so this is an appropriate second argument.) However, the * operator does not only fetch values via pointers; it can also be used to set values via pointers, when an expression involving * appears on the left-hand side of assignment operator:

```
*ip = 7;
```

This fragment stores the value 7 in the location pointed to by ip (which, if nothing has changed in the meantime, is still the variable i).

Pointers can be manipulated in a number of ways, some of which involve the pointers themselves and some of which involve the values pointed to. We've seen one example of pointer assignment, in the line

```
ip = &i;
```

The & operator created a new pointer, but naturally enough, it is also possible to assign existing pointer values. Given a second pointer variable ip2, the assignment

```
ip2 = ip;
```

creates, in ip2, a copy of the pointer in ip: ip2 now points to the same object that ip does.

When you're writing pointer expressions and verifying their correctness, it is useful to think of the & operator as adding a level of "pointerness" (or, formally, a level of indirection), and to think of the * operator as taking away a level. For example, in the assignment

```
ip = &i;
```

the & on the right-hand side adds a level of indirection (a "level of pointer-ness") to the int variable i, giving a pointer- to-int on the left, a pointer-to-int on the right, and a balanced, type-correct expression. Similarly, in

```
*ip = 7;
```

the * takes a pointer level away, leaving an int on the left, an int on the right, and another correct assignment. But none of

```
ip = i;      i = ip;
ip = 5;      i = &i2;
ip = *ip2;   *ip = ip2;
```

are correct. Those in the first column all have pointer-to-int on the left and int on the right, while those in the second column all have int on the left and pointer-to-int on the right (assuming that i2 is another int variable).

Also, notice the difference between the two assignments

```
*ip2 = *ip;
```

and

```
ip2 = ip;
```

The first assignment copies the pointed-to values (without affecting the pointers, which have to point to different locations if the assignment is to have any effect), whereas the second assignment copies the pointers (without affecting the pointed-to values). Notice that both assignments are type correct.

There is one slight exception to the rigorous type-correlation rule outlined previously; it concerns the null pointer value. This is a distinct value that can be stored in a pointer variable to record that the pointer does not point anywhere at all. The question, of course, is how to specify this value. Rather than use a special keyword (such as Pascal's nil), C uses a constant integer 0. So the pointer ip can be set to the null pointer value by writing

```
ip = 0;
```

The constant 0 is the only integer that can be assigned to a pointer variable; it is not correct to assign other constants or integer variables that happen to contain the value 0. As a convenience, several headers (see section 3.10.11) define the preprocessor macro NULL with the value 0 (or, depending on the implementation, with certain other equivalent forms of null pointer constant), allowing assignments like

```
ip = NULL;
```

(as long as one of those headers has been included).

3.6.3. Pointer Arithmetic

C supports a rich variety of pointer arithmetic, all of which presupposes that the pointers involved point into an array of adjacent elements. Consider the fragment

```
int a[10];
ip = &a[3];
```

The expression &a[3] is a straightforward application of the & operator; it generates a pointer to the int object a[3], the fourth element of the array a. The resulting array and pointer can be represented like this:

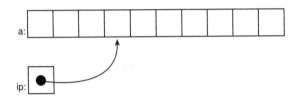

We can now compute new pointers that also point within the array a, at offsets from the element pointed to by ip. For example, the expression ip + 1 computes a new pointer that points one element past where ip points. This new pointer can either be assigned to a second pointer variable and then used

```
ip2 = ip + 1;
*ip2 = 4;
```

or be used immediately

```
*(ip + 1) = 4;
```

In both cases, the element one past the one pointed to by ip, namely a[4], is set to 4.

As might be expected, there is nothing magic about the number 1; any integer can be added to—or subtracted from—a pointer, as long as the resulting value still points within the bounds of the underlying array. For example, ip + 2 points two elements past where ip points, and ip - 1 points one element before. Naturally, the "shorthand" forms of sections 3.3.6 and 3.3.7 work with pointers as well: ip += 1 and ip++ (among other expressions) both increment ip to point one element past where it used to, and --ip is one way to decrement ip.

After the assignment

```
ip2 = ip + 2;
```

it is obvious that `ip` and `ip2` now point to elements separated by a distance of 2. Given just the two pointers, is it possible to recompute their separation? The answer is yes; the separation can be computed by subtracting the pointers. Pointer subtraction results in an integer that is the distance (in units of "elements") between the two elements pointed to. So with `ip2` set as shown here, `ip2 - ip` would give 2, and `ip - ip2` would give -2.

Given that pointers can be subtracted, it is natural that they can be compared, as well. If `ip` and `ip2` point within the same array, the `<`, `<=`, `>`, and `>=` operators all compare the relative positions of the two pointers. One pointer is greater than another if it points to a "higher" element of the array (that is, to an element with a larger subscript); two pointers are equal if they point to the same element.

Pointer addition, pointer subtraction, and the pointer comparisons that have been mentioned so far are well defined only if all pointers involved point within the same array (or single, array-like object). There is one exception: For convenience in accessing arrays via pointers, it is permissible to compute a pointer to the nonexistent element one past the end of the array, as long as this imaginary pointer is used only for comparisons. (Naturally, it would be ill defined to indirect upon this pointer to access the location pointed to because the "location" pointed to, if any, is not part of the array.) For example, here is a code fragment that sets all of the elements of an array to 0, using pointers. The pointer `endp` is used in the termination condition for the loop; it points one past the end of the array.

```
int a[10], *ip, *endp;
for(ip = &a[0], endp = &a[10]; ip < endp; ip++)
        *ip = 0;
```

Finally, two pointers can be compared for exact equality or inequality using the `==` and `!=` operators. These comparisons have fewer restrictions: The two pointers involved do not have to point within the same object, and one or both of them can be null pointers. That is, `ip == ip2` yields true if `ip` and `ip2` point to the same object or are both null pointers, and `ip != ip2` yields true if `ip` and `ip2` point to the different objects or if one is a null pointer and one is not. A pointer equality comparison is therefore another place where it is possible to use the integer constant 0 as a null pointer constant: A condition like `if(ip == 0)` asks whether `ip` has a null pointer as its value. (Again, the preprocessor macro NULL can be used as well.)

Because the definition of a "true" boolean value in C is one that compares unequal to 0, a certain abbreviation is permissible and popular in pointer testing. If `ip` is a pointer, the condition

```
if(ip)
```

is, by definition, treated identically by the compiler as if the programmer had written

```
if(ip != 0)
```

That is, it asks whether `ip` is not a null pointer. Similarly, `if(!p)` asks whether `p` is a null pointer. We have not spoken yet of the internal values used to represent pointers (which are discussed in section 3.6.8), but it is important to note that tests like `if(ip)` and `if(!ip)` work regardless of the internal representation of null pointers.

The final pointer operation to discuss is pointer conversion. Occasionally, it is necessary to manipulate an object, via a pointer, as if it had some other type. For example, we might want to access an `int` value as if it were made up of individual characters, or bytes. We could initialize a `char` pointer, pointing at an `int` object, with the code

```
int i = 0x1234;
int *ip;
char *cp;
ip = &i;
cp = (char *)ip;
```

or, more simply

```
int i = 0x1234;
char *cp;
cp = (char *)&i;
```

In each case, the cast (`char *`) requests the conversion from type pointer-to-`int` to type pointer-to-`char`. In the cast, the type name between the parentheses, `char *`, takes the form of a declaration that is missing an identifier in the declarator; that is, the declarator is the lone asterisk, indicating a pointer.

Like casts in general, pointer casts are rarely needed in modern C code. One example that still requires them can be found in section 3.10.4.4. (Also, though we have not discussed pointers to functions yet, it is worth noting that pointers to data objects cannot portably be converted to function pointers, or vice versa.)

3.6.4. Array/Pointer Initialization

Like all other variables, pointer variables can be initialized in their declarations. For example, we might write

```
int *ip = &i;
```

or, simplifying an example in the preceding section still further, we might write

```
char *cp = (char *)&i;
```

In these declarations, it is important to note that the initializer is assigned to the variable being declared, not to the expression-like construct that forms the declarator. That is,

```
int *ip = &i;
```

does not, as it might superficially appear, correspond to

```
int *ip;
*ip = &i;          /* WRONG */
```

but rather to

```
int *ip;
ip = &i;
```

Stated another way, the * in the declarator is not an actual pointer indirection operator.

When a pointer variable is global (or, more precisely, has static duration), its initializer must (as always) be a constant expression, as discussed in sections 3.2.8 and 3.3.12. The pointer-to operator & is permissible in constant expressions, with certain restrictions. It must be applied to an object that also has static duration, and the only pointer arithmetic allowed is addition or subtraction of a constant. For example, initializations such as

```
int global_i;
int *global_ip = &global_i;
```

and

```
int global_a[10];
int *global_ip2 = &global_a[0] + 2;
```

are legal.

3.6.5. Array/Pointer Equivalence

Perhaps the most significant innovation in C, and a feature that distinguishes it from most other languages, is its integration of arrays and pointers. Arrays and pointers do retain distinct identities under this "equivalence," but it is particularly easy to use pointers to access arrays or to simulate arrays.

The cornerstone of the array/pointer equivalence in C is that whenever an array appears in an expression such that its value would seem to be needed, a pointer to the array's first element is automatically generated instead. That is, if we have an array

```
int a[10];
```

and if we use it in an expression

```
a + 5
```

the effect is as if we had written

```
&a[0] + 5
```

This automatic generation of a pointer to an array's first element might seem strange, but its utility becomes obvious when we consider the second facet of array/pointer equivalence, namely that the subscripting operator [] is actually defined for pointers. Given a pointer p and an integral expression e, the construction

```
p[e]
```

is defined as

```
*((p) + (e))
```

To understand the implication of this definition, consider the array a. Successive elements of the array are accessed with expressions like a[0], a[1], a[2], or a[i]. Having learned about pointer arithmetic in section 3.6.3, we might also access the array using a pointer, by declaring

```
int *ip;
ip = &a[0];
```

and then referring to *ip, *(ip+1), *(ip+2), or *(ip+i). But we can also simply assign

```
ip = a;
```

and refer to ip[0], ip[1], ip[2], or ip[i]. By definition, the assignment ip = a is equivalent to ip = &a[0], and the expression ip[i] is equivalent to *(ip+i). So having assigned ip to point to the beginning of the array, the expression ip[e] accesses the same element as a[e]. The resulting duality between arrays and pointers makes a certain amount of sense: An array, by definition, is a set of adjacent identical elements that can therefore be accessed by index, and pointer arithmetic is defined so as to access adjacent identical elements by adding (or subtracting) integer offsets. Because pointers and arrays access the same kind of data structure (a set of identical adjacent elements) in a conceptually similar way, it is reasonable for them to be able to use the same syntax—the subscripting brackets [ ]—to do so.

Although arrays and pointers are both used to access the same kind of data structures, this does not mean that they are the same kind of data structures. An array is (by definition) a set of identical adjacent elements; a pointer is a different data type that is merely useful for accessing identical adjacent elements. In fact, as should be obvious from the fact that they are sometimes referred to as "reference" types, pointers always refer to data that is stored elsewhere. It is vital to keep in mind the distinction between the pointer itself and the data value it points to. One way of reinforcing this distinction is to consider figures like this one, representing the situation after the assignment ip = a:

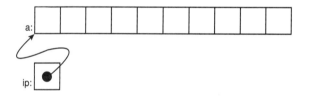

We have mentioned that C does not support assignment of entire arrays at once; the code

```
int a[10], b[10];
b = a;          /* WRONG */
```

is illegal. But pointer assignment can be used to simulate array assignment, as follows:

```
int a[10], *b;
b = a;
```

Moreover, such an assignment is likely to be quite efficient because the array contents are not copied. (Of course, since they are not copied, any change to the array pointed to by b is, in fact, a change to the array a.)

Because strings in C are represented as arrays of characters, pointers of type char * find widespread use in manipulating strings. (In fact, since attempts to manipulate an array almost always result in a pointer to the array's first element, it turns out that strings are almost always manipulated by pointers.) We see several examples of doing so in section 3.10.2. The connection between pointers to char and strings is so strong that it is common to use expressions like "the string s" or "the string pointed to by s" when the variable s is, strictly speaking, a pointer to the first character of the string.

The equivalence between arrays and pointers has several implications for function calls. If we call a function and attempt to pass an array to it, as in

```
f(a);
```

the array appears in a context in which its value is needed, so the effect is as if we had written

```
f(&a[0]);
```

The function f does not receive an entire copy of the array a; all it receives is a reference to the array, in the form of a pointer to the array's first element.

How, then, should f's parameter be declared? Strictly speaking, it seems as if f should receive a pointer, as if the definition should look like

```
f(int *x)
{
...
}
```

However, to preserve the illusion that it is possible to define functions that operate on arrays, it is also permissible to write

```
f(int x[])
{ ... }
```

The compiler knows that f does not actually receive an array as a parameter, so it quietly rewrites the declaration of the parameter x to type "pointer to int." This rewriting rule also explains why the size is optional (and usually omitted) in one-dimensional array parameters: Because the parameter is actually a reference to an array declared elsewhere, the size is immaterial, as the actual size was also set elsewhere.

Although a function like f does, in fact, receive a pointer, the pointer can be accessed within the function as if it were an array because the pointer is to the first element of the passed array and because (once again) the subscripting brackets do work with pointers.

The "conversion" of arrays to pointers during function calls occurs only for the first dimension of the array. If we have, for example, a two-dimensional array, such as

```
int a2[5][7];
```

which we pass to a function with a call like f2(a2), the compiler again passes a function to the array's first element, still as if we had written f2(&a2). In this case, however, the first element is itself an array, so the pointer actually passed is of type "pointer to array of 7 ints." The function can be defined either as having a parameter explicitly declared of that type

```
f2(int (*x)[7])
{ ... }
```

(see section 3.6.7 below for a discussion of the bewildering-looking declarator (*x)[7]), or as a seemingly two-dimensional array type

```
f2(int x[5][7])
{ ... }
```

In the second definition, the compiler performs the corresponding reinterpretation, back to "pointer to array of 7 ints" (in this case, ignoring the unneeded size 5). Notice, however, that the function

```
f2a(int **x)
{ ... }
```

is not equivalent, and it would not be correct to pass the two-dimensional array a2 to this function.

As a point of style, it is debatable whether the compiler's array parameter rewriting rules are worth using or not. Using them (that is, defining functions that look as if they accept arrays) has the advantage that the declarations look like the types of the actual arguments presumably being passed, and they are also somewhat easier to type and read in the case of multidimensional arrays. However, these rewriting rules are also responsible for a certain amount of confusion, and some programmers therefore prefer to "call a spade a spade" and declare array-like function parameters explicitly as the pointers they truly are.

Finally, you might ask what the right name for the subscripting operator [] is if it can be used with both arrays and pointers. In fact, strictly speaking, it is always used with pointers; even in a trivial expression like a[0], a strict application of the pointer equivalence rule says that a pointer to a's first element is first generated, such that the subscript [0] is actually applied to that pointer. But this is a surprising result, and it is perfectly acceptable to refer to [] as the "array subscripting operator," as long as we remember that it can also be applied to pointers.

3.6.6. Memory Allocation

One of the principal uses for pointers in C is dynamic memory allocation. The C compiler supports only the allocation of objects whose sizes are known at compile time. It is impossible to declare a true array whose size is a runtime expression. But because pointers can be used to access blocks of adjacent memory locations as conveniently as can arrays, they can be used to simulate dynamically sized arrays.

The key to doing so is the standard library function malloc, which returns a pointer to a new, contiguous area of memory having a requested size. (malloc is declared in the standard header <stdlib.h>; the line #include <stdlib.h> should be assumed to be present before all code fragments in this section.) For example, to obtain a new block of memory capable of holding n characters (and therefore capable of holding a string of length up to n-1), the first step is to declare a pointer and then allocate memory for it by calling malloc:

```
char *p;
p = malloc(n);
```

malloc's single argument is the number of bytes requested. If malloc is able to satisfy the request, it returns a pointer to a block of new memory of (at least) the requested size. Otherwise, it returns a null pointer. (Recall that the null pointer, by definition, does not compare equal with a pointer to any object and therefore points "nowhere.") Whenever you're calling malloc, therefore, it is important to check for this null pointer return before using the pointer:

```
p = malloc(n);
if(p == NULL)
        {
        printf("out of memory\n");
        return;
        }
/* ...otherwise use pointer p */
```

(Of course, in production code, it might be necessary to return an error code to the caller in the out-of-memory case, or continue processing in some different way, or perhaps to abort the program.)

Having initialized the pointer p in this way, it can be treated almost as if it were an array of size n. In particular, due to the equivalence between arrays and pointers, the rest of the program can refer to p[i] (for any index expression i), making the illusion that p is an array a very convincing one indeed.

Suppose it is necessary to dynamically allocate some number of integers, perhaps to simulate an array of int. How many bytes should be requested from malloc? You could conceivably determine how big (in bytes) one integer happens to be on the current machine and then perform the appropriate scaling before calling malloc, but doing so would needlessly tie the program to that one machine. Instead, C provides the sizeof operator, which computes the sizes of objects and allows memory-management code to be written much more portably. For example, to allocate n integers, you can call

```
int *ip = malloc(n * sizeof(int));
```

The sizeof operator takes one operand—in this case, the parenthesized type name int—and returns the size of that operand (on the current machine) in bytes. Notice that, despite its appearance, sizeof is not a function but rather an operator that does its work at compile time.

Besides a type name, the operand of sizeof can also be a variable name (or, in fact, an arbitrary expression), in which case sizeof computes the size of that variable's (or expression's) type. For example, the preceding example could be rewritten as

```
ip = malloc(n * sizeof(*ip));
```

sizeof's operand is now the expression *ip. This expression is not evaluated: no attempt is made to fetch or refer to the location pointed by ip; the compiler merely computes the size of the type of the expression, which is whatever type is pointed to by ip. With ip declared as shown here, therefore, the same answer is returned as for sizeof(int). Notice, however, that if ip's type is ever changed so that it points to data of some other size, the sizeof expression involving *ip will automatically pick up the new type and size. (When sizeof is applied to an expression, as opposed to a type name, the parentheses around the operand are optional.)

When sizeof is applied to an array or other aggregate data structure (see section 3.7), the size computed is the total size of the object. For example, given our earlier array int a[10], the expression sizeof(a) would yield 10*sizeof(int). The operand of sizeof is therefore one context in which the "equivalence" rule—that an array reference automatically generates a pointer to the array's first element—is not applied. (This makes sense because sizeof's operand is not a place where the value of the array would be needed.) To compute the number of elements in an array, an expression of the form

```
sizeof(a) / sizeof(a[0])
```

can be used.

It is important to remember that sizeof does its work at compile time, based on the actual type of the expression to which it is applied. In each of the three fragments

```
f(int x[])
{
int n = sizeof(x);
}
```

and

```
int a[10], *b = a;
int n = sizeof(b);
```

and

```
int *ip = malloc(10 * sizeof(int));
int n = sizeof(ip);
```

the sizeof operator computes (and assigns to n) not the size of an array of 10 ints, nor even the size of one int, but rather the size of one pointer-to-int—that is, the same value that sizeof(int *) would return. (Similarly, expressions like sizeof(ip)/sizeof(ip[0]), where ip is a pointer, are meaningless.)

If the pointers returned by malloc can be used to point to any data type, what is the pointer type actually returned by malloc? The answer is a special, "generic" pointer type, void *, or "pointer to void." The void type has no values, so it is meaningless to ask what a void pointer points to, but the void * type has the special property that the compiler automatically performs any appropriate conversions when a void * pointer value is assigned to some other type of data pointer or when some other type of data pointer is assigned to a void * pointer variable. That is, given that malloc is declared as returning void *, the initialization in

```
int *ip = malloc(sizeof int);
```

implies an automatic conversion, just as if we had written

```
int *ip = (int *)malloc(sizeof int);
```

See section 3.10.4.1 for more information about malloc and dynamic memory allocation, and about three more memory-management functions.

3.6.7. Pointers to Functions

Besides those pointers that point to data objects, it is also possible to declare pointers that point to functions. The syntax is slightly forbidding. The declaration

```
int (*funcptr)();
```

declares a pointer named funcptr, which will point to functions that return int. The syntax (*funcptr)() is an example of a complex declarator. The asterisk indicates that one level of indirection (one pointer level) is involved, and the second pair of parentheses indicates that a function is involved. The first pair of parentheses is there to get the precedence right, for there are precedence relationships in declarators just as there are in expressions. Without the parentheses, the declaration would be

```
int *funcptr();        /* WRONG, for pointer-to-function */
```

and would declare a function returning a pointer to int rather than a pointer to a function returning int. (We saw another example of a complex declaration in section 3.6.5, where the declarator (*x)[7] declared a function parameter x, which was a pointer to an array.)

Function pointers can also include prototypes for the parameter lists of the functions pointed to. The preceding example does not include a prototype; the second, empty pair of parentheses essentially means "taking unspecified arguments" (just as the empty parentheses in an old-style, pre-ANSI external function declaration do). If funcptr will always point to functions that accept, say, two parameters each of type float, that fact could be indicated by writing

```
int (*funcptr)(float, float);
```

(In fact, most of the time, we probably do know just what argument lists the functions pointed to by a given function pointer will accept because that list will show up in the actual calls to the pointed-to functions.)

Function pointer declarations can be simplified by the use of typedefs. For example, after declaring

```
typedef char *pc;      /* pointer to char */
typedef pc fpc();      /* function returning pointer to char */
typedef fpc *pfpc;     /* pointer to function returning... */
```

we arrive at a single type name, pfpc, embodying the type "pointer to function returning pointer to char," which can then be used to declare pointer variables of this type:

```
pfpc fp1, fp2;
```

This declaration declares `fp1` and `fp2` just as if they had been declared in "longhand," without the `typedefs`, as

```
char *(*fp1)(), *(*fp2)();
```

Pointers to functions are used analogously to pointers to data objects. Function pointer variables must first be initialized, typically with pointer values built as if by applying the `&` operator to the names of actual functions. For example, we might write something like

```
extern int f1(float, float);
int (*funcptr)(float, float);
funcptr = &f1;
```

Now `funcptr` points to the function `f1()`. However, in this case, the explicit `&` operator is optional and is usually omitted:

```
extern int f2(float, float);
funcptr = f2;
```

The syntax is unambiguous: Because the appearance of `f2` in the assignment is not followed by a parenthesized argument list, it does not represent a call to `f2`, and there is, in fact, no other interpretation than that a pointer to `f2` is required. (In other words, the rule for function names that appear in expressions where they are not being called is similar to the rule for array names in expressions where they are not being subscripted. In both cases, pointers are implicitly generated.)

Given a pointer to a function, the obvious thing to do is to call the function pointed to. Reasoning by analogy with pointers to data objects, you might attempt to use the `*` operator to "take the contents of" the function pointer, resulting in an actual function that could then be called. In fact, such a syntax does work, although an extra set of parentheses is again required to get the precedence right:

```
int n = (*funcptr)(f1, f2);
```

Without the parentheses, the call would be `*funcptr(f1, f2)`, which would attempt to call the function named `funcptr` and then take the contents of the pointer value returned, which would make sense in this case only if `funcptr` were a function returning pointer to `int`, which it is not.

However, here again a simplification is possible, and is often seen in modern code. If `funcptr` is a pointer to a function, there are only a few things that can be done with it: assign or compare it to some other function pointer, or call the function it points to. Therefore, the calling syntax

```
n = funcptr(f3, f4);
```

without the explicit * and parentheses, is unambiguous, and is also legal. A programmer using a lot of function pointers (as in object-oriented programming) may prefer the convenience of omitting the extra syntax, but when function pointers are a rarity in a piece of code, you might prefer to call attention to their exceptional use by using the exceptional-looking, explicit syntax.

Given the existence of function pointer values and variables to hold them, it is possible, naturally enough, to define functions that accept function pointers as parameters. The traditional example is a sorting function. Suppose we have a function

```
int asort(int a[], int n);
```

which sorts n elements in the array a. Suppose further that there are several different ordering relations under which the array might be sorted (perhaps normal, reverse, and odd-followed-by-even). We can define several comparison functions, each of which compares two integers and returns a result indicating whether one of the two integers should be considered greater, equal, or less than the other for the purposes of the sort. Then we modify the asort function to accept the comparison function as a third parameter:

```
int asort(int a[], int n, int (*cmpfunc)(int, int));
```

As it does its work, the new version of asort calls (*cmpfunc)(a[i], a[j]) to determine the desired relative position of two array elements a[i] and a[j]. Supposing that our several comparison functions were declared as

```
int cf1(int, int), cf2(int, int), cf3(int, int);
```

we could call any of

```
asort(a, n, cf1);
asort(a, n, cf2);
asort(a, n, cf3);
```

depending on the desired ordering. The standard C library defines a function that can sort arrays of any type (not just int) according to a caller-supplied comparison function; see section 3.10.4.4.

3.6.8. Low-Level Addressing

When C is used for low-level, "down to the bare metal" programming, it is sometimes useful to consider pointers not as abstract reference types but as the machine addresses that they typically are. Although the relationship between pointers and memory addresses and the details of low-level

memory addressing are inherently machine- and compiler-dependent, study-
ing them does provide a more concrete model for how pointers work.
(Readers uninterested in those details, or who prefer to stick exclusively to
portable programming and higher-level abstractions, may skip the rest of
this section.)

The internal representation of a C pointer is typically a machine word, of
a size appropriate for the machine's addressing architecture (e.g., 16-bit
or 32-bit words, for machines with 16- or 32-bit addressing structures). If
the global variable g sits at address 0x1234, then the assignment

```
p = &g;
```

(where p is a pointer of the appropriate type) usually stores the address
0x1234 in p. (It is for this reason that & is often referred to as the "address
of" operator.)

Pointer arithmetic is straightforward, with one twist. Continuing the preceding example, if g is type int and p is type pointer-to-int, then the
expression p + 1 should not result in 0x1235 on a byte-addressable
machine, but rather 0x1236 or 0x1238, depending on whether type int is
two or four bytes (16 or 32 bits). Therefore, on a byte-addressable
machine, the actual interpretation of an expression like p + n at the
address level is p + n * sizeof(*p). But it is rarely necessary to worry
about the multiplication by sizeof(*p), because under virtually all circumstances, it is taken care of automatically by the compiler. In particular,
explicit sizeofs in pointer arithmetic expressions often indicate that a programmer is inappropriately bogged down in assembler-style thinking, and
the extra sizeofs are actively wrong if they repeat the scaling that the
compiler would do. (In other words, do write p + n in C to compute a
new pointer n objects past the one p points to; don't write something like
p + n * sizeof(int).)

Nothing in the C language mandates byte addressability, however. It is
not at all unthinkable, for example, to implement C on a word-addressed
machine (and several such implementations have been successfully under-
taken). On a word-addressed machine, an expression like p + 1 would
likely add just 1 to p's internal value (assuming p were declared to point
to a word-sized data type). However, on such a machine, types int * and
char * would themselves have different sizes because char * would need a
few more bits to select an individual byte within a word. Moreover, on
these machines, conversions between different pointer types (e.g., as
requested by pointer casts) are actual conversions; they do much more
than just satisfy abstract requirements about type correctness.

Even on machines with flat, byte-addressed memory architectures, alignment restrictions may be significant. Conversion of, say, an arbitrary `char` `*` to an `int` `*` may lead to access violations when the `int` `*` is used. How, then, does `malloc` ensure that its callers will not get access violations when they use the pointers it returns to manipulate objects larger than bytes? The answer is that `malloc` is written so as to return pointer values suitably aligned for conversion to any type.

Finally, what about null pointers? As far as C is concerned, the only requirement is that the bit pattern that a compiler implementor chooses for a null pointer be one that can never be the address of any actual object or function. It may be desirable to pick an address that causes a memory violation when accessed, to catch programs that inadvertently attempt to use null pointers incorrectly. In fact, address 0 is commonly chosen, and attempts to access this address do indeed cause access violations under many memory-management arrangements. However, this choice is in one way a poor one, as it inevitably leads to a great deal of confusion because of the unavoidable association between the address 0 and the constant 0, which is used to request null pointers in C source code. In point of fact, it is essentially a coincidence that both the source-code and internal representations of null pointers involve the number zero; there is no reason why internal null pointers could not be represented by, say, the bit pattern `06000`. (This is not a hypothetical example; there were some old mainframes that used just this bit pattern.) A nonzero internal null pointer representation causes no problems for correctly written C code, though, because the compiler is responsible for generating that bit pattern whenever the programmer uses a constant 0 in a pointer context in source code (including when the zero appears implicitly in constructs such as `if(p)`, or is hidden behind the `NULL` macro).

When writing embedded code or device drivers, or accessing memory-mapped peripherals or display memory, it is often necessary to refer to an absolute memory address. Such access is relatively straightforward in C because it is possible to use an explicit cast to "convert" an integer into a pointer. For example, the code

```
char *p = (char *)0xb8000000;
*p = 'X';
```

would probably store the character `'X'` at address `0xb8000000`. The details of a particular compiler's integer to pointer conversion are highly machine dependent (especially under segmented memory architectures), but because code that makes use of these conversions is also machine dependent, the machine-dependent techniques are not inappropriate.

3.7. User-Defined Data Structures

C supports three user-defined data structures, along the lines of those found in many languages. C's struct type is a record of related information. A union is a variant record that can hold, at any one time, one value chosen from a selected set of types. Finally, an enum ("enumeration") is an integral type with predefined symbolic names for its values.

3.7.1. Structures

C's struct type is directly analogous to Pascal's record type and to the equivalent data structures in other languages; it is the predecessor of the class type in C++. A structure is a collection of named members (sometimes called "fields" or "elements") of potentially many different types.

One way of thinking about structures is by comparison with arrays. An array is a collection of adjacent elements, all of identical type, referenced by index numbers. A structure, on the other hand, is a collection of elements of various types, more-or-less adjacent, and referenced by name.

The syntax of a structure declaration is

```
struct tag
       {
       type1 member1 ;
       type2 member2 ;
       ...
       };
```

Within the braces, the syntax of the declarations of the individual members is identical to the syntax for declaring ordinary variables, except that no storage classes or initializers are present. Of course, the entity being declared is not a set of variables, but rather a template that can be used when declaring later instances of the actual structure. In the template, it is possible to declare several members of the same type at once (by specifying a comma-separated list of declarators following one base type, as shown in the point example next), to use complex declarators representing derived types such as arrays and pointers, and even to specify members that are themselves user-defined data structures.

A structure declaration typically also contains a tag, which is a name for this particular data structure. The tag is used when declaring later variables or functions that work with data structures of the new type so that the template does not have to be repeated each time. Tag names are chosen using the same rules as for ordinary identifiers, but they have their own namespace.

A traditional example of a user-defined data type is one to represent complex numbers. The declaration

```
struct complex
       {
       double re;
       double im;
       };
```

defines a new structure type, to be known by the tag `complex`. The template says that each instance of the structure will consist of two members, one named `re` and one named `im`, both of type `double`. Another classic example is a structure for representing points in the plane, which might be defined along the lines of

```
struct point
       {
       int x, y;
       };
```

The structure definitions here have described the templates for the new user-defined structures and have given them names ("tags"). After a new type is defined, the next thing to do is to declare some variables of that type. In the case of structures, this can be done in several ways. One is to use the keyword `struct` plus a `struct` tag as a type name, like this:

```
struct complex c1, c2;
struct point ll, ur;
```

Alternatively, variables having the new type can be declared at the same time that the new type is defined, like this:

```
struct
       {
       int x, y;
       } ul, lr;
```

The tag is optional in this case and may be omitted if no other identifiers will be declared having the new type.

Naturally, because structures are a general-purpose part of C's type system, it is possible to declare arrays of structures, and pointers to structures:

```
struct complex ca[10];
struct point *p1, *p2;
```

Formally, then, the full syntax of a structure declaration is

```
struct tag { member-declarations } declarator-list ;
```

where the *tag*, brace-enclosed member declaration list, and declarator list are all optional. This is, in fact, the same as the syntax that we have been using for declarations all along, but with the role of the base type filled by the keyword `struct`, the optional tag, and the optional member declaration. Therefore, yet another way of declaring structures is to define them as `typedef`s, as well as or instead of giving them tags. For instance, after defining

```
typedef struct
        {
        int x, y;
        } point_t;
```

the identifier `point_t` is a synonym for the new (and otherwise nameless) structure type and enables later declarations of the form

```
point_t ll, ur;
```

which do not require the keyword `struct`.

Structure variables can also be initialized when they are declared; the syntax is similar to array initialization. The initial values for the various members are all enclosed, in order, within braces:

```
struct complex c3 = {1., 0.}, c4 = {0., 1.};
```

If a partial initializer list is provided, trailing members are automatically initialized to 0.

Although we have observed a rough similarity between structures and arrays, it is important to note that the members of a structure are not guaranteed to be stored quite adjacently to each other in memory. The compiler may leave "holes"—unnamed, inaccessible memory locations—for padding between certain members so that all members are aligned appropriately for efficient access. Furthermore, a structure may have padding added at the end so that all elements of an array of structures remain properly aligned. This padding is generally only of concern when attempts are made to match structures to externally imposed data layouts, but it means that the size of a structure (as computed by `sizeof`) is often greater than the sum of the sizes of its members.

3.7.2. Structure Member Access

As mentioned, structure members are accessed by name. The basic means for doing so is the structure member access operator, which is a single dot. Continuing the preceding examples, we can refer to `c1.re`, `c2.im`, `ll.x`, `ur.y`, and so on. Just as for array and pointer access, these constructions can be used on either side of an assignment operator; that is, they can be used both to fetch and to store structure members.

The dot operator has very high precedence, on the same level as array access and function calls, and higher than that of the pointer indirection operator, `*`. Therefore, an expression like `*s.m` would mean to select the member `m` from the structure `s` and then fetch the object pointed to. (Naturally, this would work only if `s` were a structure and the member `m` had pointer type.) When you're accessing members in structures pointed to by structure pointers, therefore, a certain amount of care would be necessary. For example, if `pc` is a pointer to `struct complex`, using the `.` operator to select the member `re` requires explicit parentheses:

```
(*pc).re = 3;
```

Because pointers to structures are quite common, and because this syntax is a nuisance, a second structure access operator exists, tailored for use with structure pointers. It is the two-character `->` operator:

```
pc->re = 3;
```

Formally, `p->m` is identical to `(*p).m`, for any structure pointer `p` and member `m`.

Another difference between structures and arrays is that unlike arrays, structures are "first class types" in C. It is possible to assign entire structures from one variable to another as a unit, and to pass and return them to and from functions. Comparison, however, is not supported; structures may not be compared for equality or inequality with the `==` and `!=` operators. To compare structures, or to perform any other operations on them, typically requires writing functions. For example, here is a simple addition function, accepting two instances of `struct complex` and returning a third:

```
struct complex cpx_add(struct complex a, struct complex b)
{
        struct complex ret;
        ret.re = a.re + b.re;
        ret.im = a.im + b.im;
        return ret;
}
```

3.7.3. Unions

Closely related to structures are unions, which are somewhat analogous to Pascal's variant records. Unlike most of C's types, which (by the very definition of what a type is) can hold values of exactly one type, a union can hold values of several types, although only one value and one type at a time, and only those types that the programmer has declared as permissible. A union declaration is very similar to a structure declaration:

```
union anyval
    {
    char c;
    int i;
    long l;
    double d;
    };
```

Again, a definition of the form shown defines only a template, which in this case lists the permissible types that the union can hold and gives a name by which the value of each type can be accessed. Before the union can be used, a variable of the new type must typically be declared:

```
union anyval u;
```

Now, the member names access values within the union, using the same syntax as for structures: u.i accesses the integer stored in the union, u.d accesses the double, and so on.

Obviously, multiple values cannot be stored in a union at the same time; storing multiple values is what a struct is for. A union is just big enough to hold its largest member; the members all overlap. (In fact, an excellent way to think about a union is as a structure in which all members have offset 0, and therefore all overlap.) Also, there is no mechanism that automatically records which type of data has been most recently stored in a union; it is up to the programmer to remember somehow. One way is to wrap up a union and a code recording the current type, placing both elements in an enclosing structure:

```
struct taggedany
    {
    int which;
    union anyval value;
    };
```

The behavior is implementation defined if a value of one type is stored into a union and a different type is then extracted, but when it becomes necessary, for whatever reason, to inspect the bits that make up some value (such as a pointer or floating-point value) or otherwise "pun" unrelated types, the results are expected to be machine dependent, so a union is one way of achieving them.

3.7.4. Bit-Fields

Within structures and unions (unlike in any other declarations in C), it is possible to specify a member's size exactly, in bits. The size specification takes the form of a colon and an integer constant following the declarator:

```
struct bitfieldexamp
        {
        int i3b : 3;
        unsigned int i1b : 1;
        signed int i7b : 7;
        };
```

This declaration says that the structure bitfieldexamp consists of three members, all bit-fields. Member i3b is a 3-bit integer, member i1b is a 1-bit unsigned integer, and member i7b is a 7-bit signed integer.

Like char variables, and unlike other flavors of int, it is implementation defined whether a "plain" integer bit-field (e.g., i3b) is signed or unsigned. The keyword signed can be used to force a signed value. (Notice that a 1-bit field, if signed, can hold only the values 0 and -1.) Whether signed, unsigned, or questionably signed, bit-fields must always have a base type of int.

Adjacent bit-field members are packed into machine words, although the order is implementation defined. Bit-fields are not therefore individually addressable, and it is not possible to create arrays of bit-fields or pointers to bit-fields.

Bit-fields are useful for saving space when a structure contains multiple small, reduced-range members, such as boolean flags. (When using bit-fields, the compiler worries about the details of shifting and masking to extract ranges of bits from individual words, operations that we saw how to do explicitly in section 3.3.5.) It is also possible to utilize bit-fields when attempting to match the memory layout of a structure to some externally defined data format, although any attempt to do so is inherently machine and compiler dependent because of the imprecisely defined ordering of bit-fields within words (not to mention all the other implementation-defined aspects of numeric formats and structure layout).

When you're attempting to define the memory layout of bit-fields within a structure exactly, two additional mechanisms are available. It is permissible to omit the name (i.e., the identifier) for a bit-field member, with the result that the compiler leaves a "hole" of the specified number of bits between the surrounding bit-field members. Furthermore, it is permissible for the size of an unnamed bit-field member to be 0: An unnamed, size-0 bit-field requests that assignment of bit-field members to one machine word be completed and that succeeding bit-fields be assigned to a new word. For example, the declaration

```
struct bitfieldexamp2
    {
    int i3b : 3;
    unsigned int i1b : 1;
    signed int i7b : 7;
    int : 2;
    int i2b: 2;
    int : 0;
    int i4b : 4, i5b : 5;
    };
```

describes a structure containing 3-, 1-, and 7-bit fields as before, followed by a 2-bit hole, followed by a 2-bit field i2b, and then, in the next word, 4-bit and 5-bit fields i4b and i5b.

3.7.5. Enumerations

C's third user-defined type is the enumeration, or enum. An enumeration is simply an integral type with associated symbolic constants for certain values. Though convenient, these types are not as fundamentally important as the struct and union types; a programmer could accomplish approximately the same effect using ordinary integral variables and preprocessor macros (see section 3.8.2).

As a simple example, here is an enumeration for recording the days of the week:

```
enum wday {Sunday, Monday, Tuesday, Wednesday, Thursday,
          Friday, Saturday};
```

Besides defining the new enumeration type wday, this declaration also defines seven constants that represent seven different integer values. (As it happens, they are assigned in order, starting with 0; Sunday is 0 and Saturday is 6.) Enumeration tags (e.g., wday) share the same namespace as struct and union tags, whereas the enumeration constants (e.g., Sunday to Saturday) must coexist (that is, share a namespace) with the names of ordinary variables.

Once again, a variable or two of the new type can be declared for holding the new values:

```
enum wday today, tomorrow;
today = Wednesday;
tomorrow = Thursday;
```

It is also possible to specify the values for some or all of the enumeration constants:

```
enum cardname {ace = 1, jack = 11, queen, king};
```

Uninitialized enumeration constants always receive a value one greater than the previous constant, so `queen` is 12 and `king` is 13.

Enumerations are not particularly "strong" or "strict" types in C. It is possible to intermix them with integers, perform arithmetic on them as if they were integers, and so on. For example, there is no prohibition against writing code like

```
int i = Saturday;
```

or

```
cardname c = 10;
c++;                    /* c is now 11, which is jack */
```

In fact, because the type of an enumeration constant is `int`, it is not uncommon to see enumeration constants used freely as manifest constants (i.e., without restricting their use to `enum` variables of the corresponding type), much in the manner of preprocessor macros (which are discussed in section 3.8.2).

3.7.6. Linked Data Structures

One extremely common use of C's structure types is building linked data structures, such as trees and linked lists. The basic idea is to declare a member within a structure as a pointer to another instance of the same structure. For example, an elementary linked list node, used (for sake of example) to build lists of integers, might look like

```
struct list
     {
     int item;
     struct list *next;
     };
```

and a binary tree node (to be used for storing strings) might look like

```
struct tree
     {
     char *item;
     struct tree *left, *right;
     };
```

(Naturally, the type of data actually stored in the node depends on the application; practical node structures might have item members of various types, or multiple data members in addition to the link pointers.) These "recursive" structures are perfectly permissible; the compiler is quite willing to accept the declaration of a structure that contains a pointer to itself. Though the link pointers might look at first as if they point to "the same" structure, they almost always point to other instances of the same structure. Typically, null pointers are used to record links that do not exist (that is, for the ends of linked lists, or for leaf nodes of trees).

Working with linked data structures provides nice examples of the uses of structures, pointers, and dynamic memory allocation. For example, here is a function that inserts a new node at the beginning of a linked list, returning a pointer to the new list:

```c
#include <stdlib.h>
struct list *
listprepend(int n, struct list *oldlist)
{
        struct list *new = malloc(sizeof(struct list));
        if(new != NULL)
                {
                new->item = n;
                new->next = oldlist;
                }
        return new;
}
```

A few simple calls set up a sample list:

```c
struct list *base = NULL;
base = listprepend(1, base);
base = listprepend(2, base);
base = listprepend(3, base);
```

Traversing the list is particularly straightforward:

```c
struct list *lp;
for(lp = base; lp != NULL; lp = lp->next)
        printf("%d\n", lp->item);
```

The variable lp steps from node to node, starting at the base of the list and pointing to each node in turn until the null pointer marking the end of the list is found. In this for loop, therefore, the loop control variable is not even an integer (let alone one that steps from, say, 1 to 10). Yet this is a perfectly legal and common loop, illustrating the generality of the for loop while preserving the familiar initialize/test/increment pattern.

Working with binary trees is also straightforward. Here is a function for traversing one, using the classic inorder recursive algorithm:

```c
void treeprint(struct tree *t)
{
        if(t == NULL)
                return;
        treeprint(t->left);
        printf("%s\n", t->item);
        treeprint(t->right);
}
```

The function calls itself recursively, but the first test is whether the node pointer being examined is null, in which case the recursive descent terminates.

3.8. The C Preprocessor

C incorporates a macro preprocessor that operates conceptually before the compiler proper performs full lexical analysis and parsing. The main operations provided by the preprocessor are source file inclusion, macro definition and replacement, and conditional compilation.

All operations performed by the preprocessor are initiated by preprocessor directives, all of which begin with the # character. Preprocessor directives are unique in C in that their source layout matters: The # must be the first nonwhitespace character on the line, the directive cannot be split among several lines unless explicitly continued with the \ character, and no other source code (with the exception of comments) can follow on the same line as a directive.

3.8.1. Source File Inclusion (#include)

Lines of the form

```
#include <name>
```

and

```
#include "filename"
```

indicate that externally supplied text is to be inserted into the stream of source code seen by the compiler, just as if the programmer had typed it in manually. The externally supplied text, commonly known as a "header" or "header file," typically contains declarations and definitions that must be consistent among several source files. Placing the definitions and declarations in a header file and then using #include to copy them, verbatim, into each of the source files ensures that they will, in fact, be consistent (and may also lessen the typing burden).

The #include <name> form indicates that the external text is supplied by the compiler in some standard, central repository. For example, #include <stdio.h> brings in definitions and declarations pertaining to C's standard I/O library, including the definitions of EOF and the FILE type, external prototype function declarations for functions such as printf and getchar, and so on.

The #include `"filename"` form indicates that the external text is supplied by the programmer, in an additional source file named `filename`. Typically, the preprocessor searches for the requested file in the current directory or in the same directory as the source file doing the #include, although the exact rules are compiler dependent. The compiler may provide a way for the programmer to request additional directories where header files should be searched for. If no file by the given name is found, the preprocessor finally searches the standard, central repository, as if the #include <...> form had been used.

3.8.2. Macro Definition (#define)
A line of the form

```
#define name replacement-text
```

defines a preprocessor macro with the given name and a value consisting of the *replacement-text* (if any). Macro names follow the same rules as other identifiers (see section 3.2.4), although it is customary to give them capitalized names because it is often important to know that a given identifier represents a preprocessor macro as opposed to an ordinary variable or function.

The replacement text can be almost anything. Often it is a simple constant, but it can also be a more complicated expression, or in fact any arbitrary string of tokens, whether syntactically valid in isolation or not. The preprocessor merely replaces all later occurrences of the macro name (except inside comments and string literals) with the replacement text, and the results are passed on to the compiler proper for interpretation.

For example, we might write

```
#define MAXLINE 100
char line[MAXLINE];
char *p = fgets(line, MAXLINE, stdin);
```

This code defines a manifest constant MAXLINE with the "value" (or replacement text) 100. The macro is used in two places, as the dimension of the line array and as the second argument to the fgets function (see section 3.10.1.2). Besides making the code somewhat more self documenting, use of the macro ensures that if its value is changed—that is, to accommodate longer lines—all instances of it will be changed automatically by the preprocessor during subsequent compilations. Furthermore, because preprocessor macro replacement is performed before formal compilation, the macro MAXLINE is perfectly appropriate as an array dimension, although an ordinary (i.e., runtime) variable would not be. In other words, the code seen by the compiler after the macro is expanded is simply

```
char line[100];
char *p = fgets(line, 100, stdin);
```

Notice that a line containing a #define directive is neither a declaration nor a statement and therefore need not be terminated by a semicolon. Any semicolon in a #define line is simply treated as part of the replacement text, and would be copied blindly into the source stream at the point of invocation, which can lead to unexpected syntax errors.

A second form of preprocessor macro is also available. A line of the form

```
#define name( parameters ) replacement-text
```

defines a "function-like macro" that accepts zero or more arguments. Where the parameter names appear in the replacement text, they are replaced with the actual arguments supplied during "invocation" of the macro. For example, we might write

```
#define Square(x) x * x
```

to define a simple macro for squaring a number. (As we will see, it is a bit too simple.) An invocation such as

```
a = Square(b);
```

would be expanded by the preprocessor to

```
a = b * b;
```

If the argument text for a function-like macro involves more macro names, those macros are expanded first, before substituting for the function-like macro parameters.

Preprocessor macros, especially of the function-like variety, must be defined and used with care. When you're defining a function-like macro, there must be no space between the macro name and the open parenthesis indicating the presence of an argument list. (Otherwise, the parenthesis would be assumed to be part of the replacement text of an ordinary, non-function-like macro.) More importantly, the simple, textual substitution of preprocessor macro replacement text (of both the ordinary and function-like variety) can lead to surprising results. To see why, consider these examples:

```
a = Square(b + 1);
c = 1. / Square(d);
```

These would be expanded to

```
a = b + 1 * b + 1;
c = 1. / d * d;
```

which, due to the precedence and associativity of addition, multiplication, and division, would not be evaluated as the programmer presumably intended them to be. Defining the macro instead as

```
#define Square(x) ((x) * (x))
```

guards against both of these problems. For safety's sake, a macro that expands to an expression should always have that expression parenthesized in the definition. Furthermore, in a function-like macro, all instances of the parameters should be parenthesized if the replacement text is an expression.

One further pitfall deserves note. An invocation like

```
a = Square(b++);
```

expands to

```
a = ((b++) * (b++));
```

which is undefined, due to multiple side effects involving the same variable b. There is no good fix for this problem; function-like macros are simply not perfect substitutes for true functions. (In particular, the parentheses do not resolve the evaluation order ambiguity; see also section 3.3.9. Some compilers support "inline" functions, as in C++, and this extension is likely to be made official in the next revision of the C standard.)

Besides preprocessor macros defined by a particular source file, several macros are predefined. The ANSI/ISO C Standard specifies __STDC__ (which is always defined in a standard-conforming compiler), __FILE__ and __LINE__, which expand to the current source filename and line number, and __DATE__ and __TIME__, which expand to strings representing the date and time of compilation. Besides these macros, particular compilers may predefine their own macros, having to do with the compiler, operating system, or other aspects of the environment. (Such macros are primarily useful for directing conditional compilation; see the next section.)

3.8.3. Conditional Compilation (#ifdef, et al.)

Several related preprocessor directives support the conditional inclusion or exclusion of source code. The first form to look at is

```
#ifdef name
... source code ...
#endif
```

If a preprocessor macro of the given name is defined, the source code between the #ifdef line and the corresponding #endif is passed on to the rest of the compiler, as usual. If no macro by that name is defined, the enclosed code is discarded. The replacement text of the macro (if defined) is immaterial; the macro is simply being used as a switch, with a decision being made depending on whether or not the macro is defined at all. The conditionally included code might have to do with debugging, optional functionality, or a particular compilation environment or target operating system.

A closely related directive is #ifndef, which enables the enclosed code only if a certain macro is not defined. For more generality, the #if directive is available:

```
#if expression
... source code ...
#endif
```

The expression is a restricted form of compile-time constant expression, using only long int arithmetic. If the expression's value is nonzero, the enclosed code is enabled. One special operator is supported: defined(name) evaluates to 1 if a macro by the given name is defined; 0 otherwise. Therefore, #ifdef name is equivalent to #if defined(name), and #ifndef name is equivalent to #if !defined(name).

An #else directive may be used with #ifdef, #ifndef, and #if:

```
#ifdef name
... source code ...
#else
... alternate source code ...
#endif
```

Depending on whether the macro is defined, one set of source code or the other will be enabled. There is also an #elif directive, which can be used to simplify a cascaded chain of #if/#else/#if directives.

3.8.4. Special Replacement Operators

Within the replacement text of preprocessor macros, two special operators are available. The # operator "stringizes" a macro parameter, resulting in a string literal containing the source code text of the parameter. For example, given the macro

```
#define Str(x) #x
```

the invocation Str(abc) expands to "abc" (that is, including the quotes). In practice, abc is often itself a macro, and the goal is to obtain its replacement text as a string literal, in which case the following auxiliary macro can be used, which works by forcing an additional macro evaluation and substitution:

```
#define Xstr(x) Str(x)
```

Now, assuming the prior definition

```
#define abc def
```

the invocation Xstr(abc) expands to "def". As a more realistic example, the stringizing operator can be used (along with string literal concatenation) to construct strings containing variable names, such as in this debugging macro:

```
#define DEBUGi(x) printf(#x " is %d\n", x)
```

Given this definition, the call DEBUGi(a) expands to

```
printf("a" " is %d\n", a)
```

or, after string literal concatenation,

```
printf("a is %d\n", a)
```

and prints the value of a.

The second operator is ##, the "token-pasting" operator, which splices identifiers or other tokens together. For example, given the definition

```
#define Paste(a, b) a ## b
```

the code

```
Paste(ab, cd) = 123
```

expands to the assignment abcd = 123. (Without the ## operator, the expansion would have been ab cd = 123, which would have been a syntax error.)

3.8.5. Other Preprocessor Directives

The #line directive resets the preprocessor's and compiler's notion of the current source file and/or line number, for the purposes of error messages and the like. The syntax is either

```
#line lineno
```

or

```
#line lineno "filename"
```

This directive is useful when C source is being automatically generated from some other source, and error messages should be correlated with that other source.

The `#error` directive prints a user-specified error message during compilation. The syntax is

```
#error message
```

where `message` is any text. A programmer might use `#error` to report a mismatched or unimplemented set of conditional compilation options.

Finally, the `#pragma` directive permits any sort of compiler-specific extensions to be specified.

3.9. The Runtime Environment

Every C program begins execution with an implicit call to the function `main()`. One function named `main` must be defined by the programmer, using one of two signatures: either

```
int main(void)
```

or

```
int main(int argc, char **argv)
```

These forms are not absolute; several stylistic variations are possible. The explicit return type `int` in either form, and the keyword `void` in the first form, can both be omitted, because `int` is the default return type and because an empty pair of parentheses in a function definition indicates zero arguments (see section 3.5.1). Any names may be chosen for the parameters, but `argc` and `argv` are traditional.

3.9.1. Command-Line Arguments

When a C program is invoked, user-provided arguments may be available to it. These arguments are typically typed by the user on the command line that invoked the program, and are provided as an array of strings passed to the `main()` function. A `main()` function that wishes to receive command-line arguments is declared as

```
int main(int argc, char **argv)
```

where the parameter `argc` is the number of command-line arguments and `argv` is a reference to the array of the argument strings themselves. When passed, the strings are (as usual) represented as character pointers and the runtime startup code passes an array of these pointers to `main()`. Due to the special rules concerning arrays in expressions and as passed to functions (see section 3.6.5), `main` actually receives a pointer to the first element of the array; that is, `main` receives a pointer of type `char **`. However, `main` can equivalently be defined as accepting an array of pointers, in other words, as `main(int argc, char *argv[])`.

`argv[0]` is always the name of the program itself, if available (or the empty string `""` otherwise). Therefore, the first command-line argument is `argv[1]`. A standard example is a program that simply prints out its arguments (a la the UNIX echo program):

```
#include <stdio.h>
int main(int argc, char **argv)
{
        int i;
        for(i = 1; i < argc; i++)
                printf("argv[%d]: %s\n", i, argv[i]);
        return 0;
}
```

It is generally straightforward for a program to parse its command-line arguments and interpret them as option switches, filenames, and the like.

3.9.2. Exit Status

A C program can return an exit status to the invoking environment. The exit status is simply an integer value, with `0` indicating successful termination and nonzero values representing other conditions. The exit status is either the return value from `main` or the value passed to the `exit` function. See section 3.10.4.5 for more information on `exit` and the two predefined exit status values `EXIT_SUCCESS` and `EXIT_FAILURE`.

3.10. The Standard C Library

The Standard C runtime library is an occasionally eclectic mixture of extremely useful functions, along with a few unlikely historical warts. Most of these functions are valuable, and their use is recommended for productive and efficient programming. A few (such as `strncpy`) have foibles that must be understood for proper use, and one or two (such as `gets`) cannot be used safely, and are best avoided.

Related sets of these functions are declared in several standard headers, and before any of the functions are called, it is usually important (and always a good idea) for the corresponding header(s) to be included. Besides function prototype declarations, the headers also contain definitions for several important constants (preprocessor macros), typedefs, and structures.

This section is arranged mostly in the manner of a reference manual, although it also contains guidelines for use of these functions, examples, and even a few sample implementations, for illustrative purposes. As an overview of the kinds of functionality provided, and an index into the individual headers, we can list several classes of operations, and the headers in which functions along those lines will be found:

Functionality	Header(s)
basic definitions	`<stddef.h>`
I/O & files	`<stdio.h>`
characters and strings	`<string.h>`, `<ctype.h>`, `<stdlib.h>`, `<stdio.h>`
memory allocation	`<stdlib.h>`
mathematics	`<math.h>`
date and time	`<time.h>`
variable argument lists	`<stdarg.h>`
nonlocal jumps	`<setjmp.h>`
assertions	`<assert.h>`
signal handling	`<signal.h>`
error handling	`<errno.h>`, `<stdio.h>`, `<string.h>`
minima and maxima	`<limits.h>`, `<float.h>`
locale, internationalization	`<locale.h>`, `<stdlib.h>`, `<wchar.h>`, `<wctype.h>`
operating system interface	`<stdlib.h>`

It's also worth mentioning a few categories of functionality that are not addressed by the standard C library. There are no provisions for performing character-at-a-time input from keyboards or serial devices; screen operations such as moving the cursor, setting inverse video, or clearing the screen; graphics operations such as drawing lines; filesystem operations such as creating or listing directories; or graphical user interface operations such as working with the mouse or with windows or menus. Performing any of these operations requires using functions or system calls that are unique to a particular I/O device or operating system, and although these calls can in most cases be made from C programs, nothing more can be said about them here because they are not standard.

In the following subsections, the description of each standard library function begins with a skeletal declaration, which can be thought of either as an external prototype function declaration or the first line of the actual definition. These skeletons give the argument and return types of each function, and provide parameter names that are referred to in the descriptions.

Each standard header is described in its own subsection, as follows:

Header	*Section*	*Header*	*Section*
<stdio.h>	3.10.1	<stdarg.h>	3.10.10
<string.h>	3.10.2	<stddef.h>	3.10.11
<ctype.h>	3.10.3	<assert.h>	3.10.12
<stdlib.h>	3.10.4	<errno.h>	3.10.13
<math.h>	3.10.5	<limits.h>	3.10.14
<time.h>	3.10.6	<float.h>	3.10.15
<signal.h>	3.10.7	<iso646.h>	3.10.16
<setjmp.h>	3.10.8	<wchar.h>	3.10.17
<locale.h>	3.10.9	<wctype.h>	3.10.18

3.10.1. <stdio.h>

C's standard I/O library defines a set of functions, all declared in the header <stdio.h> , for performing efficient, buffered, portable I/O to files (and perhaps other devices), and also for performing a few filesystem-related operations. Most of the functions in the stdio library revolve around the concept of a stream, which is a sequence of bytes read from or written to some file or external device. Streams are manipulated by pointers of type FILE *, where FILE is an opaque type defined in <stdio.h>. The FILE * value (also known as a file pointer, handle, or descriptor) represents the state of a stream and is used in all operations on that stream. Streams are generally opened with the fopen function, but there are also three constant, predefined, preopened streams, stdin, stdout, and stderr, which are respectively the "standard" (or default) input, output, and error streams. These are typically connected to the user's keyboard and screen by default, but may also be redirected in various ways. (These streams are "constant" in that their identifiers cannot portably be reassigned, although they may be redirected using freopen. The standard error stream is intended to be used for error messages that should not be redirected along with the standard output.)

We have already met a few I/O functions that operated implicitly on the standard input or standard output. For example, getchar reads characters from stdin, and printf prints to stdout. For each function that implicitly uses stdin or stdout, there is a corresponding function that permits an input or output stream to be explicitly specified.

In addition to character I/O and formatted output, the stdio library also supports reading and writing individual lines of text, I/O with arbitrary blocks of text, a form of formatted input, and several other operations. The header defines several types and constants, including the FILE type and the constant EOF, which is returned by several functions to indicate end-of-file or error conditions.

3.10.1.1. Opening and Closing Streams

fopen
```
FILE *fopen(const char *name, const char *mode)
```

fopen attempts to open the file name. If successful, it returns an open stream; if not, it returns a null pointer. The mode is a string indicating how the file should be opened. The first character of the string must be r, w, or a, indicating that the file is to be opened for reading, writing, or appending, respectively. Additional characters in the mode string request optional behavior: A + character requests that the file be opened with the ability to both read and write, and a b character indicates that the file should be treated as binary, as opposed to the default text. (Text file processing implies that C's newline character, \n, is translated to and from the underlying operating system's end-of-line representation. On MS-DOS-based systems, text processing also implies that the character with value 26, control-Z or ASCII SUB, is treated as an in-band end-of-file character. Binary mode suppresses these translations.) Any additional characters in the mode string are typically ignored but may be defined as extensions in certain environments.

freopen
```
FILE *freopen(const char *name, const char *mode, FILE *fp)
```

freopen is much like fopen, except that instead of constructing a new FILE object, it reuses the existing one pointed to by fp (which is first closed, as if by calling fclose, if it was already in use). freopen is typically used to redirect one of the constant streams stdin, stdout, or stderr from within a program. For example, after calling

```
freopen("output.log", "w", stdout);
```

all future output generated by putchar and printf (and all other operations referring to stdout) will be performed on the file output.log.

fclose
```
int fclose(FILE *fp)
```

An open stream fp is closed, causing any remaining buffered output to be written out and any resources to be reclaimed, by calling fclose. The return value is EOF if there are any errors (e.g., while writing buffered output), and 0 otherwise. An fclose of all open streams is automatically performed on normal exit from a program.

fflush
```
int fflush(FILE *fp)
```

For an output stream fp, fflush causes any buffered data to be immediately written out. The return value is 0, or EOF if an error occurs (e.g., while writing the buffered data).

3.10.1.2. Input and Output Operations

getchar, getc, fgetc
```
int getchar()
int getc(FILE *fp)
int fgetc(FILE *fp)
```

getc returns the next available character from the stream fp. It returns the special value EOF to indicate end-of-file; the EOF value is distinct from all normal character values, which is why getc's return value has type int rather than char, and must be stored in a variable of type int. getchar() is equivalent to getc(stdin). fgetc is equivalent to getc except that getc may be implemented as a preprocessor macro (see section 3.8.2) and may therefore be unsafe if invoked with side effects on its fp argument.

putchar, putc, fputc
```
int putchar(int c)
int putc(int c, FILE *fp)
int fputc(int c, FILE *fp)
```

putc outputs the character c to the stream fp. putchar(c) is equivalent to putc(c, stdout). fputc is equivalent to putc except that putc may be implemented as a preprocessor macro (see section 3.8.2) and may therefore be unsafe if invoked with side effects on its fp argument. (Both putc and putchar are safe, however, in the presence of side effects on their c argument.) All three functions return the character written, or EOF in the event of an error (although write errors are usually not immediately detected, due to buffering).

printf, fprintf
```
int printf(const char *fmt, ...)
int fprintf(FILE *fp, const char *fmt, ...)
```

fprintf prints formatted output to the stream fp, under control of its fmt string. The fmt string contains either characters to be written to the output directly, or format specifiers that indicate that one of the variable arguments is to have its value formatted and inserted into the output.

printf(fmt, ...) is equivalent to fprintf(stdout, fmt, ...).

A format specifier consists of the percent sign character %, followed by optional flags, width, precision, and size modifiers, ending in a character representing the overall conversion to be performed. The complete specification of all allowable printf format specifiers and modifiers is extensive; the presentation here is somewhat simplified. See a complete C reference for all the details.

The flag characters and their meanings are as follow:

-	The formatted value should be left justified within its field width. (The default is right justification.)
+	Positive values are printed with an explicit + sign.
space	If the value is positive, an extra space is prepended (so that a column of numbers lines up if some are negative).
0	The value should be padded out to its field width with 0s rather than spaces.
#	An alternative style of formatting is used, as described under the individual format character specifications later.

The field width indicates the minimum width of the formatted field; it is padded if necessary. (A larger-than-expected value, however, effectively widens the field.) The width is either a string of digits, or a * character, indicating that the width will be taken (as an int value) from the variable argument list.

The precision indicates the number of digits past the decimal that are printed for floating-point fields, or the maximum number of characters copied and printed from the string for string fields, or the minimum number of digits printed for integer fields. The precision begins with a period, and is either a string of digits or a * character, indicating that the precision will be taken (as an int value) from the variable argument list. For styles e, f, and g, the default precision is 6.

The type size modifier is an additional character optionally appearing just before the overall formatting character, as follows:

h   The corresponding integer argument should be interpreted as short int or unsigned short int.

l   The corresponding integer argument is long int or unsigned long int. (See also NA1 note under %c and %s.)

L   The corresponding floating-point argument is long double.

Finally, the overall formatting character determines the type of conversion performed and (subject to the type size modifiers) the expected type of the argument to be printed:

c   An int argument is printed as a character. (Under NA1, the size modifier l indicates a wchar_t argument.)

d, i   An int (or, with the l modifier, long int) argument is printed as a decimal number.

e, E   A float or double (or, with the L modifier, long double) argument is printed in scientific notation. %E indicates that a capital E should be used. If the precision is 0 and the # flag is present, no decimal point is printed. Due to the default argument promotions (see section 3.5.3), no size modifier is needed to distinguish float from double arguments. (Type float has been promoted to double by the time printf sees it.)

f   A float or double (or, with the L modifier, long double) argument is printed as a decimal fraction. If the precision is 0 and the # flag is present, no decimal point is printed.

g, G   A float or double (or, with the L modifier, long double) argument is printed in the style of %e or %f, whichever gives better precision in less space. %G indicates that a capital E should be used with scientific notation (i.e., %G implies %E or %f). Trailing zeros are suppressed unless the # flag is present.

n   Nothing is printed. The corresponding argument is a pointer-to-int; the number of characters written so far is stored in that int.

o	An unsigned int (or unsigned long int) argument is printed as an octal number. If the # flag is present and the number is nonzero, a leading 0 is prepended.
p	A pointer argument of type void * is printed in an implementation-defined way.
s	A string (char *) argument is printed. If a precision is specified, no more than that number of characters from the string is used. (Under NA1, the size modifier l indicates a wchar_t * argument.)
u	An unsigned int (or unsigned long int) argument is printed as a decimal number.
x, X	An unsigned int (or unsigned long int) argument is printed as a hexadecimal number, using capital ABCDEF for %X. If the # flag is present and the number is nonzero, a leading 0x or 0X is prepended.
%	No corresponding argument is expected. A single % is printed.

To demonstrate a few of the formatting possibilities offered by printf, here are some examples:

```
printf("%d, %5d, %-5d, %05d, %5.5d\n", 1, 2, 3, 4, 5);
printf("%o %x %X %#o %#x\n", 171, 171, 171, 171, 171);
printf("%f %e %g\n", 3.14, 3.14, 3.14);
printf("%s, %.5s!\n", "Hello", "worldly");
printf("%0*d, %.*f, %*.*s\n", 2, 3, 4, 5.6, 7, 3, "abcdef");
```

Those calls print these five lines:

```
1,     2, 3    , 00004, 00005
253 ab AB 0253 0xab
3.140000 3.140000e+00 3.14
Hello, world!
03, 5.6000,     abc
```

printf and fprintf return the number of characters printed, or a negative number on error.

scanf, fscanf
```
int scanf(const char *fmt, ...)
int fscanf(FILE *fp, const char *fmt, ...)
```

fscanf is roughly the inverse of fprintf; it scans text from the stream fp and attempts to extract values from it under control of the fmt string. The fmt string contains either literal characters that are expected in the input; whitespace characters (space, tab, or newline), any of which indicate that any whitespace should be consumed from the input; or format specifiers that indicate that a value is to be converted and stored in the location pointed to by one of the variable arguments. With the exception of the %c, %n, %[, and %% conversions, all conversions also imply the consumption of leading whitespace.

scanf(fmt, ...) is equivalent to fscanf(stdin, fmt, ...).

A format specifier consists of the percent sign character (%), followed by optional flags, width, and size modifiers, ending in a character representing the overall conversion to be performed. The complete specification of all allowable scanf format specifiers is extensive; the presentation here is somewhat simplified.

The only flag character is the asterisk (*), which indicates that the converted argument should not be assigned to a corresponding pointed-to value. No corresponding argument is expected.

The field width is a string of digits indicating the maximum number of characters that will be consumed from the input for a field.

The type size modifier is an additional character optionally appearing just before the overall formatting character, as follows:

h	The corresponding argument is a pointer to short int or unsigned short int.
l	The corresponding argument is a pointer to long int or unsigned long int, or a pointer to double as opposed to float. (See also NA1 note under %c, %s, and %[.)
L	The corresponding argument is a pointer to long double.

Finally, the overall formatting character determines the type of conversion performed and (subject to the type size modifiers) the expected type of the pointed-to argument that will receive the result:

c	One character or, if a field width is present, that number of characters, is read and stored in the character or character array pointed to by the corresponding char * argument. No leading whitespace is consumed. No \0 character is added to the array. The array is quietly assumed to be big enough. (Under NA1, the size modifier l indicates a wchar_t * argument.)

d	A decimal number is read and stored in the integer pointed to by the corresponding `int *` (or, with the `h` or `l` modifiers, `short` or `long int *`) argument.
e, E, f, g, G	A decimal fraction or scientific-notation number (all five format characters accept either style of input) is read and stored in the floating-point value pointed to by the corresponding argument. The corresponding argument is of type `float *` by default, or `double *` if the `l` modifier is present, or `long double *` if the `L` modifier is present. (Notice the discrepancy with respect to `printf`, which uses `%f` for both types `float` and `double`.)
i	A number is read and stored in the integer pointed to by the corresponding `int *` (or, with the `h` or `l` modifiers, `short` or `long int *`) argument. The number is converted as if by the `strtol` function (see section 3.10.4.2) with a base of `0`; that is, it is converted from hexadecimal if it begins with `0x` or `0X`; otherwise from octal if it begins with `0`; otherwise from decimal.
n	No whitespace is consumed; no input conversion is performed at all. The number of characters read so far is stored in the integer pointed to by the corresponding `int *` argument.
o	An octal number is read and stored in the integer pointed to by the corresponding `unsigned int *` (or, with the `h` or `l` modifiers, `unsigned short` or `unsigned long int *`) argument.
p	An implementation-defined pointer representation (corresponding to the one printed by `printf`, et al., using `%p`) is read and stored in the pointer pointed to by the corresponding `void **` argument.
s	A string of nonwhitespace characters is read and stored (along with a terminating `\0`) in the character array pointed to by the corresponding `char *` argument. The array is quietly assumed to be big enough. (Under NA1, the size modifier `l` indicates a `wchar_t *` argument.)

u	An unsigned decimal number is read and stored in the integer pointed to by the corresponding unsigned int * (or, with the h or l modifiers, unsigned short or unsigned long int *) argument.
x, X	A hexadecimal number is read and stored in the integer pointed to by the corresponding unsigned int * (or, with the h or l modifiers, unsigned short or unsigned long int *) argument.
[	The complete format specifier (less the optional * flag) is %[...], with a character class or range contained between the brackets. The character class is a string of characters that is to be matched or, if a leading ^ is present, not matched. If the implementation permits it, a notation of the form a-c represents all characters in the range a to c. No leading whitespace is consumed. Characters are read from the input as long as they match the requested character class, or as long as they do not match the character class if the leading ^ is present, or until the input field width is exhausted. Characters are stored (along with a terminating \0) in the character array pointed to by the corresponding char * argument. The array is quietly assumed to be big enough. (Under NA1, the size modifier l indicates a wchar_t * argument.)

For example: the specifier %[abc] would read a string consisting only of a's, b's, and c's; the specifier %[^)] would read all characters (including whitespace) up to but not including a close parenthesis.

%	A single % character is expected in the input. No conversion is performed; no corresponding argument is expected.

scanf and fscanf return the number of conversions and assignments successfully performed (excluding those performed by %n or suppressed by the * flag). If a conversion fails or an unexpected character appears, scanning is terminated and unused characters are left on the input. If end-of-file is reached before performing any conversions, EOF is returned.

scanf is superficially powerful but inherently dangerous. It can be difficult or impossible to resynchronize in case of unexpected or erroneous input (because unmatched input is left on the input stream), and the conversion specifiers %c, %s, and %[(unless accompanied by carefully chosen field

width specifiers) can easily overflow their destination arrays. To over-
come the first difficulty, it is often a good idea to read entire lines with
`fgets` (see section 3.10.1.2) and then parse them using `sscanf` (see section
3.10.1.6).

gets, fgets
```
char *gets(char *buf)
char *fgets(char *buf, int n, FILE *fp)
```

`fgets` reads a line of text (terminated by `\n`) from the stream `fp`, and stores
the text as a string (including the `\n` and a terminating `\0`) to the character
array pointed to by `buf`. The size of the array is assumed to be `n`; if the
line is longer than n-2 characters (not counting the newline), some characters are left unread. (The stored string is terminated with `\0` in any case.)

`gets` is roughly equivalent to `fgets`, except that it implicitly reads from
`stdin`, does not place the `\n` in the string pointed to by `buf`, and does not
permit the array size to be specified. Because of the lack of an array size
specification, `gets` cannot be used safely and should be avoided.

Both `gets` and `fgets` return the string read (i.e., they return the value of
their `buf` argument), or `NULL` on end-of-file or error. Notice that if the
input happens to contain null (`\0`) characters, the string will seem to be
prematurely terminated.

puts, fputs
```
int puts(char *str)
int fputs(char *str, FILE *fp)
```

`fputs` writes the string pointed to by `str` to the stream `fp`. `puts` writes the
string pointed to by `str`, along with a trailing `\n`, to `stdout`. Both functions
return a nonnegative value, or `EOF` if an error occurs.

fread
```
size_t fread(void *buf, size_t elsize, size_t n, FILE *fp)
```

`fread` attempts to read a block of characters from the stream `fp` into the
buffer pointed to by `buf`, with no attempt being made to group characters
into lines with `\n` or strings with `\0`. Up to n*elsize bytes are read, under
the assumption that they represent n data elements, each of size `elsize`.
(Therefore, to read characters, it is most appropriate to pass `elsize` as 1
and `n` as the number of characters desired.) The return value is the number of elements (i.e., of size `elsize`) successfully read, or `EOF` on end-of-file
or error.

fwrite
```
size_t fwrite(void *buf, size_t elsize, size_t n, FILE *fp)
```

fwrite attempts to write a block of characters (not necessarily terminated by \0) from the buffer pointed to by buf to the stream fp. The number of bytes written is n*elsize, under the assumption that they represent n data elements, each of size elsize. (Therefore, to write characters, it is most appropriate to pass elsize as 1 and n as the number of characters.) The return value is the number of elements successfully written.

ungetc
```
int ungetc(int c, FILE *fp)
```

ungetc attempts to push the character with the value c back onto the input stream fp, where it will be available for reading by the next input call. One character's worth of push-back is guaranteed. The return value is the character pushed back, or EOF if an error occurs.

ungetc is useful in lexical analyzers and the like, when it is not possible to determine the end of a particular token until one character past it has been read. For example, here is a code fragment that reads a string of digits from a stream and returns their decimal value, but leaves the first nondigit character in the input stream:

```
int n = 0;
int c;
while((c = getc(fp)) >= '0' && c <= '9')
        n = 10 * n + (c - '0');
ungetc(c, fp);
```

3.10.1.3. Repositioning Streams

ftell
```
long int ftell(FILE *fp)
```

ftell returns a long integer representing the current position of the stream fp. This value may be passed to the fseek function to return the stream to the same point. For binary streams (that is, streams opened with the b modifier), the value is the offset from the beginning of the file, in bytes.

If the stream position might be too large to be represented in a long int, use fgetpos (see section 3.10.1.3) instead.

fseek, rewind

```
int fseek(FILE *fp, long int pos, int whence)

void rewind(FILE *fp)
```

fseek repositions the stream fp to the position pos, according to the whence argument.

If whence is the value SEEK_SET (defined in <stdio.h>) and pos is 0, the stream is rewound to the beginning. If whence is SEEK_SET and pos is a value returned by ftell, the stream is set to that position. If whence is SEEK_SET and fp is a binary stream, the stream is set to a position pos bytes from the beginning.

If whence is the value SEEK_CUR and pos is 0, the stream's position is unchanged. If whence is SEEK_CUR and fp is a binary stream, the stream is set to a position pos bytes forward or backward (depending on the sign of pos) from the beginning.

If whence is the value SEEK_END and pos is 0, the stream is set to its end-of-file position. If whence is SEEK_CUR, fp is a binary stream, and the implementation permits it, the stream is set to a position pos bytes forward or backward (depending on the sign of pos) from the end of the file.

If the request cannot be satisfied, a nonzero value is returned.

Except for the return value, rewind(fp) is equivalent to fseek(fp, 0, SEEK_SET).

When pos might be too large to be represented in a long int, use fsetpos (see section 3.10.1.3) instead.

fgetpos, fsetpos

```
int fgetpos(FILE *fp, fpos_t *pos)
int fsetpos(FILE *fp, const fpos_t *pos)
```

fgetpos records the current position of the stream fp by storing it in the fpos_t object pointed to by pos, in a manner potentially able to record larger positions than would fit in a long int.

fsetpos sets the position of the stream fp to the fpos_t value pointed to by pos, which must be a value previously recorded by fgetpos.

Both functions return 0 if they are successful.

3.10.1.4. Controlling Buffering

setbuf, setvbuf
```
void setbuf(FILE *fp, char *buf)
void setvbuf(FILE *fp, char *buf, int mode, size_t size)
```

These functions are used to request specific buffering strategies for the stream fp. They must be used after a stream is opened but before any I/O is performed on it.

For setvbuf, the mode argument is a constant specifying the kind of buffering to be performed. The constants (defined in <stdio.h>) are as follow:

_IONBF	Indicates no buffering; characters are always read or written immediately.
_IOFBF	Indicates full buffering; characters are read from or written to an intermediate buffer, which is filled or emptied all at once.
_IOLBF	Indicates "line buffering"; an output stream is partially buffered but is flushed whenever a \n character is printed.

If buf is a non-null pointer, it points to a caller-supplied buffer (a character array of size size) that should be used instead of the default buffer normally allocated by the stdio library.

setbuf(fp, buf) is roughly equivalent to

```
setvbuf(fp, buf, buf == NULL ? _IONBF : _IOFBF, BUFSIZ)
```

That is, if buf is null, the stream is unbuffered; otherwise, it is fully buffered using the buffer buf with a size of BUFSIZ (where BUFSIZ is a default buffer size defined in <stdio.h>).

3.10.1.5. Error Handling

feof
```
int feof(FILE *fp)
```

feof returns nonzero if end-of-file has occurred on the stream fp; 0 otherwise. It can be used to distinguish between error and end-of-file conditions when some other function has returned an exception value. (Notice that feof reports whether end-of-file has already occurred on a previous input operation; it does not predict whether the next operation will succeed. C is very different from Pascal in this respect.)

ferror
```
int ferror(FILE *fp)
```

ferror returns nonzero if an error has occurred on the stream fp; 0 otherwise. It can be used to distinguish between error and end-of-file conditions when some other function has returned an exception value, or to detect an error after a string of unchecked output function calls.

clearerr
```
void clearerr(FILE *fp)
```

clearerr clears the error and end-of-file indications (those checked by ferror and feof) on the stream fp.

perror
```
void perror(const char *prefix)
```

perror prints a message to stderr relating to the most-recent error. The message is the same one that would have been returned by the strerror function (see section 3.10.2.6) called with the current value of the global errno. If prefix is non-null, it is prepended to the message. In other words, perror(p) is roughly equivalent to

```
fprintf(stderr, "%s: %s", p == NULL ? "" : p, strerror(errno));
```

3.10.1.6. Operations on Strings

sprintf, sscanf
```
int sprintf(char *buf, const char *fmt, ...)
int sscanf(const char *buf, const char *fmt, ...)
```

sprintf and sscanf are variants of printf and scanf. Rather than working with streams, these functions work with strings. sprintf writes formatted characters to its initial buf argument, where the buffer pointed to by buf is assumed to be big enough to hold the generated string. Similarly, sscanf reads and converts characters from its buf argument, where the end of the string (\0) is interpreted as end-of-file.

3.10.1.7. Operations with Variable-Length Argument Lists

vprintf, vfprintf, vsprintf
```
int vprintf(const char *fmt, va_list argp)
int vfprintf(FILE *fp, const char *fmt, va_list argp)
int vsprintf(char *buf, const char *fmt, va_list argp)
```

These functions allow the functionality of printf, fprintf, and sprintf to be used within functions that accept their own printf-like format

arguments and additional variable arguments. In each case, they accept a
fmt string and a "pointer" to a variable-length argument list argp (that is,
rather than an actual variable-length argument list) and generate formatted output to stdout, to the stream fp, or to the string pointed to by buf,
respectively. (See section 3.10.10 for descriptions of the va_list type and
the standard facilities for manipulating arguments in variable-length argument lists.)

For example, here is an error-printing function that might be used in a
compiler. It prints an error message, perhaps incorporating additional
arguments, preceded by the program's name and the current filename and
line number (which are passed in as global variables).

```
#include <stdio.h>
#include <stdarg.h>

extern char *progname;          /* program name */
extern char *filename;          /* current input file name */
extern int lineno;              /* current input line number */
void error(char *msg, ...)
{
        va_list argp;
        va_start(argp, msg);
        fprintf(stderr, "%s: %s, line %d: ",
                progname, filename, lineno);
        vfprintf(stderr, msg, argp);
        fprintf(stderr, "\n");
        va_end(argp);
}
```

3.10.1.8. Operations on Files

rename
```
int rename(const char *fromname, const char *toname)
```

rename attempts to rename the file named fromname, giving it the new name
toname. The return value is zero if the function succeeds; nonzero if it fails.

remove
```
int remove(const char *name)
```

remove attempts to delete the file named name. The return value is 0 if the
function succeeds; nonzero if it fails.

tmpfile, tmpnam
```
FILE *tmpfile(void)    char *tmpnam(char *buf)
```

tmpfile creates a temporary file and opens it as if by calling fopen with the
mode string "wb+" (see section 3.10.1.1). tmpfile arranges that this file will
be automatically removed when it is closed, or upon program termination.

tmpnam generates a temporary filename, which the program can open or otherwise use as it wishes. The filename generated by tmpnam is different each time it is called. If buf is non-null, it is assumed to point to a character array of size at least L_tmpnam (a constant defined in <stdio.h>) into which the filename is written. Otherwise, the filename is written to an internal static buffer. In either case, a pointer to the generated name is returned.

3.10.2. <string.h>

The functions declared by <string.h> mostly provide support for C's null-terminated strings, although there are also a few functions (having names beginning with mem) that operate on arbitrary blocks of characters. The functions provided include those for copying, comparing, and performing simple searches in strings, as well as several other miscellaneous operations.

Few of these functions are at all sophisticated, and in fact many of them provide useful illustrations of the string and pointer manipulations discussed in section 3.6.5. Accordingly, several of the function descriptions here are accompanied by sample implementations.

3.10.2.1. String Length

strlen
```
size_t strlen(const char *s)
```

strlen returns the length of the string s (the number of characters up to but not including the terminating \0).

strlen is simple to implement; one possibility is

```
size_t strlen(const char *s)
{
        size_t len = 0;
        while(*s++ != '\0')
                len++;
        return len;
}
```

3.10.2.2. Copying and Concatenating Strings

strcpy
```
char *strcpy(char *dest, const char *src)
```

strcpy copies the string pointed to by src to the destination dest, and returns dest.

strcpy is also simple to implement:

```
char *strcpy(char *dest, const char *src)
{
        char *dp = dest;
        while(*src != '\0')
                *dp++ = *src++;
        *dp = '\0';
        return dest;
}
```

It is traditional to collapse the character assignment and the test for '\0'; this alleviates the necessity to append the final '\0' outside the loop:

```
while((*dp++ = *src++) != '\0')
        ;
return dest;
```

strcat
```
char *strcat(char *dest, const char *src)
```

strcat appends the string pointed to by src to the destination dest, in place, and returns dest. (Its name is somewhat of a misnomer, as it does not concatenate two strings to form a third string.)

Here is a sample implementation of strcat:

```
char *strcat(char *dest, const char *src)
{
        char *dp = dest;
        while(*dp != '\0')
                dp++;
        while(*src != '\0')
                *dp++ = *src++;
        *dp = '\0'; return dest;
}
```

strncpy
```
char *strncpy(char *dest, const char *src, size_t n)
```

strncpy copies at most n characters from the string pointed to by src to the destination dest, stopping early if there are more than n characters before the terminating \0 in src. The copied string, dest, is returned.

For obscure historical reasons, strncpy has two unusual traits. If there are fewer than n characters in the source string, the destination is padded with as many \0 characters as are required so that exactly n characters total are always written. But if there are n or more characters in the source string, the destination receives no terminating \0 at all, and is not therefore a well-formed string. A workaround is to use strncat instead of strncpy: when a call to strncpy(p1, p2, n) should create a null-terminated string, it can be replaced with the sequence `*a = '\0'`, `strncat(p1, p2, n)` (as long as the array `a` contains space for at least `n+1` characters).

strncat
```
char *strncat(char *dest, const char *src, size_t n)
```

`strncat` appends at most `n` characters from the string pointed to by `src` to the destination `dest`, in place. It appends a terminating `\0` (which is not counted against the maximum `n`). The modified string, `dest`, is returned.

3.10.2.3. Comparing Strings

strcmp
```
int strcmp(const char *s1, const char *s2)
```

`strcmp` compares the strings `s1` and `s2`. It returns the value `0` if the two strings compare equally, a negative value if `s1` is lexicographically less than `s2`, or a positive value if `s1` is greater than `s2`. The lexicographical comparison is made on a character-by-character basis using the machine's character set values.

Here is an implementation of `strcmp`. (Notice that it uses a `for` loop without an initialization expression.)

```
int strcmp(const char *s1, const char *s2)
{
        for(; *s1 == *s2; s1++, s2++)
                {
                if(*s1 == '\0')
                        return 0;
                }
        return *s1 - *s2;
}
```

The first thing to check is whether corresponding characters are equal; if they remain equal up to and including the terminating `\0`, both strings are the same. Otherwise, a simple way to obtain the ordering between the two strings is to subtract the values of the mismatched characters (which also works if one string is an initial substring of the other because the value of the character `'\0'` is, by definition, `0`). In the presence of negative character values, however (which might occur if type `char` is signed), better results would be achieved by forcing unsigned interpretation. One way to do this (at the cost of explicit casts) would be to replace the last line by

```
return *(unsigned char *)s1 - *(unsigned char *)s2;
```

strncmp
```
int strncmp(const char *s1, const char *s2, size_t n)
```

strncmp compares up to n characters from the strings s1 and s2. If the strings compare equal in their first n characters, they are considered equal even if no \0 character is found. The comparison is otherwise the same as for strcmp.

strcoll
```
int strcoll(const char *s1, const char *s2)
```

strcoll compares the strings s1 and s2, much like strcmp, except that strcoll performs a locale-dependent comparison (perhaps taking into account multinational character sets) as determined by the current LC_COLLATE category (see section 3.10.9).

strxfrm
```
size_t strxfrm(char *dest, const char *src, size_t n)
```

strxfrm creates a modified copy of the string pointed to by src in the destination buffer dest. The modified string is terminated with a \0 character, but no more than n characters (including the \0) are written to dest. The modification is such that if two strings, each converted by strxfrm, are then compared using strcmp, the same ordering will be determined as if the two original strings had been compared using strcoll, using appropriate locale-specific comparisons. strxfrm returns the number of characters written to dest, not including the terminating \0.

3.10.2.4. Searching for Characters and Strings

strchr, strrchr
```
char *strchr(const char *s, int c)
char *strrchr(const char *s, int c)
```

These functions search the strings pointed to by s for a character with the value c. strchr returns a pointer to the first such character; strrchr returns a pointer to the last (rightmost) such character. Both functions return a null pointer if the character is not found.

strstr
```
char *strstr(const char *s, const char *pat)
```

strstr searches the string pointed to by s for the first instance of the substring pat, and returns either a pointer to that substring or a null pointer if the pattern is not found.

strspn, strcspn
```
size_t strspn(const char *s, const char *set)
size_t strcspn(const char *s, const char *set)
```

These functions compute the length of the initial portion of the strings s that are composed entirely of characters found in or not found in the given string set. strspn returns the initial number of characters all of which are present in set, and strcspn returns the initial number of characters none of which are present in set.

strpbrk
```
char *strpbrk(const char *s, const char *set)
```

strpbrk searches the string pointed to by s for any character occurring within set, returning a pointer to the first one found or a null pointer if none are found.

3.10.2.5. Operations on Blocks of Characters

memcpy, memmove
```
void *memcpy(void *dest, const void *src, size_t n)
void *memmove(void *dest, const void *src, size_t n)
```

These functions copy exactly n bytes from the blocks pointed to by src to the destinations dest, returning dest. The text copied is not treated as a string; \0 characters are not searched for or treated specially. If the source and destination blocks overlap, memmove is careful to perform the copying appropriately (not overwriting characters until they have been copied); memcpy offers no such guarantee.

memcmp
```
int memcmp(const void *p1, const void *p2, size_t n)
```

memcmp compares exactly n characters from the blocks pointed to by p1 and p2. The blocks of characters are not treated as strings; \0 characters are not searched for or treated specially. The comparison is otherwise the same as for strcmp (see section 3.10.2.3).

memchr
```
void *memchr(const void *p, int c, size_t n)
```

memchr searches n characters in the block pointed to by p for the first character with the value c, and returns either a pointer to that character or a null pointer if it is not found.

memset
```
void *memset(void *p, int c, size_t n)
```

memset sets n bytes pointed to by p all to the character value c, and returns p.

3.10.2.6. Miscellaneous Operations

strtok
```
char *strtok(char *s, const char *sep)
```

A series of calls to strtok breaks up the string pointed to by s into a set of substrings, where substrings are delimited by any of the characters found in the string pointed to by sep. The first call takes the form

```
p = strtok(s, sep);
```

which picks off the first substring, terminates it by overwriting the first separator character with \0, remembers its position, and returns a pointer to the first substring. Succeeding calls take the form

```
p = strtok(NULL, sep);
```

where the null pointer argument indicates to strtok that it should resume scanning at the remembered position and break off, terminate, and return the next substring. A null pointer is returned when there are no more substrings.

For example, this fragment prints whitespace-separated substrings from a test string:

```
char teststr[] = " a b cd\tefg";
char *p;
for(p = strtok(teststr, " \t"); p != NULL; p = strtok(NULL, " \t"))
    printf("%s\n", p);
```

Because strtok necessarily uses some internal state, it is not possible to use it to break up a new string while another is still being processed.

strerror
```
char *strerror(int e)
```

strerror returns a human-readable error string corresponding to the error number e, which is typically a value deposited in the global errno after a system call or library function returns an error. See also section 3.10.13.

3.10.3. <ctype.h>

The functions declared in <ctype.h> allow testing for various classes of characters, and converting between upper- and lowercase characters.

3.10.3.1. Character Classification

```
int isupper(int c)
int islower(int c)
int isalpha(int c)
int isdigit(int c)
int isalnum(int c)
int isxdigit(int c)
int isspace(int c)
int ispunct(int c)
int isprint(int c)
int isgraph(int c)
int iscntrl(int c)
```

These functions all return nonzero if their argument character c meets some classification. isupper and islower test for upper- and lowercase alphabetic characters. isalpha tests for any alphabetic character; isdigit tests for any digit; isalnum tests for the union of the two. isxdigit tests for any hexadecimal digit (0–9 and a–f or A–F). isspace tests for whitespace characters (space, \t, \n, \r, \f, or \v). ispunct tests for punctuation characters (neither alphanumeric nor whitespace). isprint tests for any printing character, including space; isgraph tests for any printing character with a graphical representation (i.e., all except space). iscntrl tests for nonprinting "control characters."

In all cases, the value returned is 0 if the argument character does not meet the classification or nonzero (but not necessarily 1) if it does. Therefore, do not write if(isalpha(c) == 1) or if(isalpha(c) == TRUE), no matter how TRUE is defined. Simply write if(isalpha(c)) instead.

These functions all accept character values as if they were unsigned. The characters in C's standard character set all have positive values, but the values in extended character sets may not. If a character c might have a negative value, it is important to call, for example, isalpha((unsigned char)c), so that a negative number will not be passed to isalpha on machines where characters are signed by default.

3.10.3.2. Character Conversion

```
int toupper(int c)
int tolower(int c)
```

toupper converts a lowercase letter to its uppercase equivalent and leaves any other character alone. Similarly, tolower converts an uppercase letter to lowercase.

3.10.4. <stdlib.h>

The header <stdlib.h> defines several basic functions for allocating memory, converting strings to numbers, manipulating multibyte characters, and so on.

3.10.4.1. Memory Allocation

malloc, calloc
```
void *malloc(size_t n)
void *calloc(size_t n, size_t elsize)
```

malloc attempts to allocate n bytes of dynamically allocated memory. If successful, it returns a pointer to this memory; if unsuccessful, it returns a null pointer. The pointer (and hence the allocated block of memory) is suitably aligned so that it may be used for storing any kind of data. Because the return type is void *, no cast is required when assigning the return value to a pointer variable of object pointer type:

```
double *dp = malloc(10 * sizeof(double));
```

calloc(n, elsize) is equivalent to malloc(n * elsize) followed by a call to memset(p, 0, n * elsize), where p is the pointer returned by malloc (if non-null). That is, calloc initializes the newly allocated memory to all-bits-zero. (Notice that this initialization guarantees a 0 data value only for integers and characters, not necessarily for pointer or floating-point types.)

free
```
void free(void *p)
```

free accepts a pointer p, previously allocated by malloc, calloc, or realloc, and returns the formerly allocated block of memory to the free pool, where it will be available to future allocation requests by the calling program. (Note that the memory is typically not returned to the operating system immediately or otherwise made available to other programs.)

realloc
```
void *realloc(void *oldptr, size_t newsize)
```

realloc accepts a pointer oldptr to a block of memory previously allocated by malloc, calloc, or realloc, and attempts to reallocate the block to have the size newsize. If realloc is able to adjust the allocation of the existing block in place (for example, if memory following the block, out to newsize, is unused), the new allocation is simply recorded and realloc returns the original pointer, oldptr. If the block cannot be reallocated in place, realloc attempts to allocate a new block of size newsize elsewhere. If it succeeds, it copies the contents of the old block to the new (as if with memcpy), frees the old block, and returns a pointer to the new block. Otherwise, the reallocation is impossible, and realloc indicates this by returning a null pointer (in which case oldptr remains valid, albeit pointing to the old block).

As special cases, realloc(p, 0) is equivalent to free(p), and realloc(0, n) (that is, an attempt to reallocate the null pointer) is equivalent to malloc(n).

Because realloc may relocate the block, it is important that the caller update any and all pointers that point anywhere within the block. Since a null return from realloc may leave oldptr valid, it is important not to assign realloc's return value immediately back to the same pointer that was passed as oldptr. Here is a contrived example illustrating both of these points:

```
#include <stddef.h>      /* for ptrdiff_t */
#include <stdio.h>       /* for printf */
#include <stdlib.h>      /* for malloc and realloc */
#include <string.h>      /* for strstr */

ptrdiff_t p2off;
char *p = malloc(14), *p2, *newp;
if(p != NULL)
        {
        strcpy(p, "Hello, world!");
        p2 = strstr(p, "world");
        p2off = p2 - p;
        newp = realloc(p, 20);
        if(newp != NULL)
                {
                p = newp;
                p2 = p + p2off;
                }
        printf("%.5s, %s\n", p, p2);
        }
```

Notice the use of the variable p2off, which enables recomputation of p2 if the base pointer p is relocated. (The type ptrdiff_t is defined in <stddef.h>; see section 3.10.11.)

3.10.4.2. Converting Strings to Numbers

atoi, atol, strtol, strtoul
```
int atoi(const char *s)
long int atol(const char *s)
long int strtol(const char *s, char **endp, int base)
unsigned long int strtoul(const char *s, char **endp, int base)
```

These functions convert numeric strings to the corresponding integers.

The most general function is strtol. It skips over any leading whitespace, honors a leading sign character ('-' or '+'), and then converts a string of digits representing a number in the requested base. If base is less than 10, only digits from 0 to base-1 are accepted. If base is greater than 10, appropriate letters in the sets a–z or A–Z are also accepted. If base is 0, strtol infers a base by following the rule for C integer constants: base 16 if the string (sans whitespace and sign) begins with 0x or 0X; otherwise base 8 if it begins with 0; otherwise base 10. If base is exactly 16, a leading 0x or 0X is also accepted. If endp is non-null, strtol stores into *endp (that is, into the pointed-to pointer) a pointer to the first character in s that it did not consume. The caller can use the returned pointer as follows: If it equals s, no input was consumed and no part of the string s represented a valid number; otherwise, if it points to the character '\0', the string was perfectly valid; otherwise, the string began with a valid number, followed by some non-numeric characters (which *endp now points to). The return value is either the converted number, or 0 if no conversion could be performed, or the constants LONG_MAX or LONG_MIN if the number could not be represented in a long int. In the overflow cases, the global errno is set to ERANGE.

strtoul is similar to strtol except that the return value is of type unsigned long int, and the value ULONG_MAX is returned on overflow.

atoi(s) is equivalent to (int)strtol(s, NULL, 10), except that the result on overflow is undefined. Similarly, atol(s) is equivalent to strtol(s, NULL, 10). In other words, these functions perform simple base-10 integer conversions, with no special provisions for error checking.

atof, strtod

```
double atof(const char *s)
double strtod(const char *s, char **endp)
```

These functions convert numeric strings to floating-point numbers.

The more general function is strtod. It skips over any leading whitespace, honors a leading sign character ('-' or '+'), and then converts a string representing a floating-point number. The format accepted is the same as for C's floating-point constants, and can contain a decimal-point character and/or the letter e or E indicating an exponent. If endp is non-null, strtod stores into the pointed-to pointer *endp a pointer to the first character in s that it did not consume. The caller can use the returned pointer just as for strtol, et al. (see section 3.10.4.2.): to discriminate between zero returns due to errors or real zeros and to detect trailing garbage. In case of overflow, the return value is plus or minus HUGE_VAL, and the global errno is set to ERANGE.

atof(s) is equivalent to strtod(s, NULL), except that the result on overflow is undefined.

3.10.4.3. Pseudo-Random Number Generation

rand
```
int rand(void)
```

rand returns a random integer in the range 0 to RAND_MAX, inclusive, where RAND_MAX is a constant defined in <stdlib.h>. One way of obtaining random integers in a reduced range is to compute

```
rand() / (RAND_MAX / n + 1)
```

which returns integers less than n, that is, from 0 to n-1, inclusive. (This method gives good results as long as n is much less than RAND_MAX. Note, however, that RAND_MAX might be as small as 32,767.)

srand
```
void srand(unsigned int seed)
```

srand seeds the random number generator used by rand with the value seed. By default, a C program starts out as if the equivalent of srand(1) had been performed; that is, the sequence returned by repeated calls to rand will be the same for each run of the program. To achieve more truly random behavior, a program can call srand with a random seed value (perhaps derived from the time of day or a process ID). A single call to srand usually suffices for each run of the program; one simple invocation is

```
srand(time((time_t *)NULL));
```

(See section 3.10.6.1 for a discussion of the time function.)

3.10.4.4. Sorting and Searching

qsort
```
void qsort(void *a, size_t n, size_t elsize, int (*cmpfunc)())
```

qsort sorts the array a, according to an ordering relation defined by the function pointed to by cmpfunc. The array is of n elements, each of size elsize. To determine whether two elements are in order, qsort calls *cmpfunc, passing pointers to the two elements. The comparison function must therefore accept two generic void * pointers and convert them to pointers to the actual data type being sorted before comparing them. The comparison function must be declared as

```
int name(const void *p1, const void *p2)
```

and must return an integer less than, equal to, or greater than 0 according to whether the element pointed to by p1 is less than, equal to, or greater than that pointed to by p2, respectively. (Strictly speaking, then, qsort's fourth parameter is declared as int (*cmpfunc)(const void *, const void *).)

For example, to sort an array of strings represented by char * pointers, the following comparison function could be used:

```
int pstrcmp(const void *p1, const void *p2)
{
        const char *s1 = *(const char **)p1;
        const char *s2 = *(const char **)p2;
        return strcmp(s1, s2);
}
```

strcmp cannot be used directly as a qsort comparison function in this case because it compares pointers to char, whereas the qsort comparison function is passed pointers to the elements being compared, or in this case, pointers to pointers to char.

bsearch
```
bsearch(const void *key, const void *a, size_t n, size_t elsize,
        int (*cmpfunc)())
```

bsearch performs a binary search on the sorted array a, searching for an element matching the one pointed to by key. The array is of n elements, each of size elsize (as is the element pointed to by key, of course). The search is directed by a caller-supplied function pointed to by cmpfunc. cmpfunc's specification is the same as described for qsort. (In fact, qsort with the same cmpfunc is often used to sort the array prior to calling bsearch.)

3.10.4.5. Interaction with the Environment

getenv
```
char *getenv(const char *name)
```

getenv searches an implementation-defined set of environment variables for one with the given name and returns its value as a string. If no such variable can be found, getenv returns a null pointer.

exit
```
void exit(int status)
```

A call to exit requests normal termination of a program. Functions registered by atexit are called, open streams are flushed and closed, and the supplied status is returned to the operating system or other caller as the exit status of the program, just as if that same status had been returned from the initial invocation of main (see section 3.9.2). The two defined exit status values are EXIT_SUCCESS and EXIT_FAILURE. By convention, a value of 0 is also recognized as successful. The interpretation of other exit status values is implementation defined. By definition, the exit function does not return.

atexit
```
int atexit(void (*func)(void))
```

atexit arranges that the function pointed to by func be called at normal program exit (after return from main or after a call to exit). atexit returns 0 if the function is successfully registered for execution and nonzero otherwise (which should only happen if the limit of 32 registered functions is exceeded). If several functions are registered, they are called in the reverse order of their registration.

system
```
int system(const char *s)
```

system presents the string s to the underlying system's command processor for execution. The results are obviously entirely system-dependent, but the intent is that the command string be executed, and that its exit status be returned as system's return value.

abort
```
void abort(void)
```

The abort function requests immediate, unsuccessful termination of the program, as if by calling raise(SIGABRT) (see section 3.10.7.2).

3.10.4.6. Integer Arithmetic Functions

abs, labs
```
int abs(int x)   long int abs(long int x)
```

Both functions return the absolute value of their arguments.

div, ldiv
```
div_t div(int num, int denom)
ldiv_t div(long int num, long int denom)
```

These functions perform division, with two advantages over the built-in / and % operators. First, both a quotient and remainder are computed at once, in one operation. Second, the results are well defined if the numerator or denominator is negative: The quotient is rounded toward 0, and the remainder is therefore negative if num and denom differ in sign.

div's return value is of type

```
typedef struct
       {
       int quot, rem;
       } div_t;
```

(although the members may be in either order). ldiv's return type is similar, with both members having type long int.

3.10.4.7. Multibyte Character and String Functions

These functions all manipulate multibyte character sequences, which are implementation-defined (and potentially locale-specific) ways of encoding strings of wide characters (that is, arrays of elements of type wchar_t) as sequences of bytes, so that they can be manipulated as ordinary strings. Multibyte character strings are useful because they can save space, and because they can be defined (again, in a locale-specific way) so as to be compatible with existing schemes for encoding multinational characters (e.g., in text files and the like). The support for wide characters and multibyte character sequences in <stdlib.h> is limited; see section 3.10.17 for a description of the expanded functionality defined by NA1.

mblen
      int mblen(const char *s, size_t n)

mblen counts the number of characters in the string pointed to by s that form a valid multibyte character and returns that number. At most, n bytes pointed to by s are examined.

mbtowc, wctomb
      int mbtowc(wchar_t *dest, const char *src, size_t n)
      int wctomb(char *dest, wchar_t src)

These functions convert multibyte character sequences representing single wide characters to and from individual values of type wchar_t. mbtowc examines at most n bytes in the string pointed to by src and converts them, if possible, to a wide character that it stores in *dest, returning the number of characters read from src if this conversion was possible and -1 otherwise. wctomb converts the single wide character value src to a multibyte character sequence that it writes to dest, returning the number of bytes written. (This number will never be greater than MB_CUR_MAX, a constant defined in <stdlib.h>.)

mbstowcs, wcstombs
      size_t mbstowcs(wchar_t *dest, const char *src, size_t n)
      size_t wcstombs(char *dest, wchar_t src)

These functions convert multibyte character sequences representing multiple wide characters to and from strings of type wchar_t *. mbstowcs converts a multibyte character sequence pointed to by src into wide characters that it stores into dest, writing no more than n wide characters. wcstombs performs the opposite conversion, reading wide characters from src and building a multibyte character sequence in dest (but without writing more than n characters). Both functions stop early if a null character is encountered. In both cases, the return value is the number of items (wide characters or characters, respectively, exclusive of the null character) written to dest.

3.10.5. <math.h>

The header <math.h> defines the usual collection of mathematical functions. For historical reasons, on some systems, the math functions must be explicitly requested at link time (on UNIX systems by including -lm at the end of the command line).

3.10.5.1. Square Root, Exponent, and Logarithmic Functions

```
double sqrt(double x)
double pow(double x, double y)
double exp(double x)
double log(double x)
double log10(double x)
```

pow computes x raised to the power y, although it is often implemented using logarithmic identities, and so may not give the expected result if x and y are both integers. exp(x) computes e to the power x. log computes the natural (base e) logarithm; log10 computes the base 10 logarithm.

3.10.5.2. Trigonometric Functions

```
double sin(double x)
double cos(double x)
double tan(double x)
double asin(double x)
double acos(double x)
double atan(double x)
double atan2(double y, double x)
```

These functions all operate on (or return) angles in radians. atan2(y, x) is equivalent to atan(y / x) except that it returns an angle with a sign appropriate for all four quadrants of a rectangular-to-polar conversion, and works correctly if x is 0.

3.10.5.3. Hyperbolic Functions

```
double sinh(double x)
double cosh(double x)
double tanh(double x)
```

These three functions all perform hyperbolic trigonometry.

3.10.5.4. Absolute Value and Nearest-Integer Functions

```
double fabs(double x)
double ceil(double x)
double floor(double x)
```

fabs(x) returns the absolute value of x. ceil(x) returns (as a double) the smallest integer not less than x. Similarly, floor(x) returns the largest integer not greater than x.

3.10.5.5. Other Functions

```
double fmod(double x, double y)
double modf(double x, double *iptr)
double frexp(double x, int *ip)
double ldexp(double x, int exponent)
```

fmod returns the remainder when x is divided by y. modf breaks x into integer and fractional parts, storing the integer part (as a double) in *iptr and returning the fractional part. frexp splits x into its base-2 floating-point mantissa and exponent, storing the exponent in *ip and returning the mantissa. ldexp builds a floating-point number from a mantissa and base-2 exponent. For example, frexp(2.5, &i) would return 0.625 (which is 0.101 base 2) and set i to 2, and ldexp(0.625, 2) would reconstruct the value 2.5.

3.10.6. <time.h>

The header <time.h> defines several functions for dealing with dates and times. Many of these functions work with the abstract type time_t, a typedef for an arithmetic type capable of representing a date/time stamp. Note that no particular size or representation for type time_t is mandated by the C standard. Many systems implement time_t as a long integer representing the number of seconds since the beginning of January 1, 1970, but this representation is not universal.

Several other functions work with a structure that contains individual date and time components. That structure is declared somewhat as follows:

```
struct tm
         { int tm_sec;      /* 0..61 */
         int tm_min;        /* 0..59 */
         int tm_hour;       /* 0..23 */
         int tm_mday;       /* 1..31 */
         int tm_mon;        /* 0..11 */
         int tm_year;
         int tm_wday;       /* 0..6 */
         int tm_yday;       /* 0..365 */
         int tm_isdst;
         };
```

A particular implementation may add additional fields to this structure, and the fields are not necessarily in the preceding order. The ranges of several of the members are as indicated in the comments. `tm_sec` is allowed to range above 59 to accommodate the possibility of leap seconds. `tm_mon` contains 0 for January, 11 for December. `tm_year` contains the year minus 1900; it will contain the value 100 in the year 2000. `tm_wday` contains 0 for Sunday, 6 for Saturday. `tm_yday` contains 0 for January 1, 364 or 365 for December 31. `tm_isdst` contains 0 if Daylight Saving Time is not in effect, a positive value if it is in effect, and a negative value if DST information is unknown.

Several of these functions attempt to make distinctions between local time and UTC (Coordinated Universal Time, also known as GMT), or to account for Daylight Saving Time, but the information required for making these corrections is not always available from the underlying operating system.

3.10.6.1. `time`
```
time_t time(time_t *tp)
```

`time` returns a `time_t` value representing the current date and time. If `tp` is non-null, the same value is stored in `*tp`.

3.10.6.2. `localtime, gmtime`
```
struct tm *localtime(const time_t *t)
struct tm *gmtime(const time_t *t)
```

`localtime` builds a `tm` structure representing the local time corresponding to the time value `t`. `gmtime` does the same thing, if possible, but building a UTC representation. Note that the `time_t` value is passed by reference. The return pointer is to a static structure that is overwritten by each call, or is a null pointer if the conversion is impossible (e.g., if time zone information for UTC conversion is not available).

3.10.6.3. `ctime, asctime`
```
char *ctime(const time_t *t)
char *asctime(const struct tm *tp)
```

These functions construct a human-readable string corresponding to a date and time. The string is of the form
```
Tue Oct 28 07:50:28 1997\n\0
```

(and is therefore equivalent to calling `strftime` with the format string `"%a %b %m %H:%M:%S %Y\n"`). `asctime` builds the string from the information in the `tm` structure pointed to by `tp`. `ctime` builds the string from the `time_t` value pointed to by `t`; it is equivalent to `asctime(localtime(t))`. The return pointer is to a static string that is overwritten by each call.

3.10.6.4. mktime
```
time_t mktime(struct tm *tp)
```

`mktime` attempts to compute the `time_t` value corresponding to the local date and time represented by the `tm` structure pointed to by `tp`. The date is determined by `tm_mon` and `tm_mday`; `tm_wday` and `tm_yday` are ignored on input. If `tm_isdst` is negative, `mktime` attempts to determine whether DST will or would have applied on the given date, and act accordingly; if `tm_isdst` is positive or zero, the caller is asserting that the given time does or does not have a DST offset applied, respectively. If any of `tm_sec`, `tm_min`, `tm_hour`, `tm_mday`, or `tm_mon` has a value outside the expected range, `mktime` normalizes them in the process of computing a date (and also adjusts their values in `*tp`). For example, 25:70 on January 32 is converted to 2:10 on February 2. Finally, appropriate values of `tm_wday` and `tm_yday` are set in `*tp`. The return value is the converted `time_t` value, or -1 if the conversion is impossible (e.g., the date represented by the `tm` structure is outside the range representable by a `time_t`).

`mktime`'s defined handling of non-normalized dates makes it useful for performing simple calendar calculations. For example, to add `n` days to a date, it is often sufficient to store the date in a `tm` structure, increment `tm_mday` by `n`, call `mktime`, and read the corrected date out of the `tm` structure.

3.10.6.5. difftime
```
double difftime(time_t t1, time_t t2)
```

`difftime` computes the difference between two `time_t` values and returns the result `t1 - t2` as a number of seconds. It is useful for performing portable date calculations in spite of the implementation-defined encoding of `time_t` values.

3.10.6.6. clock
```
clock_t clock(void)
```

The `clock` function deals with yet a third representation of time, namely processor clock ticks, of potentially subsecond resolution. `clock` is supposed to return the number of processor ticks that have elapsed since the program began execution. The frequency of the clock ticks measured by `clock` is system dependent, but the macro `CLOCKS_PER_SEC` is defined such that a `clock_t` value, divided by `CLOCKS_PER_SEC`, yields the elapsed time in seconds. (Of course, it is also possible that the `clock_t` value, whatever its underlying type is, will have overflowed during the execution of a long-running program.)

3.10.6.7. `strftime`

```
size_t strftime(char *buf, size_t bufsize,
         const char *fmt, const struct tm *tp)
```

`strftime` performs flexible formatting of the date and time represented by the `tm` structure pointed to by `tp`, under control of the `fmt` string. Like `printf`, characters from the `fmt` string are copied through to the output, except for `%` characters, which request insertion of certain values. Like `sprintf`, the output is copied to a user-supplied character array pointed to by `buf`. Unlike `sprintf`, the size of this buffer is specified by the `bufsize` argument so that `strftime` can guarantee not to overflow it.

The format specifiers and their resulting output (and, where relevant, the corresponding member in `struct tm`) are as follow. The format specifiers must appear as shown; no `printf`-like flags or width specifiers are supported. Many of the output values are locale specific (see section 3.10.9).

`%a`	The weekday name (from `tm_wday`) as a three-character abbreviation
`%A`	The full weekday name (from `tm_wday`)
`%b`	The month name (from `tm_mon`) as a three-character abbreviation
`%B`	The full month name (from `tm_mon`)
`%c`	A complete (implementation- and locale-specific) date and time representation
`%d`	The day of the month (`tm_mday`)
`%H`	The hour (`tm_hour`) on a 24-hour clock
`%I`	The hour (from `tm_hour`) on a 12-hour clock
`%j`	The day of the year (from `tm_yday`), 1-based
`%m`	The month (from `tm_mon`), as a 1-based, two-digit number
`%M`	The minute (`tm_min`)
`%p`	An AM/PM string (from `tm_hour`)
`%S`	The second (`tm_sec`)
`%U`	The week number, where the first Sunday of the year begins week 1

%w   The day of the week (tm_wday), as a number (0 = Sunday)

%W   The week number, where the first Monday of the year begins week 1

%x   A complete (implementation- and locale-specific) date representation

%X   A complete (implementation- and locale-specific) time representation

%y   The last two digits of the year (from tm_year)

%Y   The year (from tm_year) as a four-digit number

%Z   The time zone name, if available; otherwise nothing

%%   A single % character

strftime returns the number of characters written to buf, or 0 if the given bufsize was too small to write the complete output (including the terminating \0).

3.10.7. <signal.h>

The header <signal.h> declares two functions for dealing with asynchronous interrupts or "signals." There are several possible signals, identified by integer constants, for which this header defines symbolic names:

SIGABRT   The signal generated by the abort function.

SIGFPE   A signal generated by math errors, such as divide by 0. (The spelling FPE is historical, and once stood for "floating-point exception," although the signal can occur for integer exceptions as well.)

SIGILL   A signal generated due to attempts to execute illegal instructions.

SIGINT   A signal generated by a keyboard interrupt (e.g., control-C).

SIGSEGV   A signal generated by memory access violations ("segmentation violations").

SIGTERM   A signal generated when the process is terminated by some external agent.

Many implementations define additional signal values.

3.10.7.1. signal
```
void (*signal(int sig, void (*func)(int)))(int)
```

The signal function is used to specify the action that should be taken when a signal is received. By default, all signals terminate the program, but by calling signal, the program can arrange to ignore the signal, or to have it handled by transferring control to a specified function.

sig is the signal to be handled, that is, one of the SIGxxx constants. func is either the manifest constant SIG_IGN (which requests that the signal be ignored), the constant SIG_DFL (which requests that the default handling be restored), or a pointer to a user-supplied function that is to be called when the function is received. The function should be a void function accepting one int parameter and will be called with the signal number as that parameter.

If func is a function to be called, it is implementation defined whether further instances of signal sig are somehow blocked while the function is executing, or whether the equivalent of signal(sig, SIG_DFL) is performed (that is, resetting the signal to its default action) before the function begins executing.

The signal function returns the previous disposition of the signal, whether SIG_DFL, SIG_IGN, or a function pointer. signal's declaration is therefore complex: It is a function returning a pointer to a function (a function that takes one int parameter and returns void), and its second argument is also a pointer to a function (again, one that takes one int parameter and returns void).

For example, here is a code fragment which arranges that a function exithandler be called if the interrupt signal is received, but only if that signal was not already being ignored:

```
extern void exithandler(int);
if(signal(SIGINT, SIG_IGN) != SIG_IGN)
        signal(SIGINT, exithandler);
```

3.10.7.2. raise
```
int raise(int sig)
```

The raise function sends the specified signal to the current program.

3.10.8. <setjmp.h>
The functions declared in the header <setjmp.h> allow a program to perform nonlocal jumps, achieving the approximate result of a goto between functions.

Nonlocal jumps do not use static labels, as gotos do; instead, the program calls a function (setjmp) at a point which it wishes to be able to jump to later. The "context" at this point is stashed away in an object of type jmp_buf. jmp_buf is an opaque type, although for historical reasons it is constrained to be an array type. Because a later jump to this saved spot is performed by unwinding the function call stack, these jumps must always be initiated somewhere in the calling hierarchy at or beneath the function that called setjmp.

3.10.8.1. setjmp
```
int setjmp(jmp_buf context)
```

setjmp saves the program's current location in the supplied context object and returns 0. Later, if longjmp is called with the same context object, it will appear that setjmp had returned with a nonzero value.

3.10.8.2. longjmp
```
void longjmp(jmp_buf context, int retval)
```

longjmp causes an immediate jump back to a context previously saved by setjmp. The jump is performed by unwinding the function-call stack, so the function that called setjmp must still be active (that is, the function calling longjmp must generally be a descendant of the function that called setjmp).

As the long jump completes, it will appear to the jumped-to function as if its prior call to setjmp has returned again, this time with the value retval. That function should not rely on any of its other variables, however, as it is difficult to say whether they will have their values as of the initial call to setjmp or as of the call to the function that eventually called longjmp.

3.10.9. <locale.h>
The header <locale.h> declares two functions that provide some support for localization issues. The notion is that there is some global state that guides certain locale-specific processing such as choice of decimal-point character, collating sequences, and so on. By default, a program starts out in the "C" locale, but a program can switch itself over to the user's preferred locale setting by calling the setlocale function. Furthermore, the locale-specific information is separated into several categories, and it is possible to select different locale settings for different categories.

3.10.9.1. setlocale
```
char *setlocale(int cat, const char *locale)
```

setlocale requests that locale-specific settings for the given locale be instituted. The parameter cat specifies the category of settings that should be affected. The categories are all known by symbolic constants, which affect the following areas of functionality:

LC_COLLATE	String comparison as performed by strcoll and strxfrm
LC_CTYPE	The character-classification functions in <ctype.h>
LC_MONETARY	The currency-related settings that are available through the localeconv function
LC_NUMERIC	The decimal-point character used by printf, scanf, strtod, and so on.
LC_TIME	The locale-specific formats of the strftime function
LC_ALL	The union of all the above settings

The set of available locales is, of course, locale specific and implementation defined. A locale value of "C" reverts to the default C language settings. A value of "" (the empty string) requests an implementation's or installation's locale-specific default. A null pointer value for locale does not change any settings at all. Any other values have meanings defined by a particular implementation or installation.

The return value is a pointer to a string representing the previous locale setting; the previous setting may therefore be restored by passing the returned string as the locale argument in a future call to setlocale. If setlocale is called with a null pointer as the locale argument, a pointer to a string representing the current setting is returned, without changing the current setting.

3.10.9.2. localeconv
```
struct lconv *localeconv(void)
```

The localeconv function returns a pointer to a structure containing locale-specific information, all of which is a function of the currently selected locale (perhaps as set by setlocale). With the exception of the nonmonetary decimal-point character, all of this information is advisory only; no standard C library functions make use of this information. The structure is defined somewhat as follows (although the members are not required to be in this order):

```
struct lconv
    {
    char *decimal_point;
    char *thousands_sep;
    char *grouping;
    char *int_curr_symbol;
    char *currency_symbol;
    char *mon_decimal_point;
    char *mon_thousands_sep;
    char *mon_grouping;
    char *positive_sign, *negative_sign;
    char int_frac_digits;
    char frac_digits;
    char p_cs_precedes, p_sep_by_space;
    char n_cs_precedes, n_sep_by_space;
    char p_sign_posn, n_sign_posn;
    };
```

decimal_point is the decimal point character used in ordinary numeric quantities (e.g., by printf). thousands_sep is a separator that could be used between groups of digits in large numbers; grouping is a "string" that defines the size of the groups. The string "\3" (that is, consisting of the character with value 3) would indicate repeating groups of three digits; it is also possible to indicate nonrepeating groups.

The remaining members describe (in some detail) the formatting of monetary quantities. Briefly, int_curr_symbol and currency_symbol are versions (international and local) of the local currency symbol, mon_decimal_point is the decimal point, mon_thousands_sep and mon_grouping describe the grouping (analogously to thousands_sep and grouping), positive_sign and negative_sign are sign indicators, int_frac_digits and frac_digits are the number of fractional digits to display, and the remaining values are flags controlling the arrangement of the currency symbol and sign indicator.

3.10.10. <stdarg.h>

The facilities (most of which are macros) in the header <stdarg.h> provide mechanisms that permit functions accepting a varying number of arguments (such as printf) to access those arguments.

The access mechanism revolves around an argument pointer, a descriptor used to manipulate the variable-length argument list. This descriptor is of the abstract type va_list. Facilities exist for initializing this descriptor, fetching arguments, and disposing of the descriptor. The calling function must know the expected type of each argument as it fetches it; there are no facilities for querying the type or number of arguments actually supplied during a particular call.

3.10.10.1. va_start
```
va_start(va_list argp, lastarg)
```

va_start initializes argp so that it can begin accessing variable arguments. lastarg is the name of the last of the function's fixed arguments.

3.10.10.2. va_arg
```
va_arg(va_list argp, argtype)
```

va_arg fetches a value of type argtype as the next argument from the variable-length argument list accessed by argp. argtype is specified by using the same sort of type name (base type plus optional identifierless declarator) as is used in type casts and sizeof expressions. The specified type must be the type of the corresponding argument actually passed, after the default argument promotions (see section 3.5.3) have been applied; it is the function's responsibility to know the type somehow. (printf, for example, determines the expected type of each argument by parsing the format string.)

3.10.10.3. va_end
```
va_end(va_list argp)
```

va_end indicates that the calling function is finished with variable-length argument processing. va_list must be called so that the variable-length argument machinery can reclaim any resources or otherwise clean up.

As an example of the use of the <stdarg.h> macros, here is a stripped-down implementation of printf. (It cheats and calls on sprintf to do its actual numeric formatting. See section 3.10.1.6 for a description of sprintf.)

```
#include <stdio.h>
#include <stdarg.h>

void miniprintf(const char *fmt, ...)
{
        va_list argp;
        const char *p;
        char tmpbuf[25];
        int i;

        va_start(argp, fmt);
        for(p = fmt; *p != '\0'; p++)
                {
                if(*p != '%')
                        {
                        putchar(*p);
                        continue;
                        }
```

```
switch(*++p)
{
case 'c':
    i = va_arg(argp, int); putchar(i);
    break;
case 'd':
    i = va_arg(argp, int);
    sprintf(tmpbuf, "%d", i); fputs(tmpbuf, stdout);
    break;
case 'o':
    i = va_arg(argp, int);
    sprintf(tmpbuf, "%o", i);
    fputs(tmpbuf, stdout);
    break;
case 's':
    fputs(va_arg(argp, char *), stdout);
    break;
case 'x':
    i = va_arg(argp, int);
    sprintf(tmpbuf, "%x", i); fputs(tmpbuf, stdout);
    break;
case '%':
    putchar('%');
    break;
}
}
va_end(argp);
}
```

For another example, see section 3.10.1.7.

3.10.11. <stddef.h>

The header `<stddef.h>` defines several types and macros. The types have definitions that vary from compiler to compiler but, if used with care, can result in more portable programs.

NULL   A macro expanding to a null pointer constant (generally `0` or `(void *)0`).

size_t   An unsigned integral type used for representing the sizes of objects (as computed by `sizeof` and functions such as `strlen`, and passed to functions such as `malloc`, `strncat`, and `fwrite`).

ptrdiff_t A signed integral type that is the result of pointer subtraction.

wchar_t A wide character type that may have more range than plain `char`, used for holding values in extended or multinational character sets. See also section 3.10.17.

offsetof() A macro that computes the byte offset of a member in a structure, as in `offsetof(struct tm, tm_year)`.

3.10.12. <assert.h>

<assert.h> defines one macro, assert, which is used to document (and test) runtime assertions.

```
void assert(int e)
```

The value e is any expression that the programmer asserts will be true as long as the program is functioning correctly. Should the expression ever evaluate as false, it is assumed to represent a serious programming error, and the program is aborted with a message indicating that the assertion failed.

Assertions should be used to detect "can't happen" situations during software development, not to detect expected error conditions such as end-of-file, file not found, out of memory, and so on.

If the macro NDEBUG is defined (with any value) when <assert.h> is included, assertions are suppressed. (This macro might be defined when building a production version of a program, for example, if it were felt that the "can't happen" conditions in that version truly couldn't happen.)

3.10.13. <errno.h>

<errno.h> declares the global errno in which is stored a code representing the specific reason for failure of certain library functions. (errno is set to a meaningful value only when certain library functions fail; the value is generally not meaningful otherwise.) errno can be thought of as a global variable, but it may be a macro with a clever expansion that allows distinct per-thread error codes in a threaded environment. Also defined in <errno.h> are symbolic constants for the error codes. The only error codes specified in the C standard are EDOM and ERANGE, indicating domain and range errors, respectively, for the functions in <math.h>. Most implementations define several additional error values.

3.10.14. <limits.h>

The header <limits.h> defines several macros that indicate the ranges of various types under a particular implementation. The macros are as follow:

SCHAR_MIN	SCHAR_MAX	UCHAR_MAX
CHAR_MIN	CHAR_MAX	
SHRT_MIN	SHRT_MAX	USHRT_MAX
INT_MIN	INT_MAX	UINT_MAX
LONG_MIN	LONG_MAX	ULONG_MAX
CHAR_BIT	MB_LEN_MAX	

The various MIN and MAX macros define the minimum and maximum values of the character and integer types, both signed and unsigned. CHAR_BIT is the number of bits in a char. MB_LEN_MAX is the maximum number of bytes in a single multibyte character sequence.

3.10.15. <float.h>

The header <float.h> defines several macros that describe the machine's floating-point representation(s). The macros are as follow:

FLT_RADIX	FLT_ROUNDS	
FLT_MANT_DIG	DBL_MANT_DIG	LDBL_MANT_DIG
FLT_DIG	DBL_DIG	LDBL_DIG
FLT_MIN_EXP	DBL_MIN_EXP	LDBL_MIN_EXP
FLT_MIN_10_EXP	DBL_MIN_10_EXP	LDBL_MIN_10_EXP
FLT_MAX_EXP	DBL_MAX_EXP	LDBL_MAX_EXP
FLT_MAX_10_EXP	DBL_MAX_10_EXP	LDBL_MAX_10_EXP
FLT_MAX	DBL_MAX	LDBL_MAX
FLT_EPSILON	DBL_EPSILON	LDBL_EPSILON
FLT_MIN	DBL_MIN	LDBL_MIN

FLT_RADIX is the underlying radix of the floating-point model. FLT_ROUNDS is a constant indicating the rounding model for floating-point addition: 0 if toward 0, 1 if to nearest, 2 if toward $+\infty$, 3 if toward $-\infty$, and -1 if indeterminate. The remaining macros give the properties of the types float, double, and long double. The MANT_DIG macros give the number of digits (base FLT_RADIX) in the mantissa. The DIG macros give the approximate number of equivalent base-10 digits of precision. The MIN_EXP and MAX_EXP macros give the minimum and maximum exponents, respectively, and the MIN_10_EXP and MAX_10_EXP give their approximate base-10 equivalents. The MIN and MAX macros give the minimum and maximum representable values, and the EPSILON values give the difference between 1.0 and the next larger representable number.

3.10.16. <iso646.h>

The header <iso646.h> simply defines a few macros that make it easier to write C programs on machines with restricted character sets. (It is a new header, introduced in NA1; it may not be present in all compilers.) The macro definitions are as follow:

```
#define and    &&
#define and_eq &=
#define bitand &
```

```
#define bitor |
#define compl ~
#define not !
#define not_eq !=
#define or ||
#define or_eq |=
#define xor ^
#define xor_eq ^=
```

3.10.17. <wchar.h>

This header provides companion functions for nearly all of the character- and string-related functions in the rest of the standard library, tailored for use with wide characters, that is, values of type wchar_t. <wchar.h> is a new header, introduced in NA1; it and its functions may not be present in all compilers.

Besides the wchar_t type itself and several other types and macros, this header defines a new type, wint_t, which is an integral type capable of holding all values of type wchar_t and the wide character end-of-file value, WEOF (also defined here). In other words, wint_t plays the same role (with respect to wchar_t) in functions such as wgetchar and iswalpha as int does (with respect to char) in getchar and isalpha.

Besides enlarging the set of functions available for working with wide characters, wide character strings, and multibyte character sequences, this header introduces functions for performing input and output on wide characters, with the assumption that the file or stream being read or written is composed of multibyte character sequences. In other words, as wide characters are read from or written to streams, implicit conversions from and to multibyte character sequences may be performed. Such I/O may entail partial conversions of multibyte character sequences, implying that some state pertaining to the in-progress conversion must be saved. To save this state, a type mbstate_t is defined; an mbstate_t object is potentially associated with each I/O stream, and new conversion functions are provided (see section 3.10.17.7) to accept explicit mbstate_t parameters and allow more flexibility when performing interrupted conversions. (Objects of type mbstate_t are opaque, except that it is possible to learn whether they are in their "initial state." It is also possible to reset an mbstate_t object to its initial state by assigning to it the value of a statically allocated, default-initialized, and thus 0-valued mbstate_t object.)

See sections 3.10.4.7 and 3.10.18 for information on other wide and multibyte character functions.

3.10.17.1. Wide String Functions

```
size_t wcslen(const wchar_t *s)
wchar_t *wcscpy(wchar_t *dest, const wchar_t *src)
wchar_t *wcscat(wchar_t *dest, const wchar_t *src)
wchar_t *wcsncpy(wchar_t *dest, const wchar_t *src, size_t n)
wchar_t *wcsncat(wchar_t *dest, const wchar_t *src, size_t n)
int wcscmp(const wchar_t *s1, const wchar_t *s2)
int wcsncmp(const wchar_t *s1, const wchar_t *s2, size_t n)
int wcscoll(const wchar_t *s1, const wchar_t *s2)
size_t wcsxfrm(wchar_t *dest, const wchar_t *src, size_t n)
wchar_t *wcschr(const wchar_t *s, wchar_t c)
wchar_t *wcsrchr(const wchar_t *s, wchar_t c)
wchar_t *wcsstr(const wchar_t *s, const wchar_t *pat)
size_t wcsspn(const wchar_t *s, const wchar_t *set)
size_t wcscspn(const wchar_t *s, const wchar_t *set)
wchar_t *wcspbrk(const wchar_t *s, const wchar_t *set)
```

These functions all perform analogous operations to those in sections 3.10.2.1 to 3.10.2.4, except that they work with strings of (that is, arrays of or pointers to) type wchar_t instead of char. Each function wcs*xxx* performs a function analogous to str*xxx*. For example, wcscpy copies a string of wide characters from src to dest. Where a character count parameter n appears, it is interpreted as a number of wide characters.

3.10.17.2. Operations on Blocks of Wide Characters

```
wchar_t *wmemcpy(wchar_t *dest, const wchar_t *src, size_t n)
wchar_t *wmemmove(wchar_t *dest, const wchar_t *src, size_t n)
int wmemcmp(const wchar_t *p1, const wchar_t *p2, size_t n)
wchar_t *wmemchr(const wchar_t *p, wchar_t c, size_t n)
wchar_t *wmemset(wchar_t *p, wchar_t c, size_t n)
```

These functions all perform analogous operations to those in section 3.10.2.5, except that they work with blocks of wide characters instead of characters. Each function wmem*xxx* performs a function analogous to mem*xxx*, with n interpreted as a number of wide characters.

3.10.17.3. Wide String Numeric Conversions

```
long int wcstol(const wchar_t *s, wchar_t **endp, int base)
unsigned long int wcstoul(const wchar_t *s, wchar_t **endp, int base)
double wcstod(const wchar_t *s, wchar_t **endp)
```

These functions all perform analogous operations to those in section 3.10.4.2, except that they work with strings of type wchar_t instead of char. Each function wcs*xxx* performs a function analogous to str*xxx*.

3.10.17.4. Wide String Time Conversion

```
size_t wcsftime(wchar_t *buf, size_t bufsize,
        const wchar_t *fmt, const struct tm *tp)
```

wcsftime performs the analogous operation to strftime (see section 3.10.6.7) except that the format string fmt, destination buffer buf, and destination buffer size bufsize all involve wide characters.

3.10.17.5. Wide String Tokenization
```
wchar_t *wcstok(wchar_t *s, const wchar_t *sep, wchar_t **state)
```

wcstok performs the analogous operation to strtok (see section 3.10.2.6) except that the string being split (s), the string of separator characters (sep), and the return value are all strings of wide characters. The third argument, state, is a pointer to a caller-supplied object of type wchar_t *; wcstok uses this object to save its state between calls, and so does not suffer the nonreentrancy that strtok does.

3.10.17.6. Wide String Input and Output

getwchar, getwc, fgetwc
```
wint_t getwchar(void)
wint_t getwc(FILE *fp)
wint_t fgetwc(FILE *fp)
```

These functions read wide characters, either from standard input or the stream fp, implicitly converting from multibyte character sequences as if by calling mbrtowc. WEOF is returned on end-of-file. The functions are otherwise equivalent to getchar, getc, and fgetc, as described in section 3.10.1.2.

putwchar, putwc, fputwc
```
wint_t putwchar(wchar_t c)
wint_t putwc(wchar_t c, FILE *fp)
wint_t fputwc(wchar_t c, FILE *fp)
```

These functions write wide characters, either to standard output or the stream fp, implicitly converting to multibyte character sequences as if by calling wcrtomb. The functions are otherwise equivalent to putchar, putc, and fputc, as described in section 3.10.1.2.

wprintf, fwprintf
```
int wprintf(const wchar_t *, ...)
int fwprintf(FILE *fp, const wchar_t *, ...)
```

These functions are equivalent to printf and fprintf (see section 3.10.1.2) except that the format string fmt is of wide characters, and the stream being written (either stdout or fp) is treated as a multibyte character sequence, as if by calling fputwc. In the format string, the %c and %s specifiers continue to expect parameters that are simple character values and strings of char, respectively. To print wide characters or strings of wide characters, use the new specifiers %lc and %ls.

wscanf, fwscanf
```
int wscanf(const wchar_t *, ...)
int fwscanf(FILE *fp, const wchar_t *, ...)
```

These functions are equivalent to scanf and fscanf (see section 3.10.1.2) except that the format string fmt is of wide characters, and the stream being read (either stdin or fp) is treated as a multibyte character sequence, as if by calling fgetwc. In the format string, the %c, %s, and %[specifiers read wide characters but store them, as if by calling wcrtomb, to char * arguments. To read wide characters or strings as wide characters (that is, to wchar_t * arguments), use the new specifiers %lc, %ls, and %l[.

fgetws, fputws
```
wchar_t *fgetws(wchar_t *, int, FILE *fp)
int fputws(const wchar_t *, FILE *fp)
```

These functions read or write lines of text, analogously to the fgets and fputs functions of section 3.10.1.2, except that wide characters are read or written, as if by calling fgetwc or fputwc.

ungetwc
```
wint_t ungetwc(wint_t c, FILE *fp)
```

ungetwc pushes the wide character c back on the input stream fp, analogously to ungetc (see section 3.10.1.2).

swprintf, swscanf
```
int swprintf(wchar_t *buf, size_t bufsize, const wchar_t *fmt, ...)
int swscanf(const wchar_t *buf, const wchar_t *fmt, ...)
```

These functions generate or scan formatted strings under control of their fmt arguments, analogously to the sprintf and sscanf functions of section 3.10.1.6, except that both the format strings and the strings read or written are of wide characters. Also, swprintf accepts a bufsize argument that is the size of the array pointed to by buf (in units of wide characters), so it can ensure that the array bounds will not be exceeded. See also section 3.10.17.6.

vwprintf, vfwprintf, vswprintf
```
int vwprintf(const wchar_t *fmt, va_list argp)
int vfwprintf(FILE *fp, const wchar_t *fmt, va_list argp)
int vswprintf(wchar_t *buf, size_t bufsize,
                      const wchar_t *fmt, va_list argp)
```

These functions are analogous to those of section 3.10.1.7, except that they work with wide character strings, along the lines of `wprintf`, `fwprintf`, and `swprintf`; see section 3.10.17.6. `vswprintf`'s `bufsize` argument is as for `swprintf` (see section 3.10.17.6).

fwide
```
int fwide(FILE *fp, int mode)
```

Each stdio stream has an "orientation" that reflects whether it is being used to read or write normal characters (using the functions of section 3.10.1) or multibyte characters (using the functions of this section). A stream starts out "unoriented" but is switched to either "byte-oriented" or "wide-oriented" upon the first input or output call. `fwide` attempts to set or reset the orientation of the stream `fp` to byte-oriented if `mode` is less than 0 or to wide-oriented if `mode` is greater than 0. The return value reflects the actual orientation of the stream after the call (where zero indicates unoriented).

3.10.17.7. More Wide String Conversion Functions
The functions here expand on those described in section 3.10.4.7.

btowc, wctob
```
wint_t btowc(int c)
int wctob(wint_t wc)
```

These functions convert between normal characters and their wide character equivalents. `btowc` converts the character `c` to the corresponding wide character. `wctob` attempts to convert the wide character `wc` to a normal character, returning either that character or `EOF` if the conversion is impossible.

mbrlen
```
size_t mbrlen(const char *s, size_t n, mbstate_t *state)
```

`mbrlen` is similar to `mblen` (see section 3.10.4.7) except that it can complete the computation of the length of an interrupted multibyte sequence, with the initial part reflected in the state object and the remaining part pointed to by `s`. The return value is as for `mbrtowc`.

mbrtowc, wcrtomb
```
size_t mbrtowc(wchar_t *dest, const char *src, size_t n,
                                            mbstate_t *state)
size_t wcrtomb(char *dest, wchar_t src, mbstate_t *state)
```

These functions are similar to mbtowc and wctomb (see section 3.10.4.7) except that they can work with multibyte sequences that have been interrupted, as long as the state of the conversion is accurately recorded in the object pointed to by state. mbrtowc converts a multibyte sequence at src to a wide character at dest and returns the number of bytes pointed to by src that form a valid multibyte character, or 0 if src points to a null multibyte character, or -1 if an encoding error is detected, or -2 if bytes have been read from src (and used to update *state) but no complete character has been found. wcrtomb converts the wide character src to a multibyte sequence at dest and returns the number of bytes written to dest, or -1 to indicate an encoding error.

mbsrtowcs, wcsrtombs
```
size_t mbsrtowcs(wchar_t *dest, const char **srcp, size_t n,
                                           mbstate_t *state)
size_t wcsrtombs(char *dest, const wchar_t **srcp, size_t n,
                                           mbstate_t *state)
```

These functions are similar to mbstowcs and wcstombs (see section 3.10.4.7) except that they can work with multibyte sequences that have been interrupted. The impending state of the conversion is recorded in the pointed-to object *state. The source string is passed by reference and is updated to point to the remaining unconverted string, if any. That is, if n is insufficient (as a number of wide characters for mbsrtowcs or bytes for wcsrtombs) for the destination buffer to contain the converted result, *srcp is set to point to the unconverted input, and *state is updated to reflect any interrupted conversion state.

mbsinit
```
int mbsinit(const mbstate_t *p)
```

mbsinit returns nonzero if the state object pointed to by p is in its initial state, or if p is a null pointer.

3.10.18. <wctype.h>

The header <wctype.h> declares several functions, analogous to those in <ctype.h> (see section 3.10.3) for classifying and converting wide characters, i.e., values of type wchar_t. <wctype.h> is a new header, introduced in NA1; it and its functions may not be present in all compilers. See section 3.10.17 for information on other wide character functions.

3.10.18.1. Wide Character Classification Functions

```
int iswupper(wint_t c)
int iswlower(wint_t c)
int iswalpha(wint_t c)
int iswdigit(wint_t c)
int iswalnum(wint_t c)
int iswxdigit(wint_t c)
int iswspace(wint_t c)
int iswpunct(wint_t c)
int iswprint(wint_t c)
int iswgraph(wint_t c)
int iswcntrl(wint_t c)
```

These functions all perform the same classification functions on wide characters as the correspondingly named functions of section 3.10.3.1 do on normal characters. The parameter type wint_t is related to wchar_t; see section 3.10.17 for a discussion.

3.10.18.2. Extended Wide Character Classification Functions

```
wctype_t wctype(const char *classname)
int iswctype(wint_t c, wctype_t classtok)
```

These functions permit new character classifications to be introduced without adding additional functions. wctype accepts a string classname indicating a character classification and returns a token that can be used for testing that classification. (The token type, wctype_t, is also defined in <wctype.h>.) iswctype accepts a wide character c and a token classtok previously returned by wctype, and returns nonzero if the character falls within the classification. wctype accepts the strings "upper", "lower", "alpha", "digit", "alnum", "xdigit", "space", "punct", "print", "graph", and "cntrl" (corresponding to the 11 predefined classifications), plus any implementation-defined classification strings an implementation chooses to provide.

3.10.18.3. Wide Character Conversion Functions

```
wint_t towupper(wint_t c)
wint_t towlower(wint_t c)
```

These functions perform the same conversion functions on wide characters as the correspondingly named functions of section 3.10.3.2 do on normal characters.

3.10.18.4. Extended Wide Character Conversion Functions

```
wctrans_t wctrans(const char *convname)
wint_t towctrans(wint_t c, wctrans_t convtok)
```

These functions permit new character conversions to be introduced without adding additional functions. wctrans accepts a string convname indicating a character conversion and returns a token that can be used for performing that conversion. (The token type, wctrans_t, is also defined in <wctype.h>.) towctrans accepts a wide character c and a token convtok previously returned by wctrans, and returns the appropriately converted wide character. wctrans accepts the strings "toupper" and "tolower" (corresponding to the two predefined classifications), plus any other conversion strings an implementation chooses to provide.

3.11. Acknowledgments

Thanks to Clive Feather for his invaluable summary of NA1. Thanks to Mark Brader, Jutta Degener, Dennis Ritchie, Melanie Summit, and Rob Young for reading and commenting on drafts of this manuscript.

3.12. Bibliography

American National Standards Institute. 1989. *American national standard for information systems—Programming language—C*, ANSI X3.159-1989.

Feather, C. D. W. A brief description of Normative Addendum 1, http://www.lysator.liu.se/c/na1.html.

Harbison, S. P., and G. L. Steele, Jr. 1995. *C: A reference manual* (4th ed.). Englewood Cliffs, NJ: Prentice-Hall.

Kernighan, B. W., and D. M. Ritchie. 1988. *The C programming language* (2nd ed.). Englewood Cliffs, NJ: Prentice-Hall.

Ritchie, D. M. 1993. *The development of the C language*. Second ACM HOPL Conference, Cambridge, MA. (See also this volume.)

Summit, S. 1995. *C programming FAQs: Frequently asked questions*. Reading, MA: Addison-Wesley.

PART III
Intermediate Languages

4 Intermediate Languages

CHAPTER 4
Intermediate Languages
by Ron K. Cytron

Most who program computers with some regularity are comfortable with authoring computer programs in *source* languages, such as Pascal or Java. Such languages offer extensible data and control abstractions that are conducive to algorithmic expression. However, most computers lack any native comprehension of such high-level languages but instead rely on *compilers* to translate source programs into some *target* machine language, the instructions of which typically operate on a more modest scale. Compilers and other programming-language translation tools bridge the "semantic gap" between high- and low-level program representations. For example, a compiler might accept Java programs as input and produce machine instructions for an Intel architecture.

In fact, many computer application programs can be regarded as *language translators*, in the sense that they accept an input *source* language and produce an output *target* language. For this discussion, compilers remain the primary focus; other examples include

- Text processors, which accept text and formatting specifications and produce an image to be viewed or printed

- Query processors, which accept a high-level query language and emit SQL as an intermediate language

- Theorem provers, which accept a theorem's specification and emit ML (meta-language) as an intermediate language

Although input-to-output translation is the primary, observable task of language translators, many such systems have well-defined intermediate points of arrival at which some *intermediate language* (IL) is produced. This chapter examines the nature of ILs and their importance in translator design, portability, cost, and efficiency.

4.1. Overview

The early C++ compilers did not produce machine code directly (Stroustrup, 1994). As shown in Figure 4.1, the C++ language was translated from source to standard C, with the resulting C program compiled to machine code.

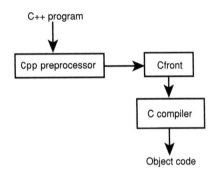

FIGURE 4.1. *Using Cfront to translate C++ to C.*

In fact, because C++ programs could use the standard C preprocessor, source programs were first translated by C's preprocessor Cpp and then translated into standard C by Cfront. Thus, in the trek from C++ to machine code, there are two well-defined points of arrival:

- From the perspective of the C and C++ programming languages, which include preprocessor directives, the output of Cpp is an intermediate step; although no name is formally given to this "language," it is a subset of C and of C++. This IL, which is preprocessor-directive-free, simplifies construction of the rest of the compiler, which need not worry about preprocessor directives.

- From the perspective of Cfront, standard C is an intermediate language, interposed between C++ and machine code.

The use of Cfront in the translation of C++ was short-lived, but it nonetheless illustrates how an existing language can be recruited as an IL to facilitate prototyping a new language.

As another example, consider the steps by which LaTeX (the language in which this chapter was authored; Lamport, 1995) is translated into print, as shown in Figure 4.2.

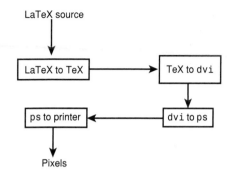

FIGURE 4.2. *Translating LaTeX into print.*

The LaTeX text-processing system does not produce print images directly; instead, LaTeX is translated into a more basic representation called TeX, which is in turn translated into a device-independent representation called dvi, which may in turn undergo several translations before arriving in print. Depending on how one views the usefulness of C in its own right, the emergence of LaTeX and its use of TeX as an IL is quite different from that of C++. Although TeX is well conceived as a typesetting tool, it lacks facilities for expressing documents in terms of their types and components. LaTeX offers such features, producing TeX as its output. In a now-standard use of ILs to enhance portability, TeX does not target any one printer but produces instead dvi. Thus, TeX need not undergo modification to accommodate a new kind of printer; instead, a new program is written to translate the (vastly simpler) dvi IL into the printer's "instruction set."

As seen with the preceding examples, use of ILs in a translation system carries some cost:

- The intermediate languages must be defined. Failure to define these languages accurately can have the same consequences as imprecise definitions of programming languages.

- Tools that process the intermediate forms must be constructed. Because such tools often operate beyond the user's focal plane (e.g., Cpp), great care must be taken to make such tools as unnoticeable as possible. Most users of C or C++ are unaware that the Cpp preprocessor is invoked.

- Connections must be made between levels. For example, if errors occur in source inputs specified in C++ or LaTeX, the error messages should reference the original source lines and not the line number of an intermediate representation beyond the user's view.

The extra steps associated with use of an intermediate language raise justifiable concerns of efficiency: A given system that uses ILs may not enjoy the performance of a competing product that avoids ILs and takes a more "direct" approach. The benefits and cost of an IL must be analyzed and compared; whereas gratuitous levels of intermediate representation are unwise, thoughtful system designs include ILs to simplify the task at hand as well as reduce the cost of adapting and maintaining the given system. In support of this, the rest of this chapter examines some principles and case studies concerning the role of ILs in an effective programming language translation system.

4.2. Patterns of IL Conception

There are primarily two "patterns" of intermediate language conception:

- Extension: An existing (source) language becomes an intermediate language of another translation system.

- Between: An intermediate language is interposed between components of a translation system.

4.2.1. The Extension Pattern

LaTeX and the early C++ compilers are examples of layering a new software system on top of an extant one. Thus, although TeX is a text-processing language in its own right, it is viewed as an intermediate language from the LaTeX perspective. Building systems in this fashion is convenient and economic because an already established language—for which robust translators have presumably already been written—is essentially adopted as an intermediate language.

If the source language L is recruited as an intermediate language, then the following problems can arise:

- L may lack facilities to ferry information from the new source language to the L's target. For example, there may not be a mechanism for transmitting source program line numbers so that error messages can be reported with respect to the source program.

- Because L was in use as a source language, it is likely that programs supplied to L were generated by humans. Ergonomic considerations may have influenced the engineering of some compilers for L. Consequently, compilers may fail when called upon to translate L programs generated automatically because such programs can exhibit complexity well beyond a human's capability to author such programs. For example, programs automatically generated in L may have

Very deeply nested scopes

Expressions involving hundreds of operands

Excessively long methods

When presented with such programs, a compiler's "failures" can be manifested as internal compiler errors: The compiler may simply not be equipped to handle such inputs, even though they are legal programs in the L language. It is also likely that the code generated by such compilers may lack the optimizations envisioned when L was recruited as an IL. Consider that L may lack support for non-local variables, whereas the new source language that uses L intermediately may require such support. Programs generated in L will require code in support of access to non-local variables (Fischer & LeBlanc, 1991); such code might maintain static links or displays, using an array to implement a stack, so that a source statement such as x=x+y would be translated into

```
stack[stack[tos]+5] =
        stack[stack[tos+5]] + stack[stack[tos+13]]
```

The compiler writer who uses L as an IL might expect that compilers for L would recognize that stack[tos]+5 need only be computed once in the preceding code, but such optimization may be difficult to obtain in a compiler for L.

These problems are troublesome, particularly because the very reason for choosing L as an IL may have been to enhance portability. If L is a popular language, then good compilers for L may exist on many platforms. Yet these compilers may appear inconsistent with respect to their ability to handle programs automatically generated in L. In summary, it can be said that nothing stresses a compiler like another compiler.

4.2.2. The Between Pattern

In the "between" pattern, an intermediate language is interposed between software components, as shown in Figure 4.3(b). The IL could be created in an extant system by dividing the system into components that create and use the IL. More frequently, a "between" IL is conceived prior to software construction so that the software development process can take advantage of the IL.

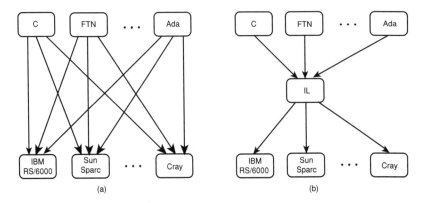

FIGURE 4.3. *An IL can reduce the effort needed to re-source or re-target a compiler.*

Suppose the compiler vendor produces a suite of compilers for *s* source languages (c, FTN, Ada, etc.) and currently supports these compilers for *t* target architectures (IBM-PC, Sun Sparc, Dec Alpha, etc.). If a different product is needed for each situation, then this company might develop and support *s*×*t* compilers, as shown in Figure 4.3(a); however, this work can be reduced to *s*+*t* if an IL can be introduced between the source and target specifications, as shown in Figure 4.3(b). Here, the company develops *s* front ends and *t* back ends. Each front end translates its source language to the IL; each back end translates the IL into native code for its architecture.

Other advantages of using a "between" IL include

- An IL allows various system components to interoperate by facilitating access to information about the program undergoing translation. For example, the IL may contain symbolic information such as variable names, variable types, and source line numbers; such information could be useful in the debugger. Similarly, program development tools such as class browsers and performance profilers, operating at different points in the software development cycle, can share and utilize program information through the IL.

- An IL simplifies testing of the system's components. Components that fit in after IL construction can be tested by (artificial) creation of IL text.

- Considering the two designs shown in Figure 4.3, work that would otherwise be duplicated in a system's front and back ends can instead

be performed in the compiler's "middle end,"[1] provided that such
work can be performed on the IL. For this reason, the "between" IL
pattern works best when most of the language translation effort can
be accomplished on the IL itself because this makes the source- and
target-specific portions simpler.

- A carefully designed and publicly accessible intermediate language
  offers the opportunity for other software systems to interface with
  the IL-bearing product, either by accepting the product's IL as input
  for some other task or by acting as a surrogate provider of the IL.
  In the compiler-suite example, a vendor could sell program optimization methods by interfacing with the compiler's IL to analyze
  and transform the intermediate representation to obtain improved
  performance.

- In a research setting, the IL can simplify the pioneering and prototyping of new ideas by providing the necessary infrastructure.
  Consider a compiler writer who wishes to experiment with new
  methods for eliminating computational redundancy. The task of
  developing a complete compiler *de novo* is daunting; if the method
  can instead be attempted on a compiler's IL, then construction of
  front and back ends can be avoided. Moreover, if the system is mul-
  tisource or multitarget, then deploying the optimization at the IL
  level can obtain benefits for multiple languages and multiple target
  platforms.

- The IL can make the compiler more portable, and numerous compilers have been developed using ILs for this reason (Chow &
  Ganapathi, 1983; Ottenstein, 1984):

Source Language	Intermediate Language
Pascal	Pcode
Java	Java VM
Ada	Diana

We'll return to the issue of portability when we consider the Pascal
Pcode system in greater detail.

---

[1]The term *middle end* has entered into common usage and refers to whatever can be pulled
out of a compiler's front and back ends, which are language and target specific, respectively.

In summary, intermediate languages play an important role in reducing the cost and complexity of translation systems. ILs work best when their role in a system can be considered with respect to present and future uses so that the IL design is appropriately general yet efficient. Finally, when an IL can be designed without a legacy of constraints from existing systems, there is typically much greater flexibility in defining the IL.

4.3. Principles of IL Design

Before examining some actual intermediate languages, it is worth considering some normative criteria for assessing the quality of an IL's design; these are expressed in the following list in terms of a "between" IL for a compiler suite, such as the one shown in Figure 4.3, but the principles can easily be extended to other IL situations:

- The IL should be a bona fide language and not just an aggregation of data structures. For example, IBM uses an intermediate language called XIL (O'Brien, O'Brien, Hopkins, Shepherd, & Unrau, 1995) in some compilers. Although those compilers are very effective, the XIL is not formally a *language* in the sense that programs are represented as strings of symbols. Instead, the front and back ends have architected interfaces for obtaining and shipping information. Consider the issue of *alias information*, which specifies when two variable names might reference the same object. Rules concerning aliasing are language specific. In XIL, such information is provided by the front end, not as a piece of text, but instead through a procedural interface for resolving specific alias queries. The result is an efficient system, but there is no "string" that fully represents the program at an intermediate level. Thus, one cannot transmit an IL form without bundling the front end and its internal structures that represent aliasing.

- The semantics of the IL should be cleanly defined and readily apparent. A good test of this criterion is the ease with which an interpreter can be written for the IL. A good example of such an IL is Pascal's Pcode, which we'll examine later in more detail. A worse example is GNU's RTL (Stallman, http://www.fsf.org):

  "People frequently have the idea of using RTL stored as text in a file as an interface between a language front end and the bulk of GNU CC. This idea is not feasible. GNU CC was designed to use RTL internally only. Correct RTL for a given program is very dependent on the particular target machine. And the RTL does not contain all the information about the program. (Section 16.18)"

It turns out that GNU has another intermediate representation, but it is poorly documented (Stallman, http://www.fsf.org):

"The proper way to interface GNU CC to a new language front end is with the "tree" data structure. There is no manual for this data structure, but it is described in the files 'tree.h' and 'tree.def'. (Section 16.18)"

If GNU's ILs have these problems, why are the GNU compilers in such widespread use? They are popular because they are easily re-*targeted* even though they are not easily re-*sourced*. Admittedly, the act of re-targeting a compiler occurs more frequently than its re-sourcing.

- The IL's representation should not be overly verbose. Although some expansion is inevitable, the IL-to-source token ratio should be as low as possible. Compression of IL representation has grown in importance with the increase of program transmission on the World Wide Web. Moreover, vendors such as Microsoft often keep portions of their software in IL format to decrease the time needed to "launch" an application because the IL format can be considerably more compact than native code.

- The IL should have a human-readable form because humans will inevitably want to examine the IL.

- The IL should be easily and cleanly extensible, although it is often difficult to predict the impact an unknown source, target, or language modification can have on the IL.

- The IL should be sufficiently general to represent the important aspects of multiple front-end languages and back-end targets.

In summary, designing a good IL is truly an engineering endeavor: Utility and generality must be considered along with efficiency.

4.4. Case Study

Although intermediate languages are frequently used in compiler construction (Chow & Ganapathi, 1983; Ottenstein, 1984), there are two efforts worth considering here:

- Pcode (Hansen, 1985; Welsh & Hay, 1986), which has served as an IL for many Pascal compilers

- Java virtual machine (Java VM; Lindholm & Yellin, 1997), which is an object-oriented IL

Both ILs are currently in use; moreover, Java VM builds heavily upon Pcode, and so we can see the evolution of one useful IL into another.

An overview of the operation of a Pcode Pascal compiler is shown in Figure 4.4. The "compiler" box is responsible for assessing the validity of the source program and generating an appropriate IL representation of the program. The program is then executed by interpretation of the IL text. Another possibility is that the IL text is subsequently translated into machine A's native code. This approach is consistent with the compiler suite shown in Figure 4.3(b).

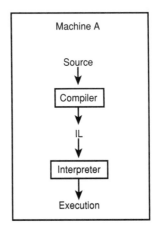

FIGURE 4.4. *An overview of a compiler/interpreter pair.*

Consider the following Pascal statement:

```
t.total := t.total + 3
```

which increments the total field of variable t by 3. The "compiler" component is a front end for Pascal and generates the following (annotated) Pcode representation of the preceding statement:

```
ldoi  9   ; pushes the value kept at slot 9 onto the
          ; run-time stack; the compiler decided that
          ; slot 9 is where t.total should be stored.
          ;
ldci  3   ; pushes the integer constant 3
          ;
adi       ; pops the stack's top two elements, forms
          ; their sum, and then pushes the result onto
          ; the stack; the previous instructions have
          ; caused the values of t.total and 3 to
```

```
                    ; be the addends for this instruction
                    ;
        sroi 9      ; stores at slot 9 (t.total) the value popped
                    ; from the stack
```

These Pcode instructions are then executed by the "interpreter" component.

Pcode is designed so that writing a Pcode interpreter is vastly simpler than writing a Pascal compiler; moreover, the compiler and interpreter components are each written in Pascal. These two design considerations were instrumental to the success of Pascal because they significantly reduce the cost of porting the compiler. A Pcode-generating Pascal compiler is ported between platforms as shown in Figure 4.5.

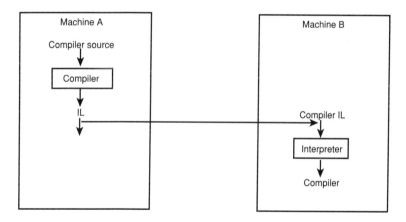

FIGURE 4.5. *Porting a compiler using its intermediate language.*

If machine A already has a Pcode-generating Pascal compiler, then Pcode generated on A can be executed on machine B after B has a Pcode interpreter. The compiler itself is compiled into Pcode on A, and when that Pcode is moved to B and interpreted by its Pcode interpreter, the result is a Pascal compiler that runs on B. Because of its portability, the UCSD Pascal compiler (Jensen, 1985) quickly became available on a great number of microcomputers and thus fostered a broad Pascal user community.

Like Pcode, Java VM uses a "stack machine" model to evaluate expressions, with instructions to place values on a stack and to perform arithmetic operations on them. Because Java is object oriented, Java VM has instructions to invoke methods (operations belonging to an object), to refer to data encapsulated within class instances, and to check object instances with respect to a class hierarchy.

To illustrate both the use of an IL as well as the cleverness with which Java VM was fashioned, consider the following code sequence:

```
t.total += 3
```

where `total` is a public data element of a class instance of type `obj`. This statement has the effect of incrementing the data item `total` by 3.[2] Translated into Java VM, the (annotated) instructions generated from the statement are

```
getfield #5 <obj.total I>     ; Slot 5 holds the reference
                              ; for t, so this instruction
                              ; pushes onto the stack the
                              ; field "total" of a reference
                              ; to type "obj" which is an
                              ; integer ("I")
                              ;
iconst_3                      ; pushes the constant 3
                              ;
iadd                          ; pops the stack's top two
                              ; elements and pushes their
                              ; sum onto the stack
                              ;
putfield #5 <obj.total I>     ; pop the result off the stack
                              ; and store it in slot 5's
                              ; (t's) integer "total" field
```

The code sequence first fetches the value of total, which places the value on the stack. After the value 3 is pushed on the stack, the iadd instruction forms the sum, and the result is then stored back to total.

Note that the design of Java VM does not permit reference to the actual address of the data within a structure. The field `total` is fetched by name rather than by specifying its location in memory. This apparent inefficiency is designed into Java VM in support of separate compilation. Suppose the structure containing `total` were to be reorganized; then any reference to the field `total` by its offset within an object instance would have to be corrected, either by recomputation at runtime or by recompilation of the source program containing the object reference. By cleverly engineering the IL, Java objects can be compiled independently. This is important because the objects, which may be defined at physically separated locations, can still interoperate correctly without recompilation. Implementations of Java VM are free to optimize object references into hardcoded offsets (addresses within a structure), but it is important that the Java IL interface not allow the direct expression of addresses.

---

[2]It is better programming style to access such data through an appropriate member function; this example is pedagogically expedient.

On the other hand, consider the Java source fragment from a public class
`test`:

```
switch (x)
    case sym.bar: y=x+1;
}
```

The reference to class `sym`'s public `bar` field appears in Java VM IL as a
constant value that is obtained at the time `test` is compiled. If class `sym` is
modified so that `bar`'s value changes, then the code in the `test` class is no
longer valid because it incorporated the value of `sym.bar` at compile time.
With no reference in class `test` to `sym.bar`, the `switch` statement's staleness
cannot be discovered. This problem arises because the IL mechanism for
expressing the `switch` statement requires that the `case` values be specified
as integer constants. This problem could be solved by

- Generalizing the IL so that its switch mechanism allows constants
  specified by name rather than just by value.

- Deferring generation of the IL switch mechanism until the class containing the `switch` statement is actually loaded. At that point, the
  value of named constants can be ascertained and the correct IL
  switch code can be generated.

4.5. Summary

Intermediate languages are an important and yet often hidden aspect
of system software. Their careful construction allows software to be
robust, portable, and efficient. As software components such as language
translators, debuggers, programming environments, and visualization
tools continue their trend toward interoperability, reasonable IL design
will continue to be an important activity. Once designed and published,
ILs will also serve as breeding grounds for new kinds of tools that span
traditional software boundaries.

4.6. Acknowledgments

The author is grateful to David Hemmendinger and Anthony Ralston for
their comments on an earlier version of this material and to Michael
Plezbert for his careful reading and comments on this material. Kitty
Jarrett's editing greatly improved this chapter. The author also thanks
Fran Allen of IBM Research for many enlightening conversations concerning the nature of intermediate languages. She has profoundly influenced the field—and especially this author.

4.7. Bibliography

Chow, F. C., and M. Ganapathi. 1983. Intermediate languages in compiler construction—A bibliography. *Sigplan Notices* 18(11):21–23.

Fischer, C., and R. Leblanc. 1991. *Crafting a compiler with C.* Redwood City, CA: Benjamin/Cummings.

Hansen, P. B. 1985. *Brinch Hansen on Pascal compilers.* Englewood Cliffs, NJ: Prentice-Hall.

Jensen, K., and N. Wirth. 1975. *Pascal user manual and report.* New York: Springer-Verlag.

Lamport, L. 1995. *LaTeX: A document preparation system.* Reading, MA: Addison-Wesley.

Lindholm, T., and F. Yellin. 1997. *The Java virtual machine specification.* Reading, MA: Addison-Wesley.

O'Brien, K., K. O'Brien, M. Hopkins, A. Shepherd, and R. Unrau. 1995. XIL and YIL: The intermediate languages of TOBEY. *ACM SIGPLAN Notices* 30(3):71–82.

Ottenstein, K. J. 1984. Intermediate languages in compiler construction— A supplemental bibliography. *Sigplan Notices* 19(7):25–27.

Stallman, R. *Using and porting* GNU CC. http://www.fsf.org.

Stroustrup, B. 1994. *The design and evolution of* C++. Reading, MA: Addison-Wesley.

Welsh, J., and A. Hay. 1986. *A model implementation of standard Pascal.* Englewood Cliffs, NJ: Prentice-Hall.

PART IV
Pascal

CHAPTER 5
Turbo Pascal
by Glenn Grotzinger

5.1. The History of Pascal

The first part of this chapter gives a brief history of Pascal, including a description of the pre-creation history of Pascal, its growth to prominence and eventual assignment of a Pascal standard, its growth since then (Pascal variants, platforms, and its descendants), and the status of Pascal today.

5.1.1. Birth

The story of the Pascal language begins in 1964 with a man named Niklaus Wirth, while he was in a group referred to as Working Group 2.1. The purpose of this group was to define a working standard for what was to become Algol 68. Ultimately, the group's deliberations to determine this new standard were reduced to two proposals, Wirth's and another individual's. Wirth's proposal was rejected in 1965, in favor of the other proposal, referred to as Algol X. Undaunted by the rejection and encouraged by the amount of dissent Algol X received, Wirth moved on to develop his proposal, which was referred to as Algol W.

In the current state of programming at that time, Algol 60 was the predominant academic language, whereas COBOL was predominant in business, and Fortran was common for scientific purposes. Fortran was clearly superior to Algol 60 in performance and features, and this is what the group sought to change.

Meanwhile, it took four years for the Algol 68 standard to reach the implementation stage. It was projected that people would abandon Algol in that time period, and many did. In this same time period, Wirth took a professorship at the Federal Institute of Technology in Zurich, Switzerland. Because of the lack of a suitable implementation of Algol (only Fortran and assembler existed) at his institution, Wirth set out to create a single pass, top-down recursive descent compiler to fill the void he saw, the necessity to teach structured programming techniques. He named this compiler Pascal, after the French mathematician and philosopher Blaise Pascal, of the seventeenth century.

Pascal was completed in 1970. In creating the language, Wirth sought to extend Algol with new data types and new abilities to combine different data types. He also sought to remove or simplify structures that were deemed confusing and unnecessary, such as the ability to place the keyword IF in the middle of a statement. The most notable additions to Pascal, inspired from other languages, was the COBOL-like record types, and the simplified for statement from Fortran (eliminating the step clause).

5.1.2. Growth

Eventually, Pascal caught on for teaching purposes but was still not efficient enough for most uses. Wirth then removed all functions but those considered useful for teaching purposes, and he called the resulting compiler Pascal-S.

After the publication of Pascal in 1970, others expressed interest in porting Pascal to other platforms besides the CDC platform which was at Zurich at the time. This led to the development of what was referred to as the "p-kit," which included most of what was needed to be able to implement a Pascal compiler in about any environment. This led to the porting of Pascal to many other platforms, though the unwillingness of people to proceed beyond the interpretative phase of porting the code led Pascal to be known as a slow language.

One group that received a copy of the p-kit was at the University of California at San Diego. At this time, the first microcomputers (PCs) were being developed, and what was to become USCD Pascal, the first compiler developed for a PC environment, was developed. What was unique for the entire case with Pascal compilers was that an interactive debugger and source editor were included along with the compiler itself.

During this time, Pascal grew to be one of the most popular languages to use in teaching, with the prevalent ability to teach the language on the microcomputers that were becoming popular (the Apple II and others). In this time, the Pascal User's Group of the University of Minnesota gained prominence in promoting the further development of Pascal, so much so that when Wirth chose to move on to other projects in 1975, this group took over much of the distribution and further development of Pascal.

Discussions to devise an official Pascal standard first occurred in 1977. As deliberations grew raucous, many factions grew out of the efforts. For this reason, standards organizations took a long time and even ratified the standard at different times. The IEEE adopted it in 1981; the ANSI, in 1982; and ISO, in 1983. Even so, after the standards were set, current distributors of Pascal compilers were very reluctant to drop many of their own extensions. The raucousness and recalcitrant nature of the participants led to several factions and standards, which still are seen today in portability problems.

5.1.3. Prominence

What was probably the single most important event to the spread and popularization of Pascal as it is today was the marketing of a Pascal compiler in 1984 from a company named Borland International. This compiler was called Turbo Pascal (Gillin, 1995). With the lack of copy protection and lower costs (the average price of work-related software at that time was $400), the Borland variant became the prominent, true compiler and development environment available to the masses, so much so that Niklaus Wirth was quoted at the HOPL-II convention as saying, "But the point is well taken that the actual [de-facto] standard for Pascal has been defined by Borland, just by producing a compiler and distributing it cheaply and widely. If you talk to anyone about Pascal today, probably Turbo Pascal from Borland is meant" (Wirth, 1996).

In the subsequent period, Borland added several extensions related to events of the period. Borland is recognized as one of the innovators and encouraging forces for the addition of object orientation to Pascal (1985) and the (agreed to be not-so-innovative) inclusion of the Borland Graphics Interface and Turbo Vision to Turbo Pascal.

Eventually, with Turbo Pascal 6 and 7, there were separated versions (Turbo Pascal and Turbo Pascal Professional for Version 6 and Turbo Pascal and Borland Pascal for Version 7). The separation was due to the inclusion of Windows compilers and later, in Version 7, a 32-bit DPMI compiler.

5.1.4. Descendants

Languages that were created and are recognized as descendants (inspired or patterned after) of the Pascal language are listed here: Concurrent Pascal (1975), Pascal-Plus (1984), Mesa (1978), Modula-2 (1982), Oberon (1989), Euclid (1978), Object Pascal (1985). Ada is also recognized as being inspired to a lesser degree by Pascal. It is interesting to note that Wirth's subsequent projects, Modula-2 and Oberon, are in this list.

5.1.5. Today

Today, Borland's implementations of Pascal are considered to be the Pascal compilers with the highest market share. Delphi was developed as a recognized continuation of Pascal into the newer "visual programming" paradigm of the Windows-only realm (targets of Delphi are Windows 32, Windows 3.1, Windows 95, and Windows NT). Even Delphi 1 is denoted in version tags in the software as "version 8."

Unfortunately, though, there has been a lack of attention to the DOS versions of Borland's Pascal compilers from the Borland company itself. Version 7 of the DOS compiler, which was last updated in 1993 (7.01), has continued to be largely usable for creating 16-bit DOS applications, though Borland has ceased to support it (yet continues to sell it). This, along with the advent of newer platforms, has resulted in a renaissance of Pascal compiler creation. As a result, compilers exist today for almost all platforms, from the Macintosh to OS/2 and even UNIX.

The newer compilers that have been developed for DOS have been full 32-bit capable (that seems to be the only target, though, so Turbo Pascal is still usable for 16-bit targets) compilers. Examples of such compilers are TMT Pascal, FPK Pascal, and GNU Pascal. They all have extended the Pascal language to be usable by today's standards and microcomputers, including the ability to compile for specific op-codes all the way up to Pentiums.

Note as well, with the advance in the capability of microcomputers today, that the use of Turbo Pascal has gained a couple of precautionary notes. With the increase of the size of hard disk drives to sizes of 2 GB and beyond, the standard DOS operating system has ceased to be able to return accurate sizes for the capacity of the disk, and the amount of space free on the disk if the size of these quantities exceed 2 GB.

In Pentium systems, a runtime error 200 (division by zero) may occur upon execution of any Turbo Pascal program that uses the CRT unit. This is due to the overflow of a variable in the initialization code for the

CRT unit's Delay procedure, as a result of the increased speed available in the Pentium processor beyond that of the older processors (greater than or equal to 200 MHz). Contrary to the statements of Borland's technical support department (its position is to update to Delphi), the problem is readily repairable, as seen by the Internet WWW sites listed next.

5.1.6. Net Resources

This is a partial listing of some Internet sites of interest (links accurate at the time of this writing) in Pascal programming:

- `http://www.geocities.com/Paris/3537/tpcont.html`—Written to provide a satisfactory source for private individuals to learn Turbo Pascal as a first language (there was none on the Net at the time), it is much more of an educational document of a textbook nature than a reference, also containing several programming exercises. These exercises demonstrate many application-related concepts in Pascal, and may be useful to those who fit the license requirements who want to study more source examples of real-life coding situations.

- `http://www.gdsoft.com/swag/swag.html`—SWAG, or the SourceWare Archival Group, is a collection of free Pascal sources, provided by programmers all over the world, as the foremost source sample reference in the Pascal language, containing Pascal source regarding 57 different types of programming questions.

- `http://www.tmt.com`—This is the home site of TMT Pascal.

- `http://home.pages.de/~FPK-Pascal/`—This is the home site of FPK-Pascal.

- `http://home.pages.de/~GNU-Pascal/`—This is the home site of GNU-Pascal.

- `http://users.southeast.net/~rdonais/tpascal/rdelay.zip` and `http://www.mi.uni-erlangen.de/~heckenb/newdelay.pas`—These are links to two different places that hold fixes, written by R.E. Donais and Frank Heckenbach, that fix the problem with the CRT unit in Turbo and Borland Pascal 7.

5.2. Pascal Constructs

This section is a tutorial on Pascal constructs related to Turbo Pascal. The constructs presented may be applicable to any kind of Pascal, though the examples were created in Turbo Pascal and are not guaranteed to work in other implementations of Pascal. It describes using the Turbo

Pascal compiler, elementary Pascal, control structures, data types, procedures and functions, units and include files, data manipulation, dynamic
memory allocation, files access, textmode manipulation, DOS command
functions, and some advanced options.

5.2.1. Using the Turbo Pascal Compiler

This section functions as a guided tour to the Turbo Pascal (TP) IDE and
highlights functions that have been found useful. To start and be able to
observe the locations of these functions in the IDE, type turbo when you
are in the \bin subdirectory of the directory in which Turbo Pascal is
installed.

After you start Turbo Pascal, move to the file menu. Note that open, save,
and print (source) are functions of interest. Most are self-explanatory.
Note that the standard extension for Pascal source files is pas. Here you
can activate the Printer Setup function.

Upon entering this function, you will see that the TP IDE prints by means
of a DOS-based print filter program called prnfltr. You may want to set
the switch to /ascii, unless you have an HP or Epson printer, or find that
erratic things happen when you attempt to print from the TP IDE. Also,
you will note later that certain keywords are highlighted by certain colors
in the source editor. The check box indicates whether you want to translate these color changes to the source printed. If you want to add support
for your printer or to study source code, the Pascal source for prnfltr
exists in the same directory as prnfltr.pas.

Now move on to the compile menu. You see the options compile, make, and
build. compile compiles the source file that is currently being worked on.
make compiles the source file worked on, as well as any other related files
needed that have been changed. build unconditionally compiles all files
that are related to the file currently being worked on. The Destination
option changes options from compiling in memory to compiling in disk.
Compiling to disk produces an EXE file.

Observe the run menu. Commands of interest are run, step over, and trace
into. run attempts to execute the code generated from the source being
edited. step over and trace into are options used for the debugger. step
over fully executes a function or procedure for which source exists, and
trace into acts on each statement.

In addition, there are other key combinations that will be of interest.
When a compiler error is presented, pressing F1 provides a better description of the error. Shift+F1 presents the index of help topics, and Ctrl+F1

performs a lookup on the index using the word that appears at the cursor. To start the debugger, debug/watch is used. Also, because multiple windows are possible in the TP IDE, Alt+0 can be used to select which window you want to view.

Turbo Pascal 7 also presents different options for compiler use as well. Turbo, which you may have just been using, is a standard 16-bit compiler with the TP IDE. TPX, which is a DPMI version of the Turbo compiler, is also available. For those who want to use the Turbo Pascal compiler as a command-line compiler, TPC exists. It can be called by typing tpc and then the filename. In any event, to ease development of Turbo Pascal programs, you may want to place the bin directory of your Turbo Pascal directory on the DOS path.

5.2.2. Elementary Pascal

This section describes the format of a Turbo Pascal program, reading variables from the screen and writing them to screen, as well as arithmetic operations on variables.

5.2.2.1. The Format of a TP Program

As shown in Listing 5.1, a valid program begins with the reserved word program. After that word is an identifier, which gives a description of the program that generally matches the first eight characters of the source file's name. The next item that must always exist in a Pascal program is the word begin, which indicates the beginning of the main program. The last thing that must exist in Pascal code is the word end, with a period. Semicolons function as statement separators.

LISTING 5.1. *A simple "Hello World!" program in Turbo Pascal.*

```
program hello;
  begin
    writeln('Hello World!');
  end.
```

5.2.2.2. Writing and Reading from the Screen

This section describes procedures used to read and write to the screen. In Turbo Pascal, they are read, readln, write, and writeln.

Listing 5.2 shows how to use these procedures. read takes a variable from the screen, and write writes a variable to the screen. readln and writeln behave in the same manner as read and write, except they move to the next line. In the example, note that another statement which is not required but which is almost always used is VAR. It denotes the start of a variable declaration section. It is terminated by another declaration identifier, such as begin. The variable named typed_variable is declared as a Pascal type string, which is a phrase of text not greater than 255 characters. Also, comments in Pascal are demonstrated here.

LISTING 5.2. *A demonstration of* reads *and* writes.

```
program fig2;
  var
    typed_variable: string;
  { This denotes a comment, between the braces }
  (* If there are no braces on your keyboard, this will also work *)
  begin
    write('Type something to me, and I will repeat it. ');
    readln(typed_variable);
    writeln('You typed: ', typed_variable, '.');
  end.
```

In the writeln statement, note that a variable may be displayed along with constant text, separated by commas, as indicated. Strings, when addressed, are to have single quotation marks (') surrounding the text. When you want to write a single quotation mark, two of them—rather than a double quotation mark (")—must be placed. A null writeln, as shown in Listing 5.3, produces movement to the next line, whereas a null readln, in a similar manner, pauses the program until Enter is pressed.

Also, another feature of the write procedures involves text placement, which can be observed in Listing 5.3. A colon may be placed after any part of a statement in a write or writeln call. The end of the section of text is placed on the column number indicated. If this is not possible, the text is placed on the screen in a left-justified manner. Included in Listing 5.3 is a number rule, which enables you to observe the result of this option.

LISTING 5.3. *A demonstration of text placement.*

```
program fig3;
  begin
    writeln('00000000011111111111222222222223333333333344444444445555',
            '555556');
    writeln('12345678901234567890123456789012345678901234567890123',
            '567890');
    writeln;
    writeln('Hi, I"m happy, are you?':50);
  end.
```

5.2.2.3. Arithmetic Manipulation

This section describes standard addition, subtraction, multiplication, division, and concatenation. For purposes of this section, variables declared as real are decimal numbers, such as 3.23, and variables declared as integer are whole numbers, such as 5. Order of operations rules and use of parentheses in Turbo Pascal are consistent with the rules of mathematics. These rules usually are consistent with all programming languages. In Listing 5.4, observe means of doing these arithmetic functions.

There are two additional mathematical functions that exist in Turbo Pascal, referred to as DIV, or integer division, and MOD, or modulo. Both are equivalent to division in the order of operations. DIV returns the integer part of a division between two integers, and MOD returns the remainder of an integer division. Listing 5.4 illustrates these functions.

An assignment of a value to a variable or a value from one variable to another variable is made by the use of the symbol := (note that this is different from = in Pascal). The data types must be similar in order for the assign to work properly. Listing 5.4 also illustrates concatenation of strings by use of the + operator. Also, a valid data identifier must not start with a number or _, and must not have any of the symbols used as a part of Turbo Pascal coding.

LISTING 5.4. *An illustration of mathematical functions, concatenation, and assigns.*

```
program fig4;
   { this is not the most efficient program, it has been expanded to }
   { purposely illustrate several ways that these things can be done }
   var
      starting: string;
      input1, input2: integer;
      output: real;
   begin
      { demonstrating concatenation }
      starting := 'Turbo' + ' Pascal';
      writeln(starting);
      { demonstrating math }
      input1 := 7;
      input2 := 3;
      writeln(input1, ' and ', input2, ':');
      writeln('Add: ', 7 + 3);
      writeln('Subtract: ', input1 - input2);
      writeln('Multiply: ', input1 * input2);
      { real division }
      write('Divide: ', input1 / input2);
      { integer division, also note that a statement can extend to }
      { multiple lines }
      writeln(' or alternatively ', input1 div input2,
              ' with a remainder of ', input1 mod input2);
   end.
```

5.2.3. Control Structures

This section describes the various control structures that are available in Turbo Pascal. They include statements of conditional execution such as `if` statements and `case` statements, loop control structures such as `for` loops, `while` loops, and `repeat` loops, and a description of boolean logic in Turbo Pascal.

5.2.3.1. if Statements

These are the basic statements for use in conditional execution of a statement. The format of an `IF` statement is shown in Listing 5.5, where a `writeln` statement is executed depending on the number entered at the beginning. Multiple conditions may be placed on `if` statements, which are described at the end of this section.

LISTING 5.5. *A demonstration of an* `if` *statement.*

```
program fig5;
  var
    entered: integer;
  begin
    write('Enter a number: ');
    readln(entered);
    if entered > 10 then
      writeln('Entered was greater than 10');
  end.
```

Any conditional statement (`if` statements, or `while` loops, and `repeat` loops) can use the following characters to represent different conditions (and more can be used, as described in section 5.2.3.6) in Turbo Pascal:

Conditional	Description
=	Equal
<>	Not equal
>	Greater than
>=	Greater than or equal to
<	Less than
<=	Less than or equal to

In addition, an `if` statement might be extended to execute another statement if the condition is not met. This is referred to as an extension to the `if` statement, called an `else` statement. That extension is demonstrated along with the method used for placing multiple statements in any control structure (a `begin-end;` pair) in Turbo Pascal in Listing 5.6. It represents a rewrite of Listing 5.5 that adds a statement which appears if the number entered is less than 10, and adds statements on each part that tell how much greater or less the number entered was from 10:

LISTING 5.6. *A demonstration of* if-else *statements.*

```pascal
program fig6;
  var
    entered: integer;
  begin
    write('Enter a number: ');
    readln(entered);
    if entered > 10 then
      begin
        writeln('Entered was greater than 10');
        writeln('It is ', entered - 10, ' greater than 10.');
      end
    else
      begin
        writeln('Entered was less than or equal to 10');
        writeln('It is ', 10 - entered, ' less than 10.');
      end;
  end.
```

5.2.3.2. case Statements

If you chain if-else statements, a program's structure might become confusing rather quickly. One solution in some cases to cut down on clutter would be to use the case statement. It uses an ordinal value (integer or char, generally) as a condition and can use set definitions as part of the checks, as defined later in this section. In Listing 5.7, the conditional statements as if statements could grow to be quite cluttered quickly. Here, the case statement would accomplish the same thing and be easier understood upon review and maintenance. Also, at the end of the case statement, note the end;, which is required at the end of a case statement.

LISTING 5.7. *A demonstration of a* case *statement.*

```pascal
program fig7;
  { this is a grade parser, which uses the general college grading
    rules: 90-100 : A, 80-89 : B, 70-79 : C, 60 - 69 : D, 0-59 : F }
  var
    grade: integer;
  begin
    write('What is your grade? ');
    readln(grade);
    case grade of
      90..100: writeln('You earned an A');
       80..89: writeln('You earned a B');
       70..79: writeln('You earned a C');
       60..69: writeln('You earned a D');
        0..59: writeln('You earned an F');
    else
      { catch all other options that grade could be as an error }
      { condition }
      writeln('The number was not between 0 and 100.  ',
              'Please re-enter your number.');
    end;
  end.
```

For the value of `grade` entered, each section of the `case` section is checked, as if an `if` statement in order from top to bottom. An equivalent listing of this program is presented in section 5.2.3.6.

5.2.3.3. `for` Loops

A loop that executes a statement or a set of statements a defined number of times is referred to as a `for` loop. It uses an index variable that it automatically increments by 1 or decrements by 1, given the way the loop is written between two set ranges. The index variable, which can be a number or an ASCII character, *should not* be changed in the loop. Valid `for` loops are defined here as well as in Listing 5.8:

```
for i := 1 to 10 do
for c := 'a' to 'z' do
for i := 10 downto 1 do
for c := 'z' downto 'a' do
```

LISTING 5.8. *A demonstration of* `for` *loops.*

```
program fig8;
  var
    i: integer;
    c: char;
  begin
    write('I can count down from 10: ');
    for i := 10 downto 1 do
      write(i, ' ');
    writeln;
    writeln('Now here"s the ABC"s');
    for c := 'A' to 'Z' do
      write(c, ' ');
    writeln;
  end.
```

The logic in execution of a `for` loop would be as follows, using the first example of a `for` loop:

1. Set an index variable, `i`, to `10`.

2. Execute statement(s) controlled by the `for` loop, and decrease `i` by 1 (because of `downto`).

3. Keep performing step 2 and stop after `i` becomes less than 1.

5.2.3.4. `while` Loops

A loop that executes while a condition is true is referred to as a `while` loop. A `while` loop is a pretest condition loop, which means it tests the condition before it executes the code. This means that if the condition is false approaching the `while` loop, the code in the `while` loop will never be executed. Also, if the condition in this loop reflects an index variable, you must be sure to have it initialized before entering the loop and increment it or decrement it before the loop re-cycles.

Demonstrated in Listing 5.9 is the method you would have to use to go from ranges in an index (the popular question "How do I do a for loop while incrementing by a number other than one?") by a while loop, noting that in this construct, the index variable can be changed in the loop. This listing is the equivalent program of Listing 5.8, minus the abc section.

LISTING 5.9. *A demonstration of a* while *loop.*

```
program fig9;
  var
    i: integer;
  begin
    write('I can count down from 10: ');
    i := 10;
    while i > 0 do
      begin
        write(i, ' ');
        i := i - 1;
      end;
    writeln;
  end.
```

Here, what is performed in the while loop is exactly what is done in the for-downto loop presented in Listing 5.8. The generic function of a while loop is to continue the statements encompassed by the while loop while the condition specified is true. If the assignment to i is changed to i := 0, the statements in the while loop will never be executed.

5.2.3.5. repeat Loops

A loop that executes statements until a condition is true is referred to as a repeat loop in Turbo Pascal. This loop always executes once no matter what condition is placed on the repeat loop; therefore, it could be referred to as a posttest condition loop. As with a while loop, any index variables used for the condition must be initialized before the loop is entered.

Listing 5.10 shows a program that performs the same actions as Listing 5.9, using a repeat loop. Note the difference in the control statement as well as the location of the control statement. As Wirth intended Pascal to be a teaching language with logic behind how the control structures are expressed, the way the constructs are written indicates the actions that happen. Because a repeat loop checks the condition after the statements are executed, the condition appears afterwards, whereas a while loop shows the control statement beforehand.

LISTING 5.10. *A demonstration of a* repeat *loop.*

```
program fig10;
  var
    i: integer;
  begin
    write('I can count down from 10: ');
    i := 10;
    repeat
      write(i, ' ');
      i := i - 1;
    until i < 1;
    writeln;
  end.
```

5.2.3.6. Boolean Logic and Control Structures

This section presents the use of boolean operators with the control structures listed previously. They include AND, OR, and NOT keywords. Generally, AND and OR would be used to indicate multiple conditions, whereas NOT negates a condition. The following is a list of standard boolean algebra:

AND	OR	NOT
True and true = true	True or true = true	Not (true) = false
True and false = false	True or false = true	Not (false) = true
False and true = false	False or true = true	
False and false = false	False or false = false	

In the order of operations, these operators are placed above all arithmetic operations and comparison operations. If a true comparison between two conditional statements is desired, parentheses must be used, as the AND or OR will be evaluated between the items nearest the word as boolean types and not the results of the two conditions as might be desired. In Listing 5.11, multiple conditions are demonstrated in the rewrite of Listing 5.7, which was the case statement grades example, to use if statements. Here, you begin to see the easily sprawling code that if statements can begin to generate.

LISTING 5.11. *A demonstration of control statements including boolean logic.*

```
program fig11;
  { this is a grade parser, which uses the general college grading
    rules: 90-100 : A, 80-89 : B, 70-79 : C, 60 - 69 : D, 0-59 : F }
  var
    grade: integer;
```

```
begin
  write('What is your grade? ');
  readln(grade);
  if (grade > 100) or (grade < 0) then
    writeln('The number was not between 0 and 100.  ',
            'Please re-enter your number.')
  else
    if grade >= 90 then
      writeln('You earned an A')
  else
    if grade >= 80 then
      writeln('You earned a B')
    else
      if grade >= 70 then
        writeln('You earned a C')
      else
        if grade >= 60 then
          writeln('You earned a D')
        else
          writeln('You earned an F');
end.
```

In any event, any control structure can be nested within another control structure numerous times deep in a proper manner with Turbo Pascal.

5.2.3.7. Boolean Logic Evaluation
Note that the manner Turbo Pascal defaults to is what is called *short-circuit evaluation*. When the final result of a multiple-condition boolean statement is apparent in short-circuit evaluation, it ceases to evaluate the particular condition statement. This behavior may or may not be desirable, if a control statement with multiple conditions does not work. The compiler directive ({$B+}) at the top of a source program sets the compiler so it fully evaluates all condition statements.

5.2.4. Data Types
This section describes most of the data types usable in Turbo Pascal. They include types to handle numerical data; types to handle character and boolean data; types to handle grouped data such as arrays, strings, records, and sets; as well as a description of enumerated types, constants, and typed data.

5.2.4.1. Numeric Data
Numeric data can be stored in a variety of ways. The most common types are integer, which represents a signed number between –32,767 and 32,768, and real, which represents a scientific number of 11 significant figures. The real numbers may be set in terms of scientific numbers or as decimal numbers. A complete listing of numeric data types and their

ranges can be found in the online help or manuals. The following are other common types of numeric representative data types:

- byte—regular storage for a byte of data: 0 to 255; 1 byte storage

- word—regular storage for a word of data: 0 to 65,535; 2 bytes storage

- integer—signed numerical storage: –32,767 to 32,768; 2 bytes storage

- longint—signed numerical storage with an even larger range than integer: 4 bytes storage

- real—scientific number, 11 digits precision, storage from about 10^{-30} to 10^{30}, 6 bytes storage

Some of the numeric types involve use of the numeric co-processor or runtime emulation routines that are inherent to Turbo Pascal. What you may want to use in this case is something referred to as a *compiler directive* to determine which way TP handles these kinds of numeric types. Compiler directives are commented codes that appear in a source program, generally at the beginning. Relevant compiler directives in this case are $N and $E. The defaults are $N- and $E+, which uses emulation by default. The + condition on each of these compiler directives signals to use either the numeric co-processor (N) or the emulation (E), whereas the - condition disables use of either.

The real data in Listing 5.4 for division resulted in output of the number in a scientific number format. In most cases of output, you may not want to output numbers for users in that format. Therefore, there is another formatting code with write and writeln that enables formatting. It is a second number, after the spacing format code, that specifies the number of digits when showing the number as a decimal. When spacing is not desired, a 0 can be used as the first character, but both formatting codes must still be used. For example, a real number can be written as a decimal number like the following:

```
{ write the real variable result, to 3 decimal places }
writeln(result:0:3);
```

5.2.4.2. Character or Boolean Data

A byte of data, translated to a character in the ASCII chart is referred to as a data type char. A character can be assigned to a char variable, such as 'A' or an equivalent ASCII number in decimal as #65 or hexadecimal such as $41. In Listing 5.12, note that even though byte and char are entirely equivalent in storage (1 byte, same value in memory), the compiler interprets these types differently. To check this fact, information is shown later (Listing 5.24) to enable you to test the statement made.

LISTING 5.12. *An illustration of* byte *versus* char.

```
program fig12;
  var
    character: char;
    byteinfo: byte;
  begin
    character := #65; { or character := 'A' would be equivalent }
    byteinfo := 65;
    writeln(character);
    writeln(byteinfo);
  end.
```

Another type of data called boolean data is stored as a byte, $00 or $FF. This type is referred to as either true or false and is assigned as such in a boolean variable. These variables are good for status flags generally.

5.2.4.3. Arrays

Arrays or tables are groups of similar data in memory. They are stored in a linear basis and can be composed of any other kind of data type that can be made. They are defined using the keyword array, along with a set defined range, encompassed by brackets, and using the phrase of <datatype>. The array bounds must be a character or integer range and must be concretely defined at compile time. Examples of valid arrays are shown here:

```
buffer: array[1..1024] of byte;
monthlydata: array[1..31] of integer;
alphabetic: array['a'..'z'] of char;
```

An array may be referred to in its entirety as a variable to write it to disk, read it from disk, or assign it to another variable of a "similar type" (defined in section 5.2.4.4). An array may also be referred to in terms of a part of its whole for writing to any device, or assigned variables of a similar type, which is the most common way. Generally, an index variable is established as well as an array, to enable to process all of the data that exists in the array sequentially.

To define what the array syntax means with the first example above, buffer is an array of 1,024 bytes, each byte referred to in a range of 1 to 1024. The first byte is referred to as buffer[1], and the 100th byte is referred to as buffer[100]. An example of declaring and accessing an array in a proper manner is shown in Listing 5.13.

LISTING 5.13. *An example of using a single-level table or array.*

```pascal
program fig13;

{ Single dimensional array demo:
  fills an array using a mathematical formula, then takes the
  average of all numbers in the array. Shows the proper way to
  access an array in Pascal, as well as process an array, and
  perform record-keeping in an array system with Pascal. }

var
   info: array[1..15] of integer;
   i, total_used: byte;
   addtemp: longint;
begin
   i := 1;
   total_used := 0;
   { use while or repeat when indefinite number of items placed in
     array }
   while (total_used * 3) < 12 do
     begin
        info[i] := total_used * 5 + 12;
        total_used := total_used + 1;
        i := i + 1;
     end;
   addtemp := 0;
   { may use for loop as well as while/repeat here. When not entirely
     filling an array, be sure to keep # of items currently used
     recorded somewhere }
   for i := 1 to total_used do
     begin
        write(info[i], ', ');
        addtemp := addtemp + info[i];
     end;
   writeln(total_used, ' numbers.');
   writeln('are averaged to ', addtemp/total_used:0:3);
end.
```

In the scheme of using arrays, it almost implies some form of loop to process each item in the grouping. Also, in cases in which it is known that all of the array is not filled with values, it is best to keep track of the number of values currently in the array.

The next question you may ask is whether an array may be of an array. The answer here is "yes." In referring to Listing 5.13, Info is an array[1..15] of integer. This array could easily be array[1..4] of array[1..15] of integer, meaning an array of four arrays of array[1...15] of integer, all indexed by the range 1..4. The first declaration here can be expressed in shorthand to be the second, though both declarations are correct. The shorthand form is considered acceptable:

```pascal
info: array[1..4] of array[1..15] of integer;
info: array[1..4,1..15] of integer;
```

More than two levels of arrays can be assigned as well, given that the memory exists in which to declare the structure. This is accomplished by adding another comma and another set range.

Memory storage of multiple-level array structures is linear, just as with the single array structures. Figure 5.1 shows how a double-level array might be stored in memory, with the info declaration sample above.

info[1]	info[2]	info[3]	info[4]

Where info[x] represents one array[1..15] of integer.

FIGURE 5.1. *An illustration of how multiple level arrays are stored in memory.*

An example of use of an array of beyond one level in a program is shown in Listing 5.14. If you keep in mind that memory storage is linear, programming for any level of array should not be difficult.

LISTING 5.14. *A demonstration of a double-level array or table.*

```
program fig14;

  { two-level array demonstration determinant of a 3X3 matrix.
    The general formula is for a matrix of:
    [ A  B  C ]
    [ D  E  F ]  is AEI + BFG + CDH - CEG - BDI - AFH = determinant
    [ G  H  I ]
  }

  var
    matrix: array[1..3,1..3] of integer;
    x, y, postx, posty1, posty2: byte;
    subadd1, subadd2, determinant: longint;
  begin
    { load a sample matrix value }
    matrix[1,1] := 3;
    matrix[1,2] := 4;
    matrix[1,3] := 2;
    matrix[2,1] := 8;
    matrix[2,2] := 7;
    matrix[2,3] := 3;
    matrix[3,1] := 1;
    matrix[3,2] := 0;
    matrix[3,3] := 4;
      { perform matrix calculation—note that y is not directly
        accessed within this for loop }
    for y := 1 to 3 do
      begin
        posty1 := y;
        posty2 := y;
```

```
subadd1 := 1;
        subadd2 := 1;
        for postx := 1 to 3 do
          begin
            if posty1 = 3 then
              posty1 := 1
            else
              posty1 := posty1 + 1;
            if posty2 = 1 then
              posty2 := 3
            else
              posty2 := posty2 - 1;
            subadd1 := subadd1 * matrix[postx, posty1];
            subadd2 := subadd2 * matrix[postx, posty2];
          end;
        determinant := determinant + subadd1 - subadd2;
      end;
    writeln('The determinant is: ', determinant, '.');
  end.
```

5.2.4.4. Strings

A special array defined in Turbo Pascal to handle character data is referred to as a string. There are two types of strings available to work with in Turbo Pascal 7: Pascal-type strings and null-terminated (or C-type) strings.

Pascal-type strings are specially defined in Turbo Pascal with the `string` identifier. Without any qualifiers, this represents an `array[0..255] of char` implicitly. The maximum length of a string type variable is 255 characters in this array, as it is stored in memory that way. The 0th position in this array holds an ASCII character equivalent in value to the dynamic (current) length of the string.

For example, if the phrase `'New York'` were placed in a string-type variable named `city`, the variable would use 256 bytes of memory, with data occupying 9 bytes of that space. Figure 5.2 shows the 9 bytes in this 256-byte array.

#8	'N'	'e'	'w'	' '	'Y'	'o'	'r'	'k'

FIGURE 5.2. *An illustration of storage of a variable type: string.*

What if you want to save all the excess space by defining a string variable as type `string` if you know that a string that long will never be assigned to that variable? If the range of possible string variables that will be stored is known, such as the case in which a program might be written involving the storage of month names, then the string variable can be further defined to have a smaller limit. That is done by placing brackets with the maximum amount inside them after the string keyword. For example, with the months, we could define a variable in the var section like this:

```
month: string[15];
```

In this case, month occupies 16 bytes of memory and holds a maximum string of 15 characters.

Another case of a string that can be supported in Turbo Pascal is the null-terminated string. This type is, as the name implies, an array of characters, starting with the text itself and ending with a null character, or #0. These types are either supportable by Turbo Pascal or can be supported by written code; though, in pure Turbo Pascal coding, the Pascal-type string is more commonly used.

5.2.4.5. Constant and Data Type Definitions

Turbo Pascal supports definition of constant values as well as data type definitions. Constant values are used for various purposes to aid in updating a program. Denoted by variables that appear under a header const, a constant type variable should be used throughout a program for values that do not change rapidly over short periods of time, such as month names and tax rates. A constant variable generally should not be modified by code in the program.

For example, in Listing 5.14, a constant variable could be placed at the top with a variable identity and have it used to change the 3s in the control statements of the program to that constant variable, as well as the 3s in the array (a constant variable may be used for arrays because the value is specified at compile time). This would result in a very easy modification to change the 3×3 nature of the matrix evaluation to an $N \times N$ evaluation of any reasonable value for N.

Data type definitions are used to help in modularity in certain ways, and are necessary to help define other data types that are described later. They are contained under a header denoted as type. When a type definition is made, generally variables that use this type definition exist in the var section or elsewhere. In essence, you are defining a new valid data type. Demonstrations of both constant variables and type data declarations are shown in Listing 5.15.

LISTING 5.15. *A demonstration of constants and data type declarations.*

```
program fig15;

  { constants and data types demonstration }

  const
    months: array[1..12] of string[3] =
  ('Jan','Feb','Mar','Apr','May','Jun','Jul','Aug','Sep','Oct','Nov',
    'Dec');
  { shows how to define a constant array, otherwise something like
    taxrate = 0.15; {will be sufficient to specify one constant
    variable }
  type
    monthtype = string[3];
  var
    answer: monthtype;
    month: byte;
  begin
    write('What number of month: ');
    readln(month);
    answer := months[month];
    writeln(answer);
  end.
```

5.2.4.6. Records

The data type used to group unrelated items in Turbo Pascal is called a *record*. This is not an intrinsic data type definition; hence, one must be defined in the type section. Any kind of variable, including another record type, may be defined within a record. A record data type might be used in the process of storing data for a phonebook program. A record definition that might be used in the type section of such a program might appear like this:

```
phonerecord = record
        firstname: string[15];
        lastname: string[10];
        midinit: char;
        areacode,
        exchange,
        number: integer;
        city: string[20];
    end;
```

There are two possible ways to access such a record structure when defined as a variable in a program. One is to specify the name of the variable, followed by a dot, and then the subidentifier as defined in the type declaration. The other is to encompass the code dealing with the particular record type in a with-do construct. There is no technical difference in either method other than the reduced typing the second method can produce. A diagram of memory storage of this construct is shown in Figure 5.3, and a demonstration of defining and using records is shown in Listing 5.16.

firstname	lastname	midinit	areacode	exchange	number	city

For a record variable defined, each type appears in order of the type declaration.

FIGURE 5.3. *An illustration of a record in memory, using the preceding sample.*

LISTING 5.16. *A demonstration of the definition and use of records.*

```
program fig16;

type
  phonerecord = record
    firstname: string[15];
    lastname: string[10];
    midinit: char;
    areacode, exchange, number: integer;
    city: string[20];
  end;

var
  phoneitem: phonerecord;
begin
  { first method used to fill record variable }
  phoneitem.firstname := 'Joe';
  phoneitem.lastname := 'Dialer';
  phoneitem.midinit := 'K';
  phoneitem.areacode := 513;
  phoneitem.exchange := 232;
  phoneitem.number := 2323;
  phoneitem.city := 'Jonestown';

  { second method used to write record variables }
  with phoneitem do
    begin
      writeln('Firstname: ', firstname);
      writeln('Lastname: ', lastname);
      writeln('Middle Initial: ', midinit);
      writeln('Phone Number: ', areacode, '-', exchange, '-',
              number);
      writeln('City: ', city);
    end;
end.
```

5.2.4.7. Sets and Set Algebra
It is possible to declare and work with algebraic sets and their operators by using the set of keyword in Turbo Pascal along with an ordinal identifier afterwards, much like an array is declared. Examples of sets of some degree

have already been shown in Listing 5.8. case statements as well as if statements can take conditions of a number, character, or set being part of a set. Operators to test sets, as well as manipulate sets are described next. Examples of valid sets are shown in Figure 5.4, along with a listing of these operators and their effects. Note that sets are always enclosed in brackets, unless they are used as conditions in case statements or enumerated types.

+	Union of two sets: Result is a set that contains both sets in the operator:
	`[0..10,21..30] + [11..20] = [0..30]`
-	Difference of two sets: Removes the second set from the first set:
	`['A'..'Z'] - ['B'..'D','F'] = ['A','E','G'..'Z']`
*	Intersection of two sets: Returns a set that is a part of both sets specified:
	`[1..100] * [50..150] = [50..100]`
<=	Subset: Every member of the set on the left side is on the right side:
	`[20..25] <= [1..50] returns true`
>=	Superset: Every member of set on the right side is on the left side:
	`[1..50] >= [40..60] returns false`
in	Inclusion: Is an element listed part of the whole set?
	`20 in [1..25] returns true`

FIGURE 5.4. *Examples of sets and set operators.*

5.2.4.8. Enumerated Types

An enumerated type is a definition that can bring a degree of clarity to programs, if possible. These types can be specified in word terms, like a constant array definition, or set terms without the brackets. They are defined in the data type definition section, as records are, or in some cases can be placed in the var section. When an enumerated type is encountered, only values specified by the type can be placed into the variable. When stored in memory, an enumerated type's label is assigned an ordinal number starting from 0 on the left-hand side. To help you fully understand, Listing 5.17 presents a short demonstration of the use of an enumerated type.

LISTING 5.17. *A demonstration of the use of an enumerated type.*

```
program fig17;
   type
      dirtype = (North, South, East, West);
   var
      i: dirtype;
      c: 1..5;
      { another enumerated type: May contain only 1, 2,3,4, or 5 }
   begin
{ actually in memory for i := 0 to 3 do, but this situation can
  tend to have more clarity as words than ordinal digits }
   for i := North to West do
      writeln('Hello');
   end.
```

5.2.5. Procedures and Functions

This section contains descriptions of methods used to write procedures and functions in Turbo Pascal, as well as the proper way to use procedures and functions written as a result. It also describes the recursion capabilities of Turbo Pascal and contains a generic discussion of the kinds of procedures and functions that are prewritten and come with the Turbo Pascal compiler.

5.2.5.1. Procedures

Procedures are grouped sets of code; this code is executed when the procedure name is called. This is the Turbo Pascal equivalent of a subprogram or subprocedure. Examples of procedures that you have already encountered in Pascal are read, readln, write, and writeln. Procedures are used generally as a function of modularity, and in order to organize code when written.

When you're writing procedures, you start with the keyword procedure and then an identifier, optionally with variable declarations inside parentheses as a parameters list. The variable declarations function as input and possibly output from these procedures.

The parameter declarations can be either of the constant form or the variable form when they are operated on within the procedure. When an identifier and a data type are listed, the variable used when calling the procedure is copied onto the stack. Any changes made to the variable are lost as the procedure ends. If the keyword var is placed before a data type group, then the original variables are passed by reference to the procedure, and they remain changed when the procedure ends.

Because procedures are similar to subprograms and can be written on their own as independent programs, constant declarations, data type statements, and variable declarations can be made within the procedure. These are considered local variables because their scope is locally defined to be the procedure itself, whereas variables defined in the main program would be considered global variables because they are globally defined for the entire program.

In addition, procedures must have data types in their data type declarations. These data types must fit the rules of variable identifiers, in that they cannot start with a number and cannot have a symbol that is used as part of the Turbo Pascal syntax. For example, arrays and defined-length Pascal string types must be redefined in the global data type definition list in order to pass them to procedures.

Examples of written procedures and procedure use are shown in Listing 5.18. Note that variable names used as local variables or procedure parameters may be the same as global variables or different. Variables at the same level must be identified uniquely, but variables at different levels may be identified using the same identifiers. The benefit of the organization of code may be seen in this listing. Also, as a function of modularity, determinants for more than one matrix could be found using the procedure, and not by recoding the determinant code.

LISTING 5.18. *A demonstration of writing and using procedures.*

```
program fig18;

   { two-level array demonstration rewritten as a procedures
     demonstration determinant of a 3X3 matrix. The general
     formula is for a matrix of:
     [ A  B  C ]
     [ D  E  F ]  is AEI + BFG + CDH - CEG - BDI - AFH = determinant
     [ G  H  I ]
   }

   type
      matrixtype = array[1..3,1..3] of integer;
   var
      matrix: matrixtype;
      result: longint;

   procedure loadmatrix(var thematrix: matrixtype);
      { var must be in front of declaration above so matrix
        declarations can survive end of procedure }
      begin
         thematrix[1,1] := 3;
         thematrix[1,2] := 4;
```

```
        thematrix[1,3] := 2;
        thematrix[2,1] := 8;
        thematrix[2,2] := 7;
        thematrix[2,3] := 3;
        thematrix[3,1] := 1;
        thematrix[3,2] := 0;
        thematrix[3,3] := 4;
    end;

procedure determinant(thematrix: matrixtype;
                      var theresult: longint);
{ local variables defined: scope is only within procedure
  determinant }
  var
    x, y, postx, posty1, posty2: byte;
    subadd1, subadd2: longint;
  begin
    for y := 1 to 3 do
      begin
        posty1 := y;
        posty2 := y;
        subadd1 := 1;
        subadd2 := 1;
        for postx := 1 to 3 do
          begin
            if posty1 = 3 then
              posty1 := 1
            else
              posty1 := posty1 + 1;
            if posty2 = 1 then
              posty2 := 3
            else
              posty2 := posty2 - 1;
            subadd1 := subadd1 * thematrix[postx, posty1];
            subadd2 := subadd2 * thematrix[postx, posty2];
          end;
        theresult := theresult + subadd1 - subadd2;
      end;
  end;

begin
  loadmatrix(matrix);
  determinant(matrix, result);
  writeln('The determinant is: ', result, '.');
end.
```

5.2.5.2. Functions

Functions, in most ways, are exactly like procedures in that the same rules of programming for procedures apply for functions. The only difference is that the function itself returns a value, a number, character, string, or pointer. Therefore, whether a variable is changed and survives in the parameter list is of no concern, as the parameter list should only contain input values.

Functions, when defined, start with the reserved word function and then a parameter list, as with procedures. The final part is a : followed by a data type that the function will return when enacted. An example of a function is shown in Listing 5.19. Functions may be used exactly in place of where a value might be, as that data type, and in that sense they function as variables of the data type they return, though some input values and code exist to evaluate or return the value.

Functions can have great value in simplifying and streamlining the coding process. Though it is hard to describe when to use functions over procedures, when you gain some slight experience in coding, the situations to use functions will become evident.

LISTING 5.19. *A demonstration of function use.*

```
program fig19;

var
  i: byte;

function power(x: real; y: integer): real;
  { function: returns result of x^y where x and y are integers }
  var
    i: integer;
    result: real;
  begin
    result := 1;
    for i := 1 to y do
      result := result * x;
    power := result;
  end;

begin
  for i := 1 to 10 do
    writeln(i, ' squared is ', power(i,2):0:2);
    { function call is treated exactly like a real number }
end.
```

5.2.5.3. Recursion, Stack Space, and Forward Declarations

Turbo Pascal has the capability of *recursion*, or the ability to execute a function or procedure within itself. Pascal recurses completely because the variables that are placed in the parameter list are recopied onto the stack along with the data to completely execute the procedure or function. In this sense, a procedure or function is called exactly the same way in a recursion action as in an iterative action.

The preference is toward iteration (linear programming) instead of recursion if the algorithm could be expressed equally well in the same way. Iteration is faster and generally easier understood than recursion. But where an iterative solution may grow messy or less elegant in nature than a recursive function, recursion may be ideal. Recursion can be seen as splitting up a large problem into several smaller problems of the same nature.

In using recursion, tremendous amounts of stack space could be used, as a recursive function or procedure could recurse many times. Hence, adjustment of the stack space may be desired. That and many other purposes are gained by adjusting values from the default in the $M compiler directive.

It is expressed by stating $M in a comment and then adding three numbers (expressed in a number of bytes). The first is the amount of stack space allowed, the second is the minimum amount of heap needed, and the third is the maximum amount of heap space needed. For concerns of this section, the first number is described. This is the amount of stack space allowed for the program. This is execution space, used for the program itself. When a procedure or function is executed, stack space lessens. The normal default for stack space is 16 KB, the minimum is 0 KB, and the maximum is 64 KB. An example of the proper way to use the $M compiler directive is as follows: {$M 32767,0,655360}. It should appear at the beginning of the code.

In recursion between functions, if the case exists, forward declarations might be useful. A forward declaration is a statement that simply declares the existence of a function or procedure and its appearance. Forwards might be useful when "function a" might call "function b" and "function b would call function a." Because the compiler has to be aware of a procedure or function before its use, this case might present a problem. Therefore, a forward declaration could be useful.

A forward declaration is made by declaring the header of the procedure/function and then, after the semicolon, stating the reserved word forward, following that with another semicolon. When the actual block of code can occur, the keyword procedure or function is given and then the name and a semicolon.

Listing 5.20 demonstrates a function written to operate recursively. A description of the execution path of the function, which is an integer power function just like the one in Listing 5.19, appears after the listing.

LISTING 5.20. *A demonstration of recursion and forwards.*

```
program fig20;

var
  i: byte;
  result: real;
  function power(x: real; y: integer): real;
    { function: returns result of x^y where x and y are integers }
    { written recursively }
    begin
      if y >= 1 then
        power := x * power(x,y-1)
      else
        power := 1;
    end;

begin
  for i := 1 to 10 do
    begin
      result := power(i,2);
      writeln(i, ' squared is ', result:0:2);
    end;
end.
```

A recursive function, such as the one in Listing 5.20, always has a condition to stop recursion and return some alternate value. In this case, when y becomes 0 when it is called in the function, the value 1 is returned, in signification that when x is anything and y is 0 in a power function, the result is always 1. Figure 5.5 illustrates the variable values and actions when power() is called.

With the preceding case, a typical algebra equation is used in the power function: x^y. Logically, in algebra, $x^y = x * x^{y-1}$. This continues until y becomes 0; in this case, x^y becomes 1, and there is no need to go any further.

Description	X	Y	Result (upon return)
Initial call, y=2 recurse to next	x:=3;	y:=2;	Result:=3*3=9
Next call, y=1 recurse to next	x:=3;	y:=1;	Result:=1*3=3
y=0 return 1	x:=3;	y:=0;	Result:=1

Note that the number gained from previous function's return is used in the computation of the next function above it.

FIGURE 5.5. *Description of the recursive power function.*

5.2.5.4. Prewritten Procedures and Functions

TP, like most programming languages today, comes with a variety of procedures and functions already written to do various things. Among those things are working with files and directories, DOS-related functions, screen output and control, enhanced keyboard input, and working with and manipulating data. You can find a description of many of these prewritten items later in this chapter.

5.2.6. Units, Unit Creation, and Include Files

This section describes TP's features of modularity. They involve the creation and use of units, as well as use of include files. The prewritten procedures and functions come in the form of units, as well, and those will be described at the end of this section.

5.2.6.1. Units and Unit Creation

A unit is a modular piece of code, with procedures and functions that may be included into any other program or unit to give access to all of the code within. Only the code in the unit that is used, generally, is compiled into the executable. Also, the code is linked into the executable at compile time, not runtime (you do not have to distribute a unit to get an executable file you compile to work).

The files in your \units directory (more than likely) are examples of unit files. These are the less commonly used units, which are included with Turbo Pascal. The more common ones, to be described later, are loaded into memory when the compiler is active. The units are not like object files and are not compatible with object files. They are optimized to a larger degree, in that only the code that is needed is included.

In Listing 5.21, note the format of a unit. Units include procedures and functions, which are generally related, in the entire listing. The interface section lists the headers of the procedures and functions, as well as any data type definitions, constant definitions, and initialization code that may be required to call any of the code that is in the unit. Note that data types cannot be duplicated.

Any type functions that are needed for unit-related functions and procedures must be declared in that unit and that unit only. The implementation section lists all the headers of the procedures and functions again, as well as the code associated with each of the headers. In implementation of a unit, all items in the interface section are made aware of the program, including type and constant declarations. Because Pascal is a strongly typed language, if a type is referred to in two locations with the same name and same description, they are still different.

LISTING 5.21. *An example of a unit file.*

```
unit fig21;
{ note, the identifier here must match the name of the file }

  interface
    function power(x:real; y: integer):real;
  implementation
    function power(x:real; y: integer):real;
    { must be exactly as above }
      var
        i: integer;
        result: real;
      begin
        result := 1;
        for i := 1 to y do
          result := result * x;
        power := result;
      end;

  end.
```

For you to use this unit, or any other unit, it must be specified after the program clause of the code in a uses clause, followed by the exact name of the identifier used in the unit clause of the unit's code. In Listing 5.22, note how the unit just created is registered and used in the resulting program. The compiled unit, as specified in Listing 5.21, should be made available to this program when created.

LISTING 5.22. *The use of a unit file in a program.*

```
program fig22; uses fig21;
{if more than 1 unit put commas between each id}
  var
    i: byte;
  begin
    for i := 1 to 10 do
      writeln(i, ' squared is ', power(i,2):0:2);
  end.
```

Here, the program executes in the same manner as Listings 5.19 and 5.20. The advantage here is that, if the unit fig21 is available, the power function does not have to be retyped and retested, just the uses clause must be typed. This kind of modularity and ability to organize code can be very useful. Also, in very large programs, units must be used, as the executable created must have a number of code segments that are a maximum of 64 KB each.

5.2.6.2. Include Files

Another not necessarily better option, but one that may be preferable, is the use of include files. When the compiler option to include a file is issued, the compiler inserts the file specified at that point in the code and compiles the code as if that file were typed in the source originally starting in the exact position the include directive was placed. A file is included into a Turbo Pascal program, at any point, by use of the $I `<filename>` compiler directive. For example, {$I STRUCT.PAS} is a valid include compiler directive.

5.2.6.3. Prewritten Units

Turbo Pascal's prewritten functions and procedures come in different units. The more uncommon ones are seen, more than likely, in the \units directory of your Turbo Pascal installation. The more common ones are loaded into memory from a "packed" file that exists in the bin directory when the compiler is evoked. Some of these common units include the CRT unit, which holds items that involve screen control and output in a text-oriented way; the DOS unit, which holds items that involve implementation of DOS-related functions; and the system unit (which need not be called in the uses clause), which contains elementary procedures and functions. write, writeln, read, and readln do not need a uses clause because they are created in the system unit.

5.2.7. Data Manipulation Procedures and Functions

This section describes some of the more commonly used functions and procedures available to perform manipulation on a data type, such as typecasting, conversions, and modifications, via mathematical evaluation or otherwise. The pseudo-random number generator and bitwise operations (or "bit fiddling") are also covered.

5.2.7.1. Typecasting and Type Conversions

Typecasting and type conversions on data are described in this section. All functions and procedures involved come from the system unit.

5.2.7.2. Typecasting

Typecasting is exactly what it implies: the interpretation of one type into another type. Generally, it is done with the typical variable types that are defined, with the type name used as a function. It is done in a function style, where the interpretation of the variable is changed, and not its format in memory. An example of typecasting (and one case in which it might be used) is shown in Listing 5.23.

LISTING 5.23. *A demonstration of typecasting.*

```
program fig23;
    { demonstrates type casting and what can be done }
    var
        a: char;
        b: byte;
    begin
        a := 'C';
        b := 45;
        writeln('a is: ', a);
        writeln('b is: ', b);
        writeln('b char: ', char(b));
        writeln('a byte: ', byte(a));
        writeln('a byte + b: ', byte(a) + b);
        writeln('a + b char: ', a + char(b));
    end.
```

ord( ) and chr( )

These two functions are most commonly used to convert characters between their ASCII equivalent character and the byte that is stored:

```
ord(x: ordinal type): longint;
chr(x: longint): char;
```

For example, ord('A') returns 65, and chr(65) returns 'A'. An example of use is shown in Listing 5.24.

LISTING 5.24. *An example of the use of* ord( ) *and* chr( ).

```
program fig24;

    { a demonstration of ord() and chr() to prove that 'A' is a byte by
      the value of 65 }

    begin
        if ord('A') = 65 then
            writeln('A character "A" is stored as a byte = 65 according ',
                    'to ord');
        if chr(65) = 'A' then
            writeln('A byte = 65 is stored as a character ''A'' according ',
                    'to chr');
    end.
```

str and val

These procedures are used to convert a number variable to a string, and a numerically oriented string to a number variable, in that order:

```
str(x: <a number>:<optional formatting as in writes>; var s: string);
val(s: string; x: <a number>; errorcode: integer);
```

str( ) takes a number, with desired formatting codes if it is a real number (if you want to have it as a decimal and not as a scientific number), like writing reals in write or writeln, and then the string the variable is going to end up in.

val() takes a string, which should have only numeric characters, as well as periods, and a numeric variable, as well as an integer-related error variable. It places the numeric equivalent of s into the variable x. errorcode is not 0, denoting the position of error if it is non-numeric, if the string s was not convertible. This variable must be checked after each and every call of val.

Demonstrations of these procedures are shown in Listing 5.25.

LISTING 5.25. *A demonstration of* val *and* str.

```
program fig25;

   { demonstrates and writes results of the use of val and str }
   var
      entry: string;
      number: real;
      error: integer;
   begin
      write('Enter something: ');
      readln(entry);
      val(entry, number, error);
      if error <> 0 then { show error at position }
         writeln('Non-numeric character found at position ', error)
      else
         writeln(number);
      number := 5.23342;
      str(number:0:2, entry); { format string may be used here }
      writeln(entry);
   end.
```

5.2.7.3. Modifications of Data Types

This section shows common procedures and functions that aid in modifying a variable data type.

upcase() **and** length()

These two functions are commonly seen together, but not always:

```
function upcase(x: char): char;
function length(s: string): byte;
```

upcase() returns the uppercased version of a letter in the alphabet, if x is a letter of the alphabet. Otherwise, it returns the exact character passed to it. length() returns the literal equivalent of ord(s[0]) in a string s, or the current real length of the string stored. length() may be preferable over ord(s[0]) in some situations, but either is usually good. An example of using both of these functions is shown in Listing 5.26.

LISTING 5.26. *A demonstration of* upcase() *and* length().

```
program fig26;

    function upstr(s: string): string;
    var
        i: byte;
        outstr: string;
    begin
        for i := 1 to length(s) do
            upstr[i] := upcase(s[i]);
        upstr[0] := s[0];
    end;

    begin
        writeln(upstr('San Francisco'));
    end.
```

copy() **and** pos()

These two functions work with strings:

```
copy(s: string, starting_postion: byte, length: byte): string;
pos(s,t: string): byte;
```

pos() returns the starting position of a string s, in the full string t, if it exists. Otherwise, it returns 0. copy() returns the partial substring described by the starting position and length byte specified in an entire string. Listing 5.27 demonstrates both functions, in a situation in which these functions are most often used, text parsing and processing.

LISTING 5.27. *A demonstration of* copy() *and* pos().

```
program fig27;
    { demo of copy and pos }
    const
        s: string = 'The brown dog jumped over the lazy cow.';
    var
        result: byte;
        subst: string;
    begin
        result := 11;
        subst := s;
        while result <> 0 do { while there still are spaces }
            begin
                result := pos(' ', subst);
                if result > 0 then
                    writeln(copy(subst, 1, result));
                subst := copy(subst, result+1, length(subst) - result);
            end;
        writeln(subst);
    { this means the last word has occurred, write it }
    end.
```

5.2.7.4. Mathematical Functions

This section describes mathematical functions and procedures. No prototypes are given because the use of most, if not all, of these functions is simple to understand. They take a numerical variable and return a numerical variable. The following are the mathematical functions (see Listing 28.5):

- `function abs`—Returns the absolute value of the number given.

- `function arctan`—Returns the arctangent of the value given in radian form.

- `function cos`—Returns the cosine of the number given, which should be in radians.

- `procedure dec`—Decreases the first `integer`/`longint` variable given by 1 and stores it in that first variable, if a second number is not given; otherwise, decreases it by the second number given (note that this is more efficient than `i := i - 1`).

- `function exp`—Returns the evaluation of `e` to the power of the number given.

- `function frac`—Returns the fractional part of a real number.

- `procedure inc`—Increases the first `integer`/`longint` variable given by 1 and stores it in that first variable, if a second number is not given; otherwise, it increases it by the second number given (note that this is more efficient than `i := i + 1`).

- `function int`—Returns the integer part of a real number.

- `function ln`—Returns the natural logarithm of the number given.

- `function pi`—This constant contains the value of pi, to the full precision capable in TP.

- `function round`—Returns the rounded number given to the nearest whole number.

- `function sin`—Returns the sine of the number given, which should be in radians.

- `function trunc`—Truncates a real number to a whole number.

LISTING 5.28. *Some mathematical functions.*

```
program fig28;
  { demonstrates some mathematical functions }
  const
    { pi = 3.1415;  DO NOT DEFINE THIS!
      It is already defined for you. }
    rad: real = pi/180; { one degree = pi / 180 radians }
    degreeparts: array[1..17] of integer =
      (0,30,45,60,90,120,135,150,180,210,225,240,270,300,315,330,360);
  var
    i: byte;
    sresult, cresult: real;
  begin
    writeln('Simple Trigonometry Table');
    writeln('Degrees','Sin':5,'Cos':10,'Tan':10);
    for i := 1 to 17 do
      begin
        sresult := sin(degreeparts[i]*rad);
        cresult := cos(degreeparts[i]*rad);
        write(degreeparts[i]:4, sresult:10:3,cresult:10:3);
        { note due to the conversion from radians that these are not
          *exactly* accurate, as denoted by the negatives on the 0
          values. }
        { done to indicate the exception in the formula for tan x,
          which is sin x / cos x ; cos x <> 0 , set won't handle
          anything beyond byte, so 30 is subtracted, and other
          values are used. }
        if (degreeparts[i] - 30) in [60, 240] then
          writeln('Invalid':10)
        else
          writeln(sresult/cresult :10:3);
      end;
  end.
```

5.2.7.5. The Pseudo-Random Number Generator

In addition, a pseudo-random number generator (PRNG) exists; it qualifies as a mathematical function. It is referred to as pseudo-random and not a truly random number generator, as it uses an algebraic equation with a seed and a given range in order to generate a number sequence that seems random.

When the seed is given to be constant in the PRNG, and consequently the program itself, it generates the same constant stream of numbers upon each execution of the program containing the PRNG statements. But a method can be used to randomize the seed from the system clock to make the number sequences appear to be random.

The seed for the PRNG is held in a longint variable called randseed, which may be set directly, if a repeating constant stream of numbers is desired. Otherwise, a procedure named "randomize" may be used in order to randomize the variable randseed in memory. Then to generate one number of the series, a function named random() may be used. Without parameters, it generates a real number between 0 and 1. With a parameter, it generates a number between 0 and (parameter − 1). For example, random(100) generates an integer between 0 and 99. A sample use of the PRNG is shown in Listing 5.29.

LISTING 5.29. *A demonstration of the PRNG.*

```
program fig29;
   { demonstration of the PRNG, distribution of 100 pseudo-randomly
     generated numbers between 1 and 10—count of occurrences }
   var
      pcount: array[1..10] of byte;
      i: byte;
   begin
      randomize;
{ call this only *once* at the beginning of the program }
      for i := 1 to 10 do
         pcount[i] := 0;
      for i := 1 to 100 do
         inc(pcount[random(10)+1]);
      for i := 1 to 10 do
         writeln(i, ' occurred ', pcount[i], ' times.');
   end.
```

5.2.7.6. Bit Manipulation

This section describes the bit operators and functions available under Turbo Pascal. As is known, a byte is made up of 8 bits, each designated either 1 or 0. The manipulation of bits involves some bit shifting or boolean algebra in any of the 1-, 2-, or 4-byte numerical variables. One-byte examples are used in this section.

Generally, when we're talking about bits, the most significant bits are to the left, as this is how most of us are used to dealing with numbers in algebra. Computer systems, though, do not necessarily deal with items in this way. Some are "big endian," meaning they deal with bits in the exact manner humans are used to dealing with them. Others, like PCs, are "little endian," meaning the least significant bit is first, when reading from left to right, in order to the most significant bit. Note that with Turbo Pascal, you will be dealing with a little endian system if you use a hex editor for observing storage methods.

Shifting Bits

In shifting bits, they can either be shifted left or right. The corresponding operators to do that in Turbo Pascal are shl, or shift left, and shr, or shift right. In shifting, the bits are physically moved, with 0s assumed on the remaining portions. If any relevant bytes are "pushed" out of the data's range for storage, they are lost. Note, in the following examples, that within storable limits, shifting bits can be equivalent to multiplying or integer division by the power of 2 the bits are shifted by in the operation.

Each operator is used by placing the value to be operated on, followed by shl or shr, and the number of places to be shifted.

```
00100100 shl 2 = 10010000    (36 shl 2 = 144)    36*2^2 = 144

00100100 shr 2 = 10010001    (36 shr 2 = 9)      36 div 2^2 = 9
```

FIGURE 5.6. *A demonstration of the effects of bit shifting (*shl *and* shr*).*

Boolean Algebra

In manipulating bits, boolean algebra or logic can be used to work with variables on a bit level. Types of boolean algebra described are AND, OR (inclusive OR), or XOR (exclusive OR). Before we continue the description, see the listing of boolean algebra rules in terms of bits. The following AND and OR rules are exactly like those encountered in control statements, when 1 is true and 0 is false:

true AND true = true

true OR true = true

true XOR true = false

true AND false = false

true OR false = true

true XOR false = true

false AND true = false

false OR true = true

false XOR true = true

false AND false = false

false OR false = false

false XOR false = false

In the case of multiple bits, each bit is evaluated depending on the rules as described here. Examples of the bit operations are shown in Figure 5.7, and appear in a TP program listing in a similar manner in decimal form.

```
┌─────────────────────────────────────────────────────────────────┐
│     10101111              10101111              10101111          │
│                                                                   │
│ AND 01010101          OR 01010101          XOR 01010101           │
│                                                                   │
│     ===========          ==========          ===========         │
│                                                                   │
│     00000101              11111111              11111010          │
└─────────────────────────────────────────────────────────────────┘
```

FIGURE 5.7. A sample of bitwise boolean algebra operators.

In using the boolean operators, the patterns of the answers can reveal the use of these operators. AND can be used quite well to test the existence of a bit or bits at specific positions. Note in the example for AND that the bytes which remain 1s or true are the ones that appear in both columns. With the OR example, any bits that are true and dissimilar are forced to true. In the XOR example, it could that in the positions the 1s are in the second object of the operator, the bits were toggled from 1 to 0, or 0 to 1. A coded example of the boolean bit operators and bit shifting are shown in Listing 5.30.

LISTING 5.30. An example of bitwise operators.

```pascal
program fig30; uses wconv;

  { visual demonstrator of effects of all bitwise evaluators,
    actually, a good tutorial/flash card program for learning
    these operators. function writebinary(inbyte: byte):string;
    is from wconv, a utility unit I have written for writing
    values in different common bases for my personal use. Code not
    included because it does not further the topic of this program.
    Such a function may be created easily with the knowledge of
    base conversions. }

var
  option, num1, num2: byte;

procedure processinfo(option, num1, num2: byte);
  begin
    writeln(writebinary(num1):23);
    case option of
      1: write('SHL');
      2: write('SHR');
      3: write('AND');
      4: write(' OR');
      5: write('XOR');
    end;
    { no point in writing out bits for 2nd number if SHL or SHR }
    if option in [1..2] then
      writeln(num2:10)
    else
      writeln(writebinary(num2):20);
    writeln('====================');
```

```
        case option of
          1: writeln(writebinary(num1 shl num2):23);
          2: writeln(writebinary(num1 shr num2):23);
          3: writeln(writebinary(num1 and num2):23);
          4: writeln(writebinary(num1 or num2):23);
          5: writeln(writebinary(num1 xor num2):23);
        end;
      end;

  begin
    option := 10;
    while option <> 6 do
      begin
        writeln;writeln;
        writeln('Enter a number from the list below:');
        writeln('1) SHL 2) SHR 3) AND 4) OR 5) XOR 6) QUIT');
        write('Enter an option [1-6]: ');
        readln(option);
        if option <> 6 then
          begin
            write('Enter first number: ');
            readln(num1);
            write('Enter second number: ');
            readln(num2);
            writeln;
            processinfo(option, num1, num2);
          end;
      end;
  end.
```

In addition, functions called lo, hi, and swap are provided. In a series of bits, they can be divided in half. The more significant bits are referred to as the high order, and the least significant bits are referred to as the low order. lo() returns the low order of the argument given, hi() returns the high order of the argument given, and swap() returns the argument with the high and low orders swapped.

5.2.8. Dynamic Memory Allocation

The PCs with the 8088 class CPUs could only deal with 64 KB of data (declared variables) at once because of the CPUs' limitations. Of course, when this computer was created, it was realized that to have 1024 KB of usable memory in it, along with the capability of accessing all this memory and not only 64 KB of it, that some way had to be devised to do this. Machine could handle only a maximum of a 16-bit address and 64 KB of data at a time.

Ultimately, it was decided for this computer to use a segment:offset combination in addressing memory, resulting in a 20-bit system for addressing memory in the DOS PC system. Also, because the limitation in memory that the CPU could handle was there, it was determined that a 4-byte address in memory could be created in order to redirect the CPU to a position in memory to find a variable or point essentially to the position in memory that holds this variable at a particular moment.

A pointer, which was described earlier, is the main means for accessing this extra memory. This 4-byte address points to a predescribed data type at a particular position in memory. Eventually, with this system of addressing memory, where 64 KB of memory was directly accessible, and the rest of the free memory up to 640 KB was referred to by pointers, special terminology was devised to refer to these portions. The portion of memory directly accessed could be referred to as the data area, and the rest of the memory accessible by pointers could be referred to as the heap. These elements are still referred to in that manner today with a 16-bit compiler because of the concern for backward compatibility.

Turbo Pascal uses a system such as this to access the other part of the 640 KB of conventional memory. In the sense that pointers can be used to dynamically place information in the heap, this section is referred to as dynamic memory allocation. This is essentially the creation, destruction, and readdressing of memory allocation at runtime instead of compile time, in which the directly accessible memory is addressed.

There are many reasons you might use pointer-based structures over static based structures. One, which has already been alluded to, is the ability to create variable data structures in excess of 64 KB. Two is the ability to dynamically allocate variables, if they are large variables that are temporarily used at one time in the program to conserve memory. Three is the ability to create pointer-based structures in many different forms, such as linear linked lists and tree-based structures, to express some algorithm that would be incredibly inefficient in other methods. Four is the sheer dynamic nature of pointer-based structures—for example, the ability to insert a new variable in any position of the structure without "shuffling" the contents currently in an array-based structure.

The means to access and use pointer-based structures is described next, as well as addressing values in memory for variables, procedures, and functions. A special exit procedure developed in Turbo Pascal called `exitproc` is also described.

5.2.8.1. Using and Accessing Pointer-Based Structures
In the sense of dynamic memory allocation, a predescribed data type can be created, destroyed, moved, or changed by use of assignments, or procedures created for dynamic allocation, such as `new()` and `dispose()`.

new() creates or assigns a position in the heap for a variable type specified in the data type for that variable, and dispose() removes the position from the heap previously allocated with new(). The designation in a program that indicates a variable is a pointer is the caret symbol (^) as part of the type or variable name. For example, observe the methods by which the simpler structures in Listing 5.31 are created and accessed. Note that this is a very inefficient way, memory wise, to use pointers (they are usually used in more complex variable types).

This listing also illustrates the difference between readdressing a pointer and modifying the contents in heap memory of that pointer. The pointer variable itself, without the caret, represents a mostly static (but sometimes dynamic) position of memory that holds a memory address to a spot on the heap, and the pointer variable (including the caret) represents the value in the memory position in the heap.

As you may expect, a pointer cannot point to a particular address in memory at all. To accomplish this, the pointer variable itself is assigned the value represented by the reserve word nil (pvar := nil;). In Turbo Pascal, this represents making the pointer point to nothing.

LISTING 5.31. *A rudimentary demonstration of pointer-based structures.*

```
program fig31;
  type
    inttype = ^integer;
{ note caret required, read "pointer to an integer" }
  var
    a, b: inttype;
  begin
    new(a);
{ note, no ^ on new or dispose as they address pointers }
    new(b);
    writeln('Largest Block Available After New: ', maxavail);
    writeln('Total Memory Available After New: ', memavail);
    a^ := 2;
    b^ := 5;
    writeln(a^, ' ', b^);

    { note that pointers are static structures which represent
      ADDRESSES, and not the INTEGER themselves. So to move the
      pointer, and eliminate the problem illustrated in Tips/Traps,
      dispose must be called BEFORE a POINTER itself is readdressed. }

    dispose(a);
    a := b; { a now points at the heap memory b points to }
    writeln(a^, ' ', b^);
```

```
{ note now this write puts out 5 on both cases }

  dispose(b);
{ to clean up in the program. Note either dispose(a) or dispose(b)
  may be called here, since dispose operates on the area reserved in
  heap memory and not the pointer, but good practice is to match up
  new() calls with dispose() calls }
    writeln('Largest Block Available After Dispose: ', maxavail);
    writeln('Total Memory Available After Dispose: ', memavail);
  end.
```

With the dynamic nature of memory allocation, a means is needed to determine how much memory is left to allocate. In this case, the variables memavail and maxavail and the function sizeof() are available. As memory can get fragmented, maxavail represents the largest continuous block of memory available to be allocated. memavail represents the total amount of memory free to be allocated. sizeof(var) returns the physical number of bytes occupied by that variable in memory.

5.2.8.2. Address of Items in Memory

In addition to pointer addresses, which may be used as indicated in the preceding section or as linked into lists or trees (one static pointer holds a record system that is allocated in the heap with pointers in that record system which are allocated for more space on the heap), an address operator may be used to refer to addresses of procedures, functions, or static variables in memory. It also can be used to aid in changing items in the program, like dynamic procedures and functions, as well as setting pointers to values returned by functions and procedures (internally, that is what is happening when procedures and functions are used). (If you are interested in the types of structures described here, locate a data structures book.) The @ symbol, or in Pascal, read as "the address of," is used in this case to represent the memory address of a variable, procedure, or function.

An example of doing this is shown in Listing 5.32. Far procedures must be used as illustrated to make something like this routine work. For example, a sort routine with options to sort by multiple functions would be ideal for this kind of coding, though this case would be ludicrous. Note that a pointer is also addressed in this listing to a static variable position in memory.

LISTING 5.32. *Demonstration of the @ operator.*

```
program fig32;
  type
    intptr = ^integer;
    proctype = procedure(a: string);
  var
    c: integer;
    d: intptr;
    callit: proctype;
  {$F+}      { this can be used or "far;" after each procedure }
  procedure yesitisafive(a: string);
    begin
      writeln('D is a 5.');
      writeln(a);
    end;
  procedure noitisnotafive(a: string);
    begin
      writeln('D is not a 5.');
      writeln(a);
    end;
  {$F-}

  begin
    @callit := nil;    { requirement to make it work }
    c := 5;
    d := @c;
    writeln('Pointer contents of d are ', d^);
    if d^ = 5 then
      @callit := @yesitisafive
    else
      @callit := @noitisnotafive;
    callit('Whatever works is fine.');
  end.
```

5.2.8.3. exitproc

exitproc is a procedure that is set up as an address system, which is executed on the compiler automatically upon completion of the program, no matter what kind of error may happen, but before a runtime error code message. A common application for this feature is the addition of runtime error-description code, or diagnostic logging features for a program, or clean-up functions for working with files. Listing 5.33 shows an example.

LISTING 5.33. *An example of the use of* exitproc.

```
program fig33;

  const
    a: integer = 3;
    b: integer = 0;
  var
    exitsave: procedure;

  {$F+}    { must be far }
  procedure myexit; {must be parameterless}
```

```
begin
  writeln;
  writeln('Exit.');
  if exitcode <> 0 then
  { exitcode used to hold run-time error number}
    writeln('There was a problem.')
  else
    writeln('Successful termination.');
  end;
{$F-}

begin
  @exitsave := exitproc;   { saving the original exit procedure }
  exitproc := @myexit;     { set to new exit procedure }
  writeln('Hello!');
  { force a division by zero RUNTIME error }
  writeln('Divide by Zero: ', a/b);
  exitproc := @exitsave;   { set the original exit procedure back }
end.
```

5.2.9. File Access

In Turbo Pascal, everything that is read from or written to is considered to be a file. This includes the keyboard and the screen as well. Turbo Pascal's behavior of having "default files" has somewhat shielded the reader from working with files for the time being. In the initialization code for a Pascal executable, a default file of input is assigned to the keyboard, and a default file of output is assigned to the monitor, as file variables "input" and "output." In this sense, a description of what file to write to has not been needed. But for other files, file descriptions have to be specified.

Remember, in the descriptions in this section, there are no such things as "different types" of files. All files are the same, though the way they are accessed is different, which is the true meaning of a "file type." These different methods of accessing files are described in this section. Among those are ASCII text files, typed and untyped binary files, and the printer.

Note, in addition, that most of the source code examples in this section use a file called INTDATA.TXT, which either may be edited or generated by a file named TESTTEXT.EXE. In the examples, the generated version is used; it is an edited ASCII text file, with a number of lines between 300 and 399, and a number of integers (as text) between 0 and 24 per line of text.

5.2.9.1. File Access in General

Any file, to be usable in Turbo Pascal, must have two procedure statements to be able to access it. The first is an assign statement, assigning a file variable to a specific filename (as a string). The specific filename may or may not have an accompanying path. After this call, the file is always referred to by the file variable. File variables, when designated in the `var` section of a program, procedure, or function, are referred to depending on the way the file is accessed.

The next is either a `reset()`, `rewrite()`, or `append()` call, with the file variable as the parameter. These procedure calls "open" the file in a particular way to be accessed. `reset()` opens a file in a read-only mode for text files and a read/write mode for other types of files at the beginning position of the file. `rewrite()` opens any type of file in a write-only mode, in the process creating the file on the drive (beware if the file already exists, that file will be gone) with that name. `append()` opens a text file and allows writes to it at the end of the current text stored in the file. Note the limitations in DOS of the maximum number of files that may be opened; this limitation is stated in the `CONFIG.SYS` of the particular system as `files=XX`.

The final procedure call, which must be used to close a file after it is used, is `close(<file variable>)`. This procedure flushes the disk cache's and buffer's contents related to that file and releases the file handle.

When a file is accessed and associated with a file variable, reading and writing of the file must generally occur. This is accomplished by adding the file variable name as the first parameter of a read or write call. Note in using the read and write procedures that the file variable must always be included as the first parameter.

5.2.9.2. Text Files

Text files, in Turbo Pascal, are files that may be read as text and interpreted into almost any variable, except for record and array structures and boolean types. To be interpreted into variables such as integers and reals, spaces must occur between each number in the file, with nothing else to read other than numerical data. In this sense, reading from and writing to a text file is exactly the same as reading from the keyboard, except in the cases of `readln` and `writeln`, which moves the "read position" in the file to the next line of text.

When experimenting with the other sources in this document, you may have observed that entering a letter when a numerical prompt was expected would crash the programs. Reading from a text file in that manner is no different because each line of text is treated like you would expect to see it treated if typed in from the keyboard. The following are some samples of the behavior of `read` with different variables:

Text file line: `30 20 30 20.5 Testament`

`read integer: 30`

`read next char: ' '`

`read next real: 20.0`

`read next string[5]: ' 30 2'`

`read next real: 0.5` (Note that if an integer is read at this point, a runtime error occurs)

Note that the current file position is always after the `read` variable. The text at the particular position is translated into whatever variable is desired. A full example of reading and writing to text files is shown in Listing 5.34, as well as proper use of the functions `eof()` and `eoln()`. These functions perform status checking to determine whether the reading is at the end of the file or the end of the line of text (in that order). These functions should always be used, as you do not always know the exact description of a file that is accessed.

LISTING 5.34. *A demonstration of reading and writing text files.*

```
program fig34;

  { demonstration of text file usage, along with eof() and eoln() }
  { Uses INTDATA.TXT as generated by TESTTEXT.EXE }

  var
    infile, outfile: text;
    total: longint;
    number_line, total_line: integer;
    objnum: integer;

  begin
    assign(infile, 'INTDATA.TXT');
    assign(outfile, 'DATARPT.TXT');
    reset(infile);
    rewrite(outfile);
    total_line := 0;
    while not eof(infile) do
      begin
        number_line := 0;
        total := 0;
        while not eoln(infile) do
          begin
            read(infile, objnum);
            inc(total, objnum);
            inc(number_line);
          end;
        readln(infile);
        inc(total_line);
```

```
              writeln(outfile, 'Line ', total_line:3, ': ', number_line:2,
                      ' numbers — Average: ', (total/number_line):10:4);
          end;
        close(infile);
        close(outfile);
    end.
```

5.2.9.3. Typed Binary Files

Another way to access a file is as a typed binary file. Binary files contain data that is stored in the file exactly as it is stored in memory. A typed binary file is a binary file in which the type of the data that is read or written is described beforehand. Therefore, the reads and writes to this type of file are always of the variable type specified (attempting to read/write any other type results in a runtime error). An example of the use of typed binary files is shown in Listing 5.35.

A typed binary file is accessed in the exact same manner as a text file with some differences. A typed binary file is described as a file of <datatype> when the file variable is written. When reset is called for a typed binary file, it may be read from as well as directly overwritten. Because this is pure binary data, readln and writeln are invalid to use with this type of file.

A procedure named seek(<binary file var>, <# of vars forward>) is used for adding random access to a binary file for purposes of reading or over-writing a position in the file, and filesize(<typed binary filevar>) returns the total number of typed variables in the file (if 38 integers are in a file, it returns 38, and not the physical size of the file on the drive). Note that eoln()'s usefulness is eliminated in this file type, but eof() is still useful in the case of reading a typed binary file.

LISTING 5.35. *An example of typed binary file use.*

```
program fig35;

    { demonstration of usage of typed binary file }

    { uses intdata.txt as input, outputs binary integer data }

    var
        infile: text;
        outfile: file of integer;
        int: integer;
    begin
        assign(infile, 'INTDATA.TXT');
        assign(outfile, 'TYPEDATA.DAT');
        reset(infile);
```

```
  rewrite(outfile);
  while not eof(infile) do
    begin
      while not eoln(infile) do
        begin
          read(infile, int);
          write(outfile, int);
        end;
      readln(infile);
    end;
  close(infile);
  close(outfile);
end.
```

5.2.9.4. Untyped Binary Files

A file can also be accessed as an untyped binary file. Here, no type is given in the file variable. In this case, filesize and seek units are always in bytes. Also, because no types are used, different procedures must be used for reading and writing to these files, as read and write work only with typed variables. blockread and blockwrite function for this purpose. The way to call these procedures is readily apparent in Listing 5.36. Note the use of sizeof(), which is the best way to indicate the size of whatever structure is used.

Also observe the reset and rewrite calls are different. Because an untyped binary file is a pure random file, a block size to read and write from must be specified. Generally, you should always specify this variable to be 1. It is this quality that also eliminates the usefulness of the eof() and eoln() variables, which makes the algorithm expressed below a requirement.

Untyped binary files have the advantage of speed and the ability to read varying data types. When the same data type is stored throughout the file, typed binary files are better.

LISTING 5.36. *An example of the use of untyped files.*

```
program fig36;

  { demonstration: untyped files, blockread, blockwrite }
  { uses TYPEDATA.DAT }
  var
    infile2, outfile: file;
    buffer: array[1..1024] of integer;
    amtread, amtwritten: integer;

  begin
    assign(infile2, 'TYPEDATA.DAT');
    assign(outfile, 'VERIFIED.DAT');
    reset(infile2, 1);
    rewrite(outfile, 1);
```

```
repeat
  blockread(infile2, buffer, sizeof(buffer), amtread);
  blockwrite(outfile, buffer, amtread, amtwritten);
until amtread = 0;
close(infile2);
close(outfile);
end.
```

5.2.9.5. The Printer as a File

The printer can also be used as a file. The printer is assigned as a write-only text file, generally to the file lptx (where x is the port number) or prn. But the printer unit is available to do this job for us, assigning a file variable named lst to the printer. Note in Listing 5.37, that a form-feed character, defined as a constant, must be written after each page.

LISTING 5.37. *An example of using the printer.*

```
program fig37; uses printer;
{ printer unit defaults to LPT 1 as the location of the printer }
  const
    ff = #12;
  var
    i: byte;
  begin
    for i := 1 to 15 do
      writeln(lst, 'Hello World! From my Printer!');
    writeln(lst,ff);
  end.
```

5.2.10. textmode Screen Manipulation

This section describes some of the common procedures and functions and their use in the CRT unit. Because this is a unit provided by Turbo Pascal, all procedures and functions require the statement uses crt;. Reading keycodes directly from the keyboard to enable use of the extended keys of the keyboard is described, as well as PC speaker usage and machine delay. Also, methods of text mode manipulation are described using code available from the CRT unit.

5.2.10.1. readkey and Extended Keys

The function readkey is a parameterless one; it reads the equivalent of a character from the keyboard. It does not echo to the screen when a character is read. Also, it continues control upon a keypress. Generally, readkey pulls in a character, or series of characters from the keyboard buffer. If it is a regular ASCII character, the function puts it into the character assigned. Otherwise, for extended keys (F1–F10, Insert, Home, Delete, PageUp,

PageDown, End, Arrow Keys), a character #0 is returned, and a subsequent call to readkey returns a unique character for each of these keys. An example of readkey and the reading of extended keys is shown in Listing 5.38.

In addition, a variable called keypressed exists. This can be used to run a process until a key is pressed.

LISTING 5.38. *A demonstration of* readkey.

```
program fig38; uses crt;

  { Demonstration of readkey }
  var
    c: char;

  begin
    write('Hit a key: ');
    c := readkey;
    writeln; {remember readkey doesn't behave like read/readln}
    write('Key codes returned by the key you pressed are: ');
    write('#', ord(c), ' ');
    if c = #0 then
      begin
        c := readkey;
        write('#', ord(c));
      end;
    writeln;
  end.
```

5.2.10.2. PC Speaker and Machine Delay

In this section, procedures that activate the PC speaker to make sounds are described. The procedures needed for this purpose are called sound(), delay(), and nosound(). sound() activates the PC speaker at a sound equivalent to the number of hertz specified, and nosound deactivates the speaker.

Generally, between the sound and nosound procedures, a procedure named delay is placed. This procedure takes a parameter of time in milliseconds. The effect of this procedure is to pause processing by the number of milliseconds specified.

Note, in addition, that a current problem with TP/BP 7.0 (since there was no such thing as a Pentium II when released) is that the delay procedure has been known to crash. Borland's position on TP 7 is to not fix this error but refer people to upgrade to Delphi. Even though Borland claims this, note that this problem can be fixed, and a description of options to fix this error (Runtime Error 200: Division by Zero) can be found at the URLs specified at the beginning of this chapter.

LISTING 5.39. *A demonstration of activating the PC speaker.*

```
program fig39; uses crt;

const
  min = 250;
  max = 3000;
var
  index: word;

procedure pcsound(hertz, milliseconds: word);
  begin
    sound(hertz);
    delay(milliseconds);
    nosound;
  end;

begin
  index := min;
  while index < max do
    begin
      pcsound(index,250);
      inc(index, 250);
    end;
  while index > min do
    begin
      pcsound(index,250);
      dec(index, 250);
    end;
end.
```

5.2.10.3. CRT Text Basics

There are some general CRT basics to remember in using the procedures for manipulating the screen. There always exists an "active window," which is the area of the screen that is being manipulated at the particular time. It may be a rectangular section of the screen or, by default, the entire screen. An active window is described by these procedures in terms of Cartesian coordinates. For example, a diagram of an active window is shown here:

```
Corner is (1,1)
   +------------------ Increasing X
   |
   |
   |
   |
   |
Increasing Y
```

The maximum X and maximum Y are dependent on the size of the active window generated, which can be manipulated.

5.2.10.4. Manipulating the Active Window

Procedures that manipulate the size and appearance of the active window are described here. They include procedures that clear all or parts of the screen and change the text mode and the size of the current active window:

clreol—Clears to the end of current line in the active window

clrscr—Clears the entire window

delline—Deletes the current line in the active window

insline—Inserts a line at the current position

window(x1,y1,x2,y2)—Changes the definition of the current active window

textmode(<*TextModeConstant*>)—Changes the text mode of the current active window

The first four procedures are described sufficiently. The window() procedure changes the definition of the current active window to (x1,y1) as the top left-hand corner and (x2,y2) as the lower right-hand corner. Incorrectly specified parameters are ignored in the case of all procedures that accept coordinates.

textmode accepts integers that are defined as constants to be BW40, CO40, BW80, and CO80, as the most common ones (BW = black and white, CO = color, 40 = 40×25 screen, 80 = 80×25 screen). In addition, with EGA and VGA cards, a parameter named Font8X8 changes the screen to 43 or 50 line mode when it is added. The default is CO80. A well-behaved program accesses the variable LastMode to store the current mode before changing it. These procedures are shown in Listing 5.40. Note that all attributes are reset when textmode and window are called.

LISTING 5.40. *A demonstration of active window manipulation.*

```
program fig40; uses crt;

var
   origmode: integer;

procedure screen(inptype: string);
   var
     j: byte;
   begin
     clrscr;
     writeln('Text Box (Active Window at 5,5 and 20,20) textmode ',
             inptype);
```

```
      window(5,5,20,20);
      for j := 1 to 40 do
        write('Fill!');
    end;

begin
    origmode := LastMode;
    textmode(CO80);
    screen('CO80');
    readln;
    textmode(CO40);
    screen('CO40');
    readln;
    textmode(Font8X8 + CO80);
    screen('Font8X8 CO80');
    readln;
    textmode(Font8X8 + CO40);
    screen('Font8X8 CO40');
    readln;
    textmode(origmode);
    writeln('Good-Bye and Have a Nice Day!');
end.
```

5.2.10.5. Text Appearance and Position

Procedures to manipulate the appearance and position of text written to the screen are described here. This includes positioning the text as well as color and type of the text and background. Procedures for this case include the following:

gotoxy(x1,y1)—Go to position indicated by x1,y1, changes definition of "current line": error is ignored }

textcolor(color)—Sets a foreground color from 0 to 15, as listed below

textbackground(color)—Sets a background color from 0 to 8

highvideo, normvideo—All these, as implied, change intensity of video

lowvideo, byte wherex, wherey—Indicate current position of the cursor (wherex, wherey)

The defaults are normvideo, textcolor(15), and textbackground(0). A demonstration is shown in Listing 5.41. Note that rote screen and color manipulation can get very lengthy in coding; also note that the designations on the colors are defined as constants in the CRT unit to represent each color, either the number as used in this program or the textmode constant seen beside the color block may be used.

LISTING 5.41. *A demonstration of text appearance procedures.*

```pascal
program fig41; uses crt;

{ Demonstration along with listing of equivalent constants }
type
  string19 = string[19];
var
  i: byte;

function returntextconstant(color: byte):string19;
  var
    rtrn: string19;
  begin
    rtrn := '';
    if color >= 128 then
      begin
        rtrn := 'Blink+';
        dec(color, 128);
      end;
    case color of
       0: rtrn := rtrn + 'Black       ';
       1: rtrn := rtrn + 'Blue        ';
       2: rtrn := rtrn + 'Green       ';
       3: rtrn := rtrn + 'Cyan        ';
       4: rtrn := rtrn + 'Red         ';
       5: rtrn := rtrn + 'Magenta     ';
       6: rtrn := rtrn + 'Brown       ';
       7: rtrn := rtrn + 'LightGray   ';
       8: rtrn := rtrn + 'DarkGray    ';
       9: rtrn := rtrn + 'LightBlue   ';
      10: rtrn := rtrn + 'LightGreen  ';
      11: rtrn := rtrn + 'LightCyan   ';
      12: rtrn := rtrn + 'LightRed    ';
      13: rtrn := rtrn + 'LightMagenta';
      14: rtrn := rtrn + 'Yellow      ';
      15: rtrn := rtrn + 'White       ';
    end;
    returntextconstant := rtrn;
  end;

procedure writeblock(color:byte);
  begin
    write(#219:6,#219,#219,#219, ' - ');
    write(returntextconstant(color));
  end;

procedure writescreenpage(start: byte);
  var
    i: byte;
  begin
    for i := start to start+15 do
      begin
        textcolor(i);
        writeblock(i);
        if (i+1) mod 2 = 0 then
          begin writeln;writeln;end;
      end;
  end;
```

```
procedure textcolordemo;
  begin
    { Does the 8 screens with backgrounds changed }
    for i := 0 to 7 do
      begin
        textbackground(i);
        clrscr;
        textcolor(white);
        writeln('Screen Demonstration: Text Background = ',
                returntextconstant(i));
        writeln;
        writescreenpage(0);
        readln;
      end;
    { does blinking screen demo}
    textcolor(white);
    textbackground(black);
    clrscr;
    writeln('Screen Demonstration: Blinking Text');
    writeln;
    writescreenpage(128);
    { start from 128; textattribute + 128 is blink }
    readln;
  end;

procedure gotoxydemo;
  begin
    clrscr;
    randomize;
    textcolor(white);
    writeln('Screen Positioning Demo: press a key when done');
    repeat
      textcolor(random(15)+1);
      gotoxy(random(79)+1, random(23)+2);
      write(#254);
      delay(500);
      gotoxy(wherex-1, wherey);
      textcolor(black);
      write(#216);
    until keypressed;
    textbackground(black);
  end;
begin
  textbackground(black);
  writeln;
  textcolordemo;
  gotoxydemo;
  clrscr;
  textcolor(white);
  clrscr;
  writeln('Thanks for your time!');
end.
```

5.2.11. DOS Command Capabilities

This section demonstrates the procedures and functions used to perform varied DOS-related capabilities in Turbo Pascal in a process-oriented illustration. Note that this includes executing another program, taking parameters from the command line for a program, listing files on the drive, confirming a file's existence, and using Pascal equivalents to DOS-based functions that work on directories as well as files themselves. In addition, most, but not all, procedures and functions described here make use of the DOS unit. Assumed is a working knowledge of using the DOS operating system, but not an expert knowledge. Because of the somewhat limited scope of this document, not all procedures and functions are demonstrated.

5.2.11.1. Executing Another Program

Executing another program from your program can be a simple matter, if you keep in mind the properties of DOS. The DOS command interpreter is always found defined in the environment variable COMSPEC. After spawning a command interpreter, which is what happens in Listing 5.42, the /C command parameter must be given before the command line desired. The command interpreter doesn't have to be spawned for specific programs, but for batch files and any command that uses any DOS features (such as redirection), the command interpreter must be called.

As shown in the listing, the first requirement is the presence of the $M compiler directive, which states the size of the stack, minimum heap, and maximum heap. The maximum heap defaults to all the memory available, leaving none to execute a program. Therefore, the maximum heap value must be defined downward.

Next is the actual call of the command. A call to swapvectors must exist before and after the exec() call. This procedure swaps the contents of the interrupt table, so an executed program cannot disrupt what the current program has done.

getenv() is a function that returns the contents of any environment variable specified as a parameter, if it exists. Here, this function is used with the environment variable COMSPEC, which is the only proper accepted method to call the command interpreter.

exec() takes the name of the program to spawn to (COMMAND.COM or another one) and then a proper parameter list (or command if COMMAND.COM is used, because the command you want to issue *is* a parameter to COMMAND.COM). The result of a proper call to exec() is execution of the program specified with all text related to the program being displayed.

All functions and procedures related to executing another program make use of the DOS unit.

LISTING 5.42. *A demonstration of shelling to execute another program.*

```
{$M 16382,0,4000}
program fig42; uses dos;
  { Demonstration of executing another program }
  var
    command: string;
  begin
    write('Enter your DOS command line here: ');
    readln(command);
    command := ' /C ' + command; { requirement for COMMAND.COM }
    swapvectors;
    exec(getenv('COMSPEC'), command);
    swapvectors;
    {an example of a command line, if it were DOS issued, would be
    c:\dos\command.com /c chkdsk /f }
    writeln;
    writeln('End of program execution.');
  end.
```

5.2.11.2. Confirming a File's Existence

The existence of a file on a drive can be determined in one of two ways, as described in Listing 5.43, with the two sample functions, in the order described. One is faster than the other for obvious reasons (presence of disk I/O), but both are in widespread use.

The first method generally involves testing a file attempting to open it using the IOResult variable after turning off I/O checking ({$I-} {$I+}). If it is not equal to 0, then a problem accessing the file is assumed.

The second method is generally faster, as it doesn't require as much disk I/O. It generally involves using any of the attribute determination functions in the DOS unit (which are described later) and checking the variable DosError for the value 2.

LISTING 5.43. *Demonstration of two methods to find whether a file exists.*

```
function slowexist(filename: string):boolean;
  var
    f: text;
  begin
    assign(f, filename);
    {$I-}
    reset(f);
    {$I+}
```

```
    if IOResult <> 0 then
      slowexist := false
    else
      begin
        slowexist := true;
        close(f); { required, since IOresult = 0, file is now OPEN }
      end;
  end;

function fastexist(filename: string): boolean;
  var
    attr: word;
    f: text;
  begin
    assign(f, filename);
    getfattr(f, attr);
    if doserror = 2 then
      fastexist := false
    else
      fastexist := true;
  end;
```

5.2.11.3. Accepting Command-Line Parameters

The functions `paramstr()` and `paramcount` are used in taking parameters from the command line for a program. In DOS batch file writing, valid parameters are %1 through %9, and in the same method, `paramstr(number)` returns a parameter equivalent to %number. `paramcount` holds the total number of parameters specified. Each part of the command line that has a space is considered a parameter.

In processing, if command-line parameters are expected, `paramcount` is called first, and then if `paramcount` is 0, then generally a call to `halt()` is issued, but not always. `halt()` terminates the program with a DOS error equivalent to the number in the parameter. Afterward, all valid `paramstr()` calls are returned into a string, and proper actions are taken depending on the parameters. An example of a proper way to handle command-line parameters is shown in Listing 5.44.

LISTING 5.44. *A demonstration of command-line parameters.*

```
{$M 16382,0,4000}
program fig44; uses dos;
  { Demonstration of parameter strings. Note the DOS unit is *NOT*
    required for the parameter systems. }
  var
    command: string;
    i: byte;
  begin
    if paramcount <> 0 then
```

```
        begin
          command := ' /C ';
          for i := 1 to paramcount do
            command := command + paramstr(i);
          swapvectors;
          exec(getenv('COMSPEC'), command);
          swapvectors;
          writeln;
          writeln('End of program execution.');
        end
      else
        begin
          writeln('Incorrect # of parameters specified.');
          halt(10);
        end;
  end.
```

5.2.11.4. Listing Files in a Directory

Listing files on the drive—in other words, being able to distinguish wild-cards in DOS—is a multistep process. The components of performing this function, the predefined searchrec record type, findfirst, findnext, and the file attribute constants are described in this section.

The definition of searchrec, which is defined in the DOS unit, is as follows:

```
searchrec = record
        fill: array[1..21] of byte;
        attr: byte;
        time: longint;
        size: longint;
        name: string[12];
    end;
```

fill represents a filler area, for which there is no purpose to access, and attr specifies the file attributes of the file described, stored additively with respect to the file attribute constants described later. time is the date and time in the standard DOS-packed format. The process of unpacking this variable is described later. size represents the size in bytes of the file, and name represents the name of the file.

findfirst and findnext are called in a manner described in Listing 5.45, using a variable defined as searchrec earlier. findfirst takes a path, attribute type, and searchrec variable and returns the first file that fits the description. A subsequent call to findnext returns the next file that fits the original description.

File attribute constants, which may be referred to in any description of file attributes, are the following:

```
ReadOnly  := $01
Hidden    := $02
SysFile   := $04
VolumeID  := $08
Directory := $10
Archive   := $20
AnyFile   := $3F
```

LISTING 5.45. *A demonstration of* findfirst *and* findnext.

```
program fig45; uses dos;

    var
        fileinfo: searchrec;
    begin
        findfirst('*.*',AnyFile, fileinfo);
        while doserror = 0 do  { doserror = 18 = no more files to list }
            begin
                write(fileinfo.name);
                if (fileinfo.attr and Directory) = Directory then
                    writeln('[DIR]':18)
                else
                    writeln(fileinfo.size:18);
                findnext(fileinfo);
            end;
    end.
```

5.2.11.5. DOS Procedures and Functions

This section provides a listing of the procedures and functions that are equivalent to DOS capabilities in Turbo Pascal's DOS unit and the system unit.

System

```
procedure ChDir(dir:string); { changes directory to dirname in string }

procedure Erase(filename: <filevar>); { erases file var }

procedure FilePos(file: <filevar>); { current position in file }

procedure Filesize(file: <filevar>); { returns size of file }

procedure GetDir(drive;path: string); { gets current directory of
    drive listed }

procedure MkDir(path: string); { makes directory }

procedure Rename(file: <filevar>); { renames file }

procedure RmDir(path: string); { removes directory }

procedure Seek(file: <filevar>); { moves position in file to read }
```

DOS

```
function Diskfree(diskno: byte): longint; { works as intended,
    ineffective for drives }

function Disksize(diskno: byte): longint; { > 1 GB }

var dosversion: word; { if DOS 6.22, Hi(dosversion) = 22,
    Lo(dosversion) = 6 }

var EnvCount: integer; { total number of environment variables }

function EnvStr(index: integer):string; { returns the env. string
    designated as index }

function FSearch(filename:PathStr; dirlist: string):pathstr;
    { searches for filename in path given by dirlist }

procedure FSplit(Path: PathStr; dir: dirstr; name: namestr; ext:
    extstr); { splits a filename up into a directory, name, and extension }

procedure Getdate(year, month, day, dayofweek: word); { Returns
    current date as set in the operating system }

function Getenv(stringname: string):string; { returns environment
    variable specified by name }

procedure GetFattr(file: <filevar>; attr: word); { obtains the
    attributes of a file in F }

procedure GetFtime(file: <filevar>; time: longint); { obtain packed
    date and time of file }

procedure GetTime(Hour, Minute, Second, Sec100: word); { gets current
    time in OS }

procedure PackTime(dnt: datetime; time: longint); { packs datetime
    record into time longint }

procedure SetDate(year, month, day: word); { sets date in OS }

procedure SetFTime(file: <filevar>; time: longint); { sets file to
    time specified }

procedure SetTime(hour, minute, second, sec100: word); { sets time in
    OS }

procedure UnPackTime(time: longint; dnt: datetime); { unpacks longint
    time to datetime record }
```

Procedures that need further explanation than what can be obtained from the preceding list are further described. For any spots at which a file variable occurs, the file must be assigned but unopened. The `longint` time variable is a packed `longint`. To be read or set, it must be unpacked and packed. The datetime record is predefined for that purpose. It is as described here:

```
datetime = record
        year, month, day, hour, minute, second: word;
```

In most of these functions and procedures, the variable doserror is set away from 0, which may be used to check for the successfulness of the statement issued. Otherwise, if this is not the case, the IOResult variable method may be used. Also, the DiskSize and DiskFree functions take a numerical value for a drive, where 0 = current drive, 1 = A, 2 = B, 3 = C, and so forth.

Listing 5.36 shows an example of a good way to copy a file. Moving a file on a drive can be accomplished by renaming the file (it works on paths), or by copying the file and then deleting it across drives.

5.2.12. Advanced Options

This section describes many of the more advanced programming options available in Turbo Pascal. Those options are creating overlay files, using object (OBJ) files, using assembler and inline statements, and calling software interrupt procedures.

5.2.12.1. Overlay Files

The overlay unit exists to enable copying of code in large applications to memory or disk. The complete construction of an overlaid application creates an EXE file as well as an overlay file. Both are required for the executable to run. The first set of statements to note is the {$O+} in the unit. This compiler directive gives permission in the unit for it to be overlaid. Note that the default is $O-. The CRT, Overlay, and System units cannot be overlaid. Also, it would be good to test self-written units for their ability to be overlaid.

The next thing to observe is the use of the {$O <TPU name>} in the main program. It is a requirement that all units to be overlaid are listed. After that, note the use of the procedures OvrInit, OvrInitEMS, and the variable OvrResult. OvrResult is the variable that returns status codes of the other two procedures, giving indication of specific problems. OvrInit initializes the automatic overlay system, with the overlay name created (note that it is always <sourcename>.OVR when compiled, although it can be renamed to work as long as the correct filename is in the procedure parameter).

If the call to OvrInit is successful, then, optionally, a call to OvrInitEMS can be made. This procedure, if successful, allows paging of the overlay to Expanded Memory Specification (EMS) memory.

Listing 5.46 and Listing 5.47 show an example of assembling an overlaid application. Generally, because the size of an application that should be overlaid is large, this example is a ludicrous one, yet good to show such a situation. Also, complete error-checking statements have been left out but may be found in the manuals or online help.

LISTING 5.46. *A sample unit for an overlaid application.*

```
{$O+}
unit fig46; { note, the identifier must match the name of the file }

  interface
    function power(x:real; y: integer):real;
  implementation
    function power(x:real; y: integer):real; { exactly as above }
      var
        i: integer;
        result: real;
      begin
        result := 1;
        for i := 1 to y do
          result := result * x;
        power := result;
      end;

end.
```

LISTING 5.47. *A sample base program for an overlaid application.*

```
program fig47; uses fig46, overlay;
{if more than 1 unit put commas between each id}
  var
    i: byte;
  {$O FIG46.TPU } { list units to be overlaid }
  begin
    OvrInit('FIG47.OVR');
    if OvrResult <> 0 then
      begin
        { note specific reasons can be stated }
        writeln('Error loading overlay!');
        halt(100);
      end
    else
      begin
        OvrInitEMS; { if overlay loadable, then try to load in EMS }
        if OvrResult <> 0 then
          writeln(#254, ' Not loaded in EMS for some reason.')
        else
          writeln(#254, ' Overlay loaded in EMS');
      end;
```

```
writeln;

for i := 1 to 10 do
    writeln(i, ' squared is ', power(i,2):0:2);
end.
```

Additionally, an overlay can be appended to the executable by use of the copy /B dos command. Then the executable name must be specified in the OvrInit procedure.

5.2.12.2. Using OBJ Files

OBJ files, which contain procedures or functions, may be used in Turbo Pascal. They should be compiled in the standard Pascal style (far, pascal). The $L variable is used to link in the OBJ file, and then the procedure or function must be restated as an external function, with types matching that in the object. Nothing may be used that is not compiled in the far pascal mode (see Listing 5.48).

LISTING 5.48. *Linking in an object file.*

```
{source for OBJ file must appear this way,
 no things linked in not compiled far, pascal }
int far pascal writeaverage(int a, int b, int c)
  {
      int temp;
      temp = a + b + c;
      return(temp / 3);
  }

Linked in program:

program fig48;

{$F+}
{$L FIG48.OBJ}
function writeaverage(a,b,c: integer):integer;external;

begin
  write('The average of 1,3, and 2 (rounded to nearest whole number) ');
  writeln('is ', writeaverage(1,3,2));
end.
```

5.2.12.3. Assembler and Inline Statements

Assembler and inline machine code are easy to implement in Turbo Pascal. You can include standard Intel assembler syntax code by enclosing it in an asm..end block. Inline statements can be included by using the inline() statement in a manner such as this: inline($9C/$42);. Do not try this example, as I made up the statement.

5.2.12.4. Software Interrupt Procedures

This section describes calling a software interrupt procedure using standard Pascal structures. The process is much like assembler, though slightly different. The predefined type registers is used in DOS. This is a record type that can be used as a set to call the interrupt procedure, with each assembler variable accessible (for example, regs.ax). After the registers type is set, then the procedure Intr() or MsDos() may be called. The intr procedure takes an interrupt value and then a registers set. MsDos takes only a register set because it is a procedure that calls Intr using interrupt $21, the common MS-DOS interrupt.

The example shown in Listing 5.49 is a little program that returns the cluster size of the current drive.

LISTING 5.49. *An example of an interrupt call.*

```
program fig49; uses dos;

function getclustersize(drive: byte): Word;
  var
    register: registers;
  begin
    register.ax := $3600;
    register.cx := 0;
    register.dx := drive;
    Intr($21, register);
    getclustersize := register.ax * register.cx;
  end;


begin
  writeln('Cluster size of current drive is: ', getclustersize(0));
end.
```

5.3. Common Questions and Answers

There may be questions that arise out of programming in Turbo Pascal. Some common questions and the answers to those questions, which are not answered by the text itself, appear in this section.

Why do I get incorrect mathematical results from Pascal?

This results from the common overflow conditions that plague any language when computations are done. Generally, when two integers are used in a computation, an integer operation is done, and an integer is assumed in the result. Although this might be valid in most cases, in some cases this assumption would not be valid. Because Pascal was designed as a teaching language, many things are not automatic about the operation of a compiler on a computer, and which must be taken into account. The following example should describe a little of what happens, illustrating the issue:

```pascal
program tnt01;

  { demonstrates type-casts and a common error due to overflow }
  const
    a: integer = 10000;   { specifically defining a type for a
                            constant }
  var
    c: longint;
  begin
    writeln;
    writeln('Note that by evaluating 10000 squared, it will create');
    writeln('incorrect results as demonstrated below in ');
    writeln('multiplying an integer by an integer, resulting in ');
    writeln('overflow of the integer type assumed by the compiler ');
    writeln('as a result, which is copied into a longint variable ');
    writeln('*after* the computation');
    c := a * a;
    writeln('10000 squared is ', c);
    readln;
    writeln('Now we typecast one of the a variables in the ');
    writeln('similar assignment pair as below. Note the correct ');
    writeln('results now show as a part of c. This is a common ');
    writeln('misjudgment made in programming for Pascal. Be ');
    writeln('aware of it. The compiler now in this case assumes ');
    writeln('longint multiplication, and assigns the result to a ');
    writeln('longint variable, therefore overflow taken care of.');
    c := longint(a) * a;
    writeln('10000 squared is ', c);
  end.
```

Why doesn't Pascal have an operator such as x**y for taking a power of a number?

Because Wirth designed Pascal as a teaching language, he wanted to make apparent the operations of the compiler. Therefore, many statements that existed in the original Pascal standard related very closely to the number of clock ticks made as a result. Such an operator is very expensive in terms of clock ticks when called. That is not readily apparent by the appearance of the operator, which existed in Fortran (and maybe still does). A realization of how expensive the x**y operator is can be seen in the next question.

So how would I evaluate powers in Pascal?

This answer comes down to an issue of mathematics knowledge. Let's start with the power functions as defined earlier. The limitations are that in x^y, y must be greater than 0. This may not be acceptable because, in some cases, you may want to take fractional and negative powers. You

can further develop the iterative algorithm, observing that signed integers in
y can be evaluated by using some algebra of powers, as in the following:

```
function power(x: real; y: integer): real;
  var
    result: real;
    i: integer;
  begin
    result := 1;
    for i := 1 to abs(y) do
      result := result * x;
    if y < 0 then
      result := 1 / result;
    power := result;
  end;
```

Note that this algorithm now takes negative integers for y and could take
any real number in x. However, a real number in place of y would be
desirable for things such as fractional powers and setting up square roots.
The ability to devise the equivalent of a real x and real y power can be
derived from calculus in a definite sense or the following simple algebra
manipulation:

```
x^y = z
ln (x^y) = ln z
y * ln(x) = ln z
e^(y * ln(x)) = z
```

Now given this relationship, we can evaluate real number powers, with a
function written rather easily. The only limitation with this function is
that a negative x may not be 0 or negative. The 0 case may be fixed easily
with the rule as stated "0 to any power is 0" in mathematics. Otherwise,
to counter the exception that x may not be negative, the other iterative
method may be used and combined into the preceding relation to gain an
expression that works with any number except where x is a real number
less than 0. Of course, it could possibly be extended to work with any
real number, when you start considering complex numbers.

To address the issue with timer ticks, if the final statement, exp(y*ln(x)),
is observed, this expression takes many more timer ticks than the average
statement.

**Why does it say two types are different between units when I name them the same thing and describe
them the same way?**

Pascal is created as a strongly typed language. Therefore, if one type is
defined, it is considered defined even if another type of the same name is
used. A problem can exist if the type is needed between two units or a
unit and the main program. What must be done is that the type must be

declared in one unit used, and then the unit must be included into the other unit or the main program by a uses statement. Note that valid uses statements and const/ type variables must exist right after the interface declaration in an unit.

Why does dispose mysteriously give me Invalid Pointer Operation **errors?**
The following source explains more specifically what happens with this error:

```
program tnt03; uses crt;

{ Demonstration of pointer heap leaks, in a ludicrous,
  but easily seen example }

type
  intptr = ^integer;

var
  a, b: intptr;
begin
  new(a);
  new(b);
  a^ := 2;
  b^ := 5;
  writeln('Note here that pointer a''s contents is ', a^);
  writeln('and pointer b''s contents is ', b^);
  writeln('When the pointer addresses are exchanged, and not the ',
          'contents,');
  a := b; {address location of pointer a to location of pointer b}
  b := a; {inactive, position of pointer a is already pointer b}
  writeln('the result is that the contents of pointer a is ', a^);
  writeln('and the contents of pointer b is ', b^);
  writeln('This is not desired, as both pointers point to the ');
  writeln('same address on the heap, one pointer''s allocated ');
  writeln('memory with new() is lost. It can happen ');
  writeln('inadvertedly, but in most cases where this occurs, ');
  writeln('it can not be easily seen. A position saved in heap ');
  writeln('memory should always be removed with dispose. Because ');
  writeln('this error occurs in this program, the first dispose ');
  writeln('issued (a) will work properly, but the second dispose ');
  writeln('will result in the runtime error listing you see ');
  writeln('below: ');
  highvideo;
  writeln('Runtime Error 204: Invalid Pointer Operation');
  writeln; writeln;
  normvideo;
  dispose(a);
  dispose(b);
  {position with 5 in it is disposed with first call, so 2nd call
    results in Runtime Error 204 Invalid Pointer Operation }
end.
```

5.4. References

Gillin, P. 1995. Give Kahn credit. *Computerworld*. 29(5):36.

Wirth, N. 1996. Recollections about the development of Pascal. In T. J. Bergin and R. G. Gibson (Eds.), *History of Programming Languages*. Reading, MA: Addison-Wesley.

PART V
Icon

CHAPTER 6
The Icon Programming Language
by Ralph E. Griswold

Icon is a high-level, imperative programming language with extensive facilities for manipulating strings and structures. It features a powerful expression-evaluation mechanism that greatly simplifies many programming tasks.

This presentation of the Icon programming language begins with a brief description of its historical origins, the languages that preceded it, and what motivated a language with Icon's capabilities.

The remainder is divided into three parts: a description of the language, examples of programming techniques, and information about getting Icon material.

6.1. Background
The origins of Icon go back to the early days of programming languages—to 1962 with the first SNOBOL language (Farber, Griswold, & Polonsky, 1964).

SNOBOL was developed at Bell Laboratories by a small group with no prior experience in programming language design. Their goal was to provide a tool for manipulating text on computers. That was a relatively novel idea at a time when computation was viewed by most persons as an entirely numerical activity.

SNOBOL deals only with strings of characters and has a high-level pattern-matching facility that was novel at the time. SNOBOL adapted control flow concepts from contemporary assembly languages and from COMIT, a language designed for natural language translation (Yngve, 1958). SNOBOL uses the concepts of success and failure with conditional gotos, rather than boolean values, to control program flow. SNOBOL has no other control structures.

A SNOBOL program consists of a sequence of statements. The parts of a statement are

```
[label]    subject    pattern    [replacement]    [goto]
```

The components in brackets are optional. The `label` identifies the statements for the purpose of transferring control by gotos. The `subject` provides the string to which the pattern is applied. If the `pattern` matches, the `replacement`, if any, replaces the matched part of the subject, changing it. There are three kinds of gotos: unconditional, success, and failure. In the case of the last two, transfer is made depending on whether the pattern matches.

SNOBOL has four kinds of patterns:

- strings, matching only a specified string

- arbitrary, matching any string

- balanced, matching only strings balanced with respect to parentheses

- fixed-length, matching strings of a specified length

Except for strings, which can be specified literally or by string-valued variables, a pattern is indicated by bounding asterisks and other characters to indicate what kind of pattern it is. Names of variables to which matched components of the subject are assigned can be included. Examples are

`*HEAD*`, which matches an arbitrary string and assigns it to HEAD

`*(EXPR)*`, which matches a parenthesis-balanced string and assigns it to EXPR

COL/10, which matches a string of 10 characters and assigns it to COL

An example of a SNOBOL statement is

```
REMOVE    EXPR    "("  *(EXPR)*  ")"          /S(REMOVE)
```

which removes all outer parentheses from EXPR. Note that if the pattern matches, a new value is assigned to EXPR and control is transferred back to the beginning of the statement.

SNOBOL quickly became popular at a time when there was no commercial software and no other generally available programming languages for manipulating strings. It found users in diverse disciplines. Many researchers in computing in the humanities adopted SNOBOL. By contrast, it was widely used by systems programmers for file creation and modification.

As a result of interest in SNOBOL and the demand for more features, a series of increasingly more powerful SNOBOL languages was developed, culminating in SNOBOL4 (Griswold, Poage, & Polonsky, 1971).

In SNOBOL4, patterns are data objects that can be constructed during program execution. SNOBOL4 uses a much more sophisticated pattern-matching algorithm than SNOBOL. It also provides high-level data structures including tables with associative lookup.

Here is a SNOBOL4 program that counts the "words" in the input file:

```
          wordcnt = table()

          lower =  "abcdefghijklmnopqrstuvwxyz"
          upper = "ABCDEFGHIJKLMNOPQRSTUVWXYZ"
          letters = lower upper

          findword = break(letters)    span(letters) . word

  read    line = input                          :f(list)
  next    line    findword =                     :f(read)
          wordcnt[word] = wordcnt[word] + 1      :(next)

  list    convert(wordcnt, "array")

  loop    i = i + 1
          output = wordcnt[i, 1] " : " wordcnt[i, 2]    :s(loop)
  end
```

The program is initialized by assigning a table to wordcnt, a string containing the upper- and lowercase letters to letters, and a pattern that finds and then matches a string of consecutive letters to findword. The variable word in this pattern is assigned the string of letters that are matched. Concatenation for both strings and patterns has no explicit operator; components are just written in succession.

A line of input is read and assigned to `line` by the statement labeled `read`; reference to `input` reads a line automatically. When an end of file is reached, this statement fails and control is transferred to the statement labeled `list`. If the statement succeeds, `findword` is applied to `line` to find another word, assign it to `word`, and delete the initial part of `line`. If the pattern match succeeds, control continues to the next statement, where the table `wordcnt` is subscripted by the word and the count for that word is incremented. If the pattern match fails, control is transferred to the statement labeled `read` to read another line.

When the input is exhausted, control is transferred to the statement labeled `list`, where `wordcnt` is converted from a table into a two-dimensional array in which the first column contains the words that were found and the second column contains the respective counts.

At the statement labeled `loop`, the value of `i`, `0` initially, is incremented by one. In the following statement, a line containing the word, a separating colon, and the count is written (assigning a value to `output` causes its value to be written). As long as `i` is in bounds, control is transferred back to the statement labeled `loop`. When `i` exceeds the length of the array, however, the statement fails and the program terminates by flowing into the statement labeled `end`.

SNOBOL4, which is still in use today, is one of the most powerful programming languages ever developed. It has problems, however: an idiosyncratic syntax, a lack of control structures, and a separation of language facilities into two quite different sublanguages—pattern matching and traditional computation.

Work on the SNOBOL languages moved to the University of Arizona in 1971 with attempts to resolve the problems with SNOBOL4. This work led to SL5 (SNOBOL Language 5; Hanson & Griswold, 1978), which generalized the concepts in SNOBOL4 and provided a more conventional syntax with control structures. SL5 used a very general coroutine mechanism to support the search-and-backtracking facilities of pattern matching. The result was a very powerful but large and complicated language that is difficult to use and understand. SL5 never became popular, but it provided the inspiration for Icon.

Icon arose from the realization that a full coroutine mechanism was not necessary to support pattern matching. Instead, pattern matching could be accomplished using generators and goal-directed evaluation.

Generators in Icon are expressions that can produce more than one result and suspend computation between results. Goal-directed evaluation automatically searches for a successful result, using alternative results from generators.

At the time, this approach was seen as a simplification of SL5's pattern-matching mechanism. In fact, generators and related control structures became a pervasive aspect of Icon and are useful in many different kinds of computation. Icon is a much more powerful and general programming language than was originally perceived and, in fact, pattern matching became a natural consequence of generators and goal-directed evaluation.

The first version of Icon appeared in 1978 (Griswold, 1978), followed by successive versions that smoothed out rough spots and added additional facilities. The last major version of Icon, Version 9, added extensive graphics facilities.

The heritage of SNOBOL, as well as the different approach taken by Icon, can be seen in this Icon program for counting words:

```
procedure main()

    wordcnt := table(0)

    while line := read() do {
        line ? {
            while tab(upto(&letter)) do
                wordcnt[tab(many(&letters))] +:= 1
        }
    }

    wordcnt := sort(wordcnt, 3)

    while write(get(wordcnt), " : ", get(wordcnt))

end
```

Unlike the SNOBOL languages, Icon has a familiar syntax and conventional control structures. The concepts of success and failure are still used, as in controlling loops. Instead of the patterns of SNOBOL4, Icon uses matching procedures and string-analysis functions to provide more control over string analysis.

6.2. The Language

6.2.1. Basics

6.2.1.1. Program Structure

As in most imperative programming languages, an Icon program consists of declarations: procedure declarations that include executable code, declarations for record structures, scope declarations for identifiers, and so on.

Icon uses a reserved-word syntax; `procedure`, `end`, `global`, `if`, `then`, and so forth have special syntactic meanings.

Every Icon program must have a main procedure; program execution begins with the invocation of this procedure. Here's a simple Icon program that just writes a greeting:

```
procedure main()

    write("Welcome to Mars.")

end
```

Computation is performed by evaluating expressions, such as the function `write()` in the example. The main kinds of expressions are

operators, such as `countdown - 1`

function and procedure calls, such as `write("Earthling go home!")`

control structures, such as `if countdown = 0 then write("Ignition.")`

Icon is an expression-based language. It has no statements; even control structures produce values. Icon also has no block structure. Expressions are separated by semicolons and can be grouped using braces, as in

```
if countdown = 0 then {
    write("Ignition.");
    write("Lift off.")
    }
```

When an expression ends at the end of a line, no semicolon is needed, as illustrated by

```
if countdown = 0 then {
    write("Ignition.")
    write("Lift off.")
    }
```

6.2.1.2. Assignment

The operation `:=` assigns a value to a variable, as in

```
count := 0
   ...
countdown := countdown - 1
```

As in this assignment, the assigned value often is obtained by a computation on the value of the variable to which the assignment is then made. Icon provides augmented assignment operations that combine the assignment operation with the operation to be performed on the variable. An example is

```
countdown -:= 1
```

which decrements the value of `countdown`.

There are augmented assignment operations for all infix (binary) operations except assignment itself.

6.2.1.3. Comments

The character # indicates the beginning of a comment. The # and all subsequent characters up to the end of the current line are ignored.

An example is

```
write("Welcome to Mars.")    # might as well be friendly ...
```

6.2.1.4. Control Flow

Expressions are evaluated in the order in which they appear unless a control structure is encountered. By definition, a control structure is an expression that may change the sequential order of evaluation.

An important and distinguishing characteristic of Icon is that control decisions are based on the success or failure of conditional operations and not on boolean values. For example,

```
countdown = 0
```

compares the value of `countdown` with 0. If `countdown` is equal to 0, the comparison expression *succeeds*; otherwise, it *fails*.

An example of the use of success and failure to control program flow is

```
while line := read() do
    process(line)
```

The function `read()` attempts to read a line of text from standard input. It succeeds if there is a line and produces the line as its value, which is then processed. However, if there is no more data, `read()` fails. The `while-do` control structure uses the failure of `read()` to terminate the loop.

Failure is not an error; failure occurs when an operation is meaningful but cannot be carried out in a specific situation.

6.2.1.5. Data Types

Icon has no type declarations; a variable can have a value of any type. Values are typed, however, and when computations are performed, types are checked to be sure they are appropriate.

Icon has several data types. The numeric types are integer and real (floating point). Icon has no character type, but instead it has a string type. A string is a sequence of characters in which order is significant. Strings can be arbitrarily long. Icon also has a cset (character set) type. Csets are unordered collections of distinct characters.

Icon supports four structure types: records, lists (vectors), sets, and tables with associative lookup.

Types are converted (coerced) automatically when possible. For example, in

```
year := 2010
write(year)
```

the integer 2010 is automatically converted to a string for the purpose of writing.

A type that cannot be converted to an appropriate one causes a runtime error that terminates program execution. For example, in

```
countdown - "1"
```

the string "1" is converted to the integer 1, but

```
countdown - "i"
```

is erroneous and causes program termination because "i" does not represent an integer.

The type of any value can be determined during program execution by using the function type (x), which produces the string name for the type of x. For example, type(year) produces "integer".

Values can be converted from one type to another explicitly, as in

```
date := string(year)
```

which assigns the string "2010" to date. Explicit type conversion fails instead of causing error termination if the conversion cannot be performed. For example, integer("i") fails.

The null value is a special value that is the initial value of variables. The null value is illegal in most computations, so attempting to perform an operation on a variable that has not been assigned a value explicitly usually produces an error.

The operations /x and \x succeed and fail if x has a null or non-null value, respectively. They can be used to determine if a value has been assigned to a variable, as in

```
if /state then ...    #initialize state
```

6.2.1.6. Control Structures
Icon has a large repertoire of control structures that includes ones that are common to most imperative programming languages. These are

```
if expr1 then expr2 else expr3
while expr1 do expr2
until expr1 do expr3
```

The control structure

```
repeat expr
```

evaluates *expr* repeatedly and is equivalent to an expression such as

```
while 1 do expr
```

Any looping control structure can be terminated by the expression break, as in

```
repeat {
    ...
    if faults > 0 then break
    ...
}
```

if faults is greater than 0, the repeat loop is terminated and control is transferred to the point immediately after it.

The expression next, on the other hand, returns control to the beginning of the loop in which it appears, as in

```
while countdown > 0 do {
    ...
    if okay = 0 then next else correct()
    ...
}
```

The not control structure inverts success and failure. It fails if its argument succeeds and succeeds, producing the null value, if its argument fails. For example,

```
if not expr then write("evaluation failed")
```

writes evaluation failed if *expr* fails.

The case control structure selects an expression to evaluate based on a value. For example,

```
case name of {
    "Napoleon":  write("French")
    "DeGaulle":  write("French")
    "Hitler":    write("German")
    "Churchill": write("English")
       ...
    default:     write("unknown")
    }
```

The values can be of any type and need not all be of the same type.

Icon has several unconventional control structures. One is alternation ("or"):

```
expr1 | expr2
```

In alternation, expr1 is evaluated first. If it succeeds, its value is the result of alternation. If it fails, expr2 is evaluated; if it succeeds, its value is the result of alternation. If both expr1 and expr2 fail, the alternation control structure fails. For example, in

```
if (countdown > 0) | (hold > 0) then report()
```

report() is evaluated if either countdown or hold is greater than 0.

Many expressions can be linked together in alternation to produce the alternation of many values:

```
expr1 | expr2 | expr3 | ... | exprn
```

Control structures that use other aspects of expression evaluation are described in section 6.2.2.

6.2.1.7. Procedures

A procedure consists of a sequence of expressions bounded by the reserved words procedure and end. The name of the procedure and its parameters enclosed in parentheses follow procedure. An example is

```
procedure max(i, j)

    if i > j then return i else return j

end
```

which produces the maximum of i and j. The expression return returns its argument as the value of the procedure call.

A procedure may fail instead of producing a result by using `fail` instead of `return`. An example is

```
procedure posmax(i, j)

    if i > j then {
        if i > 0 then return i else fail
        }
    else if j > 0 then return j else fail

end
```

which produces the maximum of `i` and `j` provided it is positive but fails otherwise.

Flowing off the end of a procedure without a `return` also causes the procedure to fail.

Procedures may be called recursively, directly, or through a sequence of other procedure calls. An example is provided by the familiar factorial operation, $n! = 1 \times 2 \times \ldots \times n$:

```
procedure factorial(n)

    if n < 2 then return 1
    else return n * factorial(n - 1)

end
```

Procedures are values. That is, they can be assigned to variables, passed as arguments, and so on. Consider

```
procedure nonneg(p, n)

    if n < 0 then fail
    else return p(n)

end
```

This procedure fails if `n` is less than zero but otherwise returns the value produced by `p(n)`. For example,

```
nonneg(factorial, n)
```

produces the factorial of `n` if it is greater than or equal to zero but fails otherwise.

6.2.1.8. Scope

Icon provides three kinds of scope for variables: global, local, and static. Variables have the null value initially, except for global variables that are the names of functions and procedures.

The values of global variables are available to all procedures and for the duration of program execution. Global declarations occur outside procedure declarations. For example,

```
global state
global mode
```

declares state and mode to be global and available throughout the program.

Local and static variables belong to procedures and are declared inside them. Local variables are created when a procedure is called and destroyed when it returns. For example, in

```
procedure revolve(x, y)
    local z
    ...
```

z is local to revolve(). Parameters, in this case x and y, are local, also.

Static variables belong to all calls of the procedure in which they are declared but last throughout program execution and are available to all calls of the procedure. This allows variables to be shared by all calls of a procedure. Static variables can be initialized in an initial expression, which is evaluated only the first time a procedure is called. For example, in

```
procedure fracture(s)
    static vowels

    initial vowels :=  "aeiouAEIOU"
        ...
```

the static variable vowels is initialized in the first call of fracture() and that value is available in all subsequent calls of fracture().

6.2.1.9. Input and Output
As indicated by previous examples, read() and write() read and write lines of text, respectively. In the absence of a specified file, read() reads from standard input and write() writes to standard output. Files can be specified, as in

```
read(database)
write(log, entry)
```

A file is opened by

```
open(name, options)
```

where name is the name of the file and options specifies how it is to be opened. The default option, if the argument is omitted, is opening for reading, as in

```
database := open("backup.db")
```

The option "w" opens a file for writing, as in

```
log := open("newlog.txt", "w")
```

The function open() fails if the named file cannot be opened in the specified manner. It is important to check for this, as in

```
database := open("backup.db") | stop("*** cannot open backup")
```

Note the use of alternation to evaluate another expression if the first one fails. The function stop() is like write(), but it writes its argument to standard error output and terminates program execution.

Three *keywords*, indicated by an initial ampersand, have values for the standard files:

&input—Standard input

&output—Standard output

&errout—Standard error output

Thus,

```
write(&errout, " ignition failure")
```

writes an error message to standard error output but does not terminate program execution like stop() does.

In addition to line-oriented input and output, Icon supports binary input and output and random access to files.

6.2.1.10. Preprocessing

Icon has an integrated preprocessor that allows files to be included, symbols to be defined, and so forth. Preprocessor directives begin with $, as illustrated by

```
$include "constants.defs"
```

which inserts the file constants.def in place of the preprocessor directive. Similarly,

```
$define Width 10
```

defines the constant Width to have the value 10. Subsequently, appearances of Width are replaced by 10.

6.2.1.11. Storage Management

Many values in Icon require storage space in memory; strings and structures are examples. Icon allocates storage for values when they are created. This is done automatically without explicit allocation expressions in the program.

If there is not enough memory to provide space for a newly created value, memory is garbage-collected to reclaim space that no longer is in use. This also is an automatic process and occurs only as needed.

6.2.2. Generators and Goal-Directed Evaluation

In the preceding section, the concept of alternation was introduced. As noted there, alternation may produce more than one value. Expressions that are capable of producing more than one value are called *generators*.

A generator produces more than one value only if the context in which it is evaluated requests more than one value. The values are produced in succession as they are requested.

There are two contexts in which a generator may be requested to produce more than one value: *iteration* and *goal-directed evaluation*.

6.2.2.1. Iteration

Iteration is produced by the control structure

```
every exp1 do expr2
```

In this control structure, the generator *expr1* is requested to produce all its values. For each one produced, *expr2* is evaluated. For example,

```
every i := 1 | 2 | 3 do
    write(i)
```

writes 1, 2, and 3.

A generator that is useful in iteration is

```
i to j by k
```

which generates the integers from i to j with increments of k. The by clause is optional; if it is omitted, the increment defaults to 1. For example,

```
every i := -5 to 5 do
    write(i)
```

writes -5, -4, ... -1, 0, 1, ... 4, 5.

The do clause in iteration is optional, and this expression can be written more compactly as

```
every write(-5 to 5)
```

The function seq(i, j) generates an infinite sequence of integers, starting at i and incrementing by increments of j. If i or j is omitted, it defaults to 1. Thus, seq() generates the positive integers.

6.2.2.2. Goal-Directed Evaluation

Goal-directed evaluation, which is implicit in expression evaluation in Icon, attempts to obtain a successful result for a computation by requesting additional values from generators if necessary.

Failure drives goal-directed evaluation; it is failure that causes requests for additional values from generators.

A simple example is

```
if (i | j) = 0 then proceed() else pause()
```

The generator (i | j) first produces the value of i, which is compared with 0. If the comparison succeeds, the then clause is evaluated. If, however, the comparison fails, another value is requested from (i | j), which produces the value of j. If the comparison succeeds, the then clause is evaluated. If it does not succeed, the failure causes another value to be requested from (i | j). Because it has no more values to generate, (i | j) = 0 fails and the else clause is evaluated. The net effect is that the then clause is evaluated if i or j equals 0, but the else clause is evaluated otherwise.

From an operational point of view, a generator that produces a value and is capable of producing additional values *suspends*. It is *resumed* to produce another value by a request in the context in which it is evaluated. If the context for evaluation leaves an expression in which there is a suspended generator, the suspended generator is discarded.

The extent of expression evaluation is limited by *bounded expressions*; after evaluation in a bounded expression is complete, suspended generators in the bounded expression are discarded and cannot be resumed. The control expressions in control structures are bounded. For example, in

```
if expr1 then expr2
```

expr1 is bounded. If *expr1* succeeds, any suspended generators in *expr1* are discarded. Consequently, they cannot be resumed if *expr2* fails. Expressions followed by semicolons or ends of lines also are bounded.

Therefore, in

```
expr1; expr2
```

after the evaluation of expr1 is complete, whether successful or not, any suspended generators in it are discarded and evaluation moves on to expr2.

6.2.2.3. Procedures as Generators

A procedure can generate a sequence of results by using suspend in place of return. An example is

```
procedure power(i, j)

    k := i

    every 1 to j do {
        suspend k
        k *:=  i
        }

end
```

This procedure generates the powers of i from 1 through j. It suspends for each power. If it is resumed, it computes the next power and produces it. If it reaches the end of the every loop, control flows off the end of the procedure, producing failure as mentioned earlier. This indicates that the procedure has no more values to produce.

Note that a generator may be capable of producing an unlimited number of values. Removing the limit on the powers in the previous procedure illustrates this:

```
procedure power(i)

    k := i

    repeat {
        suspend k
        k *:=  i
        }

end
```

Because a generator only produces values on request, a generator that is capable of producing an unlimited number of values may produce only a few. For example, the loop

```
every j := power(i) do
    if j > 1000000 then break else write(j)
```

stops writing powers when a value exceeds 1,000,000. At this point, break terminates the loop and the suspended generator is discarded.

6.2.2.4. Other Control Structures

Limitation

The number of results that a generator is allowed to produce can be limited by using the control structure

```
expr \ i
```

which limits `expr` to at most `i` results. For example,

```
every write(power(i) \ 10)
```

writes only the first 10 powers of `i`.

Repeated Alternation

The control structure

```
| expr
```

generates the values of `expr` repeatedly.

This can be useful for producing sequences, as in

```
|(1 to 3)
```

which generates 1, 2, 3, 1, 2, 3, and so on.

6.2.2.5. Conjunction

Sometimes it is useful to bind several expressions together for goal-directed evaluation. As mentioned earlier, if the expressions are separated by semicolons or, equivalently, written on separate lines, goal-directed evaluation goes from one to the next. For example, in

```
expr1; expr2
```

after the evaluation of `expr1` is complete, it no longer is involved in goal-directed evaluation. In particular, if `expr2` fails, there is no resumption of generators in `expr1`. They have, in fact, been discarded.

To prevent this, the expressions can be combined using conjunction:

```
expr1 & expr2
```

In conjunction, failure of `expr2` causes the resumption of suspended generators in `expr1`. The net effect of this is that

```
expr1 & expr2
```

succeeds only if both `expr1` and `expr2` succeed. This sometimes is referred to as "and" in contrast with the "or" of alternation. For example,

```
if (i = 0) & (j = 0) then proceed()
```

evaluates the `then` clause only if both `i` and `j` are equal to 0.

As with alternation, many expressions can be combined for goal-directed evaluation using conjunction:

```
expr1 & expr2 & expr3 & ... & exprn
```

If a conjunction succeeds, its value is the value of the last expression in it. In the preceding example, it is the value of `exprn`.

6.2.2.6. Backtracking

The process of resuming suspended generators, which returns control to sites of earlier evaluation, is called *control backtracking*. Control backtracking is implicit in expression evaluation in Icon and occurs automatically.

Data backtracking is the process of restoring previous values during control backtracking to undo the effects of previous assignments. Icon ordinarily does not perform data backtracking. For example, in

```
(count := 0) & expr
```

if `expr` fails, the value of `count` remains 0 regardless of its value before the assignment.

Icon provides a form of assignment that is reversible. This operation is <-. For example, in

```
(count <- 0) & expr
```

if `expr` fails, the value of `count` is restored to what it was prior to the reversible assignment.

6.2.3. String Processing

Icon has powerful facilities for manipulating strings of characters. It does not, however, have a character data type. Instead, it has two data types that are composed of characters:

- *csets,* which are unordered collections of distinct characters

- *strings,* which are ordered sequences of characters

All 256 characters in the 8-bit extended ASCII character set can be used in csets and strings.

6.2.3.1. Csets

Icon has several built-in csets, including:

&digits—The 10 decimal digits

&ucase—The 26 uppercase letters

&lcase—The 26 lowercase letters

&letters—The 52 upper- and lowercase letters

&cset—All 256 characters

Csets can be specified literally by enclosing characters in single quotation marks, as in

```
vowels := 'AEIOUaeiou'
```

The empty cset, containing no characters, is specified literally by two single quotation marks: ''.

Csets can be constructed by set operations on other csets:

c1 ++ c2, the union of c1 and c2; all the characters in either of them

c1 ** c2, the intersection of c1 and c2; all the characters in both of them

c1 -- c2, the difference between c1 and c2; all the characters c1 not in c2

-c, the complement of c with respect to &cset; all the characters not in c

6.2.3.2. Strings

Strings can be arbitrarily long. They can be specified literally by enclosing a sequence of characters in double quotation marks, as in

```
place := "Mars"
```

The empty string, containing no characters, is specified by two double quotation marks: " ".

The operation *s produces the length of s—the number of characters in it. For example, *place produces 4.

String Construction

The most basic operation for constructing strings is concatenation, one string followed by another. Concatenation is specified by s1 || s2, as in

```
salutation := "Hi there"
greeting := salutation || " " || place || "."
```

which assigns the string "Hi there Mars." to greeting.

Multiple copies of a string can be concatenated at one time using the function repl(s, i), which produces i copies of s, as in

```
banner := repl("+-", 20)
```

which assigns to banner a 40-character string of alternating +s and -s.

There are three functions for producing strings of a fixed length:

> left(s1, i, s2)—Produces a string of length i with s1 starting at the left and copies of s2 used for padding at the right, if necessary
>
> right(s1, i, s2)—Produces a string of length i with s1 ending at the right and copies of s2 used for padding at the left, if necessary
>
> center(s1, i, s2)—Produces a string of length i with s1 centered and copies of s2 used for padding at the left and right, if necessary

For example, right("61", 4, "0") produces "0061".

If *s1 is less than i, it is truncated at the right, left, and ends for the three functions, respectively. If s2 is omitted, it defaults to a blank.

The function trim(s, c) returns the result of trimming all the characters in c off the right end of s. If c is omitted, blanks are trimmed.

String Positions and Substrings

Positions in strings are between characters, numbered starting at 1 before the first character, and there is a position after the last character, as shown by this example:

```
  m   a   n   t   r   a
↑   ↑   ↑   ↑   ↑   ↑   ↑
1   2   3   4   5   6   7
```

Substrings are specified by bounding positions. For example, the substring between positions 2 and 5 in "mantra" is "ant".

Subscripting can be used to produce substrings. For example, if

```
word := "mantra"
```

then word[2:5] produces the substring of word between positions 2 and 5— "ant" in this case.

The expression s[i] is shorthand for specifying the ith character of s (the character after position i). For example, word[1] is "m".

There also are nonpositive position specifications starting at 0 after the last character and decreasing toward the left:

```
  m   a   n   t   r   a
  ↑   ↑   ↑   ↑   ↑   ↑
 -6  -5  -4  -3  -2  -1   0
```

For example, the positions 5 and –2 in "mantra" are equivalent. Positive and nonpositive position specifications can be intermixed and given in any order. Thus, word[2:5] and word[-2,2] are equivalent.

A string can be assigned to a subscripting expression to replace the specified substring. For example, if

```
word := "thesis"
```

then

```
word[1] := "T"
```

changes word to "Thesis".

The replacement need not be the same length as the substring it replaces. For example,

```
word[4:0] := ""
```

replaces the substring "sis" of "Thesis" by the empty string to change the value of word to "The".

The operation !s generates the one-character substrings of s, from beginning to end. For example,

```
every write(!"Hello")
```

writes H, e, l, l, o on separate lines.

String Comparison

As mentioned earlier, Icon uses the 256-character extended ASCII character set. The ASCII codes for characters impose an ordering on the characters.

Strings can be compared on the basis of the codes for their characters. The character c_1 is less than c_2 if the internal code for c_1 is less than the code for c_2. For example, the (ASCII) code for "D" is 68, and the code for "Q" is 81, so "D" is less than "Q". The codes for letters have the same order as ordinary alphabetical order, but the lowercase and uppercase letters have different codes.

The codes for the digits are smaller than the codes for letters, and the uppercase letters have smaller codes than the lowercase letters. Other characters, such as punctuation, have various codes.

For strings, order is determined by the order of their characters, from left to right. Therefore, in ASCII "DQ" is less than "dQ" and "dQ" is less than "dq". If one string is an initial substring of another, the shorter string is less than the longer. For example, "DQa" is lexically less than "DQaaa". The empty string is less than any other string. Two strings are equal if and only if they have the same length and are the same, character by character.

There are six comparison operations for strings, which succeed and return the right operand if the comparison is successful but fail otherwise:

s1 == s2—equal

s1 ~== s2—not equal

s1 << s2—less than

s1 <<= s2—less than or equal

s1 >> s2—greater than

s1 >>= s2—greater than or equal

String Analysis

Icon has several functions for analyzing strings. They all return positions in strings. The string-analysis functions include

upto(c, s)—The first position in s of a character in the cset c

many(c,s)—The position in s following the longest initial sequence of characters in c

find(s1, s2)—The position of the first instance of s1 in s2

match(s1, s2)—The position in s2 after the initial substring s1

These functions fail if there is no match. The functions upto() and find() are generators that produce positions of successive matches.

An example of using string-analysis functions is

```
while instruction := read() do {
    j := upto(" ", instruction) | next        # skip bad lines
    command := instruction[1, j]
    if match(command, "comment") then next     # skip comments
    else  ...                                  # process command
    }
```

6.2.3.3. String Scanning

String scanning is a high-level facility for string analysis. It suppresses much of the detail otherwise involved in string analysis and uses a navigational metaphor.

In string scanning, there is a *scanning subject* to which all scanning operations apply. There also is a *scanning position*, initially 1, that may change during string scanning. Changes in the position occur as the result of successful matching in the subject.

String scanning has the form

```
subject ? expr
```

where the subject string is scanned by expr. The value produced by a scanning expression is the value of expr; it fails if expr does.

Matching Expressions

Matches in the subject occur as the result of *matching functions*:

tab(i)—Moves the position to i

move(i)—Increments the position by i

If the specified position is within the subject, it is changed accordingly; if it is not, the function fails. In the case of a successful match, the matching function returns the substring of the subject between the former position and new position.

Here is a simple example of the use of matching functions:

```
line ? {
      while write(move(1)) do    # write one character
            move(1)              # skip the next one
      }
```

As indicated by the comments, this scanning expression writes every other character in line. The loop terminates when the end of the string is reached because move(1) fails if the new position would not be in the range of the subject.

The power of string scanning comes from using string-analysis functions to provide the argument for tab(), thus moving through the subject to portions of interest. In this usage, the second argument of a string-analysis function is omitted and defaults to the subject of scanning. The string-analysis functions also work starting at the current position in the subject.

This is illustrated by the following segment of code, which converts lines of comma-separated fields to fields of fixed width:

```
while line := read() do {
   result := ""
   line ? {
      while field := tab(upto(',')) do {
         result ||:= left(field, width)
         move(1)
```

```
        }
      }
    write(result ||:= left(tab(0), width))
  }
```

For each line of input, `result` starts with an empty string. The line is scanned, repeatedly looking for a comma with `upto(',')`, which returns its position. `tab(upto(','))` moves to that position and matches the substring prior to it. This substring is put at the left of a blank-filled field of the specified width and concatenated onto the evolving result. Before looking for another comma, `move(1)` skips the current one. When there are no more commas, the `while` loop terminates, and the remainder of the subject up to the last character, matched by `tab(0)`, is appended in another field. The final result is written before a new line is read. Notice that lines are assumed to have fields separated by commas, but with no comma after the last field. Otherwise, the `tab(0)` would not be needed.

Note that in string scanning, it is not necessary to specify the actual positions at which the characters are found. In addition, the subject is implicit in the processing and does not have to be mentioned.

Another example is provided by the following code segment, which converts fixed-width fields to comma-separated fields:

```
while line := read() do {
    result := ""
    line ? {
        while field := move(width) do
            result ||:= trim(field) || ", "
        }
    write(result ? tab(-1))
}
```

Successive fields are matched by `move(width)` and assigned to `field`, which is trimmed of trailing blanks and concatenated onto the evolving result. When there are no more fields, the result is scanned to produce the substring up to the last character (at position -1 in the subject) and it is written.

The operation `=s` is shorthand for `tab(match(s))` and is useful for matching a specific string. This is illustrated by rewriting the earlier string-analysis example that does not use string scanning:

```
while instruction := read() do {
    instruction ? {
        if ="comment " then next           # skip comments
        else  command := tab(upto(' '))
            ...                            # process command
```

Scanning Environments

The subject and the position in it constitute a *scanning environment*. Before beginning a scanning expression, the current scanning environment is saved, and it is restored when the new scanning expression terminates. This allows scanning expressions to be nested.

An example is

```
while line := read() do {
   result := ""
   line ? {
      while field := tab(upto(',')) do {
         field ? {
            if ="X" then next
            }
         result ||:= left(field, Width)
         move(1)
         }
      }
   write(result ||:= left(tab(0), Width))
   }
```

which omits fields that begin with "X".

The function pos(i) succeeds if the current position in the subject is i but fails otherwise. The argument of pos(i) can be a nonpositive specification. For example, pos(-1) succeeds if the position is before the last character in the subject.

The keywords &subject and &pos contain the values of the subject and position in the current scanning environment. They change when the scanning environment changes.

The position in the subject can be changed explicitly by assignment to &pos. For example,

```
&pos := 1
```

sets the position to the beginning of the subject. Assignment to &pos fails if the position would be outside the range of the subject.

In most situations, it is not necessary to refer to &subject and &pos explicitly. There are situations, however, in which this is useful. See section 6.3.2.

Procedure calls do not change the scanning environment. This allows procedures to be used for scanning within a scanning expression. An example is

```
procedure blankx()
```

```
    if ="X" then return " " else return tab(0)

end
```

which could be used to replace fields that begin with an "x" by blank
fields, leaving other fields unchanged, as in

```
while line := read() do {
    result := ""
    line ? {
        while field := tab(upto(',')) do {
            field := {
                field ? blankx()
                }
            result ||:= left(field, width)
            move(1)
            }
        }
    write(result ||:= left(tab(0), width))
    }
```

6.2.4. Structures

Icon provides four kinds of structures for organizing and accessing collections of values in different ways:

- records, which are fixed in size and accessed by named fields

- lists, which are one-dimensional arrays that can be accessed by position or as stacks and queues

- sets, which are collections of distinct values

- tables, which provide associative lookup

Structures are created during program execution. The values in structures
can be of any type, and a structure can contain values of different types.
All structures except records can change in size during program execution.

6.2.4.1. Records

Records are declared, as in

```
record rational(numer, denom)
```

which declares a record named rational with field names numer and denom.

Instances of records are created during program execution by using a
function whose name corresponds to the record name and whose arguments correspond to the fields, as in

```
portion := rational(2, 3)
```

A record declaration adds a type corresponding to the record name to Icon's built-in type repertoire. For example, type(portion) produces "rational".

Record fields are accessed by name using the binary dot (.) operator, as in

```
portion.numer := 1
```

which changes the numer field of portion to 1.

Record fields also can be accessed by position, as in

```
portion[2] := 5
```

which changes the denom field of portion to 5.

6.2.4.2. Lists
A list consists of a sequence of zero or more values. A list is created by an expression in which the values are enclosed in square brackets, as in

```
primaries := ["red", "blue", "green"]
```

A list also can be created by the function list(i, x), which produces a list of i values, all of which are x. For example,

```
grades := list(35, 0)
```

assigns to grades a list of 35 values, all of which are 0.

An empty list, which contains no values, can be produced by [] or list(0).

The values in a list are called elements. The elements in a list can be accessed by using subscripts, as in

```
write(primaries[2])
```

which writes blue. Elements also can be changed by assigning to a subscript, as in

```
grades[21] +:= 10
```

which adds 10 to the twenty-first element of grades.

Nonpositive specifications can be used for subscripting lists. For example,

```
write(primaries[-1])
```

writes green.

Two lists can be concatenated to produce a new list using the operation L1 ||| L2, as in

```
newgrades := grades ||| list(5, 0)
```

which assign to `newgrades` a list of 40 values.

The section operation, `L[i:j]`, produces a new list consisting of elements `i` through `j` of `L`.

6.2.4.3. Using Lists as Queues and Stacks

There are five functions for adding or removing values from the ends of lists, allowing lists to be used as stacks and queues. In this usage, the first element of a list is at its right end and the last at its left. The functions are

`put(L, x)`—Puts `x` on the right end of `L`

`push(L, x1)`—Pushes `x` onto the left end of `L`

`get(L)`—Removes the leftmost element of `L` and produces its value; `get()` fails if `L` is empty

`pop(L)`—Is a synonym for `get()`

`pull(L)`—Removes the rightmost element of `L` and produces its value; `pull()` fails if `L` is empty

The way these functions work is illustrated by this diagram:

An example of using stack and queue access is this code segment that writes the input file in reverse order:

```
lines := []              # start with empty list

while push(lines, read())   # add lines at beginning

while write(get(lines))     # write lines from beginning to end
```

6.2.4.4. Sets

A set is an unordered collection of distinct values. The function `set()` creates a set that initially is empty, as in

```
words := set()
```

The function `insert(S, x)` inserts `x` into the set `S`. For example,

```
insert(words, "cornucopia")
```

adds `"cornucopia"` to `words`. If the value already is in the set, `insert()` does nothing.

The function `delete(S, x)` deletes the member `x` from the set `S`. For example,

```
delete(words, "cornucopia")
```

deletes "cornucopia" from words, if it is contained in words. Attempting to delete a value that is not in a set does nothing.

The function member(s, x) succeeds if x is in s but fails otherwise.

The following operations on sets are available:

s1 ++ s2—Produces the union of s1 and s2

s1 ** s2—Produces the intersection of s1 and s2

s1 -- s2—Produces the difference between s1 and s2

An example of the use of sets is the following code segment, which creates a set containing all the different letters in the input file:

```
letters := set()

while line := read() do
    every insert(letters, !line)
```

6.2.4.5. Tables
A table is a collection of elements. An element is a pair, consisting of a *key* and a value associated with the key.

The function table(x) creates an empty table, where x is a *default value* that is associated with new keys. For example,

```
wordcount := table(0)
```

assigns to wordcount an empty table whose default value is 0.

Tables are subscripted like lists, but the subscripts are keys that can be any type of value. For example,

```
wordcount["cornucopia"] := 1
```

assigns the value 1 to the key "cornucopia" in wordcount. Subsequently,

```
write(wordcount[["cornucopia"]])
```

writes 1.

The value associated with a key can be changed, as in

```
wordcount[["cornucopia"] := 13
```

Augmented assignment is useful for changing the values associated with keys. For example,

```
wordcount["cornucopia"] +:= 1
```

increments the value associated with the key `"cornucopia"`.

The size of a table increases by 1 every time a value is assigned to a key that is not already in the table. An element is added to a table only when an assignment is made to a new key. Therefore, if the key `"tumbler"` has not been assigned a value in wordcount, the expression

```
wordcount["tumbler"]
```

produces the default value of `0`, but `"tumbler"` is not added to wordcount and the size wordcount does not change. On the other hand,

```
wordcount["tumbler"] +:= 1
```

adds `"tumbler"` to wordcount and increases the size of wordcount by 1.

An example of the use of tables is the following code segment, which creates a table containing all the different letters in the input file and the number of times each one occurs:

```
letter_count := table(0)
while line := read() do
    every letter_count[!line] +:= 1
```

There are several other functions that apply to tables. The function key(T) generates the keys in T. The order of generation is not predictable. Note that it is always possible to get from a key to its corresponding value.

The functions insert(), delete(), and member() apply to tables as well as sets. The function member(T, x) succeeds if x is a key in the table T. The function insert(T, x, y) is equivalent to T[x] := y.

6.2.4.6. Operations on Structures
Several operations apply to all kinds of structures:

    *x—Produces the size of (number of elements in) x; for tables, the size is the number of keys.

    ?x—Produces a randomly selected value from x; ?x fails if x is empty.

    !x—Generates the values in x. For records and lists, they are generated from first to last. For sets and tables, the order is not predictable. For tables, the values, not the keys, are generated.

6.2.4.7. Serial Numbers
Every structure has a serial number, and each structure type has a separate series of serial numbers. Serial numbers start at 1 for the first structure created of that type and increase as new structures are created. Each record type has its own series.

The function `serial(x)` returns the serial number of the structure x.

6.2.4.8. Sorting Structures

A structure can be sorted to produce a list with the values in the structure in sorted order. Sorting is first by type, in the order null, integer, real, string, followed by other types. Sorting for numbers is in order of nondecreasing magnitude. Sorting for strings is in nondecreasing lexical (alphabetical) order.

Lists, sets, and records are sorted by `sort(X)`, which produces a list with the values of X in sorted order.

Sorting tables is more complicated because a table element consists of a key and a value. The way a table is sorted depends on the second argument of `sort()`:

> `sort(T, 1)`—Produces a list of two-element lists, where each two-element list corresponds to an element of T; sorting of the two-element lists is by key.

> `sort(T, 2)`—Is like `sort(T, 1)` except that the two-element lists are sorted by value.

> `sort(T, 3)`—Produces a list of alternating keys and associated values sorted by keys; the resulting list has twice as many elements as T.

> `sort(T, 4)`—Is like `sort(T, 3)`, except that sorting is by value.

The result of sorting often can be used directly. For example, to write all the letters in the set `letters`, all that is needed is

```
every write(!sort(letters))
```

In the case of tables, a sorted list with alternating keys and values can be conveniently formatted using queue access. As an example, to write a list of letters and their counts from `letter_count`, the following will do:

```
letter_list := sort(letter_count, 3)
while write(get(letter_list), right(get(letter_list, 10)))
```

The letters are followed by their counts right adjusted in a 10-character field with blanks for padding.

6.2.4.9. Pointers

Structure values are pointers to collections of values. The result of

```
S := set()
```

may be visualized as follows:

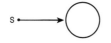

Every structure-creation operation creates a new structure that is different from all other structures; it points to a different object. Even if two structures have identical values, they are not the same. For example, the expressions

```
S1 := set()
S2 := set()
```

create two different empty sets:

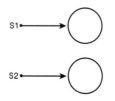

The comparison operation x1 === x2 compares the values of x1 and x2. In order for the comparison to succeed, x1 and x2 must be of the same data type, and if they are structures, they must be the same. Thus, for the preceding example,

```
S1 === S1
```

succeeds, but

```
S1 === S2
```

fails.

Assignment of a structure to a variable copies the pointer to the structure, not the structure itself. Thus, after

```
S3 := S1
```

S1 and S3 point to the same structure, and

```
S1 === S3
```

succeeds:

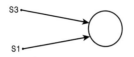

It is important to understand that changing a value in a structure changes it for all values that point to the structure. For example, since s1 and s3 are the same, after

```
insert(S1, "the")
```

the expression

```
member(S3, "the")
```

succeeds:

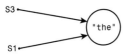

Similarly, if a structure is the value of an argument in a procedure call, a pointer to it is passed to the procedure. If the procedure changes values in that structure, they are, of course, changed in all pointers to it, including ones outside the procedure.

Because structure values are pointers, a structure can contain (pointers) to other structures. For example,

```
insert(S3, set())
```

produces the following situation:

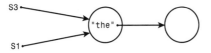

The function copy(x) can be used to copy a structure and create a new structure value. For example, after

```
S4 := copy(S1)
```

s4 is a different structure from s1, but it has the values in s1 at the time of the copy.

Such a copy is a "one-level" copy; if the structure being copied contains pointers to other structures, the pointers are copied but what they point to is not copied. For example,

```
S4 := copy(S1)
```

produces this situation:

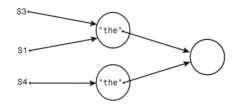

6.2.5. Numerical Computation

Although Icon emphasizes computations related to strings and structures, it has an extensive repertoire of operations for numerical computation.

Integers can be arbitrarily large. Real numbers are represented by floating-point values and depend for their precision and range on the platform on which Icon runs.

In mixed-mode operations involving both integer and real values, integers are "promoted" to reals and the result is real.

6.2.5.1. Literals

Integers

Integers are represented literally in the usual way. By default, integer literals are in base 10.

Radix literals can be used to specify bases other than 10. Radix literals have the form i r j, where i, in base 10, specifies the base for j. The base can be any value from 2 through 36. The letters a, b, ..., z are used to specify "digits" in j that are larger than 9. Examples are

> 2r110—Represents the integer 6
>
> 8r100—Represents the integer 64
>
> 16r1a—Represents 26
>
> 36rtree—Represents 1,388,534

Real Numbers

Real numbers can be represented literally using either decimal or exponent notation. For example, 31.2e3 and 31200.0 are equivalent and represent the real number 31,200.0.

6.2.5.2. Arithmetic

The precedence and associativity for infix (binary) arithmetic operations follow the conventional rules:

Expression	*Operation*	*Precedence*	*Associativity*
N1 ^ N2	exponentiation	3	right to left
N1 % N2	remaindering	2	left to right
N1 / N2	division	2	left to right
N1 * N2	multiplication	2	left to right
N1 - N2	subtraction	1	left to right
N1 + N2	addition	1	left to right

In addition, the prefix (unary) operation -N produces the negative of N, and abs(N) produces the absolute value of N.

In integer division, the remainder is discarded; that is, the value is truncated toward 0. For example,

```
-11 / 5
```

produces -2.

The remaindering operation, N1 % N2, produces the remainder of N1 divided by N2 with the sign of N1. For example,

```
-11 % 2
```

produces -1, but

```
11 % -2
```

produces 1.

Division by zero and raising a negative real number to a real power are erroneous and cause program termination.

6.2.5.3. Numerical Comparison

The numerical comparison operations are

N1 = N2	equal to
N1 ~= N2	not equal to
N1 < N2	less than
N1 <= N2	less than or equal to
N1 >= N2	greater than or equal to
N1 > N2	greater than

Numerical comparison operations succeed and return the value of the right operand if the relationship holds. They fail otherwise.

6.2.5.4. Numerical Computation

Icon supports the following trigonometric functions:

sin(r)	sine of r
cos(r)	cosine of r
tan(r)	tangent of r
asin(r)	arcsine of r
acos(r)	arccosine of r
atan(r1, r2)	arctangent of r1 / r2

Angles are in radians. If r2 is omitted in atan(), the default is 1.0.

The following functions convert between radians and degrees:

dtor(r)	the radian equivalent of r given in degrees
rtod(r)	the degree equivalent of r given in radians

The following functions for numerical calculations also are provided:

sqrt(r)	square root of r
exp(r)	e raised to the power r
log(r1, r2)	logarithm of r1 to the base r2

The default for r2 is e.

Common mathematical constants are provided by keywords:

&e	base of the natural logarithms, 2.71828...
&phi	golden ratio, 1.61803...
&pi	ratio of circumference to diameter of a circle, 3.14159...

6.2.5.5. Pseudo-Random Numbers

If i is a positive integer, ?i produces a randomly selected integer j in the range 1 = j = i. For example, the expression

```
if ?2 = 1 then "odd" else "even"
```

produces the string "odd" or "even" with approximately equal probability.

If i is 0, ?i produces a randomly selected real number r in the range 0.0 = r < 1.0.

Icon's pseudo-random number generator uses a linear congruence relation with an initial seed of 0. The seed can be changed by assigning an integer value to &random.

6.2.5.6. Bit Operations

Icon has five functions that operate on the bit patterns of integers:

iand(i, j)—Produces the bitwise *and* of i and j

ior(i, j)—Produces the bitwise inclusive *or* of i and j

ixor(i, j)—Produces the bitwise exclusive *or* of i and j

icom(i)—Produces the bitwise complement of i

ishift(i, j)—Produces the result of shifting i by j places

If j is positive, the shift is to the left, and vacated bit positions are filled with zeros. If j is negative, the shift is to the right with sign extension.

6.2.6. Co-Expressions

Generators are powerful tools for formulating many kinds of computations. A generator, however, can only produce its values at the place in the program where it appears. Furthermore, goal-directed evaluation prevents generators from producing their values in parallel.

A co-expression "captures" an expression, provides an environment for its evaluation, and allows the expression's values to be produced at any desired place and time in a program.

The expression

```
create expr
```

creates a co-expression that contains *expr*, but the evaluation of *expr* is deferred until its values are needed.

Co-expressions are values that can be assigned to variables, passed as arguments to procedures, and so on. Therefore,

```
intseq := create 1 to 100
```

creates a co-expression containing 1 to 100 and assigns it to intseq.

The values of the expression in a co-expression are produced by *activating* the co-expression, using the operation @c. One value is produced for each activation until there are no more values, in which case activation fails. For example,

```
while write("L", @intseq, ":") do {
        ...                          # process data
    }
```

writes the L1:, L2:, up to L100:, interspersed by any output produced by processing data.

As another example, consider producing a file in which the octal, decimal, and hexadecimal numbers for the 256 characters are given in columns. The expression

```
(0 to 3) || (0 to 7) || (0 to 7)
```

generates the octal numbers 0 through 377 in order. The expression

```
0 to 255
```

generates the decimal numbers 0 through 255, and the expression

```
!"0123456789abcdef" || !"0123456789abcdef"
```

generates the hexadecimal numbers 00 through ff. To write these in parallel columns, all that is needed is to create co-expressions for these expressions and activate each of them in a `while` loop:

```
octal := create (0 to 3) || (0 to 7) || (0 to 7)
decimal := create 0 to 255
hexadecimal := !"0123456789abcdef" || !"0123456789abcdef"

while write(@octal, " ", @decimal, " ", @hexadecimal)
```

Expressions in co-expressions can be procedure calls. For example,

```
lseq := create labels()
```

assigns to `lseq` a co-expression for producing the values from labels.

In fact, Icon program execution begins with the activation of a co-expression for `main()`.

6.2.7. Graphics

Icon supports a wide variety of graphics facilities. Shapes can be drawn, and text can be written in various fonts and styles in windows. Image files can be read and written, users can interact with windows using a mouse, and so on.

6.2.7.1. Windows

Here is a typical window, with a frame provided by the graphics system:

A window consists of a rectangular array of small dots called *pixels*. Pixels can be illuminated and colored. The window shown here is 500 pixels wide and 200 pixels high.

The upper-left pixel in a window has x,y coordinates (0,0). Pixel positions increase to the right (in the x-direction) and down (in the y-direction):

Note that the axes are arranged in a way that corresponds to reading and writing. For drawing, however, the orientation of the y axis is the opposite of the familiar Cartesian coordinate system.

Because pixel numbering starts at 0, the lower-right pixel in the window shown is numbered (499,199).

Windows are created in a manner similar to opening files. The function WOpen() opens a window. Its arguments specify attributes of the window. For example,

```
WOpen("size=500,200")
```

opens a window that is 500 pixels wide and 200 pixels high like the one shown.

There are many other window attributes. There are defaults for all of them, and most can be changed after the window is opened.

A window has a background color and a foreground color. The background color initially fills the window. Drawing and writing text to a window are done in the foreground color, replacing pixels already in the window. The default background and foreground colors are white and black, respectively.

Other background and foreground colors can be specified when a window is open, using the attributes fg and bg. For example,

```
WOpen("size=500, 200", "bg=dark gray", "fg=white")
```

produces the window:

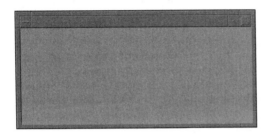

Subsequent drawing and writing are done in white.

The function WAttrib() is used to change window attributes after a window has been opened. For example, the foreground color can be changed to black by

```
WAttrib("fg=black")
```

Subsequent drawing and writing are done in black.

6.2.7.2. Drawing
Drawing can be used to produce points, lines, and various shapes in a window. Any portion of a shape that falls outside the boundaries of the window is not drawn.

Icon has a large repertoire of drawing functions, including

DrawPoint(x, y)—Draws a point (x, y).

DrawLine(x1, y1, x2, y2)—Draws a line from (x1,y1) to (x2,y2).

DrawRectangle(x, y, w, h)—Draws a rectangle whose upper-left corner is at (x,y) and whose width and height are w and h, respectively.

DrawPolygon(x1, y1, ... xn, yn)—Draws a polygon with vertices at (x1,y1) ... (xn,yn); if the first and last vertices are not the same, a line is drawn from the last to the first to close the shape.

DrawCircle(x, y, r)—Draws a circle of radius r with its center at (x,y).

For closed shapes, there are corresponding functions that fill the interior with the foreground color: FillRectangle(), FillPolygon(), and FillCircle().

All drawing functions take multiple sets of arguments to draw multiple shapes with a single call.

Here is a code segment that produces a simple drawing:

```
WOpen("size=400,400")
```

```
every i := 5 to 150 by 2 do
   DrawCircle(i + 50, i + 50, i)
```

The result is shown here:

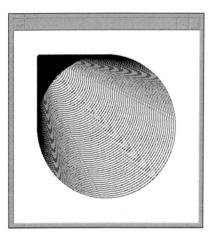

The artifacts are produced by the moiré effect resulting from interference when attempting to draw on an array of pixels of fixed size with values of a higher resolution.

6.2.7.3. Writing to Windows

Writing to a window is similar to writing to a file, except the function used is WWrite() instead of write(). For example,

```
WWrite(" Earthling go home!")
```

produces the following result on a window with a white background and a black foreground:

Character positions are numbered by rows and columns. The initial position is at character (1,1). Positions increase to the right as characters are written. WWrite() ends a line and advances the text position to the beginning of the next row. Text in a window scrolls when it reaches the bottom.

In the preceding example, the initial blank in the string written provides space so that the E does not touch the frame.

The size and appearance of text are determined by the font used. A font specification consists of a *family* that determines the font's general appearance, a size in pixels that determines the text height, and style characteristics. The fonts available depend on the platform on which Icon runs. The font is specified by the font attribute, as in

```
WAttrib("font=Times,10,italic")
```

which specifies the Times family in a 10-pixel size, italicized.

6.2.7.4. Color

Colors can be specified by name using a system based on Berk (1982). Examples are "red", "greenish-blue", and "light blue green". The syntax of a color name is

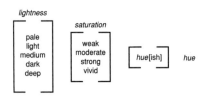

The available *hues* are red, blue, green, cyan, yellow, magenta, violet, brown, orange, purple, pink, white, gray, and black. The items in brackets are optional modifiers. Words are separated by blanks or dashes, as indicated by the previous examples.

Names that fall outside this naming system are passed to the underlying graphics system, allowing the use of system-dependent color names.

Colors also can be specified numerically according to the amount of red, blue, and green light they contain. Amounts vary from 0 (no light) to $2^{16}-1$, representing the maximum intensity. A numerical specification is given as a string in which the intensities are separated by commas. For example,

```
WOpen("bg="0,0,50000")
```

opens a window with a bright blue background.

6.2.7.5. Image Files

Image files can be read into a window. Similarly, a rectangular portion of a window can be saved as an image file. Icon supports GIF, the CompuServe Graphics Interchange Format (Murray & vanRyper, 1994). Additional image file formats are supported on some platforms.

An image can be loaded into a window when it is opened by using the image attribute with the name of an image file. The size of the window is set automatically to the size of the image. An example is

```
WOpen("image=fire_engine.gif")
```

which opens a window using the GIF file fire_engine.gif. The result might look like this:

6.2.7.6. User Interaction

A user can interact with a program through a window at a low level using the keyboard and mouse or at a high level using dialogs and interface tools such as menus and buttons.

Low-Level Interaction

Pressing a mouse button or typing a character with the mouse cursor in the window produces an *event* that the program can detect. The program can determine what the user action was and where in the window it occurred. User events are queued until the program requests them.

The function Event() produces the next event in the queue. For example,

```
repeat {
    case Event() of {
        "o" :    draw_outline()
        "f" :    draw_fill()
```

```
    "q" :    break
    }
}
```

is an *event loop* that performs different operations depending on the characters a user types: `"o"` causes `draw_outline()` to be called, `"f"` causes `draw_fill()` to be called, and a `"q"` terminates the loop. All other events are ignored.

A three-button mouse is standard, with left, middle, and right buttons that can be pressed and released, each of which produces an event. If the mouse is moved while a button is pressed, a "drag" event is produced. These events are represented by keywords:

`&rpress`	right button press
`&mpress`	middle button press
`&lpress`	left button press
`&rdrag`	right button drag
`&mdrag`	middle button drag
`&ldrag`	left button drag
`&rrelease`	right button release
`&mrelease`	middle button release
`&lrelease`	left button release

When an event is processed, the position in the window where the event occurred is automatically assigned to the keywords `&x` and `&y`.

An example of using the mouse coordinates when a mouse event occurs is the following event loop, which draws lines between points at which the left mouse button is pressed:

```
repeat case Event() of {
    &lpress:  {
        DrawLine(\x, \y, &x, &y)
        x := &x
        y := &y
    }
    "e":    EraseArea()
    "q":    break
}
```

If `e` is entered, the window is erased. If `q` is entered, the loop terminates. The non-null test prevents an attempt to draw a line the first time the left mouse button is pressed. An example produced by the event loop is shown here:

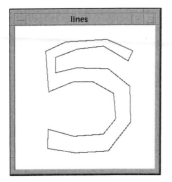

Dialogs

A dialog is a temporary window that a program can produce to provide information to the user or get information from the user. The notice dialog informs the user of a situation such as an error and requires the user to acknowledge the notice. The function Notice(s) produces a dialog with the message s. For example,

```
Notice("Launch aborted!")
```

produces the following dialog window:

The dialog window remains open until the user dismisses it by clicking on the Okay button. Other kinds of dialogs are provided for common situations, such as selecting one of several alternatives, as in

```
SelectDialog("Pick a color:", ["red", "blue", "green"])
```

which produces the following dialog:

Other forms of dialogs allow the user to enter text in fields, turn switches on or off, and select colors interactively.

Visual Interfaces

A visual interface provides for user interaction using tools such as menus, buttons, and sliders.

Icon provides several kinds of interface tools:

- Menus in which the user can select an item from among several choices

- Buttons with several kinds of functionality and in a variety of styles

- Sliders and scrollbars that allow a user to specify a numerical value by moving a "thumb"

- Scrolling text lists

- Text-entry fields in which the user can enter information

- Regions that define rectangular areas and accept low-level events

In addition, text and lines can be used to decorate an interface.

This is the visual interface for an application that performs symmetric drawing:

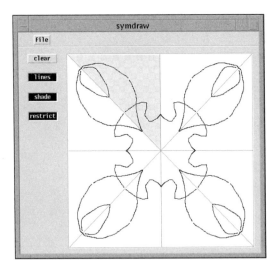

The user draws in the shaded area, called the *generating region*. What is drawn is reflected by "mirrors," indicated by the straight lines, to produce the "sunflower" symmetry, whose technical designation is *p4m*.

The construction of programs with visual interfaces is described in section 6.3.4.

6.2.8. Running Icon Programs

The implementation of Icon is based on the concept of a virtual machine—an imaginary computer that executes instructions for Icon programs. The Icon compiler translates Icon programs into assembly language for the virtual machine and then converts the assembly language into virtual machine code. This virtual machine code is then "executed" on a real computer using an interpreter. This implementation method allows Icon to run on many different computer platforms.

Compiling and running Icon programs is easy. It is not necessary to understand Icon's virtual machine, but knowing the nature of the implementation may help in understanding what is going on in some situations. This section describes the rudiments of running Icon programs.

How Icon programs are run necessarily varies from platform to platform. On some platforms, Icon is run from the command line. On others, it is run interactively through a visual interface. This chapter describes how Icon is run in a command-line environment. Even for this environment, details depend on the platform. In any event, the user manual for a specific platform is the best guide to running Icon.

6.2.8.1. Basics

The name of a file that contains an Icon source program must end with the suffix .icn, as in hello.icn. The .icn suffix is used by the Icon compiler to distinguish Icon source programs from other kinds of files.

The Icon compiler usually is named icont. To compile hello.icn, all that is needed is

```
icont hello.icn
```

The suffix .icn is assumed if none is given, so that this can be written more simply as

```
icont hello
```

The result is an executable *icode* file. The name of the icode file depends on the platform on which Icon is run. On some platforms, notably UNIX, the name is the same as the name of the source file, but without the suffix. On these platforms, the compilation of hello.icn produces an icode file named hello. On other platforms, such as MS-DOS, the icode file has the suffix .icn replaced by .exe, as in hello.exe. For Microsoft Windows, the suffix is .cmd, and so on.

After compilation, entering

```
hello
```

runs the program.

An Icon program can be compiled and run in a single step using the -x option following the program name. For example,

```
icont hello -x
```

compiles and executes hello.icn. An icode file also is created, and it can be executed subsequently without recompiling the source program.

There are command-line options for icont. Options must appear before file names on the icont command line. For example,

```
icont -s hello
```

suppresses informative messages that icont ordinarily produces.

6.2.8.2. Input and Output Redirection
In a command-line environment, most input and output is done using standard input, standard output, and standard error output. Standard input typically is read from the keyboard, whereas standard output and standard error output are written to the console.

Standard input and standard output can be redirected so that files can be used in place of keyboard input. For example,

```
hello < hello.dat > hello.out
```

executes hello with hello.dat as standard input and hello.out as standard output. (The directions that the angular brackets point relative to the program name are suggestive of the direction of data flow.)

6.2.8.3. Command-Line Arguments
Arguments on the command line following an icode file name are available to the executing Icon program in the form of a list of strings. This list is the argument to the main procedure. For example, if showargs.icn consists of

```
procedure main(arguments)

    every write(!arguments)

end
```

then this program prints the arguments on the command line with which it is executed. Thus,

```
icont showargs
showargs Hello world
```

writes

```
Hello
world
```

When -x is used, the arguments follow it, as in

```
icont showargs -x Hello world
```

Arguments are separated by blanks. The treatment of special characters, methods of embedding blanks in arguments, and so forth, vary from platform to platform.

6.2.8.4. Library Modules

The -c option to icont stops processing after the production of assembly-language code and produces a pair of *ucode* files that can be incorporated in other Icon programs. These files constitute a *library module*, which usually contains one or more procedures. For example,

```
icont -c mylibe
```

produces ucode files from mylibe.icn. The ucode files have the suffixes .u1 and .u2—in this case, mylibe.u1 and mylibe.u2.

Ucode files can be incorporated in a program using the link declaration, as in

```
link mylibe
   ...
procedure main()
   ...
```

The ucode file suffixes are not used in link declarations. In the preceding example, any procedures in mylibe.icn are available in the program that links their ucode files.

6.2.8.5. Environment Variables

Environment variables can be used to configure Icon and specify the location of files. For example, the environment variable IPATH can be used to specify the location of library modules. If the library module graphics is in

```
/usr/icon/ipl/gprogs
```

and IPATH has that value, then

```
link graphics
```

finds it.

6.2.9. Debugging Facilities

6.2.9.1. Diagnostic Output

The first thing most programmers do when faced with a problem in a program is to add diagnostic output. In Icon, this takes the form of write() expressions. However, write() can handle only values that are strings or convertible to strings.

For other kinds of values, the function image(x) is particularly useful. It produces a string representation of x for all types of values. In addition, the type can be determined from the value image() produces.

For numeric values, image() simply produces a string showing the value. For example,

```
write(image(137))
```

writes 137 and

```
write(image(-23.3))
```

writes -23.3.

For strings and csets, image() produces the value with enclosing double and single quotation marks, respectively. For example,

```
write(image("Hello world"))
```

writes "Hello world", and

```
write(image('aeiou'))
```

writes 'aeiou'. Because image() encloses strings and csets in quotation marks, such values can be told from other values with corresponding characters. For example,

```
write(image("137"))
```

writes "137", not 137.

For structure types, image() produces a string with the type name, the serial number of the structure, and its size. The form of the string produced is illustrated by

```
write([2, 3, 5, 7, 11, 13])
```

which writes `list_21(6)`, assuming this is the twenty-first list created during program execution.

Some values produced by `image()` are in the form of keywords that produce the value. For example,

```
write(image())
```

writes `&null`.

6.2.9.2. Error Messages
Icon detects errors, according to the phases of program processing:

- Preprocessing

- Compilation

- Linking

- Execution

An error produces a message, which is written to standard error output. An error in one phase prevents program processing from proceeding to the next phase.

Preprocessor Errors
Preprocessor error messages are largely self-explanatory. For example, in

```
$define "constants.icn"
```

if the file `constants.icn` does not exist, the error message is

```
$include: invalid file name
```

Syntax Errors
Syntax errors are detected during compilation. Some error messages are self-explanatory, such as

```
invalid context for next
```

which simply means that a `next` expression occurs in a context in which there is no enclosing loop.

Other error messages are less informative, largely because an expression that is valid at the time it occurs may become invalid at a later point in the program, at which time the source of the error is no longer known. An example is

```
procedure parse()                          # 1
    every 1 to count do                    # 2
        s := goal                          # 3
```

```
        repeat {                                        # 4
            if not upto(&ucase,s) then break            # 5
            if not(s ? replace(!xlist)) then break next # 6
            until s ?:= replace(?xlist)                 # 7
            }                                           # 8
        write(s)                                        # 9
        }                                               # 10
    end                                                 # 11
```

Here, the error is a missing left (opening) brace following the do on line 2. The subsequent code is syntactically correct until the end of the procedure is reached. At that point, the message

```
... Line 10 # "}": missing semicolon or operator
```

occurs.

The use of a consistent indentation style not only makes it easier to find the source of such errors but also to avoid them in the first place.

Linking Errors

Only one error message can occur during linking:

```
inconsistent redeclaration
```

This error occurs if two procedures have the same name, a procedure and a record have the same name, and so on. (It is legal to have a global declaration name that is the same as the name of a procedure or record.)

Runtime Errors

Many errors manifest themselves as errors during program execution. When such a runtime error occurs, there is an error message, a traceback of the procedure calls leading to the place of the error, and the offending expression. Runtime error messages are numbered and divided into categories, depending on the nature of the error.

Error messages with 100 numbers indicate an invalid type or form. An example is

```
103 string expected
```

Error messages with 200 numbers indicate an invalid value or computation, as in

```
201 division by zero
```

Error messages with 300 numbers indicate a capacity has been exceeded. An example is

```
301 evaluation stack overflow
```

This error usually results from excessively deep recursion in procedure calls.

An example of error reporting and the traceback as the result of a run-time error is

```
Run-time error 106
File recorder.icn; Line 32
procedure or integer expected
offending value: &null
Traceback:
    main()
    &null("Summary information ...") from line 32 in recorder.icn
```

Such error termination messages generally are self-explanatory. For example, the error that resulted in the preceding output occurred in the main procedure. The offending expression was an invocation, but instead of a function, procedure, or integer, there was an attempt to apply the null value. This often is the result of a misspelling. In the program in which this error occurred, two letters were transposed, resulting in `wirte` instead of `write`.

6.2.9.3. Termination Dumps

If the value of the keyword `&dump` is nonzero when program execution terminates, whether normally or as the result of a runtime error, a dump of variable values at the time of termination is given. Here is an example:

```
Run-time error 103
File csgen.icn; Line 137
string expected
offending value: &null
Traceback:
    main(list_1 = [])
    subst(list_4 = ["X","abc"]) from line 127 in csgen.icn
    find(&null,"X",&null,&null) from line 137 in csgen.icn

Termination dump:

co-expression_1
subst local identifiers:
    a = list_4 = ["X","abc"]
main local identifiers:
    args = list_1 = []
    line = "X:10"
    goal = "X"
    count = 10
    s = "X"
    opts = table_1(0)

global identifiers:
    any = function any
    close = function close
    find = function find
    get = function get
```

```
integer = function integer
main = procedure main
many = function many
map = function map
move = function move
open = function open
options = procedure options
pos = function pos
pull = function pull
push = function push
put = function put
randomize = procedure randomize
read = function read
real = function real
stop = function stop
string = function string
subst = procedure subst
tab = function tab
table = function table
upto = function upto
write = function write
xlist = list_3 = [list_4(2),list_5(2),list_6(2), ...,
        list_8(2),list_9(2),list_10(2)]
xpairs = procedure xpairs
```

Note that the functions used by the program are listed.

6.2.9.4. Tracing

Tracing of procedures occurs if the value of &trace is nonzero. (The initial value of &trace is 0.) The value of &trace is decremented for each trace message, so if &trace is set to a positive value, it turns off automatically, provided procedure activity continues long enough. Assigning a negative value to &trace, as in

```
&trace := -1
```

results in unlimited tracing. The value of &trace can, of course, be changed at any time during program execution.

Trace messages occur for the following:

- Invocation (call)
- Return
- Failure
- Suspension
- Resumption

Here is an example of tracing resulting from testing the procedure factorial() shown earlier:

```
ftest:    5   | factorial(5)
ftest:   12   | | factorial(4)
ftest:   12   | | | factorial(3)
ftest:   12   | | | | factorial(2)
ftest:   12   | | | | | factorial(1)
ftest:   11   | | | | | factorial returned 1
ftest:   12   | | | | factorial returned 2
ftest:   12   | | | factorial returned 6
ftest:   12   | | factorial returned 24
ftest:   12   | factorial returned 120
ftest:    7   main failed
```

Each line of tracing shows the name of the source file in which procedure activity occurs (ftest.icn in the preceding example). Following a separating colon after the file name, the line number in the file where the activity occurred is given, followed by vertical bars that indicate the level of procedure call.

The rest of the line indicates the type of procedure activity with an associated value if the activity has one.

6.3. Programming Techniques and Examples

6.3.1. Programming with Sequences

When learning a new natural language that is not familiar, it is typical to start by learning grammar and vocabulary and then translating mentally from the new language into a familiar one. To really master a new language, however, it is necessary to *think* in it.

The same situation exists in programming languages. The first steps are to learn the syntax and the computational repertoire. The computational repertoire involves more than just vocabulary; the semantics may be very different from familiar programming languages.

It is much more difficult to grasp how to program in a new language—to use it to formulate solutions to problems. As with natural languages, the first approach usually is to formulate programs in a familiar language and then try to translate them into the new language.

If the two languages are similar, this approach may be successful to a point. But to really take advantage of the features in a new programming language that a familiar programming language does not have, it is necessary to learn to think in the new language.

Since Icon has many features that are not found in other programming languages, translating from another language into Icon inevitably means that many features of Icon will not be used or not used as well as they might be. For example, if a programmer thinks in C and translates into Icon, generators and goal-directed evaluation cannot be used to their full advantage; C simply does not have the concepts.

One way to approach learning to think in a new programming language is to deliberately avoid thinking in a familiar language and translating to the new one. Although it may be difficult at the beginning to write even simple programs in an unfamiliar language, it pays off in the long run. Another approach is to concentrate on the essential features of the new language and see what can be done with them, independent of a pre-planned project. Recreational topics work well because of their inherent interest.

In Icon, the most difficult concepts to master are related to expression evaluation: success, failure, and particularly generation.

If there is one single thing that most characterizes thinking in Icon, it is formulating solutions to problems in terms of sequences produced by generators. Because few programming languages have generators, and none have them in the style of Icon, thinking in terms of sequences produced by generators not only means thinking in Icon but also using a uniquely powerful programming tool.

Icon has subtleties in generators and the control structures related to them that are not described in preceding material. More aspects of these matters will be brought out in what follows, but many can be understood by deciding what is most natural and how specific features might be generalized.

6.3.1.1. Generative Expressions
Working with expressions without the benefit of procedures is a good way to learn what generators are all about. The following sections provide some examples and pose some problems that may be helpful in learning to think in Icon.

Problems: Analyzing Expressions
It generally is easier to figure out what an expression does than to craft one to produce a desired result. Here are some expressions for generating sequences of values. Try to determine their sequences. For example,

```
(1 to 10 by 2) \ 3
```

has the sequence 1, 3, 5.

1. `(1 to 3) | (3 to 1 by -1)`

Solution: 1, 2, 3, 3, 2, 1. The sequence for alternation consists of the sequence for its first operand followed by the sequence for its second operand.

2. (1 | 2) to 3

   Solution: 1, 2, 3, 2, 3. The expression (1 | 2) to 3 is equivalent to (1 to 3) | (2 to 3).

3. 1 to (2 | 3)

   Solution: 1, 2, 1, 2, 3. The expression 1 to (2 | 3) is equivalent to (1 to 2) | (1 to 3).

4. (1 to 3) | (3 to 1 by -2)

   Solution: 1, 2, 3, 3, 1.

5. 3 to (1 | 2)

   Solution: *Nothing.* If the first operand of to-by is greater than the second and the increment is positive (1 by default here), no value is produced.

6. 1 & 2

   Solution: 2. Conjunction generates the sequence for its second operand, which is just 2 in this case.

7. (1 to 3) & 2

   Solution: 2, 2, 2. In the expression, (1 to 3) & 2, (1 to 3) generates three results; for each one the conjunction is evaluated, producing its second operand, 2. This expression is equivalent to (1 & 2) | (2 & 2) | (3 & 2).

8. (1 | 2) & 2

   Solution: 2, 2.

9. 1 & (1 to 3)

   Solution: 1, 2, 3. See the comment in the solution to problem 6.

10. (3 to 5) & (1 to 3)

    Solution: 1, 2, 3, 1, 2, 3, 1, 2, 3. Because the first operand of the conjunction, (3 to 5), produces three results, and the second argument, (1 to 3), is evaluated three times. The values produced by the first operand of conjunction are irrelevant.

11. |(1 to 3)

Solution: 1, 2, 3, 1, 2, 3, 1, 2, 3, ... Repeated alternation produces the sequence for its operand repeatedly. In this case, it is equivalent to (1 to 3) | (1 to 3) | (1 to 3).... Although the sequence is infinite, the number of results actually produced depends on the context in which it is evaluated.

12. |((1 to 3) | (3 to 1 by -1))

Solution: 1, 2, 3, 3, 2, 1, 1, 2, 3, 3, 2, 1, 1, 2, 3, 3, 2, 1, ... See the comments on the solution to problem 1.

13. |3

Solution: 3, 3, 3, ...

14. |((1 to 10 by 2) \ 3)

Solution: 1, 3, 5, 1, 3, 5, 1, 3, 5, 1, 3, 5, 1, 3, 5, 1, 3, 5, 1, 3, ... The expression (1 to 10 by 2) generates 1, 3, 5, 7, 9, but the limitation to three values truncates this to 1, 3, 5.

15. |(3 to (1 | 2))

Solution: *Nothing.* Because the expression (3 to (1 | 2)) produces no value as mentioned in the solution to problem 5, repeated alternation produces no value.

16. ¦(1 & 2)

Solution: 2, 2, 2, ... See the solution to problem 6.

17. |(1 \ 2)

Solution: 1, 1, 1, ... Limiting the expression 1 to two values has no effect because 1 produces only one value.

18. |((3 to 5) & (1 | 2))

Solution: 1, 2, 1, 2, 1, 2, 1, 2, 1, 2, 1, 2, 1, 2, 1, 2, 1, 2, ... See the solution to problem 10.

19. (|((1 to 3) & (1 | 2))) \ 5

Solution: 1, 2, 1, 2, 1. The operand of repeated alternation produces 1, 2, 1, 2, 1, 2, and repeated alternation would produce this repeatedly except for the limitation to five values, which occurs before any repetition.

20. !&lcase

Solution: `"a"`, `"b"`, `"c"`, ..., `"x"`, `"y"`, `"z"`. Because &lcase is a cset and the element generation operation applies only to strings, &lcase is converted automatically to a string of the 26 lowercase letters. Note that the values are strings, not csets.

21. `|!&lcase`

Solution: `"a"`, `"b"`, `"c"`, ..., `"x"`, `"y"`, `"z"`, `"a"`, `"b"`, `"c"`, ..., `"x"`, `"y"`, `"z"`, `"a"`, `"b"`, `"c"`, ..., `"x"`, `"y"`, `"z"`....

22. `!reverse(&lcase)`

Solution: "z", "y", "x", ..., `"c"`, `"b"`, `"a"`.

23. `reverse(!&lcase)`

Solution: `"a"`, `"b"`, `"c"`, ..., `"x"`, `"y"`, `"z"`, `"a"`, `"b"`, `"c"`, ..., `"x"`, `"y"`, `"z"`, `"a"`, `"b"`, `"c"`, ..., `"x"`, `"y"`, `"z"`.... The function reverse() is applied to the sequence for !&lcase as given in the solution to problem 20. Reversing a one-character string has no effect.

24. `|?"HT"`

Solution: `"H"`, `"H"`, `"H"`, `"T"`, `"H"`, `"H"`, ... The sequence for ?"HT" is produced repeatedly. The values are `"H"` and `"T"` with approximately equal probability. The actual sequence produced varies from evaluation to evaluation as the pseudo-random sequence advances.

25. `?|"HT"`

Solution: `"T"`, `"T"`, `"H"`, `"T"`, `"H"`, `"T"`, ... The expressions |?"HT" and ?|"HT" are essentially the same. The first corresponds to ?"HT" | ?"HT" | ?"HT" | ..., and the second corresponds to ?("HT" | "HT" | "HT" ...).

26. `!100`

Solution: `"1"`, `"0"`, `"0"`. This one is subtle. As mentioned in the solution to problem 20, the element generation operation applies only to strings and structures. The integer argument 100 therefore is converted automatically to the string `"100"`.

27. `!(1 to 3)`

Solution: `"1"`, `"2"`, `"3"`. The expression (1 to 3) produces the integers 1, 2, and 3. Each is converted to a string as described in the solution to the preceding problem. Element generation applied to a one-character string just produces the string.

28. (1 to !3)

Solution: 1, 2, 3. The expression !3 produces "3", which is converted to an integer automatically.

29. (1 to |3)

Solution: 1, 2, 3, 1, 2, 3, 1, 2, 3, ... The expression |3 produces 3, 3, 3, ..., so the repeated alternation is equivalent to (1 to 3) | (1 to 3) | (1 to 3).... Note that (1 to |3) is equivalent to |(1 to 3).

30. !12 to 3

Solution: 1, 2, 3, 2, 3. The expression !12 has the sequence "1" , "2". Therefore !12 to 3 is equivalent to ("1" | "2") to 3, which is equivalent to ((1 | 2) to 3), which is equivalent to (1 to 3) | (2 to 3).

Problems: Creating Expressions

Now here are some sequences. Show expressions that generate them. Do not use procedures, and make the expressions as concise as possible.

31. An infinite sequence consisting of randomly selected characters.

Solution: |?&cset. In this expression, &cset produces a cset of all 256 characters. The random-selection operation converts this cset to a string and selects a one-character substring at random. Repeated alternation causes the operation to repeat indefinitely.

32. An infinite sequence consisting of the squares of the positive integers: 1, 4, 9, 16, ...

Solution: The general approach to the problem of generating a sequence of values based on the sequence of positive integers is to generate the positive integers and then apply a function to the results to get the desired sequence. One model for this is

```
i := 0 & |(i +:= 1) & f(i)
```

where f(i) produces the desired value (which need not be an integer, of course). This also can be written as

```
(i := 0, |(i +:= 1), f(i))
```

For the squares, this becomes

```
(i := 0, |(i +:= 1), i ^ 2)
```

33. An infinite sequence consisting of the Fibonacci numbers: 1, 2, 3, 5, 8, 13, 21, 34, ...

Solution: The Fibonacci numbers are defined by the recurrence relation

```
f (i )  = 1                  i = 1, 2
f (i )  = f (i - 1) + f (i - 2)    i > 2
```

It is easy to formulate a recursive procedure based on this recurrence relation, but because procedures are not allowed in solutions to these exercises, a recursive approach cannot be used. An iterative procedure suggests a method:

```
procedure fibseq()

    suspend (i | j) := 1

    repeat {
      i :=: j
      suspend j +:= i
    }

end
```

It takes a little cleverness to get from this procedure to a procedure-free expression:

```
((i | j) := 1) | |((i :=: j) & (j +:= i))
```

There are more parentheses here than are necessary to make the grouping clear. The expression `(i | j) := 1` initializes the two variables and also produces the first two values in the Fibonacci sequence. The remainder of the expression mimics the iterative procedure, using repeated alternation and conjunction in place of `repeat` and the two expressions in the procedure.

34. An infinite sequence consisting of the factorials of the positive integers: 1, 2, 6, 24, 120, 720, ...

Solution: `(i := 1) & |(i *:= seq`. The repeated alternation can be moved inside the parentheses because all that is necessary is for the variable to be generated repeatedly, yielding `(i := 1) & (|i *:= seq())`.

35. An infinite sequence consisting of the "triangular numbers," which have the form $i(i + 1)/2$, yielding: 1, 3, 6, 10, 15, 21, ...

Solution: The triangular numbers are an instance of the *polygonal numbers*, the two-dimensional part of the more general *figurate numbers* (Beiler, 1966). As the name suggests, these numbers have geometrical interpretations. The first four triangular numbers are given by the number of nodes in the following figures:

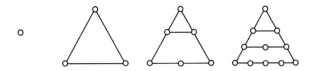

The sequence for the triangular numbers can be produced simply by using the formula `i(i + 1)/2`, incrementing `i` at each step as in previous expressions. There is an easier approach, however, and one that's recommended for unknown sequences: Take the first difference of successive terms and see if it suggests something. In the case here, the first difference yields 2, 3, 4, 5, 6, ... In other words, if `t(i)` is the `i`th triangular number, then

```
t(i) = t(i - 1) + i
```

From this, a sequence to generate the triangular numbers is just

```
(i := 1) | (i +:= seq(2))
```

36. An infinite sequence consisting of the prime numbers: 2, 3, 5, 7, 11, 13, ...

Solution: Although there is no known method for computing primes efficiently in sequence, a brute-force method is simple: Just generate all the integers and filter out those that are not prime. The trivial observation that 2 is the only even prime leads to the following expression:

```
2 | ((i := seq(3, 2)) & (not(i = (2 to i) * (2 to i))) & i)
```

The second operand of the conjunction, `not(i = (2 to i) * (2 to i))`, fails if `i` cannot be represented as the product of two integers. Otherwise, the result of the expression is just `i`, the third operand of the conjunction. It is, of course, not necessary to check all the way to `i * i`. A much better test is

```
not(i = (k := (3 to sqrt(i) by 2)) * (i / k))
```

37. An infinite sequence consisting of *n* copies of each positive integer *n*:
1, 2, 2, 3, 3, 3, 4, 4, 4, 4, ...

Solution: This one is entirely different from the preceding exercises. This solution uses limitation in combination with repeated alternation:

```
i := seq() & (|i \ i)
```

38. A sequence consisting of strings representing the times in minutes in the 24-hour day, starting at midnight and ending at the minute before midnight: `"00:00"`, `"00:01"`, ... `"00:59"`, `"01:00"`, ... `"23:59"`.

Solution: The solution to this problem has two components: a generator for the hours and a generator for the minutes. `0 to 23` generates the hours, and `0 to 59` generates the minutes, but the values need to be padded with zeros:

```
right(0 to 23, 2, "0")
right(0 to 59, 2, "0")
```

All that remains is a concatenation with colons added as separators:

```
right(0 to 23, 2, "0") || ":" ||
   right(0 to 59, 2, "0")
```

6.3.1.2. Recursive Generators

Recursion is a powerful tool for formulating solutions to problems that are defined in self-referential ways. Recurrences such as the ones for factorials, the triangular numbers, and the Fibonacci numbers given earlier provide simple examples. Such formulations are easily cast in terms of recursive procedures.

Procedures also can be recursive generators—suspending with calls of themselves either directly or through a chain of other procedure calls.

Because few programming languages support generators, the concept of recursive generation may seem strange, and it may be difficult initially to understand what is going on or how to use it. Examples follow.

Recursive generators often arise naturally for computations that have more than one value. Consider the permutations of a string—the different ways in which the characters of a string can be rearranged. For example, the permutations of `"abc"` are

```
"abc"
"acb"
"bac"
"bca"
"cab"
"cba"
```

In general, there are $n!$ permutations of an n-character string.

The obvious approach to producing the permutations of a string is to extract each character and concatenate it with the permutations of the remaining characters. Thus, the preceding permutations can be constructed from

```
"a" || permute("bc")
"b" || permute("ac")
"c" || permute("ab")
```

where permute(s) produces (generates) the permutations of s. The step to recursion is clear, and is easily formulated as a recursive generator:

```
procedure permute(s)

    if *s = 0 the return ""

    every i := 1 to *s do
        suspend s[i] || permute(s01:i] || s[i+1:0]])

end
```

The test for an empty string provides termination for the recursion. (The empty string, by convention, has only itself as a permutation.)

Another example of the utility of recursive generation is the "closure" of a set of characters: all the strings that can be composed from the characters, given in order of increasing length. For example, the closure of 'abc' is "", "a", "b", "c", "aa", "ab", "ac", "ba", ... A procedure that generates the closure of a set of characters is

```
procedure closure(c)

    suspend "" | (closure(c) || !c)

end
```

In order to understand the sequence of results for this procedure, consider

```
closure('abc')
```

The first value is the empty string, produced by suspending with "". The subsequent values consist of each value in the sequence produced by closure('abc') concatenated with each character in 'abc'. Because !c is repeatedly resumed for each value generated by closure(c), each character in c is appended to the first value in the results for closure(c). Therefore, the results are "", "a", "b", "c", ... When closure(c) is resumed for its second result, it produces "a", onto which are appended in succession "a", "b", and "c", and so on.

Recursive generators also can be used to generate the sequences for many recursively defined functions. For example, the Fibonacci numbers are generated by fibseq(1, 1) using the following procedure:

```
procedure fibseq(i, j)

    suspend i | fibseq(j, i + j)

end
```

Other examples of recursive generators are noted in subsequent sections.

6.3.2. Pattern Matching

The term *pattern matching* refers to a view of string scanning in which expressions are thought of in terms of the strings they can match instead of how they do it. For example, move(i) can be thought of in two ways: (1) as an expression that adds i to the current position and returns the substring between the previous and new positions, or (2) as a pattern that matches any string that is i characters long.

Although pattern matching is primarily a matter of viewpoint, it provides a powerful conceptual tool for analyzing strings.

Patterns are composed of *matching expressions*. There are two built-in matching expressions: move(i) and tab(i). More complicated matching expressions can be built by combining the built-in ones and by writing *matching procedures*.

6.3.2.1. The Matching Protocol

A matching expression is defined in terms of a protocol that specifies what is allowed:

- A matching expression cannot decrease the position in the subject.

- When a matching expression establishes a new position, it suspends, producing the substring of the subject between the previous and new positions.

- If a matching expression is resumed and has no alternatives, it restores the position to its original value and fails.

The requirement that the position cannot be decreased is not essential to the concept of pattern matching, but it simplifies some of the discussion that follows. It also is natural for most string analysis in Icon and fits nicely with string-analysis functions, which always produce positions at the current position or to its right. Note that `tab(i)` and `move(i)` can be used in ways that violate this requirement. The discussion that follows assumes they are not used to decrease the position in the subject.

There are two fundamentally different aspects to these rules of protocol: what a matching expression produces (the matched portion of the subject) and data backtracking (maintenance of the position).

The idea behind producing the matched portion of the subject is that a matching expression, viewed as a pattern, produces a specific string from among all those that the pattern can match. Thus, while `move(i)`, as a pattern, characterizes all strings of length `i`, evaluating `move(i)` at a particular position in a particular subject produces a specific string of length `i`.

Because matching expressions may advance the position when they match, they have the nice property that the string matched by two matching expressions in succession is the concatenation of the strings they match. For example,

```
move(i) || move(j)
```

is a matching expression.

Data backtracking is more subtle. It means that a matching expression is responsible for maintaining the position and, in particular, leaving it as it was if it fails. This assures that alternative patterns are applied at the same place in the subject, and it corresponds to the intuitive notion of matching one pattern or another. For example, in

```
(move(3) || =".") | move(5)
```

if `move(3)` succeeds but `="."` fails, `move(5)` matches starting at the same place as `move(3)` did.

In order for a matching expression to restore the position, it must suspend so that it can regain control if a subsequent matching expression fails. In the preceding example, `move(3)` suspends and is resumed when `="."` fails. The suspension has nothing to do with producing alternative matches: Although some matching expressions are generators, `move(3)` can match in only one way. It suspends only so that it can be resumed to restore the position if a subsequent matching expression fails. Of course, a matching expression that does not change the position need not suspend (but it does need to return the empty string).

6.3.2.2. Composing Matching Expressions

The ability to build up complicated matching expressions from simpler ones is essential to the use of pattern matching. The rules of protocol given in the preceding section determine how matching expressions can be combined to form other matching expressions. The two basic forms of combination are concatenation and alternation. If *expr1* and *expr2* are matching expressions, then

    expr1 || expr2

and

    expr1 | expr2

are matching expressions. And, of course, =s is a matching expression because it is just a shorthand for tab(match(s)).

Note that, in general,

    expr1 & expr2

is not a matching expression because it produces the string matched by *expr2*, not the concatenation of the strings matched by *expr1* and *expr2*.

Most operations on matching expressions do not yield matching expressions. Some do not because they do not produce a matched substring, as in

    expr1 + expr2

Of course, adding two matched substrings is an unlikely operation. The more serious limitations arise with control structures.

By definition, control structures alter the flow of control. Most control structures have control expressions that determine what expression is evaluated next. Control expressions are bounded, so that if they produce a result, they cannot be resumed. Bounded expressions are fatal to matching because they prevent the backtracking that is required to maintain the position. For example, if *expr1* and *expr2* are matching expressions,

    if expr1 then expr2

is not, in general, a matching expression, because *expr1* is bounded and cannot be resumed to restore the position if a subsequent matching expression fails.

Despite other possibilities, matching expressions usually are composed by the concatenation and alternation of other matching expressions. These two operations correspond to "match this then match that" and "match this or match that," respectively.

6.3.2.3. Matching Procedures

The obvious approach to extending the built-in repertoire of matching expressions is to write *matching procedures*—procedures that obey the matching protocol.

Showing how `move(i)` and `tab(i)` can be written as procedures illustrates the principles. This is one way to write a procedure `tab(i)`:

```
procedure tab(i)
   local saved_position

   saved_position := &pos

   if &pos := i then {
      suspend &subject[saved_position : &pos]
      &pos := saved_position
      }

   fail

end
```

The local identifier `saved_position` is used to save the position. If the assignment of `i` to `&pos` succeeds (that is, if `i` is in range), `tab()` suspends with the matched substring of the subject. If `tab()` is resumed, it restores the saved position and fails.

This procedure is an instance of a more general model for matching procedures:

```
procedure tab(i)
   local saved_position

   saved_position := &pos

   every &pos := new_pos do {
      suspend &subject[saved_position : &pos]
      &pos := saved_position
      }

   fail

end
```

where *new_pos* indicates an expression that generates values for the position. An example of the use of this model is

```
procedure gap()
   local saved_position

   saved_position := &pos
```

```
every &pos := saved_position to *&subject + 1 do {
   suspend &subject[saved_position : &pos]
   &pos := saved_position
   }

fail

end
```

This procedure matches strings of length 0, 1, and so on through the end of the subject.

As mentioned earlier, a pattern abstractly characterizes a set of strings without any particular order among them. A procedure like gap() may match several different strings, but, of course, there is an order. The preceding procedure is "pessimistic" and tries the shortest possible string first, matching longer strings only if it is forced to do so by resumption resulting from the failure of subsequent matching expressions. An optimistic version of this matching procedure is

```
procedure gap()
   local saved_position

   saved_position := &pos
   every &pos := *&subject + 1 to saved_position by -1 do {
      suspend &subject[saved_position : &pos]
      &pos := saved_position
      }

   fail

end
```

6.3.2.4. Matching Procedures as Arguments to Matching Procedures

One of the potentially most powerful aspects of pattern matching is to use matching procedures as first-class values—passing matching procedures as arguments to other matching procedures.

Consider a matching procedure, p(), and the common situation in which a match is wanted for p() or the empty string. This can be written as

```
p() | ""
```

However, matching something or the empty string is a concept that can be encapsulated in a way that is independent of any particular matching procedure—in another procedure, say orempty(p). The idea is that orempty(p) applies p in the desired context:

```
procedure orempty(p)

   suspend (p() | "")

end
```

To understand orempty(), follow through the evaluation. The call p() is evaluated first. If it fails, the empty string is evaluated next, orempty() suspends with the empty string, and what happens next is clear. If p() succeeds, orempty() suspends with the value it matched; that is, it does just what p() alone would have done. If orempty() is resumed, p() is resumed because it suspended (as required of matching expressions).

Sometimes a particular construction in a string—a pattern—occurs several times in a row; perhaps zero or more. Suppose p() matches this pattern. What is needed is a matching procedure arbno(p) that matches what p() matches, zero or more times in a row:

    "" | p() | (p() || p()) | (p() || p() || p()) | ...

Of course, there must be some context that causes the alternatives to be evaluated.

Such an open-ended construction suggests a closed form, using recursion:

```
procedure arbno(p)

    suspend "" | (p() || arbno(p))

end
```

arbno(p) first matches the empty string (zero occurrences of p(p). If it is resumed, it matches p() followed by arbno())—which matches the empty string first, so this amounts to one match of p(), and so on.

Note that arbno() is a recursive generator.

6.3.3. Procedures with Memory

There are situations in which a procedure is called many times with the same argument values and always returns the same value for those arguments. Obviously, recomputation is expensive in terms of time and in some cases in terms of space. Also, in some cases, the amount of such redundant computation is so great that it limits what is possible to compute.

6.3.3.1. The Problem

The problem with redundant computation is particularly serious when a computation is defined recursively, so one call may lead to many other calls. The examples of this situation that are easy to understand are somewhat artificial in the sense that they are not likely to occur in "real" programs. Nevertheless, the basic problem *is* real and can occur when searching databases, traversing structures, and so forth.

The Fibonacci numbers, mentioned earlier, provide an example. The Fibonacci numbers are defined by the recurrence relation:

```
f (i )  = 1              i = 1, 2
f (i )  = f (i - 1) + f (i - 2)    i > 2
```

The resulting sequence is 1, 1, 2, 3, 5, 8, 13, 21, 34, and so on. The numbers get large quickly. For example, f(35) is 9,227,465.

A straightforward procedure for computing the ith Fibonacci number follows directly from the recurrence:

```
procedure f(i)

    if i = (1 | 2) then return 1
    else return f(i - 1) + f(i - 2)

end
```

The problem with this kind of a formulation is not that any one call is expensive. The problem is that one call leads to another, and many of the calls have the same argument and hence result in redundant computation. For example, f(8) calls f(7) and f(6), f(7) calls f(6) and f(5), and so on. The way the calls add up is illustrated by the computation of f(10), where the numbers of calls are

f(10)	1
f(9)	1
f(8)	2
f(7)	3
f(6)	5
f(5)	8
f(4)	13
f(3)	21
f(2)	34
f(1)	21
total	109

Note that except for f(1), the number of calls itself forms the Fibonacci sequence. This is not a coincidence, and the consequences are significant, considering how rapidly the Fibonacci numbers grow.

Of course, computing Fibonacci numbers recursively is not the best approach. An efficient iterative method was given earlier.

Although there are general methods for converting recursive formulations to iterative ones (Kleene, 1952), they are impractical in many cases. Consider this nested recurrence (Hofstadter, 1979):

```
q (i )   = 1                                        i = 1, 2
q (i )   = q (i -  q (i  - 1)) + q (i -  q (i  - 2))     i > 2
```

The sequence for this recurrence is "chaotic" in the sense that values do not get progressively larger. Instead, a value sometimes is less than the preceding one, although on the average the values increase. Here's how the sequence starts: 1, 1, 2, 3, 3, 4, 5, 5, 6, 6, 6, 8, 8, 8, 10, 9, 10, 11, 11, 12, 12, 12, 16, 14, 14, 16, and so on. The underscores show values that are less than their predecessors.

A recursive procedure based on the preceding recurrence is trivial to formulate:

```
procedure q(i)

    if i = (1 | 2) then return 1
    else return q(i - q(i - 1)) + q(i - q(i - 2))

end
```

Although redundant computation clearly is a problem in the recursive computation of the Fibonacci sequence, it is a much more serious problem here. The calls for computing q(10) are

q(10)	1
q(9)	1
q(8)	2
q(7)	3
q(6)	5
q(5)	9
q(4)	22
q(3)	77
q(2)	284
q(1)	77
total	481

For q(11), q(12), and q(13) computed in this way, the total numbers of calls are 813, 1,393, and 2,325, respectively. Getting values of q(i) for large i in this manner is impractical.

6.3.3.2. Adding Memory to Procedures

It is clear that redundant computation must be avoided if there is to be any hope of computing many values in such a sequence. The obvious way to avoid duplicate procedure calls is to keep track of calls and record their values. Then, when a call occurs that has occurred before, its value can be produced without performing the computation again. In other words, add memory to the procedure. This idea is an old one (Mitchie, 1967), and it is an important component of dynamic programming (Horowitz & Sahni, 1978).

The basic idea is simple: Provide memory in the form of a data structure that is subscripted by argument value. When a procedure is called, the memory is checked. If there is a value for the argument in the memory, the value is returned. If there is not, the computation is performed as before, and the resulting value is added to the memory before the procedure returns.

For Icon, tables provide a particularly convenient form of memory. They can be subscripted by any value; it is not necessary to worry about out-of-range references, and they grow in size automatically as information is added to them.

Here is how the procedure for computing the chaotic sequence looks with memory added:

```
procedure q(i)
   static memory

   initial {
      memory := table()
      memory[1] := memory[2] := 1
      }

   if value := \memory[i] then return value
   else return memory[i] := q(i - q(i - 1)) + q(i - q(i - 2))

end
```

The use of a static variable allows all calls of q() to access previously computed values.

The first time q() is called, memory is set up, and the two initial values in the sequence are placed in it so that it is not necessary to check for them in subsequent calls. Because the default value for the table is null, it is easy to check whether an argument is in memory. If it is not, the computed value is added to memory before returning.

Using this formulation, the speed of computation is nearly linear in i. Values for q(i) easily can be computed for large i.

A thousand values are more than enough to reveal some startling properties of this chaotic sequence, as shown in this plot produced using Icon's graphics facilities:

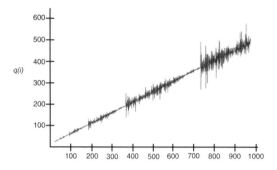

The average value of `q(i)` appears to be linear and close to `i/2`. Notice also the self-similarity in the oscillations—a suggestion of a possible relationship to fractals.

6.3.4. Visual Interfaces in Icon

Most programs now provide visual interfaces through which a user can control the program in a high-level manner using interface tools such as menus and buttons.

As mentioned in section 6.2.7, Icon supports a variety of interface tools. The (Icon) program VIB ("visual interface builder") provides a visual environment for building interfaces. This section provides an overview of the process of building a visual interface and writing a program to use such an interface. A slightly simplified version of the symmetric drawing application shown in section 6.2.7 is used as an example here:

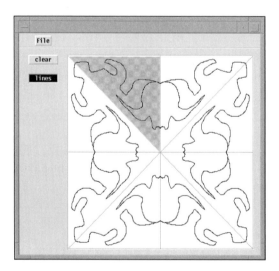

6.3.4.1. The Interface

It is not necessary to know how the functionality of an application is accomplished in order to create a visual interface for it. Interface design—how functionality is expressed and arranged visually—is a complicated and difficult subject. This section does not deal with these topics but instead shows how to create a given interface, such as the one shown previously.

The interface for the symmetric drawing application has four interface tools:

- A menu at the top left
- Two buttons below the menu
- A square region in which the drawing is displayed

In addition, there is a line that separates the menu bar from the rest of the interface.

The file menu has three items:

The save item allows the user to save the current drawing in an image file. The help item leads to information about the application and how to use it. Finally, the quit item terminates execution of the application.

The clear and lines buttons clear the display and toggle the visibility of the lines that indicate the "mirrors" around which drawing is reflected, respectively. The two buttons differ in functionality. The clear button simply causes an action. The lines button retains a state according to whether the mirror lines are shown. This toggle button is highlighted (by reversing colors) when it is on so that its state can be seen on the interface.

The region in which the drawing is displayed accepts mouse events that are translated into drawing that is mirrored to create the symmetry.

Producing this interface involves defining the size of the interface, creating the tools, positioning them, and giving them appropriate attributes.

6.3.4.2. VIB

VIB provides a visual interface on which tools can be placed, arranged, and configured. Mouse actions and dialogs provide the means.

The VIB window for a new interface looks like this:

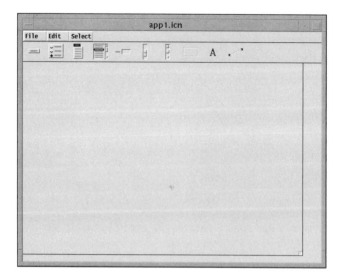

The menu at the top provides various features. Below this is a toolbar with icons representing the kinds of tools and decorations that can be placed on an interface.

From left to right, these are

- Buttons
- Radio buttons
- Menus
- Text lists
- Text-entry fields
- Sliders
- Scrollbars
- Regions
- Labels
- Lines

Below the toolbar is a rectangular area that indicates the size of the interface that is being constructed. The box at its lower-right corner can be dragged to change the size of the area.

An instance of a tool is created by pressing on its icon and dragging onto the interface area. The attributes of a newly created tool usually need to be changed. This is done by using the mouse for positioning and sizing and by dialogs for other attributes as well as setting precise locations and sizes.

A dialog for configuring a tool is produced by pressing the right mouse button with the mouse cursor on the tool. For example, the dialog for the clear button, after editing, looks like this:

The label, clear, is what appears on the face of the button. The ID is used to identify the tool; a mnemonic value, perhaps the same as the label, is useful for keeping track of tools. The callback field contains the name of an Icon procedure that is called when the user presses the button. Thus, the code for the symmetric drawing application contains a procedure clear_cb() that clears the display region so that a new drawing can be started. The other fields in this dialog relate to the button's appearance and functionality. For example, for the lines button, toggle is checked to indicate that the button maintains a state.

The dialog for a menu provides fields for the items the menu supports:

As indicated by this dialog, there are provisions for adding and deleting items and creating submenus for items.

The dialog for a region provides four options for the visual appearance of the region's border:

The callback procedure for a dialog is called when an event occurs in the region.

The final interface for the symmetric drawing application, as seen in VIB, looks like this:

6.3.4.3. Integrating the Interface and the Program

VIB produces code to create the interface. The complete application consists of the VIB interface code, code to support user interaction, and code for the functionality of the application itself.

The code produced by VIB contains a procedure, `ui()`, that opens a window for the interface, draws the tools, and initializes them. This procedure also returns a table whose keys are the tool IDs and whose corresponding values are records that implement the tools.

A program that has a VIB interface typically begins in this way:

```
procedure main()
   tools := ui()
         ...
```

The tools are enclosed within and managed by a *root* tool that has the ID "root". User events are handled by a procedure that takes the root as an argument:

```
GetEvents(tools["root"])
```

This procedure produces callbacks for user actions on tools. GetEvent() never returns; all program activity occurs as the result of callbacks.

6.3.4.4. Callbacks

A callback procedure has two arguments: the tool that caused the callback and a value associated with that tool.

In the case of a menu, the value is a list that contains the selected items and items from successive submenus, if any. The callback procedure for the file menu is

```
procedure file_cb(tool, value)

   case value[1] of {
      "save":    save()
      "help":    help()
      "quit":    exit()
      }

   return

end
```

Because the items on the file menu do not have submenus, the list has only one element. The procedures save() and help() save an image file for the current drawing and provide access for information on how to use the application, respectively. The function exit() simply terminates program execution.

The callback procedure for the clear button is simpler. Because no value is associated with a button without a state, no arguments are needed:

```
procedure clear_cb()

   EraseArea(pane)
   if \lines then drawmirrors()
```

```
    return

  end
```

The global variable `lines` is non-null if lines for the mirrors are to be drawn.

Activity related to symmetric drawing occurs within the region tool. For a region, the callback values are the events themselves, such as mouse button presses. The symmetric drawing application has several modes, including drawing points, drawing lines, and erasing. The portion of the region callback associated with drawing points illustrates the procedure:

```
procedure pane_cb(vidget, event)

        &lpress: {     # free-hand drawing
            every DrawPoint(pane, &x | (W - &x), &y | (H - &y))
            every DrawPoint(pane, &y | (W - &y), &x | (H - &x))
            x := &x
            y := &y
            }
            . . .
```

Note that alternation is used to draw in symmetric positions.

6.3.5. Anatomy of a Program

The preceding sections describe Icon and explore various aspects of programming in Icon. This section presents a complete Icon program, including how it is designed and written.

6.3.5.1. A Recognizer Generator

The problem is to convert a description of a context-free language (Griswold & Griswold, 1996) into a recognizer for the language; that is, to write a program that writes another one—a recognizer.

The context-free languages used here are written in a version of Backus-Naur Form in which nonterminal symbols are enclosed in angular brackets and alternatives are separated by vertical bars (Backus, 1959).

A simple grammar that illustrates this syntax-description notation is

```
plist> ::= [ ] | [<args>]  | [<plist>]
<args> ::= , | ,<plist> | ,<args>
```

Each line contains a definition, or *production*, that defines a *nonterminal* symbol. `<plist>` and `<args>` are nonterminal symbols, `::=` stands for "is defined to be," and vertical bars separate alternatives as mentioned previously. All other symbols (here brackets and commas) are *terminal* symbols that stand for themselves.

The language defined by <plist> contains strings such as "[,[ ]]", "[,,,]", and "[[ ]]".

An Icon recognizer for <plist> is

```
procedure plist_()
    suspend {
        (="[ ]") | (="[" || args() || ="]") | (="[" || plist() || ="]")
        }
end

procedure args_()
    suspend {
        (=",") | (="," || plist()) | (="," || args())
        }
end

procedure main()
    while line := read() do {
        writes(image(line))
        if line ? (plist() & pos(0)) then write(": accepted")
        else write(": rejected")
        }
end
```

6.3.5.2. The Structure of a Production

The problem is a conceptually simple one: Analyze each production in the grammar, and construct a corresponding recognizing procedure.

String scanning is the obvious tool to use for the analysis of the productions, but some care is needed to avoid a messy, bug-ridden program.

The analysis should be organized around the syntax of productions, which have the form

```
production -> < name > ::= rhs
```

where *rhs* stands for "right-hand side." A right-hand side, in turn, is a sequence of alternatives separated by vertical bars:

```
rhs -> alt | alt | ... | alt
```

and an alternative is a sequence of symbols:

```
alt  ->  sym sym  ... sym
```

The point is that the hierarchical structure of a production should be reflected in the structure of its analysis.

6.3.5.3. Transforming a Production

The components of a production as described in the preceding section also need to be transformed to produce a recognizing procedure:

```
τ(< name > ::= rhs) =      procedure name()
          suspend t(rhs)
      end

τ(alt | alt | ... | alt) = τ(alt) | τ(alt) | ... | τ(alt)

τ(sym sym ... sym) = (τ(sym) || τ(sym) || ... || τ(sym))

τ(terminal) = ="terminal"

τ(nonterminal) = nonterminal()
```

6.3.5.4. Organization of the Program

The hierarchical structure of a production is reflected in a hierarchy of
procedures that analyze and transform a production:

```
transprod()   Transform a production
     ↓
transalts()   Transform the alternatives
     ↓
transseq()    Transform a sequence of symbols
     ↓
transsym()    Transform a symbol
```

6.3.5.5. Writing the Program

There are two main issues in actually writing the program:(1) how to perform the analysis and (2) how to produce the required transformed output.

The approach taken here uses string scanning exclusively, with matching
procedures doing the work. These matching procedures operate in the
context of a scanning environment that is established before they are
called. For example, the transformation loop in the main procedure is

```
while line := read() do
    line ? transprod()
```

Thus, the procedure transprod() is called with the appropriate scanning
environment already in place. transprod() needs to get the name of the
nonterminal symbol being defined by the production, write a procedure
heading, provide the "shell" for suspension, call tranalts() to transform
the alternatives, and then finish off the procedure declaration:

```
procedure transprod()

    {
        ="<" &
        write("procedure ", tab(many(nchars)), "()") &
        =">::="
        } | error()

    write("    suspend {")
```

```
        transalts()
        write("       }")
        write("end")

        return

   end
```

The global variable nchars contains a cset consisting of the characters that are acceptable in a nonterminal name. Note that in writing the procedure heading, the second argument of write() is the result of string scanning, inserting the name in the proper place in the procedure declaration. Conjunction is used to bind the three expressions involved in analyzing the production into a single unit, so that only one call of error() is needed. In this program, an error in the syntax of a production terminates program execution.

The procedure transalts() is next. It is called with the same scanning environment as for transprod() but with the position now at the first character of the right-hand side.

Because a right-hand side is a sequence of alternatives separated by vertical bars, a loop is the natural control structure to use. Since vertical bars *separate* alternatives, an alternative is matched by

```
   tab(upto('|') | 0)
```

This construction is useful when items are separated by some marker but there is no marker after the last one. It matches up to the marker or else matches the remainder of the subject.

If there were no transformation to apply to the subject, the analysis loop would look like

```
   repeat {
       tab(upto('|') | 0) ? transseq()
       move(1) | break
       }
```

where

```
   move(1) | break
```

either moves past the separator or terminates the loop in the case of the last alternative.

To construct the required output, however, parentheses are needed around each alternative, and vertical bars are needed between them. The complete procedure, therefore, is a bit more complicated:

```
procedure transalts()

    writes("        ")
    repeat {
        writes("(")
        tab(upto('|') | 0) ? transseq()
        if move(1) then writes(") |")
        else {
            write(")")
            return
            }
        }

end
```

Note that an alternation symbol is only written when there is another alternative to process.

The procedure `transseq()` is invoked as a matching procedure in

```
tab(upto('|') | 0) ? transseq()
```

The scanning environment for `transseq()` is just the current alternative. There is a question of how to terminate the loop: by checking in `transseq()` or having `transsym()` fail. To allow for the possibility of an empty alternative, which is reasonable, it is more convenient for `transseq()` to check when `transsym()` has processed the last symbol. Note that the symbols for concatenation are provided only when there is another symbol to process:

```
procedure transseq()

    repeat {
        transsym()
        if not pos(0) then writes(" || ")
        else return
        }

end
```

As noted previously, there are two kinds of symbols, and the translations are quite different in the two cases. Analysis and transformation of a nonterminal symbol involves a straightforward scanning expression with conjunction again used to bind the component subexpressions. A terminal symbol, on the other hand, requires a prefix equal sign and enclosing quotes:

```
procedure transsym()

    if ="<" then {
        {
            writes(tab(many(nchars)), "()") &
            =">"
            } | error()
        }
```

```
    else writes("=", image(tab(upto('<') | 0))))

    return

end
```

The function `image()` is handy for producing the enclosing quotes; otherwise, escaped quotes in literal strings are required. These are hard to read and easy to get wrong.

Note that if several terminal symbols occur in a row, they are combined into a single matching expression. For example, `abcd` gets transformed into

```
="abcd"
```

rather than

```
="a" || ="b" || ="c" || ="d"
```

as specified formally in the transformation given earlier. The result is the same, and the first form is, of course, not only more compact but also more efficient.

There are a few more things that need to be taken care of in the complete program, such as writing out a main procedure that reads in lines and determines whether they are sentences in the grammar. It is necessary to identify the "goal" nonterminal symbol, which by convention is the one for the first production.

Here is the complete program:

```
global goal                     # nonterminal goal name
global nchars                   # characters allowed in a  name

#
# Translate a grammar into a recognizer.
#

procedure main()
    local line         # a line of input

    nchars := &letters ++ '_'

    while line := read() do {       # process lines of input
        line ? transprod()          # transform the production
        }          # end while

    write("procedure main()")            # write out the main procedure
    write("    while line := read() do {")
    write("        writes(image(line))")
    write("        if line ? (", goal, "() & pos(0)) then ")
    write("            write(\": accepted\")")
    write("        else write(\": rejected\")")
```

```
      write("        }")
      write("end")

end


#
#  Transform a production.
#

procedure transprod()
      local sym                          # the symbol being defined

      {
        ="<" &                           # begin the procedure
        write("procedure ", sym := tab(many(nchars)), "()") &
        =">::="                          # skip definition symbols
        } | error()                      # catch syntactic error
      write("   suspend {")              # begin the suspend expression
      transalts()                        # transform the alternatives
      write("        }")                 # end the suspend expression
      write("end")                       # end the procedure declaration
      write()                            # space between declarations
      /goal := sym                       # first symbol is goal

      return

end


#
#  Transform a sequence of alternatives.
#

procedure transalts()

      writes("        ")                 # write indentation
      repeat {                           # process alternatives
        writes(" (")                     # parenthesis for alternative
        tab(upto('|') | 0) ? transseq()  # transform the symbols
        if move(1) then writes(") |")    # if more, close the parentheses
                                         # and add the alternation

        else {
           write(")")                    # no more, close parentheses
           return
           }                             # end else
        }                                # end repeat

end


#
#  Transform a sequence of symbols.
#

procedure transseq()

      repeat {
        transsym()                       # process a symbol
        if not pos(0) then writes(" || ") # if more, provide concatenation
        else return                      # else get out and return
```

```
        }                                    # end repeat

end

#
#   Transform a symbol.
#

procedure transsym()

    if ="<" then {                       # if it's a nonterminal
        {                                # write it with suffix
            writes(tab(many(nchars)), "()") &
            =">"                         # get rid of closing bracket
        } | error()                      # or catch the error
    }                                    # end then; otherwise
                                         # transform nonterminal
    else writes("=", image(tab(upto('<') | 0)))

    return

end

#
#   Issue error message and terminate execution.
#

procedure error()

    stop("*** malformed production: ", tab(0))

end
```

6.4. Icon Resources

Many resources are available to Icon programmers. These include implementations for many platforms, a program library, source code, books, technical reports, newsletters, and a newsgroup.

Most Icon material, except for books, is available free of charge.

6.4.1. Online Access

On the World Wide Web, the Icon home page is located at

```
http://www.cs.arizona.edu/icon/
```

From there, links to general information about Icon, reference material, the current status of Icon, implementations, the Icon program library, documentation, technical support, and so on can be found.

The address for anonymous FTP is

```
ftp.cs.arizona.edu
```

From there, `cd /icon` and get README for navigational instructions.

6.4.2. Implementations

All implementations of Icon are in the public domain and available as described in the preceding section.

The current version, Version 9, presently is available for the Acorn Archimedes, the Amiga, Macintosh/MPW, Microsoft Windows, MS-DOS, many UNIX platforms, VAX/VMS, and Windows NT.

There also are earlier versions for several other platforms. Icon's graphics facilities presently are supported for Microsoft Windows, UNIX, VAX/VMS, and Windows NT.

6.4.3. Documentation

Documentation on Icon is extensive. In addition to the material here, there are three books devoted to Icon:

> *The Icon Program Language* (Griswold & Griswold, 1996) contains a description of Version 9.3 of Icon, including a detailed reference manual.
>
> *Graphics Programming in Icon* (Griswold, Jeffery, & Townsend, 1998) describes Icon's graphics facilities and how to build applications with visual interfaces.
>
> *The Implementation of the Icon Programming Language* (Griswold & Griswold, 1986) contains a detailed description of how Icon is implemented. Although it describes an earlier version, it still is a useful reference.

There are two newsletters:

> *The Icon Newsletter* (Griswold, Griswold, & Townsend, 1978–) is published by the Department of Computer Science at The University of Arizona and The Bright Forest Company, Tucson, AZ, three times a year and contains material of a topical nature, such as work in progress and new implementations.
>
> *The Icon Analyst* (Griswold, Griswold, & Townsend, 1990–) provides in-depth coverage of technical matters related to Icon, including programming techniques and applications. It is published bimonthly by the Department of Computer Science at The University of Arizona and The Bright Forest Company, Tucson, AZ.

There also are many technical reports and user manuals for various platforms.

6.4.4. The Icon Program Library

One of the most useful resources available to Icon programmers is the Icon program library. It contains hundreds of programs, thousands of procedures that can be used in other programs, as well as documentation and useful data.

The library is divided into two parts, a basic part and a part concerned with graphics. Within these parts are directories for data, documents, include files, large programs in separate packages, procedures, and stand-alone programs.

The directory structure looks like this:

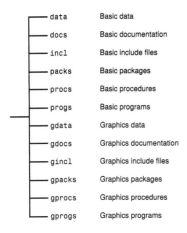

data	Basic data
docs	Basic documentation
incl	Basic include files
packs	Basic packages
procs	Basic procedures
progs	Basic programs
gdata	Graphics data
gdocs	Graphics documentation
gincl	Graphics include files
gpacks	Graphics packages
gprocs	Graphics procedures
gprogs	Graphics programs

The `packs` and `gpacks` directories contain subdirectories, each devoted to a packaged program and the material it requires. For example, VIB is included in `gpacks`.

The directories `procs` and `gprocs` contain modules that are useful in building programs, including many extensions to Icon's built-in computational repertoire. Modules that contain commonly used procedures are designated as *core modules*. The core modules are

convert	Type conversion and formatting procedures
datetime	Date and time procedures
factors	Procedures related to factoring and prime numbers
io	Procedures related to input and output
lists	List manipulation procedures
math	Procedures for mathematical computation

numbers	Procedures for numerical computation and formatting	
random	Procedures related to random numbers	
records	Record manipulation procedures	
scan	Scanning procedures	
sets	Set manipulation procedures	
sort	Sorting procedures	
strings	String manipulation procedures	
tables	Table manipulation procedures	

There are listings and cross-reference indexes to help locate programs and procedures. A section of the listing for progs looks like this:

Keyword	File	Description
character	findstr	Find embedded character strings
character	ruler	Write a character ruler
character	xtable	Show character code translations
characters	delamc	Delaminate file using tab characters
characters	fileprnt	Display characters in file
characters	tablc	Tabulate characters in a file
check	adlcheck	Check for bad address list data
check	chkhtml	Check HTML files
christmas	sing	Sing The Twelve Days of Christmas
code	isrcline	Count code lines in Icon program
code	iwriter	Write Icon code to write input
code	lindcode	Produce Icon code from L-system
code	morse	Convert string to Morse code
code	ostrip	Show virtual-machine op-code strip
code	what	Identify source-code information
code	xtable	Show character code translations
code	zipsort	Sort mailing labels by ZIP code

A section of a listing for procs looks like this:

Keyword	File	Description
case	noncase	Case-independent matching
caseless	caseless	Perform caseless scanning
character	allpat	Produce all n-character patterns
character	asciinam	ASCII name of unprintable character
character	escapesq	Deal with character string escapes
characters	inbits	Read variable-length characters
characters	outbits	Write variable-length characters
characters	strip	Strip characters from a string
chart	ichartp	A simple chart parser
check	dif	Check for differences
classify	tclass	Classify values as atomic or composite
close	openchk	Aid in open/close debugging
code	identgen	Meta-translation code generation
code	gen	Meta-variant code generation
code	evtmap	Map event code names to values
code	gen	Meta-variant code generation
code	identgen	Meta-translation code generation
code	itokens	Tokenize Icon code
code	morse	Convert string to Morse code

Procedure indexes provide information about specific procedures and where they can be found. A section of the index for procs looks like this:

Keyword	file:procedure	Description
decimal	numbers:decipos	Position decimal point
decollation	strings:decollate	String decollation
decomposition	factors:prdecomp	Prime decomposition
default	tables:tbldflt	Table default
delete	lists:ldelete	Delete list elements

delete	strings:deletec	Delete characters
delete	strings:deletes	Delete string
depth	trees:depth	Depth of tree
detect	numbers:large	Detect large integers
difference	tables:tbldiff	Table difference
digits	digitcnt:digitcnt	Count digits in file
digits	numbers:digred	Sum digits of integer
directory	io:dosdir	Process DOS directory
directory	io:dosdirlist	Get list of DOS directory
directory	io:getwd	Get DOS working directory
divide	factors:pfactors	Primes that divide integer
division	numbers:div	Real division
divisor	numbers:gcd	Greatest common divisor

The program and procedure files themselves contain documentation about their contents.

6.4.5. Icon Newsgroup

The newsgroup comp.lang.icon handles news related to Icon. There also is a mailing list connected to the newsgroup via a gateway. To subscribe, send mail to

icon-group-request@cs.arizona.edu

6.4.6. The Icon Project

Information about Icon also is available from

Icon Project
Department of Computer Science
The University of Arizona
P.O. Box 210077
Tucson, Arizona 85721-0077
U.S.A.
voice: 520-621-6613
fax: 520-621-4246
e-mail: icon-project@cs.arizona.edu

6.5. Acknowledgments

Some of the material presented here was adapted from *The Icon Programming Language*, third edition (Griswold & Griswold, 1996) and is used by permission of the publisher, Peer-to-Peer Communications, Inc. Portions of the material on graphics facilities and interface design are based on material in *Graphics Programming in Icon* (Griswold, Jeffery, & Townsend, 1997), also by permission of the publisher, Peer-to-Peer Communications, Inc. Some of the material on programming techniques was derived from *The Icon Analyst* (Griswold, Griswold, & Townsend, 1990) and is used by permission of the editors.

The author is indebted to his wife, Madge T. Griswold, for careful readings of the manuscript and numerous helpful suggestions.

6.6. References

Beiler, A. H. 1966. *Re-creations in the theory of Numbers; The queen of mathematics entertains* (2nd ed.). New York: Dover Publications.

Berk, T., L. Brownston, and A. Kaufman. May 1982. A new color-naming system for graphics languages. *IEEE Computer Graphics and Applications* pp. 37–44.

Farber, D. J., R. E. Griswold, and I. P. Polonsky. 1964. SNOBOL, a string manipulation language. *Journal of the ACM*, 11:21–30.

Griswold, R. E. *User's Manual for the Icon Programming Language*. 1978. Technical Report TR 78-14. Tucson, AZ: The University of Arizona, Department of Computer Science.

Griswold, R. E. and M. T. Griswold. 1986. *The implementation of the Icon programming language*. Princeton, NJ: Princeton University Press.

Griswold, R. E. and M. T. Griswold. 1996. *The Icon programming language* (3rd ed.). San Jose, CA: Peer-to-Peer Communications.

Griswold, R. E., C. L. Jeffery, and G. M. Townsend. 1996. *Version 9.3 of the Icon programming language*. Technical Report IPD278. Tucson, AZ: The University of Arizona, Department of Computer Science.

Griswold, R. E., C. L. Jeffery, and G. M. Townsend. 1998. *Graphics programming in Icon*. San Jose, CA: Peer-to-Peer Communications.

Griswold, R. E., J. F. Poage, and I. P. Polonsky. 1971. *The SNOBOL4 programming language* (2nd ed.). Englewood Cliffs, NJ: Prentice Hall.

Hanson, D. R., and R. E. Griswold. 1978. The SL5 Procedure Mechanism. *Communications of the ACM*, pp. 392–400.

Hofstadter, D. R. 1979. *Gödel, Escher, Bach: An eternal golden braid.* New York: Basic Books.

Horowitz, E. and S. Sahni. 1978. *Fundamentals of computer algorithms.* Potomac, MD: Computer Science Press.

Kleene, S. C. *Introduction to metamathematics.* 1952. Princeton, NJ: Van Nostrand Company.

Mitchie, D. 1967. *Memo functions: A language feature with rote learning properties.* DMIP Memorandum MIP-R-29. Edinburgh, Scotland.

Murray, J. D. and W. vanRyper. 1994. *Encyclopedia of graphics file formats.* Sebastopol, CA: O'Reilly.

Townsend, G. M. and M. Cameron. 1996. *VIB: A visual interface builder for Icon; Version 3.* Technical Report IPD265. Tucson, AZ: The University of Arizona, Department of Computer Science.

Yngve, V. H. 1958. A programming language for mechanical translation. *Mechanical Translation* 5:25–41.

INDEX

Symbols

! (exclamation mark) (Fortran 95
  comments), 13
#define preprocessor directive (C), 178
#else preprocessor directive (C), 179
#error preprocessor directive (C), 181
#if preprocessor directive (C), 179
#include preprocessor directive (C), 176
#pragma preprocessor directive (C), 181
& (ampersand) (Fortran 95 continued
  statements), 12
& (standard I/O) keywords (Icon), 339

A

Abort function (C), 211
Abs function (C), 211
absolute value functions (C), 214
accessing
  arrays (in C via pointers), 151
  pointers (in Turbo Pascal), 295, 297
  record files (in Fortran 95), 53
  Turbo Pascal files, 299-300
ada (Diana intermediate language), 243
advancing I/O record files (Fortran 95),
  53-54
Algol 60, 68, 72, 253
Algol W, 253
Algol X, 253
aliases, 47, 244

ampersand (&) (Fortran 95 continued
  statements), 12
arguments
  C functions, 137-138
  procedures in Fortran 95, 28-29
arithmetic operators
  C, 106-108
  Fortran 95, 15
  Icon, 360-361
  Turbo Pascal, 261
arrays
  B, 66
  BCPL, 66
  C, 70-71, 80-81
    accessing via pointers, 151
    declaring, 97-98
    initializing, 102
    integration with pointers, 154-158
    nested, 98
    operation constraints, 98
    references, 141
    versus pointers, 155
    versus structures, 169
  Fortran 95, 31
    assignment, 33
    computing shape, 32
    constructors, 32
    declaring, 31
    dynamic, 32
    indexed parallel assignment, 35-36
    masked assignment, 34
    operators, 34
    returning true values, 36
    sections, 33
  Turbo Pascal, 269, 271

U

V

W

X-Y-Z